Energy, Ecology, and the Environment

Energy, Ecology, and the Environment

Richard Wilson

Harvard University

William J. Jones

Massachusetts Institute of Technology

ACADEMIC PRESS, INC.
111 Fifth Avenue, New York, New York 10003

United Kingdom Edition published by
ACADEMIC PRESS, INC. (LONDON) LTD.
24/28 Oval Road, London NW1

LIBRARY OF CONGRESS CATALOG CARD NUMBER: 74-10064

ISBN 0–12–757550–2

PRINTED IN THE UNITED STATES OF AMERICA

*Cover photograph courtesy of Portland General Electric Power Co.,
Portland, Oregon*

Contents

Contents

Contents

Contents

Contents

Contents

List of Technical Notes

List of Worksheets

Preface

"Energy, Ecology, and the Environment," the title of this book,
is a concise statement of conflicting interests. Extraction of the
sources of energy and the methods of harnessing and utilizing energy
can adversely affect the ecology and environment of our world. Highly
developed nations depend on cheap energy to maintain their standard of
living. The hopes of the developing countries are based on the similar
harnessing of cheap energy and spreading of its benefits. Only if we
are careful can we minimize damage to the ecology and, at the same time,
maintain and achieve the above.

In the United States, there is an apt example of conflict. The
southern hot-weather states after World War II developed as an industrial and cultural force with the widespread introduction of air conditioning. In the hottest parts of the year, air conditioning is as
necessary in the South as is heat in the North during the winter months.
Air conditioning, with the common compression- or absorption-type unit,
is unfortunately one of the most inefficient ways of using energy to
condition working and living space.

We might be able to develop more efficient ways of using energy for
this purpose, but barring a total shortage of energy, it is unlikely
that we will, as a general national policy, discontinue the use of air
conditioning where it is most needed. To do so would drastically affect
the economy and structure of this country.

Aside from the question of how much energy is available, we know about pollution caused by emissions from electrical generating plants, effluent from extraction of fuels, and the like. We shall discuss all of these matters in detail and endeavor to do so from a foundation of facts.

This is a book dealing with science and technology. Most of the material in the book is text. Technical Notes in the body of the book may be skipped without effect on the continuity of the text. They provide detailed information about scientific principles or technology. Some of these Technical Notes require the use of mathematics, but all can be used as a point of departure for the instructor who may want to add special topics to the course. References are provided to encourage further reading.

In addition to covering a subject of importance to us all, this book provides the reader with a good idea of how physicists and engineers approach problems. The reader is asked to make "ball park" estimates to show whether or not an effect is important, in some cases where he might not even realize he was capable of so doing. The reader is taught to distinguish between goals that are theoretically possible but not yet technologically feasible, and those that violate basic physical principles. He is shown how to find solid data.

The book also reveals something about the social concerns of scientists.

This book is dedicated to our wives, Dorothy J. and Andree W., who have lived with it more than the reader will have to.

Several persons have helped us with criticism and suggestions. Special note is made of the contributions of Academic Press.

1
Energy

INTRODUCTION

Energy is a mainstay of our economic life. Five percent of our Gross National Product is spent on electricity, more than twenty-five percent on automobiles, their use, and their maintenance. All indications are that our demands for energy will increase. Yet we now see that our fuel supplies such as gasoline and electricity will have to be rationed in the very near future... 1974, 1975, 1976?

Some experts say that continual exploration will find new oil and gas fields or that nuclear power, if rapidly brought into the picture, will go a long way toward forestalling the need to impose restrictions on the use of energy. Other experts say that the price we will have to pay in terms of environmental damage and health hazards for these immediate solutions will be great.

Whenever questions of energy resources come up, so too do questions of technology, economics, social need, and environmental effects. Which, in each case, is the more important factor? Too often each spokesman seems to work with a different set of facts, and different numbers for these effects.

What are the facts? How accurately can we project the amount of petroleum that remains in the Earth? How safe are nuclear power reactors? Are they as accident proof as some say, or as vulnerable as

1

others say? Is there such a concept as "absolutely safe"? Are other forms of fuel any better than nuclear fuels? How can the scientist and engineer fit human and economic factors into his equations? How does the concerned citizen determine whether industry is making realistic projections for the long- and short-term benefit of society or whether a political leader may be just accepting the popular viewpoint on an issue?

We shall try to work toward the answers to these questions. In the process we will develop a formal definition of energy and become familiar with the terminology of the scientist and engineer. This aspect of the subject will not prove particularly difficult since most of the terms fit our intuitive everyday use of the same words.

We shall see how important it is to decide what data we need and to express this as quantitatively (numerically) as we can; then we will be able to compare the cost of obtaining energy, of the associated environmental dislocation, and of loss of life in accident, with the gain to society of easily available energy.

When we can express the data quantitatively, decisions become easier. They become hard to make when the data is quantitatively unreliable.

ENERGY CONSUMPTION: A BRIEF HISTORY

Early in geologic time our mineral resources and fossil fuels were laid down in limited, or finite, amounts. Coal, like petroleum and natural gas, is a fossil fuel, a fuel believed to have evolved from buried organic matter over the course of thousands of centuries through a combination of chemical changes and intense pressures from the tons of earth over it. Once used, we cannot expect these minerals and fuels to be replaced.

Figure 1-1 shows the various periods of geologic time. Man has lived in the latter part of this time and is now rapidly consuming these resources. [Refer to Worksheets 1-1 and 1-2.]

Man's use of energy has grown slowly. At first it was limited to what he ate: then as now about 2000 Calories* per day. This energy was obtained from the sun via animal and vegetable life.

As man learned to control his environment to some extent, he tamed animals and used them to bear a number of his burdens of labor. He invented the wheel to improve his efficiency in energy use. As he did so, he obtained an advantage over other species and was able to divert more and more of the world's resources to his use. The

---

* The Calorie is defined in Chapter III. [See Worksheet 3-1.]

human population increased quite slowly until the beginning of the industrial revolution, about 400 years ago; at that time several marked changes came about.

Wood had long been burned for heating and cooking, but its use was limited by the supply. By 1700 the wood of England was essentially all cut, and the population was saved from being exceptionally cold by the discovery of coal near the northeast coast of England, near Newcastle, in the 12th century. The development of coal mining followed.

The use of various power sources for motive power developed more slowly. Animal hauling, wind for sails in ships, and the steam engine came about over a long period of time.

The water wheel and the windmill were used for milling quite early. Hero's aeolipile, a simple steam engine demonstrated to the ancient Greeks 1900 years ago, was regarded as a toy rather than a machine.

The steam engine of James Watt (lab assistant to the Professor at the Physics Department, University of Glasgow) was first used in mining, to pump out water and to haul men and coal up from the pits. By 1800, all pit mines in England were so equipped. The use of the steam engine for motive power appeared in 1828, first on the mine railroads, which had previously employed horses. It was so successful that railroads expanded all over the world within half a century.

Two further important steps took place soon thereafter. The first, Michael Faraday's discovery of electromagnetic induction, was followed at the end of the century by the electric motor and dynamo. Its application to electric trains and streetcars came very fast, by about 1890. Edison's electric light was, perhaps, even more profound in its effect on society; but the electric light is not a major factor in energy consumption.

The second step was the invention of the internal combustion engine, combined with the discovery of large quantities of oil. The internal combustion engine has shown itself to be extraordinarily robust and reliable; gasoline (or fuel oil) has a very high heat content.

In all this time, a growth in human population has taken place. Early man appeared nearly a million years ago. How fast did his numbers increase? Let us look at the conservative side of things, and at the same time introduce the concept of *doubling time*.

If man doubled his population regularly every 30,000 years, he would have increased from, shall we say, two to four hundred million in half a million years. Four hundred million was the Earth's population in the year 1600. Yet, in the last two hundred years, the world's population has doubled every sixty years! With this growth in population has come a demand for energy; indeed, it can be argued that without even more energy *per person* the population increase would not have been possible.

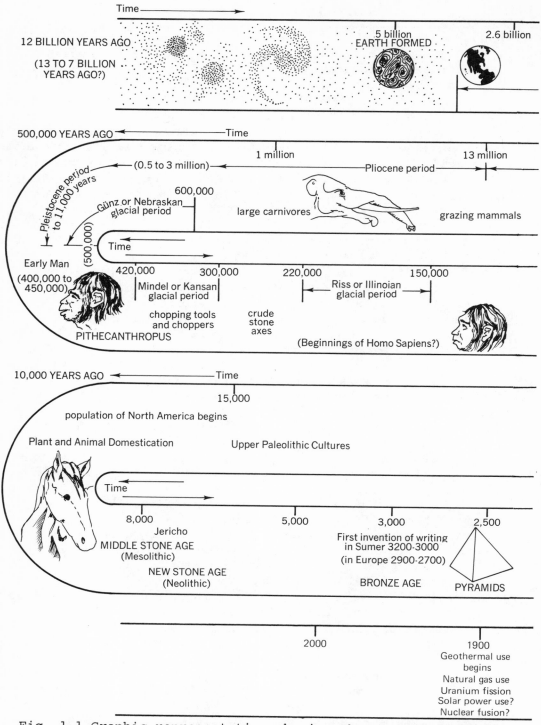

Time ───────────►

12 BILLION YEARS AGO

(13 TO 7 BILLION
YEARS AGO?)

5 billion
EARTH FORMED

2.6 billion

500,000 YEARS AGO ◄─────── Time

1 million

13 million

Pleistocene period
to 11,000 years

(0.5 to 3 million) ◄─────── Pliocene period ─────────►

Günz or Nebraskan
glacial period

600,000

large carnivores

grazing mammals

(500,000)

Time ───────────►

Early Man
(400,000 to
450,000)

420,000   300,000   220,000   150,000

Mindel or Kansan
glacial period

chopping tools
and choppers

crude
stone
axes

Riss or Illinoian
glacial period

PITHECANTHROPUS

(Beginnings of Homo Sapiens?)

10,000 YEARS AGO ◄─────── Time

15,000

population of North America begins

Plant and Animal Domestication

Upper Paleolithic Cultures

Time ───────────►

8,000   5,000   3,000   2,500

Jericho
MIDDLE STONE AGE
(Mesolithic)

First invention of writing
in Sumer 3200-3000

(in Europe 2900-2700)

NEW STONE AGE
(Neolithic)

BRONZE AGE

PYRAMIDS

2000   1900
Geothermal use
begins
Natural gas use
Uranium fission
Solar power use?
Nuclear fusion?

Fig. 1-1 Graphic representation showing the vast difference in
time between our rapid use of fossil fuels (bottom segment) and their
early formation.

4

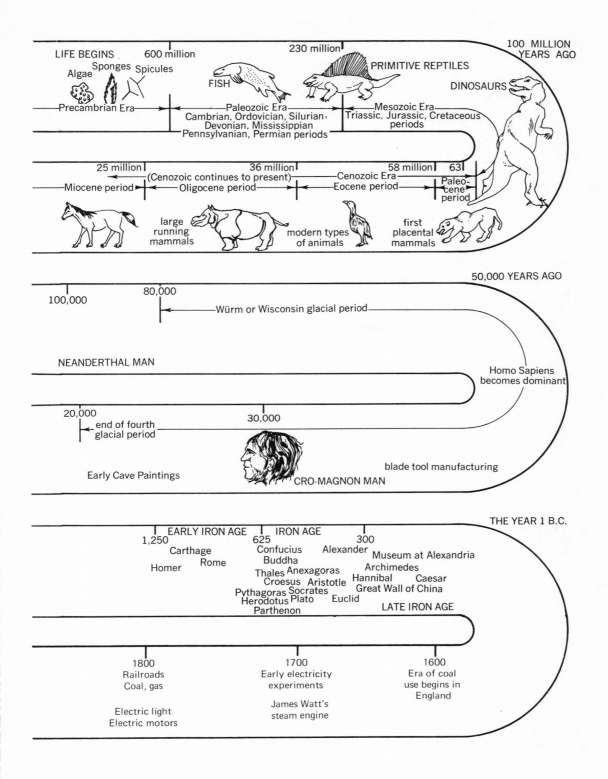

LIFE BEGINS   600 million   230 million
                                                                    PRIMITIVE REPTILES   100 MILLION
    Algae Sponges Spicules   YEARS AGO
                              FISH   DINOSAURS

─Precambrian Era─────→├───────Paleozoic Era────────→├──Mesozoic Era──
                          Cambrian, Ordovician, Silurian,   Triassic, Jurassic, Cretaceous
                            Devonian, Mississippian   periods
                          Pennsylvanian, Permian periods

      25 million   36 million   58 million   63│
├──────────────────(Cenozoic continues to present)←───────Cenozoic Era──   Paleo-
─Miocene period→├────Oligocene period────→├──────────────Eocene period──   cene
                                                                              period

                              large   first
                              running   modern types   placental
                              mammals   of animals   mammals

                                                                    50,000 YEARS AGO

      100,000   80,000
                        ├←──────Würm or Wisconsin glacial period────────

NEANDERTHAL MAN
                                                                    Homo Sapiens
                                                                    becomes dominant

      20,000   30,000
        ├←─end of fourth──────────
             glacial period
                                                                    blade tool manufacturing
    Early Cave Paintings   CRO-MAGNON MAN

                                                                    THE YEAR 1 B.C.

            ├ EARLY IRON AGE ├ IRON AGE
        1,250   625   300
            Carthage   Confucius   Alexander   Museum at Alexandria
              Rome   Buddha   Archimedes
      Homer   Thales Anexagoras   Hannibal   Caesar
                          Croesus Aristotle   Great Wall of China
                    Pythagoras Socrates   Euclid
                      Herodotus Plato   LATE IRON AGE
                        Parthenon

        1800   1700   1600
        Railroads   Early electricity   Era of coal
        Coal, gas   experiments   use begins in
                                                   England
        Electric light   James Watt's
        Electric motors   steam engine

5

1. Energy

TECHNICAL NOTE 1-1

Doubling Time

Population growth affects the environment and is related to the increasing rate of energy consumption. However, this aspect of the problem is not directly related to the main thrust of this book. Therefore, let us simply acquaint the reader with some few facts about this subject.

Biological species reproduce and double their populations after a certain period of time called the doubling time, provided that the environment, including food supply, remains favorable. The limit is usually set by food supply, and then the population becomes constant. Poisoning by waste products can destroy the whole population. For example, the bacteria which feed on grapes eventually drown in their own waste (wine). If man is to be wise enough to avert such a catastrophe, he must understand the phenomenon.

Suppose that the doubling time for man is about 60 years (about the figure for the last two centuries) and that this figure is applicable to the biblical concept of creation, two initial humans. When would the world population have been two people?

In 1972, the population of the world was about 4 billion. Let us set up a table.

Time (years)	Population
$0 = 0 \times 60$	$2 = 2^1$
$60 = 1 \times 60$	$4 = 2^2$
$120 = 2 \times 60$	$8 = 2^3$
$180 = 3 \times 60$	$16 = 2^4$
.	.
.	.
.	.
$n \times 60$ (in general)	2^{n+1}

Continuing in this way, we find

Time (years): $1800 = 30 \times 60$,   Population: $4,000,000,000$

(To check this figure, calculate for 60 multiplied by 9, 19, and 29.) This is not in accord with the anthropologically accepted figure of man first appearing $1,000,000$ (one million) years ago. For this figure, the average doubling time is found by dividing $1,000,000$ by 30. The

WORKSHEET 1-1

Energy Consumption: Projections

The table gives data for world energy consumption for the last several hundred years and projections of consumption for the next several hundred years. Plot this data on the graph below. The shape of the curve is extremely informative.

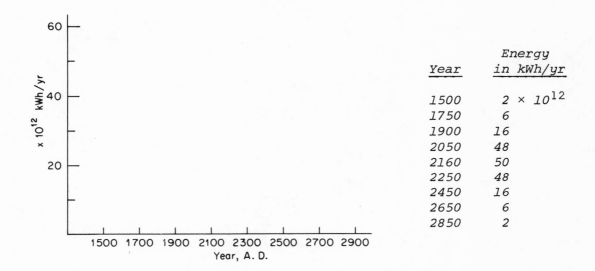

Year	Energy in kWh/yr
1500	2×10^{12}
1750	6
1900	16
2050	48
2160	50
2250	48
2450	16
2650	6
2850	2

A host of conclusions can be drawn from this curve. What information can you extract from this curve? (See Problem 2.)

Note. From your electric bills, you know that energy consumption is often measured in units of kilowatt hours. The units on this graph are the number of kilowatt hours consumed per year. These units will be discussed later in the chapter.

Note. The shorthand notation for 1,000,000,000,000 is 10^{12}, that is, 10 multiplied by itself twelve times. Similarly 100 is represented as 10^2.

To make this picture still more striking, replot the data in a rough way on a scale of years extending from 5000 years ago to 5000 years in the future.

6a

WORKSHEET 1-2

Energy Consumption and Population Growth

Here are some rough data, but accurate enough to give a feel for the relation between energy consumption and population growth. Set up your data in the table using the information in Worksheet 1-1 and the graph below. Plot a curve of energy used versus population.

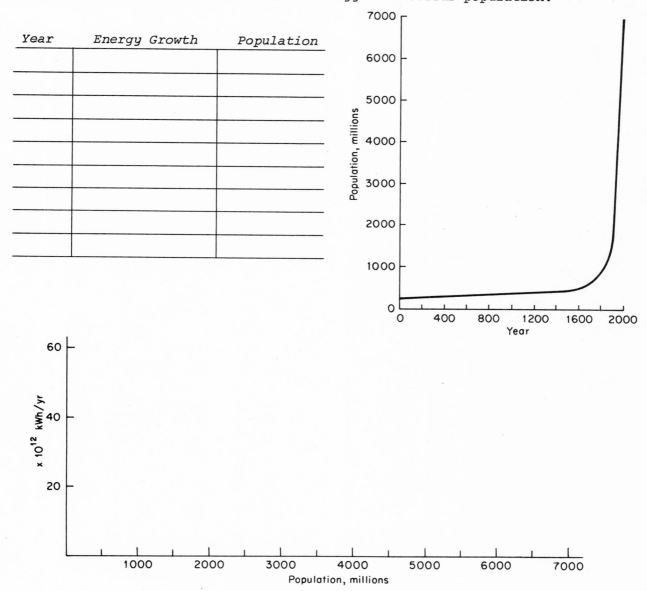

Year	Energy Growth	Population

Using the data, develop arguments to show that the availability of energy influences the growth rate of population. If you consider the historical availability of energy sources, you will realize that this is not simply a question of more people using more energy, as is the case today, for the most part.

*30 is still valid from the above calculation, since it tells us that
the population would have to double thirty times to go from 2 to 4
billion:*

1,000,000/30 = 33,000 years for each doubling

*This average seems about correct until the last two centuries when
the rate increased dramatically.*

ENVIRONMENTAL EFFECTS

Ideally, we would like to use energy without leaving any undesirable
traces. This is not completely possible. If we use energy to move us
from one place to another, friction converts some of the energy into
heat, which can change the climate. In addition, due to our inability
to control completely the sources of energy, there are many diverse
environmental effects. These are the effects discussed in this book.

It would be pleasant to be able to write that one source of energy
is cheap, is plentiful, and can be used without any environmental
problems. If that were so, this book would be unnecessary. No source
of energy is completely free of environmental effects. In every case
the use of energy may lead to disease in or the death of some person
or persons. Thus society agrees to accept risks in return for what it
deems to be adequate benefits. This concept of balancing benefit and
risk was first introduced in discussions of allowable radiation dose
levels by the International Commission of Radiological Protection
(ICRP). The members of this commission have been accused of "playing
God"; yet, they may be the first to recognize explicitly and admit the
environmental hazards in human actions, and hence to assign the blame
for accidents and diseases to man instead of calling them "acts of God."

In the United States, the National Environmental Policy Act
of 1969 (NEPA) enjoins every federal agency to make such comparisons
of risk and benefit when it contemplates any action: such as licensing
a power plant or building a dam or highway. The full text of the act
is available in JCAE [1]. In this age when a concern for the environment is popular, every man claims to be an environmentalist. We believe
that such a title can only be given to those who try at all times to
compare the environmental consequences of alternative courses of action
in the most detailed possible way. Such is the message of NEPA. This
law is binding on federal agencies and should be strongly enforced;
the same spirit guides this book.

In some cases we will assign numbers to risk in terms of death
rates. The assessment of benefit is harder, but necessary.

1. Energy

The benefit of energy in comfort of a heated or air-conditioned home is clear; man can work harder when he is comfortable. The benefit of cheap transportation is also obvious. Less easy to express in quantitative terms is the benefit of reliability of the energy supply, but we have only to consider the effect of an electricity failure on a major hospital to realize its importance.

In this book, we put a great deal of emphasis on the hazard to human life as the major environmental hazard. There are other environmental effects; those on animals and plants are similar to those on humans and need not be considered separately. Others, the destruction of natural beauty or of the balance of nature, *must* be considered separately.

THE CONCEPT OF ENERGY

Perhaps you know or have heard that heat is a form of energy. Energy can be found in many forms, such as sound and light. You may or may not be familiar with such phrases as electrical, chemical, or kinetic energy. In this general context we will try to get an intuitive grip on the following definition of energy:

> Energy is the ability to do work.

√ If you exert a force to push a box across the floor, you do work, and to do work, you have to expend energy.

√ If you lift a weight to a certain height, you exert a force to overcome the force of gravity and you do work; to do work, you expend energy.

√ Steam may be used to drive a generator of electricity. When you use some of this electricity to run a motor, which in turn generates a force and does work, you will have taken advantage of the process:

heat energy (steam) ⟶ electrical energy ⟶ work

That heat and electrical energy can be harnessed to do work is not unfamiliar, but light and sound are not commonly harnessed to do work in our everyday world. Chemical energy is: in fuels to power vehicles, and in storage batteries, where it is converted into electrical energy.

In the next several paragraphs we shall quickly tie together in perhaps a slightly formal way the terms *force, work,* and *energy,* so that we may use them in an unambiguous manner.

The Concept of Energy

Force

(1) We exert a force whenever we move an object, or whenever we stop a body that is moving. A force is involved in throwing a baseball, and a force is involved in catching a baseball. An automobile engine exerts a force when it puts a car into motion, and its brakes exert a force when they stop it. In each of these cases, to bring the force into play, something came in physical contact with something else.

(2) If you drop a book from a given height, it will fall to the ground under the influence of the gravitational force. The book and the earth were not in contact when the force of gravity started the book falling downward.

A magnet of sufficient strength placed near a piece of iron will attract the iron. This is an example of magnetic force; as in the gravitational case, the force can act without contact being made between the bodies. And, as you know, if two north magnetic poles are placed near each other, the magnets will move apart. Therefore, be careful not to assume that all forces are attractive; some are repulsive.

(3) In common use, we generally measure force in pounds. To say that you weigh 100 pounds is a short way of saying that the gravitational force between you and the earth has a strength of 100 pounds weight.

(4) It is important that we understand the following. A force is acting if a body changes its motion:

      if it starts to move from rest;
      if it speeds up or slows down while in motion;
      if it changes direction;
      if it stops from a state of motion.

In short, if a body changes its state of motion, that is, if it *accelerates,* it does so only because a force is acting on it. [See Worksheet 1-3.]

(5) There are five classes of force that are known:

Type of force	"Use" in nature
✓ Gravitational	Coagulation of matter in galaxies, stars, planets; creation of tides
✓ Electromagnetic (the combined effect of electrical and magnetic forces as they most often appear in nature)	Binding of atoms; chemistry; electricity

√ Strong	Binding of nuclei; the fusion process in the sun and other stars
Weak	Transmutation of elements, radioactivity
Superweak	Not known, but found to exist from experiments in high-energy physics

In the course of this book we shall deal with the first three forces.

Each force can act to produce energy, just as the gravitational force acting on water can make it fall. We see that there are three major classes of energy in use today, corresponding to three of these forces:

(1) Gravitational (which is used to produce electricity when water falls through a turbine, which in turn drives a generator);

(2) Electromagnetic (which includes all chemical processes, such as the burning of gasoline to run an automobile). We do not always think of chemistry in terms of electrical energy. The force that attracts electrons to an atomic nucleus is electromagnetic, and chemical energy arises from moving these electrons between different atoms;

(3) Nuclear (which may be controlled in a nuclear reactor to produce electricity).

Two additional classes of force have been discovered in recent years, but are not yet controlled to produce useful energy. One is the *weak force* which acts between particles in the nucleus of an atom; it controls the radioactive decay of nuclei. Radioactive materials are used, in special applications, to provide electricity; the amount available is small, but radioactive materials have been used to construct a battery of long life, and such batteries are particularly well suited for space technology and heart implants (cardiac pacemakers).

The other, or fifth, force is the *superweak force*, which was only recently discovered and which is still less well understood. It appears only in one place in nature - in the decay of a subatomic particle known as the neutral K meson (no, you don't have to remember the name) - and appears to have no utility in generating or transforming energy for man's use.

Of course, it is not only man that makes changes from one type of energy to another. The energy in the sun begins as gravitational energy; nuclear interactions (strong force) then take place, and the energy is radiated in the form of electromagnetic radiation, visible

light, and ultraviolet and infrared rays. This electromagnetic
radiation is absorbed on the earth by the chlorophyll in plants and
trees and then enters into chemical reactions. By the heating and
the evaporation of water, the winds which turn windmills are formed,
as are the rains which fall (gravitationally) and produce hydroelectric
power.

Work

Let us apply a force to a body and in so doing move it a certain
distance. The work done in moving this body is most simply *defined*
by use of an equation which reads:

$$\text{Work} = \text{Force} \times \text{Distance}$$

TECHNICAL NOTE 1-2

Newton's Laws

*Newton's laws relate forces and motion. The first law appears
to be a self-apparent, common-sense statement. We can, in effect,
deduce it from our own experience. For example, let us assume a body
is at rest... and nothing in any way disturbs it. We shall assume no
gravity acts on it, temperatures are unchanged, it is truly undisturbed.
Will it start to move? Certainly not; there is nothing that is going
to make it move on its own.*

*Take a parallel case. A body is moving along with a steady speed
far away from the influence of anything else. Will it speed up or slow
down? What's to make it change its speed? Will it change direction?
Thus, Newton postulated as his first law that a body at rest will so
remain and that a body in motion will continue in straight-line motion
at a steady speed unless subject to external influences.*

*For his second law, Newton introduced the concept of a force, the
influencing factor that will cause the motion of a body to change.
A change in motion is called an acceleration. The change in motion
means a change in the direction in which a body is moving or a change
in the speed with which it moves. Newton codified this law in a profound but simple-looking equation:*

$$Force = Mass \times Acceleration$$

or, as more commonly written,

$$F = ma$$

11

1. Energy

As we look at this statement again, we find that it is intuitively true. The bigger the force (the more powerful the car motor), the greater the acceleration. A body with little mass is easier to get into motion (to accelerate from rest) than a body with a great deal of mass.

Mass is a fundamental quantity telling "how much" substance you are dealing with. In the metric system it is measured in grams or kilograms (1000 grams). Mass is discussed in the section on kinetic theory.

Newton's third law is the one of action and reaction, the law which, for example, predicts that a gun will recoil. The logic of the law can be seen from this example: Assume that you and a person of equal mass stand on ice, which we shall regard as a friction-free surface, and one of you pushes the other. Both parties will move apart with the same acceleration. Nature sees the problem as symmetrical and does not decide that one is pushing the other, but rather that there is a mutual force between the two. Hence, when the bullet leaves the gun, nature says, on the one hand, that the gun exerts a forward force on the bullet, and, on the other, that the bullet exerts an equal but rearward force on the gun.

Work implies that a force is applied and that motion results. The more force applied, the more work done. The farther the body is moved, the more work done.

The classic illustrative problem is that of a box pushed across a floor at a steady speed. Because of friction, the box would slow to a stop once the force was removed.

To lift a weight, you must apply a force upward. The higher you lift the weight, the more work you must do. And, the faster you lift the weight, the more work you must do. For to lift the weight more quickly means that more force is being used in the lifting process. It is more fatiguing to lift a heavy weight quickly than to do so slowly. As an example, think about how you feel after running up a flight of stairs.

Kinetic Energy

Does a moving baseball possess energy? Let us look at the instance where it is thrown at a can. The can will move. It will have accelerated from rest. Therefore the baseball must have exerted a force on the can while in contact with it. Short as the time may have been, the baseball and can moved together, and therefore we have a force being applied through a distance; work was done. If we return to our definition of energy as the ability to do work, we must conclude that the moving baseball possessed energy. It possessed energy by virtue of its motion, and this energy is known as *kinetic energy*. All moving bodies possess kinetic energy.

A fast-flowing river or waterfall possesses kinetic energy. This energy can be harnessed to drive electric generators or, as in days of yore, run a mill to grind flour.

The formal definition of kinetic energy is given in a concise formula, and, of course, this formula is used to get numerical values for the kinetic energy:

$$\text{Kinetic Energy} = (1/2)\text{Mass} \times \text{Speed}^2$$

Mass and weight are related, to be sure, but mass is the more fundamental idea. In space, in the absence of gravity, bodies are weightless (remember, weight is a force, the force of gravitational attraction). Yet, even in space, were you to throw a baseball and a similar sphere made of lead, you would not be able to get as much speed on the lead ball as on the baseball. The lead ball has the greater mass. Mass is a way of telling you "how much" of a substance you have. In the metric system, the gram is the unit of mass. A penny is about three grams.

We shall return many times to kinetic energy as a principle. Indeed, you will find that it will become a familiar and comfortable concept to you.

The Units of Energy

We shall discuss the units used to measure energy: the calorie, the watt, and the joule. These are the terms used by power companies and dropped in conversation at licensing hearings. If we are to appreciate the numbers involved in the energy "game," we have to know how big these units are.

British and American engineers tend to use one set of units, and scientists another. In large part the situation parallels the use of the metric system in most parts of the world and British units in the United States and Great Britain.

The metric system is logically constructed [see Technical Note 1-3]:

√ Distances are measured in centimeters (one centimeter is about the length of the nail on your pinky) or meters (one meter is roughly three inches longer than a yard). 100 centimeters is equal to one meter.

√ Mass is measured in grams (a penny has a mass of about three grams) or kilograms. 1000 grams equal one kilogram.

√ Force is measured in units called newtons. The newton is smaller than the pound, equal to about 1/4 pound. (The unit of force to which the reader is most accustomed is the pound.)

13

1. Energy

The British system, as we know, uses the foot as the basic unit of length, and the pound as the basic unit of force. The unit of mass is one that you are not likely to be familiar with; it is called the slug. We will not have occasion to use the slug.

TECHNICAL NOTE 1-3

The Metric System; Units

Here is a brief table for the conversion of British and metric units. Try to visualize the actual sizes involved:

Length: *1 inch (in.) = 2.54 centimeters (cm)*
                   10 millimeters (mm) = 1 cm
                   100 cm = 1 meter (m) = 3.28 feet (ft)

Force: *1 newton (N) = 0.225 pounds (lb), weight*
                   1 lb = 4.45 N

Energy: *1 calorie (cal) = 4.18 joules (j)*
                   1 kilowatt-hour (kWh) = $3.60 \times 10^6 j$
                   1 British thermal unit (Btu) = 252 cal = 1055j

Mass: *1 kilogram (kg) will weigh 2.2 lb on Earth*

Every quantity that we work with has a label which gives the units of measure. Length, for example, whether measured in feet, inches, or meters, must be properly tagged, e.g., 10 ft, 3 m, etc.

Speed is the rate at which distance is covered per unit time. Instinctively, we give a car's speed in miles per hour. A steady speed of 60 miles/hr means we would cover 60 miles in an hour. In two hours of such travel we would cover 120 miles. Let's make our point by writing out this calculation.

We very naturally multiplied:

$$60 \ \frac{miles}{hour} \times 2 \ hours = 120 \ miles$$

Notice how the units of time cancel out to give the proper final units. This is a simple example of "dimensional analysis"; it is a principle that is never violated. The units must be consistent.

Notice, too, that we have used a formula without even thinking about one:

$$Speed \times Time = Distance$$

The Concept of Energy

Three of the quantities just discussed are the fundamental quantities for the system of science man has built. They are

mass,   length,   time.

Refer to Worksheet 1-3 to see how straightforward it is to apply the definition of kinetic energy to get numbers and to see how the units are defined. You must remember that the unit of energy in the metric system is the *joule,* if masses are in kilograms, and distances in meters.

We will also be concerned with how fast we consume energy. The watt (w) is the rate or speed at which energy is being used. It is defined as the number of joules used per second:

one watt = one joule/second

In summary:

The joule is the measure of energy.   The watt is the measure of the rate at which energy is being used.

Let us get a feel for the size of the numbers involved in these problems. A 6 kg mass (equivalent to a body weighing 13.3 lb)* moving with a speed of 10 m/sec (about 20 mph) has a kinetic energy of 300 j. [See Worksheet 1-3.]

To relate this figure to the everyday world, let us note that a 60-w lamp consumes (or more properly, converts to light and heat) 60 j of electricity every second. If a river with a current of 20 mph drives a generator, and if all of the kinetic energy of the river is converted into electrical energy - *an impossible circumstance* - 13.3 lb of water (about 13.5 pints) flowing through the generator turbine blades every second is required to keep the lamp lit for 5 sec.

We will talk about energy loss at an appropriate point further on in the book. The problem of efficiency, how well we can convert one form of energy into another form without waste, is another key to our understanding of the energy problem.

Potential Energy

We must understand the concept of potential energy; the concept is quite straightforward. Energy is somehow stored over a period of time and when released is in a form which can be harnessed to do work.

All of our energy supply systems are describable in terms of potential energy. Let us look at three examples.

---

* Remember, mass and weight are not the same. On Earth, a mass of 6 kg will feel a force of 13.3 lb due to the pull of gravity. In the parentheses we have shifted from mass to weight and from the metric system to the British system of units.

Example 1. A dam holds a large amount of water. When the gates
of the dam are opened, the water that rushes out possesses a large
amount of kinetic energy. The energy was stored in the body of water
itself in the form of gravitational *potential energy*.

Example 2. The storage battery in an automobile possesses potential
energy in the form of chemical potential energy. When released, this
potential energy becomes electrical energy which does work in driving
an electric motor, the starter, which spins the automobile engine over
to get the internal combustion cycle started.

Example 3. Ball-point pen refills have a small spring around their
lower tip. When the refill is clicked into the writing position, the
spring is compressed. You do work to compress the spring. You exert
a small force via your thumb and move it through a small distance.
This work becomes potential energy when it is stored in the compressed
spring. When the button on top of the pen is pressed again, a simple
latch is released, and the spring expands to release its potential
energy and do work on the ink cartridge in shooting it up into the
body of the pen.

Example 1 illustrates gravitational potential energy; Example 2
illustrates chemical potential energy; Example 3 illustrates a form
of mechanical potential energy stored in a spring.

THE CONSERVATION OF ENERGY

Without so stating, we have been employing the principle known as
the conservation of energy. This is a cornerstone principle in physics,
and there is no indication that nature under any circumstances violates
the conservation of energy. It applies in biological systems as well
as physical systems. The understanding of this principle is essential
for an understanding of our energy problems.
Rather than work from a formal definition, let us see the conservation of energy in action and work first toward an intuitive grasp of
the concept. To do this we will step by step analyze the case of a
falling mass, say, a stone.

(1) The stone in Fig. 1-2 is said to possess gravitational
potential energy when held above the ground. In our example, it is
not in motion and therefore does not possess kinetic energy.

WORKSHEET 1-3

Newton's Law; Work and Kinetic Energy

Here are a few problems to illustrate the use of the formulas. Because the units of energy of concern to us are in the metric system (e.g., the kilowatt-hour), we will use the metric system in our problems. We shall make only one or two points in illustrating the application of Newton's second law: $F = m \times a$. We start by analyzing a, the acceleration:

(1) All bodies near the Earth's surface are accelerated by gravity at 9.8 m/sec^2. We are, of course, neglecting air friction.

(a) Speed, the rate at which you cover a distance, is measured in meters/second. The acceleration of a body falling straight down is the rate at which it increases its speed. Explain, therefore, why units of acceleration are meters/second^2.

(b) What is the gravitational force on a mass of 10 kg?

$$F = m \times a$$

$$= \underline{\hspace{1cm}} \text{ kg} \times \underline{\hspace{1cm}} \text{ m/sec}^2$$

$$= \underline{\hspace{1cm}} \text{ kg-m/sec}^2$$

The kilogram × meters/second^2 is called a newton, the unit of force in the metric system. Thus, the answer would simply be given in newtons.

(c) 1 lb = 4.45 N. Calculate the above gravitational force in pounds. The gravitational force is given the special name weight.

$$F = \underline{\hspace{1cm}} \text{ lb}$$

(2) A force of 67 N (about 15 lb) is used to lift a box 5 m (about 16.5 ft). Calculate the work done:

$$\text{Work} = \text{Force} \times \text{Distance}$$

$$= \underline{\hspace{1cm}} \text{ N} \times \underline{\hspace{1cm}} \text{ m}$$

$$= \underline{\hspace{1cm}} \text{ N-m}$$

The Newton-meter is called a joule, and the joule is a unit of work and energy.

16a

(3) A mass of 10 kg has a speed of 9.9 m/sec just as it strikes the ground. Find its kinetic energy at that moment:

(a) $KE = (1/2)m\text{-}s^2$

$= 1/2$ _____ kg

$=$ _____ kg

$=$ _____ j

(b) Show that kg $(m^2/sec^2) = N\text{-}m$.

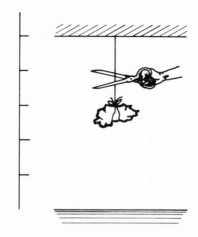

Fig. 1-2

(2) At any point in midflight (Fig. 1-3a), the stone has both kinetic and potential energy. It has kinetic energy, quite obviously, because it is in motion. That it still possesses some potential energy can be seen by thinking of the stone in terms of Fig. 1-3b.

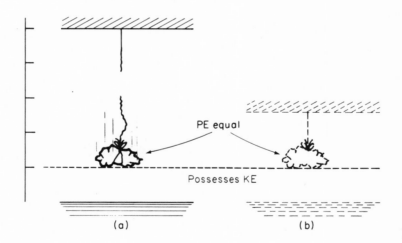

PE equal

Possesses KE

(a)   (b)

Fig. 1-3

(3) Just at the microscopic split second that a point of the stone first makes contact with the ground, or, if you prefer, at the split second before it hits the ground (Fig. 1-4), it has no potential energy and has all kinetic energy. (This is the split second before the stone stops moving.)

17

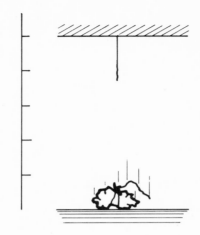

Fig. 1-4

Now we shall introduce the conservation of energy into this problem. According to the conservation of energy, we start with a certain amount of energy and that is how much energy we must have when we are finished. We cannot suddenly create energy, nor can we destroy it. It can be changed from one form to another, as in our example here, from potential energy to kinetic energy.

To be specific, let us say the stone in Fig. 1-2 has 20 j of potential energy. According to the conservation of energy, the stone will have 20 j of kinetic energy as it hits the ground, the same total amount of energy as we started with.

What about Fig. 1-3, the intermediate situation? When the stone is halfway between the starting point and the ground, it will have 10 j of potential energy and 10 j of kinetic energy. The closer it gets to the ground, the faster it goes, and the more kinetic energy it has, the less potential energy it will have. However, at every point, the total of the kinetic plus potential energy will be 20 j.

As the stone hits the ground and comes to rest, the energy is dissipated in the form of heat and sound and diffuses into the atmosphere. The energy is not "destroyed," it just moves on in another form.

Strictly speaking, the stone will not hit the ground with 20 j of kinetic energy. Some small amount of this energy will be lost in the form of heat due to air friction as the stone falls to the ground.

An engineer or scientist would refer to the components of this example as a *system*. He would draw mental boundary lines around those things that must be considered in the problem and generally exclude all else, as in Fig. 1-5. In our case, the *system* had a given amount of energy to start with. Thereafter, we neither added nor removed

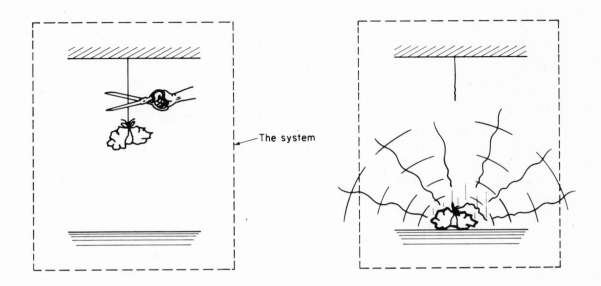

Fig. 1-5

energy from the *system*. Thus, we have looked at a problem confined
to a limited region of space and studied over a small period of time.
    To determine what happened to the 20 j of energy after it became
heat and sound, we would have to enlarge our system and study it for
a longer period of time. For the problems of concern to us, the system
will be a restricted one. [See Worksheet 1-4.]

Electrical Energy

    Let us look at the conservation of energy in terms of producing
electrical energy (see Fig. 1-6):

(1) Coal is burned to heat
water to produce steam;

(1) Chemical potential energy
is converted into heat, then
into a form of mechanical energy
(expanding gases);

(2) The steam drives a turbine, which turns an electric
generator;

(2) Mechanical energy does work
(more mechanical energy);

(3) The generator produces
electricity to light lamps,
drive motors, etc.;

(3) Mechanical energy is converted into electrical energy,
and electrical energy into light,
heat, work.

19

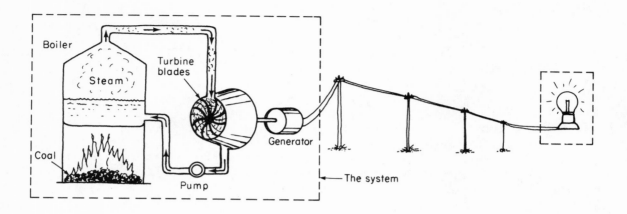

Fig. 1-6

Not all of the chemical energy in the coal is recovered in the form of electrical energy. The losses are substantial:

(1) Not all of the heat from the burning coal produces the steam. There is heat loss at the walls of the furnace and elsewhere.

(2) Not all of the steam does "productive" work. It cools down a bit, there are losses due to internal friction in the gas, etc.

(3) Friction in the turbine blades and generator produces waste heat. The wires conducting the electricity have a certain amount of electrical resistance which causes energy losses in the form of heat as the electricity is transmitted to the home.

Not counting the losses due to the appliances in the home, the system in the diagram, in the case of a typical power plant, is only 30% efficient. Sixty percent of the chemical potential energy of the coal is wasted.

If we enlarge our definition of the system and measure all the waste heat along with the useful energy generated, we would find that the total energy would equal the chemical potential energy of the coal.

At the time of this writing, a pumped-storage facility is being proposed as a backup source of power for New York City. We will discuss a pumped-storage system in Chapter III, along with its implications. For now, we want briefly to describe it in the context of the conservation of energy.

In such a facility, water is stored in a large man-made reservoir a goodly number of feet above an adjacent river. When there is a peak

WORKSHEET 1-4

Conservation of Energy

We shall look at a 10 kg mass lifted 5 m above the ground.

(1) Find the work done in lifting this mass:

Work = Force × Distance

= _____ × _____

= _____ j (=N-m)

This work has now become gravitational potential energy. By the conservation of energy the potential energy must be _____ j. To determine a formula for gravitational potential energy, we take into consideration:

(a) The potential energy increases with the height above the ground.
(b) The potential energy increases with the weight of the body.

(2) Justify statements (a) and (b) with simple intuitive arguments.
We know the units of PE are the joule = newton-meter. It would seem, therefore, that the simplest formula we can guess at is:

PE = weight (N) × height (m)

This formula is in accord with statements (a) and (b) and can be shown to be a "special case" of the formula for work.

(3) Explain in words why this is so.

(4) Use the principle of the conservation of energy to find the kinetic energy of the body just as it hits the ground, the split instant before its motion stops:

_____ j

(5) When the body was falling and was 2 m above the ground, its potential energy was 196 j. What was its kinetic energy at that point?

Total energy = _____ j + _____ j

Kinetic energy = _____ j

20a

20b

demand for electricity, the water is released to drive generators, which provide additional power to the area. However, to get the water into the reservoir, it must be pumped uphill using heavy-duty motors, which are driven by electricity. Hence, the reservoir is filled during periods when there is low demand on the community power supply.

Consider the energy losses in this process. To start with, as we have just seen, in generating the electricity that drives the pumps, there are energy losses of 60%. There are further losses in the pumps and in the resulting friction when the water is pushed uphill, and the usual friction losses when the water runs back down to drive the generators. In terms of fuel supplies, this is a terrible waste, but we shall deal later with the advantages and drawbacks of pumped-storage facilities.

To be flippant, there is a moral to all this. In real life, you get back less usable energy than you put in. Even to get back exactly what you put in would require an ideal world, free of friction and other opposing forces. That, in short, is why a perpetual motion machine cannot be made. To keep the machine going, the system would have to be free of any losses whatsoever.

REFERENCES

[1] US Congress, Joint Committee on Atomic Energy (1972). "Selected Materials on the Calvert Cliffs Decision." Available from Superintendent of Documents, USGPO, Washington, D.C.

General References

Note the excellent value for money of the government reports and, in particular, the congressional hearings reports. These contain appendices with reprints of many of the important articles in the field. All US Government reports are available from the Superintendent of Documents, US Govt. Printing Office (USGPO), Washington, D.C. 20402.

Darmstadter, J., et al. (1971). "Energy in the World Economy." Johns Hopkins Univ. Press, Baltimore, Maryland.
Du Pree, W.G., and West, J.A. (1972). "U.S. Energy through the Year 2000." US Dept. of Interior, Washington, D.C. (December).
Hammond, A.L., Metz, W.D., and Maugh, T.H., II (1973). "Energy and the Future." American Association for Advancement of Science, Washington, D.C.
Holdren, J., and Herrara, P. (1972). "Energy." Sierra Club Books, New York.

1. Energy

International Atomic Energy Agency (1970). Report of Conference of the IAEA, Vienna 1970. Available from IAEA, Vienna, or United Nations, New York.

Landsberg, H., and Schurr, S.H. (1968). "Energy in the United States." Random House, New York.

MIT Technology Review Editors (1972). "Energy Technology to the Year 2000." MIT Technology Review (whole issue), Cambridge, Massachusetts.

Rorer, D. (1972). "Resource Letter on Energy and the Environment." American Physical Society, New York. (Also published in American Journal of Physics.) [Lists many references.]

Royal Swedish Academy of Sciences (1973). "Energy in Society," Symposium at Royal Swedish Academy of Sciences, Ambio., Vol. 2, No. 6.

Scientific American Editors (1971). "Energy and Power." Scientific American (whole issue), September; also published by Freeman, San Francisco, California.

Sporn, P. (1973). "Energy." Pergamon, Oxford.

US Congress, Joint Committee on Atomic Energy (1969). "Selected Materials on Environmental Effects of Producing Electric Power." USGPO (August).

US Congress, Joint Committee on Atomic Energy (1969). "Hearings before the JCAE," Vols. I, II (with combined index at end of Vol. II, Part II). USGPO (October, November).

US Council on Environmental Quality (1971). "Environmental Effects of Nuclear Power Stations." USCEQ, Washington, D.C.

US Council on Environmental Quality (1973). "Energy and the Environment - Electric Power." USCEQ, Washington, D.C. (August).

US Govt. (1970). "Electric Power and the Environment." USGPO.

US Govt. (annual). "Statistical Abstract of the United States." USGPO.

Wilson, C.L., and Matthews, W.H., eds. (1970). "Man's Impact on the Global Environment." MIT Press, Cambridge, Massachusetts.

PROBLEMS

1. Environmentalists are now saying we must conserve energy. What relevance does this have to the scientific principles of the conservation of energy? Is conservation of fuel a better expression? If not, what might be?

2. Do you agree with the projections for future energy use given in Worksheet 1-1? Make your own now, and another when you have finished this book.

3. Write an essay outlining the reasons that could have contributed to the dramatic increase in world population in the last three

Problems

centuries. State all the facts that you can imagine have any relevance, but do not be afraid to make tentative judgments on their
relative importance. Stress particularly the role you conceive energy
has played in the process.

4. Refer to the graph in Worksheet 1-2. (You need not have gone
through the Worksheet to do this problem.) From the curve, make an
estimate of how the doubling time has been changing over the centuries.

5. What is your weight in the metric system? How many meters are
in a mile? Find the speed of a car going 60 mph in terms of meters/
second.

6. What must a spaceship do to make a left turn?
   Explain your answer to this question: does the moon accelerate
in its motion around the earth?

7. Twelve kWh is a measure of energy. Give the equivalent amount
of energy in joules.

8. Refer to the definition of a watt. If 5 W of power are used
per second, then 5 j of energy are consumed. With this example as a
guide, write out a simple formula relating energy, time, and power.

9. Which gives off more light, a 40-W incandescent lamp or a 40-W
fluorescent lamp? Justify your answer by applying the conservation of
energy. What happens to the rest of the energy? Why do large office
buildings leave their lights on at night in the winter?

10. A lake is 10 m deep and 1 km × 1 km in area; all of the water
goes over a waterfall 300 m high. How much electricity can be generated
at 100% efficiency from this energy supply? (Each cubic meter of water
weighs 9800 Nm^3.)

11. Describe the conservation of energy in terms of your body, from
energy input to output.

2
Man's Energy Resources

Any discussion of the energy problem must begin with a consideration of the several sources of energy available for use by man. Available energy resources are not inexhaustible. Some new energy sources fall into the classification of those that we do not yet know how to utilize and those that we find too costly to use.

SOLAR POWER

The Sun's Radiation

The sun, like other stars, was formed from a massive cloud of interstellar hydrogen, a cloud so massive that it developed a sizable internal gravitational pull. One part of the cloud attracted another, and the cloud moved in upon itself at ever increasing speeds, to the point where the atoms possessed sufficient kinetic energy for their nuclei to react with each other in a process known as fusion, the process used in the hydrogen bomb [1]. (Fusion is discussed in Chapter 5, along with more details of the sun's processes.) These reactions involve temperatures of several million degrees.

Solar Power

The radiant heat presently emitted at the outer surface of the sun is roughly that emitted by any hot body at 5000° C (about 9000° F).

It is not at all surprising that early man worshipped the sun, for he knew that his life and comfort depended upon it.

TECHNICAL NOTE 2-1

Fahrenheit to Centigrade

The two key temperatures for defining the centigrade scale are the freezing point of water, designated 0° C, and the boiling point of water, designated 100° C. On the fahrenheit scale, the scale we normally use, the freezing point of water is 32° and the boiling point 212°. Comparing the scales, we see that each degree centigrade is larger than each degree fahrenheit, since the difference between the freezing point and boiling point is 100° on the centigrade scale, while it is 180° on the Fahrenheit scale. Thus each degree fahrenheit is equivalent to (5/9 × °C [that is, (100/180) × °C]. To get a conversion formula then,

$$F = (5/9)\ C + 32$$

The reason for adding 32 becomes obvious if you set C = 0.

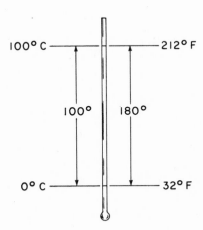

Fig. 2-1.

However, nature is not so agreeable as to take the freezing point of water as zero on its temperature scale. Temperature is a measure of the average kinetic energy of the molecules in a substance: The higher the temperature, the greater the kinetic energy of the molecules. This picture makes sense in terms of our earlier discussions of the conservation of energy.

Nature's zero temperature is the point at which each molecule of a system is in its lowest energy state. Absolute zero is 273° C below 0° C. Scientists use this absolute scale, or Kelvin scale as it is known (after William Thompson, first Lord Kelvin), which is

$$K = C + 273$$

The role of the sun's energy in a number of nature's processes is shown in a general way in Fig. 2-2. In this figure we see that energy arriving at the Earth from the sun is balanced by the reradiation of most of it back into space and a little energy radiated into space by other processes. All balancing acts are delicate, and the energy balancing act at the Earth is no exception: The Earth neither heats up nor cools down except in terms of geological time periods.

The incoming radiation shown in Fig. 2-2 is made up of visible light, ultraviolet rays (short-wavelength radiation), and infrared rays (long-wavelength radiation). Invisible to the eye, ultraviolet radiation causes the skin to tan and burn. About 35% of the ultraviolet rays that reach the outer rim of the Earth's atmosphere are reflected by the atmosphere. Were an increased amount of ultraviolet radiation to reach the Earth's surface, our life systems would change. The rate of skin and other forms of cancer would increase greatly: A drastic increase in ultraviolet radiation could destroy life on Earth. For example, a possible consequence of a large fleet of supersonic jet transport planes (SST) flying at high altitudes would be to generate nitrogen oxides (see Chapter 8) that remove ozone from the atmosphere, and thereby additional amounts of ultraviolet radiation would arrive at the Earth with resulting unpredictable but probably adverse biological effects.

Continuing down the incoming beam on the diagram, we see that another 43% of the incoming energy is radiated back into space in the form of what most people would call "ordinary" heat, which is, in fact, mostly infrared radiation. Heated by the sun, the land, water, etc., in turn become surfaces which radiate heat energy.

The remaining processes of reradiation or storage of the sun's received energy should be understandable from the diagram itself.

On the other hand, the Earth generates heat in some of its own internal processes, from nuclear, thermal, and gravitational reactions within the core of the planet, and from the friction of the seas as

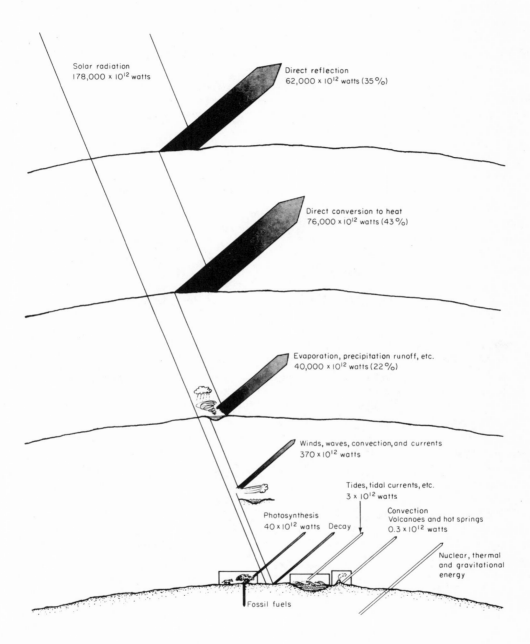

Fig. 2-2· World energy flow broken into its major components.

a result of tides and currents. The radiation of energy into space
from these energy sources, although relatively small, also contributes
to the energy balance of the planet on which we live.

When it falls on the Earth squarely, 0.139 W/cm^2 of the sun's
energy reaches the outermost part of the Earth's atmosphere. (At the
poles, the sun's rays "graze" the Earth, and the figure is considerably
smaller.) Keep in mind that 0.139 W/cm^2 is a statement that in each
second 0.139 j of energy is falling on an area of about the size of
your fingernail. This amount of energy is small and would barely light
a flashlight bulb. But, the surface of the Earth is large, and if we
total the incident energy over the whole surface, we find 1.78×10^{17} W,
which is 10,000 times what we need to supply world energy needs in the
year 2000. If we could envisage a direct economic way of capturing and
using this energy, it would be one of the major triumphs of the human
intellect.

TECHNICAL NOTE 2-2

Waves and the Electromagnetic Spectrum

*We know that the mutual gravitational attraction of the Earth and
moon keeps the moon in orbit around the Earth. But how is the gravitational effect transmitted between the two bodies? At first, this
specific question wasn't answered; it was observed that there was an
interaction without contact through the vacuum of space. The name
given to such phenomena was action at a distance.*

*In the 1800's, the concept of "field" evolved. A planet is said
to be surrounded by a gravitational field. If another body comes
under the influence of the field, that body and the field interact,
with the body experiencing a force. A magnet is said to be surrounded
by a magnetic field, and an electric charge by an electric field.*

*Let us generate an electric field of varying strength - it can
be done easily enough. We'll start with no field (or zero field),
smoothly built to a maximum value, or, in short, we vary the strength
of the field so that a graph of its intensity versus time (Fig. 2-3)*

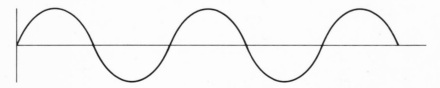

Fig. 2-3.

looks like a sine curve. In scientific terminology, we say that we have generated a wave.

One of the variables of a wave is its frequency. One cycle is a single complete wave form; the frequency is the number of cycles generated per second (expressed in units called Hertz, Hz).

(1) Electromagnetic waves are combined electric and magnetic waves generated by the same source simultaneously.

(2) Radio waves are electromagnetic waves of low frequency.

(3) Gamma rays are electromagnetic waves of high frequency.

(4) Light waves are electromagnetic waves of "intermediate" frequency.

Thus, just as low notes and high notes are sound waves of different frequencies, the radiation that we will discuss in this book refers to electromagnetic waves of different frequencies (see Table 2-1). A better overall picture is given by Fig. 2-4.

TABLE 2-1

Type	Typical frequency (Hz)	Wavelength (cm)
Radio (long wave, AM)	10^6	30,000
Television	6×10^6	500
Radar	10^{10}	3
Infrared	10^{13}	0.003
Visible light	5×10^{14}	6×10^{-5}
Ultraviolet light	10^{16}	3×10^{-6}
X Rays	10^{18}	3×10^{-8}
Gamma rays	10^{20} and over	3×10^{-10}

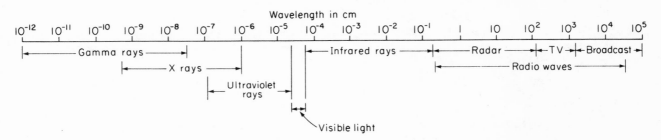

Fig. 2-4. Electromagnetic spectrum. "Hertzian" waves are generated by moving charges (electric currents), infrared by hot bodies (heat). The labels on the axis give the length of a single wave expressed in cm.

2. Man's Energy Resources

TECHNICAL NOTE 2-3

Photocells

In Technical Note 2-2, light was described as an electromagnetic wave. This wave carries energy. In an atom, electrons are kept in orbit around a nucleus by the mutual attraction of their negative charge to the positive charge of the nucleus. To remove an electron from an atom requires work. A particle with sufficient kinetic energy could knock an electron free.

Light carries enough energy to free an electron from an atom of a photoelectric material. Most photoelectric materials require light in the ultraviolet region to free electrons. The amount of energy required to free the electron varies from material to material and is called the work function. We will designate the work function by W. If after being freed from the atom, the electron has kinetic energy, the conservation of energy demands that the sum of the parts equal the whole, that is,

$$E_{light} = W + E_{electron}$$

Although there are many experiments that can only be explained by assuming that light travels as a wave, the photoelectric effect and a number of other experiments provide evidence that light interacts with matter like a collection of particles.

Do not expect to feel comfortable with this idea. Thanks to quantum theory and confirming experiments, we now know that the wave concept is correct and in other circumstances the particle concept is correct.

An individual particle in a light beam is called a photon. Whether viewed as a moving electromagnetic wave or a beam of photons, light travels at a speed of approximately 186,000 miles/sec. This statement applies to the entire electromagnetic spectrum. A gamma ray is a high-energy photon, and it too moves at 186,000 miles/sec.

Because it appears so often, by convention, the speed of light is represented by the letter c. In the metric system the speed of light is 30,000,000,000 cm/sec.

It has been theoretically demonstrated and experimentally shown that the higher the frequency of a photon, the higher its energy. Thus ultraviolet light is more energetic than, say, red light, and gamma rays are the most energetic of all forms of electromagnetic radiation. This is described by the equation $E_{light} = \hbar\nu$, where $\hbar$ is Planck's constant (Planck was the originator of the quantum theory, in 1905) and ν the frequency.

Feasibility is not the problem, for there are several feasible ways of utilizing solar power. Using nature's way, trees can be planted, and we can wait for them to turn into coal or burn the wood directly. In fact, a scheme for accelerating the biological transformation of carbon dioxide to a hydrocarbon fuel using bacteria and anaerobic fermentation was proposed by Oswald and Golueka [2].

Harnessing Solar Power, I

Photocells, which convert sunlight directly into electricity with a conversion efficiency in excess of 10%, have been successfully used on satellites. That is, something amounting to 10 to 15% of energy in the form of sunlight that falls on the photocell is converted into energy in the form of electricity. In these cells, sunlight falls on a photoelectric material and ejects electrons from the material. [Refer to Technical Note 2-3.] These electrons are then constrained to flow along a wire. What we loosely refer to as electricity is an electric current in a wire, that is, a flow of electrons through a wire. The larger the current, the more electrons flow through any given section of the wire.

Only the most expensive photocells reach the efficiencies cited above. On space vehicles where these are used capital cost is secondary to weight and size considerations, and these cells are indeed a lightweight source of power.

Photocells are common in the laboratory and are used in small applications. Assume, however, we wish to use them in a large application, as in a 1000-MW generating station. At an efficiency of 10%, we would need to collect 10,000 MW of solar power to generate 1000 MW of electrical power. If our solar facility is at the equator and we allow for night time and occasional cloud cover, our solar cells will receive, on the average, only about 1/6 of the sunlight that reaches the uppermost part of the Earth's atmosphere. To produce the 1000 MW of power, our solar station would have to cover an area of 4×10^{11} cm^2, or equivalently, be a square 4 miles on a side. In Worksheet 2-1, you are asked to carry this calculation through.

The food that we grow provides man with about 100 W per person on 100 times the area the stations would occupy. It may therefore not be unreasonable to consider devoting space to solar stations for the generation of electricity. However, the expense of building such stations is great; to make the photocells one must secure costly raw materials and expend much effort to process them into final form. Moreover, we have yet to develop an energy storage mechanism to take over during darkness. It might be well to remind ourselves, as shown in Chapter 1, that the process of storage will cost us energy, since we cannot transfer energy with 100% efficiency.

Harnessing Solar Power, II

A truly elaborate technological feat would be to mount mirrors
on satellites which orbit the earth and to focus the sun's rays onto
an area of the earth smaller than required for the photocell proposal.
The size of the power station would be relatively small and therefore
more practical to build [3]. The danger inherent in this proposal is
all too obvious: death and destruction would result were the mirror
to get out of control.

A more recent proposal suggests the conversion of energy at the
satellite into microwaves for transmission to earth [4, 5]. Several
potentially expensive and certainly complex technologies are involved
in this proposal. It is being studied under a research contract with
the National Aeronautics and Space Administration (NASA).

Were we able to accomplish this mode of harnessing solar energy,
for the scientific dreamer the next step would be to make the satellite
orbit the sun and collect more energy than falls on the Earth. We
leave to the science-fiction writers the search for energy throughout
the galaxy when the sun can no longer adequately supply the Earth. At
that point, surely the Earth's energy balance would be grossly upset.

Both of these methods, photoelectric cells on the Earth's surface
and the satellite-mounted photoelectric cells, convert sunlight *directly*
into electricity. However, direct conversion devices themselves cause
problems, but we shall leave a full discussion of direct energy conversion devices to Chapter 12. We therefore look at ways of generating
electricity from sunlight through intermediate steps, such as using
the sun's rays to operate a steam engine, which in turn would drive
a generator.

Harnessing Solar Power, III

Thus we turn our attention to producing electricity in the rather
conventional way, except that instead of using a fossil fuel such as
coal to generate steam, we shall use solar radiation.

As a first step in this discussion, it would be valuable to look
at a coal-fired power station which produces 1000 MW of electricity.
The laws of thermodynamics as applied to this class of problems tell
us that a thermal plant cannot have better than a 38% efficiency
[Technical Note 2-4]. Thus, this power station will require about
3000 MW of heat. Its boiler might be a cube about 20 ft on a side.

To collect 3000 MW of thermal power from the sun would require
an area on the Earth of 2 miles^2 (3 km^2). We must find a way of:
(1) collecting the sun's heat; (2) storing the sun's heat; (3) seeing
that very little heat is lost by reradiation.

WORKSHEET 2-1

Solar Farms

(1) You have been told to decide on the practicality of "solar-cell farms" for electrical energy. Each farm, 4 square miles in area, will generate 1000 MW. We need to generate 500,000 MW. What percentage of U.S. land would this involve? (Area of U.S. = 3.63 million square miles = 3.63×10^6 miles^2.)

(2) On the accompanying map of the U.S., select a limited number of favorable sites for the farms and note the area they would "feed."

(3) Develop a thesis on the geographic and cost considerations from the location of these farms.

(4) What environmental opposition might develop from your choice of sites? While you can be sure of a quiet and clean energy source, environmental opposition might still develop. To what might the environmentalists object?

(5) Assume that a 1000-MW electric power station must cost no more than 500 million dollars (megabucks) to be practical, and only half this cost can be photocells. What is the maximum allowable cost of a photocell section 1 m × 1 m in size?

32a

32b

Solar Power

The husband and wife team of Arden P. and Marjorie P. Meinel, both of whom are astrophysicists, have examined a scheme for carrying out steps (1)-(3) in several optimistic papers that are receiving a good deal of attention [6, 7]. They propose to collect the sun's rays on a bank of tubes containing liquid sodium, a fluid that is being used and further studied to conduct heat from some nuclear reactors. These tubes will convey heat at high temperatures to the central power station.

TECHNICAL NOTE 2-4

The Carnot Engine and Efficiency

There are two valuable lessons to be learned in this Technical Note:

(1) An understanding of the maximum efficiency at which any engine can operate;
(2) The difference between a theoretical restriction on a design and a technological limitation;

Sadi Carnot, a French military engineer, was involved in the study of steam engines, the dominant manmade power source of the 1800's. He addressed himself to the question of what might be the maximum efficiency of an engine, assuming there were no engineering limitations. The details of how the engine was put together were unimportant. His goal was to determine the best performance for an ideal engine: No real engine would perform to that standard, but here was something to aim for.

A steam engine takes heat from a heat source (the boiler), and then eventually the steam is condensed and heat given up to a heat sink (the air or a special condenser). All the heat is not available for doing mechanical work or generating electricity. This is true whether we use steam or any other working fluid.

This Carnot engine, as it is now called, was devised in 1824. Whatever the working fluid was, such as steam, it would absorb heat at some temperature T_h and give it up at some temperature T_c. During its change from one temperature to another, it would be perfectly insulated, exchanging work with surroundings, but no heat. Carnot found the efficiency η of such an ideal engine was given by

$$\eta = \frac{T_h - T_c}{T}$$

where T is the absolute temperature.

2. Man's Energy Resources

In a steam engine, the steam under conditions of proper pressure reaches temperatures of about 1000° F, and the maximum efficiency of an ideal steam engine is about 68%, but in practice it is much less, about 40%.

The efficiency of any energy process can be defined in the general terms

$$\eta = \frac{\text{useful energy out}}{\text{energy from fuel source}}$$

Can someone invent a steam engine that will have a better η than 68%? If the laws of physics as we understand them hold, the answer is no. This is a theoretical limitation of the same kind that's imposed on any perpetual motion machine. It is not a question of better engineering.

On the other hand, the question, "will man ever be able to create complex life forms in a laboratory?" could best be answered by, "why not?" Life exists; therefore it is theoretically possible to produce life. But here is an engineering problem of the first rank. There are many aspects of life systems we don't understand fully and many processes we can't carry through at present. But there is no reason to believe that we will not be able to do so at some time in the future.

Thus you see we must distinguish between not being able to do something because it violates the laws of nature or because we just do not yet know how to do it.

To collect the sun's rays on the tubes most efficiently, a large bank of glass focusing lenses will be used. The concentration of sunlight will thereby be improved by a factor of two.

Heat loss in the tubes can come from two factors:

(1) Conduction of heat away from the tubes: The heat will be partially transferred to whatever is in contact with the tubes, the ground, the air, etc. In the Meinel system, the tubes will be isolated in a vacuum using the best available vacuum technology.

(2) Reradiation of heat away from the tubes: All warm bodies emit infrared radiation [see Technical Note 2-3], your own body included. So, too, will these hot tubes emit infrared radiation, and this reradiation normally prevents a high temperature from being reached. For example, the Earth is heated up by the sun, and it reradiates infrared rays to space. The amount of radiation reradiated depends upon the temperature of the body: The higher the temperature, the more energy

will be reradiated. The mean temperature of the Earth adjusts itself so that exactly as much radiation is reemitted as is absorbed. Unless we take care to prevent reradiation, we cannot raise the temperature of an object very much above the Earth's mean temperature.

The Meinels propose to take advantage of recent technology that has made it possible to manufacture *interference filters* inexpensively [Technical Note 2-5]. Properly designed, these filters will allow sunlight to pass through them but only allow 2% of the infrared light to escape. Thus the temperature of the collecting surface can exceed that of the Earth and can be raised to 1260° F, a temperature high enough to operate a conventional steam-generating power station.

TECHNICAL NOTE 2-5

Interference Filters

Technical Notes 2-1 and 2-2 described light in terms of its description as a wave as well as a particle. To deal with the phenomenon of interference, we will regard light as a wave. We want to take a closer look at what a wave is.

Look at the piece of string stretched taut in Fig. 2-5a. If we pluck the string (Fig. 2-5b), a "disturbance" will travel along its length (Fig. 2-5c).

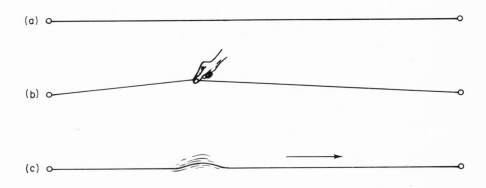

Fig. 2-5.

Notice two things:

(1) No part of the string moves from left to right: only the "disturbance" moves;

(2) The "disturbance" has a definite speed, and it carries energy with it.

If we could set up a pair of identical pulses as shown in Fig. 2-6a,

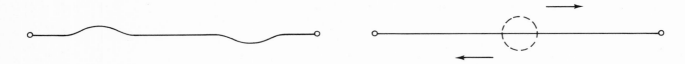

Fig. 2-6.

as they pass each other, they would cancel each other out at the moment of overlap (Fig. 2-6b). This cancellation of waves is called destructive interference.

Interference filters, as a general rule, are made up of two layers, a glass base and a thin layer of a metal evaporated onto the glass. The layers are normally about 0.00005 to 0.000006 in. thick. The thickness must be very uniform.

Light reflected from the front surface of the film interferes with that from the back, if, the thickness of the film is the right distance to allow the cancellation shown about to occur.

Think carefully about this: The light is not able to escape. The energy remains trapped beneath the filter.

For the storage of heat energy during daylight hours for use at nighttime, molten salt will be tried. We shall discuss such energy storage devices in Chapter 3.

Figure 2-7 is a photograph of a solar-power farm in the desert. Is this a feasible scheme from the point of view of both cost and technology? Hottel and Howard [8], who have studied solar energy for some time, disagree with the detailed numbers obtained by the Meinels. They claim the Meinels are overly optimistic about the hours of sunlight in Arizona, the ability to achieve low heat conductivity over large areas, and a number of other matters. Given these facts, would it be wise now to make a large-scale commitment to such a project? Probably not. But in this sense large scale is a 1000-MW power station; small-scale studies of a solar farm up to 1 MW in size are in progress.

Fig. 2-7 Model of a solar-power farm on typical desert terrain. Note
that the rows of collectors noticeably darken the desert. This 250-MW
power station would use turbine waste heat to desalinate seawater.

Another approach to the problem is given in a proposal by Ford
[9]. Large plastic lenses would be used to collect the sun's rays.
Estimated costs for each square yard of lenses is about $35, and for
each square yard of boiler area $10. However, if this plan is worth
developing, research would have to be inaugurated on plastics that
would not deteriorate in strong sunlight. Ford's energy-storage scheme
is a clever and efficient one. At 2700° F water will decompose into
hydrogen and oxygen. He proposes to collect sunlight at this temperature so that energy will be stored as chemical potential energy. However, to achieve such temperatures is at present extremely difficult.
An alternative is to search for a catalytic reaction that enables the
water to decompose at a lower temperature.

Some Conclusions

These pessimistic remarks do not mean that solar energy should
not be studied. In fact, an historical analogy may be in order. By
1920 we already knew that the atomic nucleus was an energy source,
and we also knew that this was the way the sun derived its energy.
Yet, even a physicist as great as Lord Rutherford, the man who proposed
and established the existence of the atom's nucleus, believed that
the "secret" of nuclear energy would never be unlocked by man. When
the "secret" was finally discovered in early 1939, it was as an out-
growth of fundamental research on the structure of the atom, research
intended only to increase man's understanding of the universe, research
having no "practical" objective.

2. Man's Energy Resources

The very fact that we can consider sophisticated schemes for directly harvesting the sun's energy is a result of basic research carried out for what may be called intellectual reasons. For example, interference filters were invented because we had studied the fundamental nature of light. Photocells have reached their present level of efficiency because the quantum theory had come into existence to account for experimental results that contradicted older theories that had worked for so many other phenomena.

The quantum theory of atoms was truly an esoteric area of study insofar as the world of 1900 was concerned. When the theory was found to work for atomic phenomena, it was applied to ordered arrays of atoms, that is, to solids with relatively simple structures. From these first theoretical steps came an understanding of solids. When enough was known about submicroscopic interactions in solids, it was possible to say, "What if...?" and conceive of the transistor, if not actually invent it. Similarly, one can now say about the present photocell, "What if...?" and then proceed to try to do what he has in mind to improve the properties of the photocell.

In the case of solar energy, we should continue fundamental research in many areas, including some that might never be of use, as well as conduct directed research on interference filters and vacuum technology.

We need research in many areas. Basic research requires much less money than development projects and is usually a very good value.

Since solar power is not at the developmental stage, we should not yet stop those projects that are, e.g., breeder reactors and gasification of coal, which use engineers and not pure scientists, or those which are even further advanced and at a manufacturing stage, e.g., present nuclear power and ordinary coal- and oil-fired stations. These facts indicate that we would best benefit from a balanced budgetary attitude to these projects and that one should not displace the other.

One direct use of solar energy is already possible and almost economically practicable. Experimental houses have been built that are heated by solar heat, with other sources as supplemental or standby heating.* We could probably obtain half of our space-heating requirements in this way by drastic redesign of houses. But this would supply only 20% of our total fuel consumption. Certainly we should avoid obvious waste. Large glass-walled apartment buildings allow the sun's heat to pass (while inhibiting reradiation), and this is good on a sunny day in winter. But in the summer it can lead to excessive demands for air conditioning: One building in Montreal, Canada, used air conditioning in October! A means of controlling the solar absorption

---

* Supplemental heat by electric heat using "heat pumps" [Technical Note 2-7] will help.

is vital. General references on solar energy are given in the reference list [10-13].

We will not dwell on environmental problems of solar energy. They are probably few, but not until projects reach the development or manufacturing stage do we usually bother to examine environmental effects.

POWER FROM THE RIVERS AND SEAS

Hydroelectric Power

The next most obvious energy source (which also seems to cost nothing in operation) is hydroelectric power. Water mills have been used since prehistoric times, but water power came into major vogue only with the use of electricity to transmit power over long distances. Before then, the farmer had to bring his grain to the mill by the river.

Most commonly, hydroelectric power is a utilization of the kinetic energy of a fast-moving body of water, such as a river or rapids. Manmade dams of large size have been built across rivers to raise the height of the water and release it over a falls. The environmental effects of manmade dams are discussed in Chapter 4.

The development of hydroelectric power in the U.S. has been very rapid. Large and small power stations have been built at all convenient locations, and about 27% of possible sources were already developed in 1965 [14, 15]. In the populous northeastern states, more than half the available hydropower sites have been developed; to develop the rest may involve environmental dislocation. The ultimate available hydropower for the United States is fairly definite: 170,000 MW.

Western Europe has much less water power available, but because of the high population density more of the ultimately available hydroelectric power is already developed. Other parts of the world have not developed hydropower to such an extent. Africa, in particular, has huge undeveloped resources, and the development of these resources is certain as industry and technology expand.

The world's water power resources are shown in Table 2-2. Note that development in the U.S. and Western Europe has reached 30%, which is probably a practical maximum [16].

We have not devoted much space to this power source simply because most of what can be done both technologically and geographically has been done. But, as we see in the next section, another, less exploited, source of water power exists.

TABLE 2-2

Summary of World's Water-Power Capacity, 1962

Region	Potential (10^3 MW)	Percent of total	Development (10^3 MW)	Percent developed
North America	313	11	59	19
South America	577	20	5	
Western Europe	158	6	47	30
Africa	780	27	2	
Middle East	21	1		
Southeast Asia	455	16	2	
Far East	42	1	19	
Australasia	45	2	2	
U.S.S.R., China, and satellites	466	16	16	3
Total	2857	100	152	

Tidal Power

The source of tidal energy is the gravitational energy of the earth-moon-sun system. The motion of the moon around the earth, combined with the rotation of the earth, produces tides with a tidal period (T) of 12 hr and 24 min in most places.

As the oceans move backwards and forwards under the influence of these tides, the energy is dissipated in friction between water molecules and between the water and the land. The direct calculation of the tidal energy seems difficult. However, it has been noticed that the rotations of the moon around the earth and of the earth around itself are slowing down, and the day is lengthening by 0.001 sec per century. This does not seem like much, but it corresponds to an energy loss of 3×10^{12} j/sec or 3×10^{12} W. We will not go into the details of this process, but we suggest that you read the excellent book by Munk and Macdonald [17] that deals with this subject.

As before, we want to think about this process as a function of the conservation of energy. If the earth gives up kinetic energy at a rate of 3×10^9 kW, this energy must go into some other form of energy. Indeed it does, and not unexpectedly, as with frictional processes in general, the kinetic energy becomes heat energy. We would like to capture some of this tidal energy before it is converted into heat and siphon it off to produce electricity.

The calculation which gives the rate of energy loss is quite reliable and suggests that even by the year 2000 tidal power, if completely harnessed, could supply 10% of the world's energy use (see Table 2-5). However, in practice most of this energy is not available. A water turbine has friction in its bearings and works well when a small quantity of water exerts a large force, as with a high waterfall. In the mid-Atlantic, for example, the differences in water heights due to tides are small.

Accordingly, we can only consider sites in the shallow seas for tidal power projects. Here, the tidal range (R), the difference in height between low and high tide, can be large. Large bays are particularly useful; the Bay of Fundy between Nova Scotia and New Brunswick in Canada is a well-known possible power source site. In practice, we would place a dam across the mouth of the bay and allow water to pass only through turbines [see Technical Note 2-5]. This power is available only at certain times of day, so that to be useful an energy-storage mechanism is needed.

The efficiency of such a tidal power station can be quite high; at La Rance in France, 25% of the theoretically obtainable power (given by the formula in Technical Note 2-6) is generated as electricity [18].

TECHNICAL NOTE 2-6

Tidal Power

We are going to develop an expression which gives the energy involved in the raising and lowering of water levels. We define our terms in Figs. 2-8, 2-9, and 2-10. The distance R is the tidal range (Fig. 2-8).

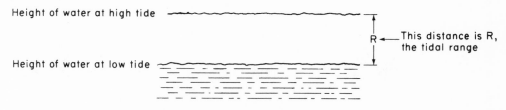

Fig. 2-8.

We designate the area of the bay by A (Fig. 2-9). The volume of water that comes into the bay with the tide (Fig. 2-10) is:

$$\text{Volume} = \text{Area} \times \text{height}$$
$$V = A \times R$$

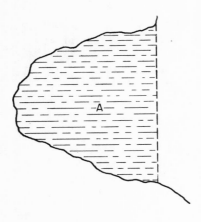

Fig. 2-9.

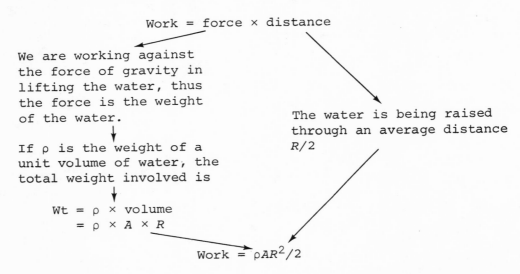

Fig. 2-10.

The work involved in raising the water level of the bay is:

Work = force × distance

We are working against
the force of gravity in
lifting the water, thus
the force is the weight
of the water.

The water is being raised
through an average distance
R/2

If ρ is the weight of a
unit volume of water, the
total weight involved is

Wt = ρ × volume
   = ρ × A × R

Work = $\rho AR^2/2$

*We would generate energy from the tides when the water comes in and
when it goes out, so that the total work done, or the energy available,
is twice the above formula:*

Energy = ρAR^2

*Power is the rate of flow of energy and thus is found by dividing the
energy by the time it takes for the water to flow in and out, measuring
the time in seconds and all other quantities in the metric system in
order to get the answer in watts.*

42

A list of possible tidal power sites is shown in Table 2-3. The main North American sites are in the Bay of Fundy, and mostly in Canada. From the table, we can calculate that only 6×10^{10} W is readily available: 2% of the total energy in the tides, and a small fraction of the world's energy needs.

TABLE 2-3

Selected tidal power sites	Potential power (kW, average)
Passamaquoddy (U.S.)	1800×10^3
Minas-Cobequid (U.S.)	$19,900 \times 10^3$
Shepody (U.S.)	2520×10^3
La Rance (France)	1550×10^3
Mont Saint-Michel (France)	9700×10^3
San Jose (Argentina)	5870×10^3
White Sea (U.S.S.R.)	$14,400 \times 10^3$

The environmental impact of tidal power is the effect of its use on the coastal waters. It will markedly change the habits of fish, although whether for better or worse is a matter that is probably under our control. Since not many tidal power sites are available in the United States, it seems exaggerated to dwell further on this point. [See Worksheet 2-2.]

Thermal Power from the Sea

We here make brief mention of a possible system for extracting energy from the seas; most experts believe it holds very little promise for large-scale utilization.

The surface waters of the world change their temperature with changes in climatic conditions. The deep waters do not. Therefore, there is often a temperature difference between the surface and the deep waters, and perhaps this temperature difference can be utilized to run a steam engine or other heat engine. To do so, one must find an adequate difference in temperature within a relatively small volume of water.

The Caribbean Sea appears to be a good place to seek out such a power source. A discussion of a preliminary study for a 100-MW power plant was published in 1966 [19]. This, however, on a worldwide basis, will also be a power source of limited energy output.

There has recently appeared an excellent review of the potential and the problems of thermal power from the oceans by Clarence Zener [20], under the title, "Solar Power from Seawater." The title emphasizes that the origin of these temperature gradients, like so many things, is the sun's radiation. Zener points out that to cope with the small temperature gradients, large and very costly engines are needed.

We will have a bit more to say about these matters when we discuss heat pumps in Chapter 4.

POWER FROM THE WINDS

It is a good practice to look back at old solutions to problems that are still with us and to see if modern technology might be able to improve on them. The harnessing of wind power is a case in point.

For centuries, man relied on the winds to transport his goods across the globe. The wind was used to grind grain, pump water, and in the case of Holland to pump water not for convenience, but for the necessity of keeping the country dry. Although somewhat irregular and rather unreliable, in sum total the winds did these tasks well.

Winds at levels of 25 to 30 mph, constant almost 24 hours per day for 11 months of the year, are not uncommon throughout many parts of the world. The periods of calm compare favorably with the "down time" of fossil-fuel power plants. Economically poor parts of the world would most benefit from wind power. If only a small amount of power was generated by the wind, it would be more economical than human power (in cases where large families are necessary for life-supporting tasks, but in themselves consume more than they produce) or animal power (which is most expensive in the areas where it is presently most relied upon).

For what we would call "low-level" energy applications, wind power can be stored. Storage batteries can be charged; water can be pumped uphill and held for future energy use. This, in fact, is done in Seteía (Crete), where the pumped water is used to assure the regular operation of watermills.

In 1945, a very large windmill was set up in Vermont to generate 1.2 MW of electricity (Fig. 2-11). It proved to be an uneconomical source of power when compared with the cost of readily available fossil fuels of that date. The serious student of the energy problem should refer to Putnam, "Energy from the Wind" [21], for a history of this project and a general discussion of harnessing the winds. More recent references on wind power can be found in a United Nations report of 1963 [22] and a NATO Seminar of 1963 [23].

There are both environmental and socioeconomic reasons to justify further research on wind power. The new technology of which we spoke can contribute new materials, stronger and lighter than those known in the past, computer design of the optimum shape of the blade or

WORKSHEET 2-2

Tidal Power

Passamaquoddy Bay is located on the U.S./Canada border, between Maine and New Brunswick. Here are the facts:

The area of the bay is 250×10^3 meters^2.
The mean tidal range is 5.5 meters.
Using the units of weight in the metric system (the newton instead of the pound), the density of water is 9800 N/m^3.

(a) Convert these numbers into the British system so that you have a better picture of what they mean:

area _____,   tidal range _____,   density _____

(b) To show that this station can produce 2000 MW of power, calculate:

The volume of water raised _____

The gravitational force involved _____

The potential energy of the water at high tide _____

The station's power capability by using the fact that the tide moves in and out every six and one-half hours. The answer is to be given in kilowatts _____

44b

Fig. 2-11.

"wings," and more efficient energy converters. There is much that can be done on a worldwide basis in this area, but it is not likely to be a major source of energy.

GEOTHERMAL ENERGY

Below the Earth's crust lies a molten layer, the mantle, and below (or more precisely, within) this layer lies the core. The base of the crust, which is some 25 to 50 km (15 to 30 miles) beneath the surface of the Earth, is estimated to be at temperatures which range from 200 to 1000° C (400 to 1800° F) [24]; a result of millions of years of radioactive decay within the Earth. Here then is nuclear energy going to waste.

Only a fraction of this interior heat of the Earth may ever be available to man, but geothermal sources are now grossly underdeveloped. They hold the potential for a significant increase in the energy resources of the United States.

One can make a qualitative estimate of the total amount of available geothermal energy. In order to be a little conservative, we assume that we can remove only the heat from a layer 100 km (about 62 miles) thick, lying 32 km (about 19 miles) below the surface, as shown in the schematic drawing of Fig. 2-12.

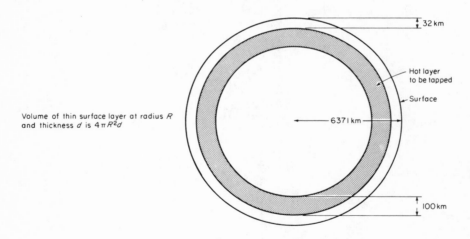

Volume of thin surface layer at radius R and thickness d is $4\pi R^2 d$

32 km

Hot layer to be tapped

Surface

6371 km

100 km

Fig. 2-12. Cross section of the Earth.

As Worksheet 2-3 shows, the total amount of heat in the Earth's interior is 3×10^{21} kWh. This calculation, for simplicity, ignores the fact that the extracted heat must be replaced at the same rate at which it is withdrawn by the heat further down in the earth in order for a power station to operate on a continuous basis. If we

WORKSHEET 2-3

The Amount of Heat within the Earth

We are fully capable of carrying out a fair estimate as to how much heat energy we can extract from the Earth. To be conservative, we assume that we can remove heat only from a layer 100 km thick lying 30 km below the surface. We start with a bit of laboratory-measured data.

(1) It requires about 700 j of heat energy to raise the temperature of 1 kg of earth by 1° C. Thus we first calculate how many calories it would take to raise 1 kg of earth by 1000° C, a good rough value for the temperature at the bottom of the crust. It is

_____ .

(2) We next have to determine what mass of earth we are dealing with. From laboratory measurements we find that each cubic meter of earth has a mass of approximately 1500 kg. And, using the diagram and formula below, the mass in question can be calculated as

_____ .

(3) From (1) and (2) you can find the energy stored within the Earth's mantle. It is

_____ .

(4) To convert your answer to kilowatt-hours,

$$\text{\_\_\_\_\_ } j = \text{\_\_\_\_\_ } j \times \frac{1 \ hr}{3600 \ sec} = \frac{\text{\_\_\_\_\_}}{3600} \ (j/sec) \ hr = \text{\_\_\_\_\_ } kWh.$$

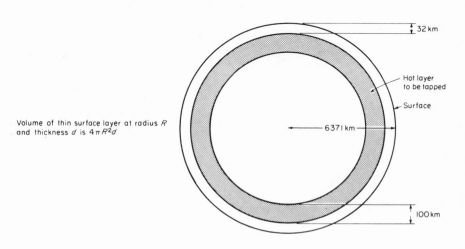

Volume of thin surface layer at radius R and thickness d is $4\pi R^2 d$

32 km

Hot layer to be tapped

Surface

6371 km

100 km

took 1000 years to extract this energy, there would still be available 3×10^{17} kWh per year, which is 10,000 times the present world demand. Thus we list this source as a continuous one on our list of economically recoverable fuels (Table 2-5).

At the present time, no clearly promising scheme has been proposed to bring all of this energy to the surface, but we are encouraged to look further and to see what fraction of it can be used.

Directly beneath the crust of the Earth, the molten mass of the mantle (called magma) is still in the process of cooling. In some places, earth tremors of the early Cenozoic era have caused fissures to open and the magma to come quite close to the surface. This can cause active volcanoes and, where there is surface water, hot springs and geysers.

The hot magma is also responsible for steam vents called fumaroles. These steam vents are natural escape lines for the mass that boils below. The steam that originates from the cooling magma itself is called magmatic steam. When surface water seeps down into porous rock heated by magma, the steam formed is called meteoritic steam.

There are three principal ways in which geothermal energy may be utilized. In one, the steam that is generated from contact between existing underground reservoirs of water and very hot rock or originating from the molten rock is used directly to actuate generators (Fig. 2-13). In the second, hot, salty water coming naturally out of

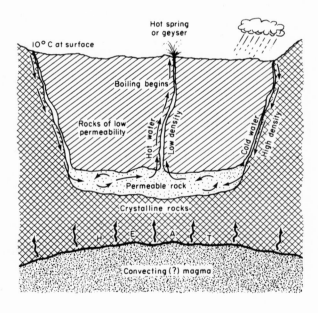

Fig. 2-13. Illustrations of a geothermal field showing how heat can be tapped. Adapted from Muffler, L.J.P., and White, D.E. (1972). "Geothermal Energy." The Science Teacher 39 (3), p. 40.

47

the ground will be used. In the third, cold surface water from a lake
or river is artificially forced through pipes into underground areas
of hot, dry rocks (for example, near volcanoes) where the water is
turned into steam and allowed to return to the surface to move the
turbines. This third method is speculative, however.

Natural steam spouts from the earth in a number of places around
the world. Roman documents 2100 years old tell of a steam field at
what is now Larderello, south of Florence, Italy. During the 19th
century, Larderello natural steam was used for industrial heating and
mechanical power. Today, Italy produces more than 400,000 kW of electricity from natural steam. New Zealand, U.S.S.R., Japan, Iceland,
and Mexico also have geothermal electric plants (see Figs. 2-14 and
2-15).

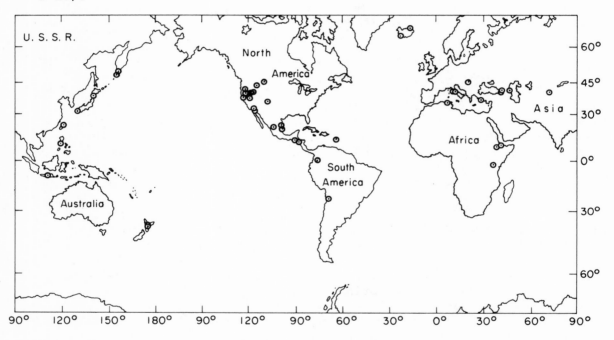

Fig. 2-14. Outline map showing locations of major geothermal fields.

Natural underground steam is now being used to generate electricity
at The Geysers Power Plant in Sonoma County, California, the only geothermal power plant in North America. The Geysers Power Plant does
not, in fact, use geysers, which like Old Faithful in Yellowstone
National Park send up fountainlike jets of hot water and steam at
intervals. The Geysers' field uses fumaroles, fissures in volcanic
areas that emit vapors steadily, and also artificial steam vents.
In 1922, drillers had already successfully tapped the meteoric
steam fields at The Geysers. But the piping and tubing of that time
could not withstand the corrosive and abrasive effects of the natural
steam and the impurities it contained.

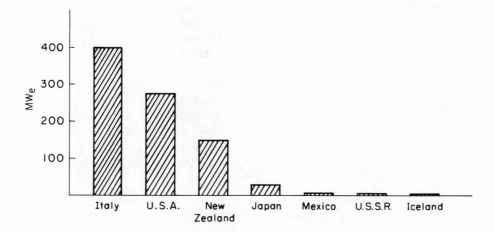

Fig. 2-15. Present relative geothermal generating capacity of several countries. Data from Muffler and White (1972).

In 1956, a second successful attempt was made to utilize the natural steam and generate electricity. Stainless-steel alloys that could withstand corrosion and efficient extractors for the impurities had been developed. Today The Geysers has a total generating capacity of 302,000 kWh.

In such installations the natural steam leaves the wellheads at about 350° F. After it leaves the turbines, it is condensed by combining it with cooling water and further reduced in temperature in cooling towers. In Fig. 2-16 we show a part of The Geysers' fields with a cooling tower in the background.

This system's major problem is the disposal of the condensed steam and the impurities that were extracted from it. The "insult" to the environment lies in bringing to the surface enormous quantities of salts and other chemicals at an unnatural rate.

While geothermal sources do not produce atmospheric particulate pollution as fossil fuels do, they do produce greater amounts of gaseous emissions, particularly hydrogen sulfide. Projected adverse effects include the possibility of subsidence, due either to fluid withdrawal [25] or to thermal contraction of the underground rock as heat is withdrawn, and the increased possibility of earthquakes due to the reinjection of cold water into the fault zones.

Scientists at the Los Alamos scientific laboratory have proposed a demonstration test for a scheme in which they would drill into the hot but dry underground region near a volcano, force water into one hole, which upon contact with the hot rock would become steam and be forced out of an adjacent hole for use in a turbine-generator [26].

Fig. 2-16. A typical geyser field. (Courtesy Pacific Gas & Electric Co.)

The Earth's temperature increases on an average of one fahrenheit degree with every 100 ft of depth. If temperatures of about 350 to 600° F are required to heat water for efficient power generation, holes 15,000 ft in depth would be sufficient. This is a relatively easy engineering task.

According to the Los Alamos concept, the drilled hole would be fitted with a perforated steel pipe to a point several hundred feet above the bottom of the hole. A high-pressure pump at the surface would force water into the well at pressures of about 7000 lb/in.^{2}, great enough to flow through the perforations and crack the surrounding rock. This is a common technique in oil-well drilling and is known as hydraulic fracturing.

The resulting fracture zone would be shaped like a pancake on edge and have a radius of about 1500 ft. To keep the cracks open, a "propping agent," sand or high-strength glass beads, could be injected into them when the pumping pressure is released. A second hole would then be drilled about 20 to 30 ft from the first and would intersect the upper parts of the cracks. Water would be pumped down the first hole. It would circulate through the network of cracks, where it would be heated and then forced up the second hole as steam to operate a turbine.

Once a moderate temperature difference has been established between the cold water descending in the first hole and the hot water rising in the second, circulation through the system should be maintained by natural convection. Pumping could be discontinued except for the injection of additional water as needed (Fig. 2-17).

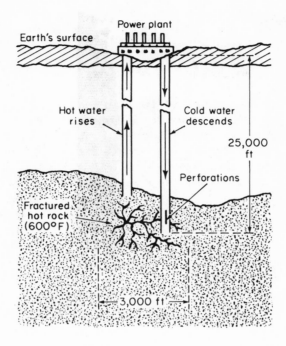

Fig. 2-17. One technique for generating geothermal energy.

Eventually, as heat is removed from the hot rocks, the rocks will tend to shrink. This is expected to cause new cracks reaching far beyond the original fracture zone and should enable a well to produce geothermal energy for years.

It may be desirable to create large caverns at the bottom of the well for steam collection. A nuclear explosive could efficiently create such a cavern [27]. The use of nuclear explosives for peaceful purposes poses many problems, not the least being the psychological one, but this is not a topic which we shall consider here.

There are several questions that must be investigated:

(1) Will the rock cracking spread as forecast?
(2) Will serious seismic activity result that could touch off small earthquakes?
(3) Will the depleted well cause the surface terrain to collapse?
(4) Can we control the gaseous emissions?

Then too there remains the problem mentioned earlier, that of the soluble minerals extracted from the rock by the water, which could corrode the overall system if not removed. If the impurities must be removed, then their disposal poses another challenge.

Effluent from either hot-water- or vapor-dominated systems can pollute streams or ground water. Federal and state regulations require reinjection of objectionable fluids back into a deep reservoir.

The prospects for geothermal power seem so attractive that the question of why its development is so slow is a natural one to ask. Two reasons might be given:

First, until now we have had to use geothermal energy where it was found. In many cases, to do so would have meant a very costly installation of transmission lines over long distances. However, since we find many sources in southern California where there is a huge demand for energy, this excuse alone is inadequate.

Second, the magnitude of the presently exploitable reserves may have been underestimated. As recently as 1967, experts argued that only the first two methods were practicable and that the total possible capacity of geothermal energy in the United States was only 20,000 MW, mostly in southern California, and would last no more than 30 years [28]. This supply must of course be exploited, but it scarcely deserves a large outlay of Federal research funds. Now, however, the outlook seems more promising. More recent estimates suggest a lifetime of 1000 years for a geothermal field, although individual wells must be replaced [29, 30]. Although the estimates of 20,000 MW for the Imperial Valley of California remain essentially unchanged, the total Western U.S. capacity is now being estimated at 10^5 to 10^7 MW.

Since the liquid basalt magma at over 1000° C is everywhere, we may consider, in the absence of hot water or steam fields, extracting heat from the Earth's interior by direct heat-extraction techniques, including heat pipes and injection of water to form steam. Nevertheless, for the pages that follow we will restrain our imaginations and restrict ourselves to the comparative reality of the 1967 estimates.

For local considerations, however, we note at once that the 20,000-MW projections for the Imperial Valley in California suggest that geothermal energy could supply electrical needs of Los Angeles, a city which has recently banned fossil-fuel power stations and which may ban nuclear power stations.

The cost of geothermal energy is competitive with other sources. The actual price of electricity at The Geysers field in northern California is less than 5 mils/kWh compared to the California average price of 7 mils/kWh [31]. Clearly, a major development is already under way. At this cost, utilities will develop the known fields quickly. Research should, presumably, be directed at exploration of new areas and at the tapping of the earth's heat at places where no steam or hot-water wells exist.

Some years ago the National Science Foundation began the MOHOLE project for drilling into the earth's crust; MOHOLE was abandoned by Congress when the cost estimate rose high. Perhaps it should be reconsidered. If, in the estimates cited above, the lower limit of

10^5 MW is correct, then geothermal power is already important; if 10^7 MW is more like it, geothermal power could supply the needs of the entire world.

The energy sources we have thus far discussed are continuous supply sources; we do not expect to deplete them. In the last section of this chapter we provide tables giving the amount of energy we can economically expect to extract from these sources.

FOSSIL-FUEL RESERVES

Crude Oil

Over three-quarters of U.S. energy use is from fossil fuels. That the United States is running out of oil is now all too well known. Oil reserves elsewhere in the world are similarly being depleted. The oil of the Middle East may not last for more than 100 years.

Estimates of the present U.S. reserves have ranged from 150 to 600 billion barrels. (In 1973, from both domestic and foreign sources, we consumed 5 billion barrels.) Optimists, usually people in the oil industry, tend to derive the higher figures. In 1962, one rather interesting nonindustry optimistic projection was made by Zapp, a Department of Interior geologist [32]. More recently, King Hubbert [33, 34] has reexamined Zapp's projections and expressed them in a simpler form. Looking at his calculations is rather instructive, for it illustrates the kind of assumptions that are brought into play in such estimates.

Geologists assume that oil deposits are found in specific regions around the Earth; the location of all of these regions may not be known, but presumably the oil is confined to specific locales.

But to find these locales from the Earth's surface is hard. The only way of being sure is to drill a hole and to see if oil is there. Therefore, projections of oil reserves, such as that of Zapp, tend to assume that it was equally likely that oil might be found in one place as in another; in other words, equal success might be achieved by drilling randomly as by picking spots based on the best geological information.

To set up the problem in a way that would yield usable numbers, Zapp laid a rectangular grid over a map of the United States, each rectangle being representative of two miles on a side. On each corner an oil well was to be drilled to a depth adequate to discover oil, or to a maximum depth of 20,000 ft in searching for oil. The total possible drilling on this basis is 5×10^9 ft cumulative, of which, in fact, 1.5×10^9 ft had been drilled by 1968.

If Zapp's assumption of randomness is valid, then for every *x* number of wells tried, one should yield oil. Thus, the rate of discovery should be constant. You will recall that to graph a constant, one draws a line parallel to one of the axes. In Fig. 2-18, the dashed horizontal line is the constant rate of discovery when the number of feet drilled (cumulative footage) is plotted against the number of barrels found per foot.

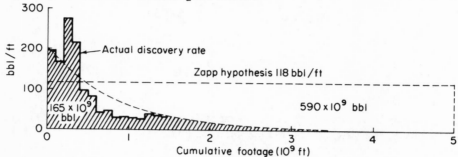

Fig. 2-18. Comparison of Zapp hypothesis with actual U.S. discovery data. The thick line represents the curves used for prediction that we usually see. The light dashed curves are the actual statistical data. This prediction was first made about 1962, and the data still follow the curve closely. (Source, Hubbert [33].)

In actuality, we have so far discovered 169×10^9 barrels, so that future exploration should, according to Zapp, extend this to 590×10^9 barrels. The actual discovery rate of oil is shown in the shaded area, and does not follow Zapp's hypothesis. It was initially high and is now diminishing. Moreover, more effort and sophistication is being spent on exploration than every before.

Hubbert [33, 34] fits a simple exponential "decay" curve to the discovery curve and thereby deduces that we have already discovered most of the available oil in the U.S.

In Fig. 2-19, following Hubbert [33], we show the rate of discovery of oil in the U.S. and the rate of production. Discovery is falling off, and production is still rising; the reserves are dwindling. Ignoring these indications that we are running out of oil, oil companies argue that oil prices are too low to encourage exploration and that all we need is more financial incentive, higher prices, and a higher depletion allowance.

From this, we realize that the citizens of the U.S. have consumed half the total stock of oil that nature laid down for us over millions of years, and much of this has been consumed in the last 20 years. This gives us the prospect of running out of oil in 20 years, even if we moderate our demands.

The world supply of oil can be similarly evaluated, but the numbers are not as reliable. The Middle East has three times the reserves of the U.S.

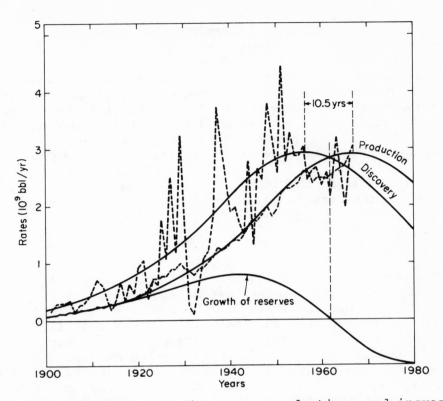

Fig. 2-19. Rates of proved discovery, production, and increase of
reserves of crude oil in the U.S., exclusive of Alaska. Solid lines
are actual yearly data; dashed lines are analytical derivatives. (Source:
Hubbert [33].)

All of the above discussion pertains to *easily available* oil and
to *proven* and *estimated reserves*. Presently, only 30% of the oil is
extracted from any oil field; 70% usually stays behind as sludge. As
the price of oil rises, it will become economic to use more sophisticated
"secondary" and "tertiary" extraction systems to get at this "sludge"
oil. Secondary recovery schemes include injecting gas or water under
pressure.

The oil reserves are therefore a function of price and are about
twice those discussed here as the price of oil becomes twice the amount
it was in early 1973.

But other easily accessible oil is not there; the best that can
be expected is an early development of the tar sands and oil shales,
which, as noted below, are available but expensive both in money and
environmental damage to extract.

There are other liquid-fuel reserves than the crude oil noted
here; there is a small amount of "natural-gas liquid" associated with
natural gas discoveries. Also, heavy oil is found in "tar sands"

(the Athabasca Sands in Canada). Removal of useful fuel is hard and is only economic on a large scale. This is nevertheless now being done and can increase the oil reserves.

The largest extra reserve is shale oil, found in a *solid* form. These shales are hard to extract and refine. Although there is a huge amount of shale oil available, most of it seems to be unrecoverable.

There is, therefore, a great need for research on recovering these shale oils and oil from tar sands. Alternatively, we can intensify a search for ways of converting coal to oil. (See Chapters 6 and 12.)

Again, we refer to the last section of this chapter where tables present data on the Earth's initial oil resources and our remaining supplies.

Natural Gas

Natural gas tends to be discovered together with oil. Therefore, estimates of natural gas reserves can be made similarly as for crude oil. According to Hubbert [33], we in the U.S. have already used up about one-third of the available natural gas, and that in the last 20 years. Gas is also running out. Twenty years ago natural gas went to waste at the oil fields, where it was vented or burned because of inadequate pipelines. This still happens in some parts of the world, where little demand exists in close proximity to the source of supply. Fortunately, it is now technically and economically feasible to liquefy the gas and transport it by ship to users. Sometimes it is forced back into the ground so that it can push oil to the surface.

There is some gas in widely dispersed pockets in the Western U.S. The natural gas reserves of the U.S. could be increased by a factor of 2 if this gas could be extracted. One proposed method is to coagulate these pockets by means of many underground atomic bomb explosions. Some initial studies have been made by the U.S. Atomic Energy Commission under the Plowshare program, and have been variously code-named "Project Gasbuggy," "Wagonwheel," etc. The explosion of 4000 atom bombs could release enough natural gas to double the U.S. reserves [34].

Short-lived radioactive materials would be allowed to decay before the gas would be made available for use. The long-lived radioactive wastes produced by these bombs would stay underground (except for Krypton 85 and tritium), and these long-lived wastes would be 10 to 100 times less than those from the direct production of the same amount of energy in nuclear-fission reactors. If this gas were used industrially, the krypton and tritium would cause no hazard; if used in a kitchen stove without ventilation, it would produce an increase in radiation of only 20% over background. However, the explosion of so many bombs is anathema to any peace lover, and there is a risk that the bomb explosions could vent short-lived radioactivity to the surface. It is unlikely, therefore, that this gas will be used in the foreseeable future.

The use of gas is so convenient that the exhaustion of resources may be serious, and accordingly gas may again be made from coal. (See Chapters 6 and 12.)

In fact, there are several pilot plants and much research on new and improved techniques under way.

Coal

The coal resources of the world are comparatively plentiful and much easier to assess than are other fossil-fuel reserves. In the U.S., for example, there is a plentiful supply of low-grade coal in the Western states. World estimates are shown in Fig. 2-20 [35]. In the summary which follows we will take 60% of this estimate as the actually mapped, easily available number, as discussed by Hubbert [33, 34].

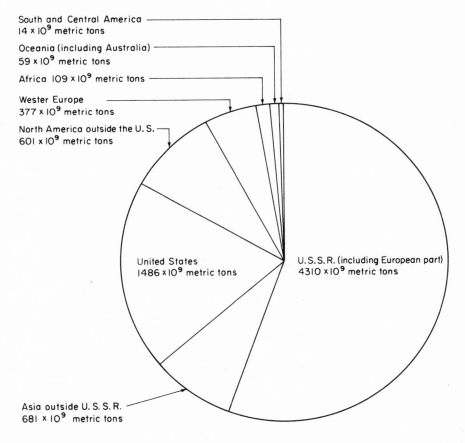

South and Central America 14 × 10⁹ metric tons

Oceania (including Australia) 59 × 10⁹ metric tons

Africa 109 × 10⁹ metric tons

Wester Europe 377 × 10⁹ metric tons

North America outside the U.S. 601 × 10⁹ metric tons

United States 1486 × 10⁹ metric tons

U.S.S.R. (including European part) 4310 × 10⁹ metric tons

Asia outside U.S.S.R. 681 × 10⁹ metric tons

Fig. 2-20 Coal resources of the world, following Averitt [35]. These estimates are double those used in Table 2-6. See text.

Coal was originally found close to the surface in 14th-century England on the coast of Northumberland, where it acquired the name, "sea-coales." However, in the last 300 years, coal has been dug from below the ground by coal miners.

More recently, coal near the surface has again been used by strip mining. In the United States the total amount of coal used has been constant over the decade 1960 to 1970 as factories and utilities have switched to oil and gas, whose pollution effects are less. Projected demand for coal will increase by the year 2000; this is shown in Fig. 2-21. The huge expansion of strip mining is evident. We discuss related environmental problems in Chapter 6.

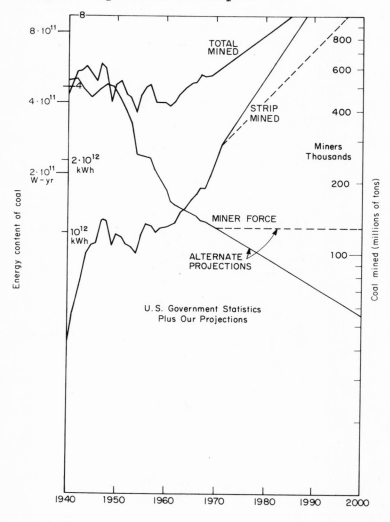

Fig. 2-21 Coal mining: underground versus strip miner force; U.S., 1940 to 1970 and projection to the year 2000.

Coal is at present our most plentiful fossil fuel. Because it is a raw material for many chemical products, its uses extend beyond its fuel value. Coal is clumsy to store compared to oil and gas, and it is essentially a "dirty" fuel, which yields a high degree of particulate waste. However, there are processes to turn coal into a gaseous fuel, but these gasification processes are as yet uneconomical. In World War II, Nazi Germany turned to liquification of coal as it was cut off from the oil resources of Eastern Europe. Here too is an area that should be the subject of extensive research.

URANIUM AND THORIUM

The total uranium and thorium supplies of the world, or even of the United States, are not known with any certainty. The heavy metals, such as these, are much rarer than fossil fuels. However, the amount of energy obtained from a given mass of these metals is 10,000,000 times greater than from the same mass of fossil fuel.

In 1939, there were three major uranium mines: Joachimstal in Czechoslovakia (in use for many centuries), Union Meuniére d'Haute Katanga in the Congo, and the Eldorado Mining Company in Canada.

After the atomic bomb explosions in 1945, the major countries in the world began a search for uranium for military purposes. This search did not, at first, lead to a free competitive market with a lot of exploration. The military market was saturated after a few years, and nuclear power was slow in coming. About 1967, however, 50 large, new nuclear power stations were ordered in the U.S., all using uranium 235 only (an isotope* which is present only to 0.72% in natural uranium). It immediately became apparent that a shortage might develop, and more exploration began. The effect has been dramatic: the proved reserves in the U.S. have doubled in two years! Exploration is by no means complete, and it seems that more uranium may yet be found.

In Fig. 2-22 we show how the recent additions to uranium reserves have come from increased drilling, and how these reserves have increased in a manner roughly proportional to the increase in drilling.

In the case of oil, we have seen that increased exploration now leads to much smaller returns. If Fig. 2-18 is valid for all energy resources, that is, if the decay curve represents not only oil but every energy resource, then we may conclude that we have a long way to go before we reach the point of diminishing returns for uranium.

The information in Table 2-4 is extremely important, for it shows in some detail that just having energy resources within the ground is

---

* To be discussed in detail in Chapter 5.

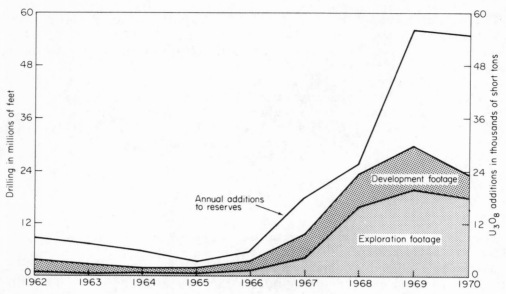

Fig. 2-22 Reserve additions, and exploration and development drilling, U_3O_8 [36].

not sufficient to assure a supply of energy. The numbers, however, deal specifically with the uranium resources of the United States as their extent was known in 1971.

Refer to column 1. At 1971 prices, we had available 5×10^5 tons of uranium oxide which could have been extracted from the ground and processed into uranium suitable for use in a reactor at a cost of $8/lb. Once this 5×10^5 tons of uranium is exhausted, we must extract that ore which is next most accessible and/or easy to process into usable form; if we had had to use this ore in 1971, it would have cost $10/lb. The major portion of our known uranium resources would cost 12.5 times as much as the material we are presently mining and processing [36].

Column 2 shows the amount of this mineral resource available at the given cost.

Column 3 states how much more electrical power will cost as each "level" of uranium ore is depleted; the ore costing $8/lb is taken as the base entry, or zero point.

Before we turn our attention to the last two columns, let us quickly note that when uranium is processed, two forms are isolated, the more abundant U^{235} and the more "energy-packed" U^{238}. In Chapter 5 we will discuss these two species in some detail.

The most popular reactor in use is the water reactor which employs U^{235}. Column 4 gives the total power we can obtain by consuming all of the uranium in each "level."

As we shall later come to understand, U^{238} can be used in the breeder reactors that are now coming into use throughout the world. Breeder reactors derive their name from the fact that in the normal course of matters they create a byproduct, plutonium, which can itself be used as a nuclear fuel.

The last column gives the total energy figures appropriate to that type of reactor. We have allowed for 0.25% of the U^{235} remaining unextracted in the separation plant, but with plutonium produced in the reactor of about the same amount to compensate. Note that with a breeder reactor the cost of fuel is negligible.

TABLE 2-4

U.S. Uranium Resources, 1971*

Price ($/lb)	Resource (tons)	Increase in electricity cost due to higher uranium price (mils/kWh)		Energy content ($\times 10^{12}$ kWh)	
		Water reactor	Breeder	Water reactor	Breeder
8	500,000	0	0	102	13,700
10	950,000	0.1	0	162	21,600
15	1,500,000	0.4	0	255	34,000
30	2,200,000	1.3	0	375	50,000
50	10,000,000	2.5	0	1700	230,000
100	25,000,000	5.5	0	4300	570,000

* Partial exploration only. For comparison, 1965 total energy was 13.5×10^{12} kWh. Table adapted from [36].

We see that we could use power from light-water nuclear reactors for 200 years at the $100/lb fuel cost, with our estimated year 2000 capacity (one-fourth of the U.S. energy supply and one-half of the electricity supply), even without new uranium being discovered by further exploration. This would, however, require a 5 mil/kWh increase in cost (a 50% increase), and we must remember that together with this cost will go environmental damage: progressively larger uranium mining trailings and strip mining. Electricity demand may increase faster than we estimate, and the environmental costs of the necessary strip mining and fuel reprocessing may be too much to tolerate. Therefore, the U.S. policy is to build a breeder reactor as soon as possible, after which the output from an equivalent fuel supply increases one hundredfold.

The increase in fuel usage with a breeder reactor is even greater than indicated here. If we are willing to pay $1000/lb for uranium or thorium in a breeder reactor, then reserves are enormous and have not even been extensively surveyed. We list here only the thorium available in the Conway granite in the White Mountains of New Hampshire. The thorium crops out (comes to the surface) over an area of 750 km^2 and may be 10 km deep. This rock [37] averages 56 g/metric ton, or 150 g/m^3, fuel for *tens of thousands* of years. The environmental cost of the strip mining may be large, but less than mining the greater quantity of coal.

In estimating the time by which a breeder will be necessary, we must remember that we cannot use the fuel immediately after it is mined. A seven years' advance supply is needed for concentration of the U^{235} isotope, purification, and the initial "charge" of the reactor. The AEC, estimating twice the electricity demand by the year 2000 that we do here, compiled figures on consumption in the U.S. They deduce that uranium at $10/lb or less will be depleted by about 1993, and $15/lb or less by 1998.

The world supplies of uranium are not as well known as are U.S. supplies. Presently known reserves are double the U.S. supplies [33], but authorities estimate that ultimate resources will be ten times U.S. resources.

Further details and figures of the world's energy sources may be found in [33, 34, 38, 39, 40, and 41].

ECONOMIC FACTORS OF FUEL RECOVERY

It is not enough to talk about our total fuel resources; it is necessary to understand that not all of the fuel may be available to us at reasonable cost and effort. Tables 2-5 and 2-6 separately consider the fuels in terms of those continuously available and those that are depletable. The figures are given in terms of the energy we can extract from them rather than the volume or weight amounts, and thereby we can make direct comparisons. Thus the tables give the sum total of energy available to us. That more fuel energy exists is a fact that we shall probably not be able to take advantage of.

Table 2-7 presents figures on crude-oil refining capacities: For in the case of oil, it is not enough to collect it, it must also be processed. Refining capabilities have a direct effect on consumption.

We have only guessed at the amount of oil in the U.S.S.R. and China, and the numbers included here may be a serious underestimate; although oil in Alaska is included in the domestic oil reserves estimates, the amount of oil in the continental shelf is still unknown.

TABLE 2-5

Economically Recoverable Fuels (Continuous Supply)*

Type	World ($\times 10^{12}$ W)		U.S. ($\times 10^{12}$ W)	
	Maximum	Possible by year 2000	Maximum	Possible by year 2000
Solar	28,000		1600	
Fuel wood	3	1.3	0.1	0.05
Farm waste	2	0.6	0.2	0
Photosynthesis	8	0.01	0.5	0.001
Hydropower	3	1	0.3	0.1
Wind power	0.1	0.01	0.01	0.001
Direct conversion**	?	0.01	?	0.001
Space heat	0.6	0.006	0.01	0.001
Nonsolar				
Tidal	1	0.06	0.1	0.06
Geothermal***	50	0.06	10	0.02
Total	68	3	11	0.2
Annual demand				
1970		4.5		2
2000 (expected)		15		6

* Table adapted from [42].
** Direct-conversion solar power supplies potentially more power than shown but does not now seem economically recoverable.
*** The maximum geothermal estimates vary; see text.

TABLE 2-6

Economically Recoverable Fuels (Depletable Supply)*

	World		US (including Alaska)	
	Original supply	Remaining, 1972	Original supply	Remaining, 1972
Coal	37,000	34,800	6800	6470
Oil and natural gas liquids	2700	1800	380	180
Oil tars**	508	508	–	–
Oil shales[†]	350	350	150	150
Natural gas	2300	1900	375	235
U^{235} (up to $20/lb UO_2)[††]	700	680	235	228
U^{238} (up to $100/lb UO_2)[††]	5×10^5	5×10^5	10^5	10^5
Thorium 232[§]	large		10^7	10^7
Deuterium (1% of seawater)	2×10^{10}	2×10^{10}	5×10^9	5×10^9
Lithium	10^5	10^5	2×10^4	2×10^4
1970 annual use	40		18	
2000 annual use[§§] (projected)	300		60	
1965-2000 use (projected)	4200		1000	

* Sources: [28, 36], updated by National Petroleum Council, 1972 statistics; and Keystone Coal Industry Manual (McGraw-Hill, New York, 1973). Data are given in 10^{12} kW$_t$h = 1.14 × 10^{11} W-yr = 3.61 × 10^{18} j.

** Oil tars are relatively unexplored. These figures are for the Athabasca sands, Canadian fields.

[†] The economically recoverable shales only.

[††] Uranium exploration is incomplete, and reserves are increasing.

[§] Thorium exploration has barely begun.

[§§] As we are willing to pay more for fuel, the amount available increases by up to a factor of 2.

TABLE 2-7

1971 World Petroleum Statistics [43]

	Production		Use		Refining output	
	bbl, millions*	% of world	bbl, millions*	% of world	bbl, millions*	% of world
U.S.	3,454	19.5	5,555	31.4	4,423	24.7
Canada Central America South America	2,363	13.4	1,607	9.1	2,460	13.8
Western Europe	131	0.7	4,712	26.6	4,714	26.4
Middle East	5,979	34.0	460	2.7	881	4.9
Africa	2,067	11.6	288	1.6	263	1.5
Asiatic Area	581	3.3	2,451	13.8	2,264	12.7

Total
  Noncommunist
    world
	14,575	82.5	15,073	85.2	15,005	84.0

Sino-Soviet	3,098	17.5	2,622	14.8	2,843	16.0
World total	17,673	100.0	17,695	100.0	17,848	100.0

* 1 bbl = 42 gal = 5.8×10^6 Btu (energy) = 1700 kWh (electricity).

TABLES OF ENERGY CONVERSION FACTORS

We close this second chapter with two important tables to which we shall refer throughout the remainder of the book. Table 2-8 allows one to convert from one unit of energy to another and to see at a glance comparable energy values of our natural resources. Table 2-9 presents some very practical data, such as the amount of energy in terms of barrels of oil carried by a single supertanker. The data for this table were obtained directly from various power companies and in part from the Statistical Abstract of the United States.

TABLE 2-8

Conversion of Energy Units

Unit		kWh	j	cal	W-yr	Btu
One kilowatt-hour (kWh)	equals	1	3.60×10^6	8.60×10^5	0.114	3410
One joule (j)	equals	2.78×10^{-7}	1	0.239	3.17×10^{-8}	9.48×10^{-4}
One calorie (cal)	equals	1.16×10^{-6}	4.18	1	1.33×10^{-5}	3.97×10^{-3}
One watt-year (W-yr)	equals	8.77	3.16×10^7	7.54×10^6	1	2.99×10^4
One British thermal unit (Btu)	equals	2.93×10^{-4}	1054	252	3.21×10^{-5}	1
One metric ton of coal ($=10^6$ g)	yields	8600	3.10×10^{10}	7.40×10^9	981	2.93×10^7
One barrel (bbl) of oil (=42 gal)	yields	1700	6.12×10^9	1.46×10^9	194	5.80×10^6
One cubic foot (ft^3) of natural gas	yields	0.29	1.05×10^6	2.52×10^5	0.033	1000
One gram (g) of U^{235}	yields	2.30×10^4	8.28×10^{10}	1.98×10^{10}	2620	7.84×10^7
One gram (g) of deuterium	yields	6.60×10^4	2.38×10^{11}	5.68×10^{10}	7.53×10^3	2.25×10^8

Tables of Energy Conversion Factors

	Coal (tons)	Oil (bbl)	Natural gas (ft^3)	U^{235} (g)	Deuterium (g)
	1.16×10^{-4}	5.88×10^{-4}	3.41	4.35×10^{-5}	1.51×10^{-5}
is	3.23×10^{-11}	1.63×10^{-10}	10^{-6}	1.20×10^{-11}	4.21×10^{-12}
derived	1.35×10^{-10}	6.84×10^{-10}	3.97×10^{-6}	5.82×10^{-11}	1.76×10^{-11}
from	1.02×10^{-3}	5.16×10^{-3}	30	3.80×10^{-4}	1.33×10^{-11}
	3.41×10^{-8}	1.72×10^{-7}	10^{-3}	1.28×10^{-8}	4.44×10^{-9}
	1	5	2.94×10^{4}	0.37	0.13
is	0.2	1	5800	0.07	0.026
equivalent					
to	3.41×10^{-5}	1.72×10^{-4}	1	1.27×10^{-5}	4.44×10^{-6}
	2.7	13.5	7.84×10^{4}	1	3.5
	7.7	39	2.25×10^{5}	2.9	1

TABLE 2-9

"Practical" Fuel-Energy Conversion Constants

Fuel	Usual unit	Heat content (rough average)	Amount necessary for operation of one large power station (1000 MW_e and 3000 MW_t)*
Coal	metric ton $= 10^6$ g $= 1.102$ short tons $= 0.9842$ long tons	≈ 8600 kWh/ton $= 8.6 \times 10^{-3}$ kWh/g	10,000 ton/day ≈ 1 train/day
Oil	barrel (U.S.) $= 42$ gal $= 158.98$ liter $= 1.43 \times 10^5$ g	≈ 1700 kWh/bbl $= 11.9 \times 10^{-3}$ kWh/g	40,000 bbl/day ≈ 1 supertanker/week
Natural gas (95% methane)	cubic foot $= 20.3$ g $= 2.83 \times 10^4$ cm^3	≈ 1000 Btu/ft^3 $= 0.29$ kWh/ft^3 $= 14.7 \times 10^{-3}$ kWh/g ($\Delta H = 19.8 \times 10^{-3}$ kWh/g)	2.5×10^8 ft^3/day $\approx 10^4$ m^3/day LNG ≈ 1 ship/5 days
U235 (fission)	gram	23,000 kWh/g $= 2620$ W-yr/g	3 kg/day (negligible compared to container weight)
Deuterium (fusion)	gram	66,000 kWh/g	1 kg/day

* Subscript e is electrical, t is thermal.

REFERENCES

[1] Gamow, G. (1940). "Birth and Death of the Sun." Viking, New York.
[2] Oswald, W.J., and Goleuka, C.G. (1960). Advan. Appl. Microbiol. Vol. 2, p. 223.
[3] Ehriche, K.A. (1971). Bull. At. Sci. Vol. 27, p. 18.
[4] Glaser, P.E. (1968). Science Vol. 162, p. 857.
[5] Glaser, P.E. (1969). Trans N.Y. Acad. Sci. Vol. 31, p. 951.
[6] Meinel, A.B., and Meinel, M.P. (1971). Bull. At. Sci. Vol. 27.
[7] Meinel, A.B., and Meinel, M.P. (1972). Phys. Today (February).
[8] Hottel, H.C., and Howard, J.B. (1972). "New Energy Technology." MIT Press, Cambridge, Massachusetts.
[9] Ford, N.C., and Kane, J.W. (1971). Bull. At. Sci. Vol. 27, p. 27.
[10] US Govt. (1967). "Statistical Abstract of the United States." USGPO.
[11] Federal Power Commission (FPC) (1968). "Hydroelectric Power Resources of the United States." USGPO.
[12] Daniels, F. (1964). "Direct Use of the Sun's Energy." Yale Univ. Press, New Haven, Connecticut.
[13] Lof, G.O., Duffie, J.A., and Smith, C.O. (1966). "World Distribution of Solar Energy," Rept. No. 21. Solar Energy Labs, Univ. of Wisconsin, Madison, Wisconsin.
[14] US Govt. (1965). "Statistical Abstract of the United States." USGPO.
[15] FPC (1968). Op. cit.
[16] Hubbert, M.K. (1962). "Energy Resources." Rept. to the Committee on Natural Resources, National Academy of Sciences, Publ. 1000 D.
[17] Munk, W.H., and Macdonald, G.J.F. (1961). "The Rotation of the Earth." Cambridge Univ. Press, London and New York.
[18] Charlier, R.H. (1969). Sea Frontiers Vol. 15, p. 339.
[19] Anderson, J.H. (1966). Mech. Eng. Vol. 88, p. 41.
[20] Zener, C. (1973). "Solar Power from Seawater." Phys. Today (January).
[21] Putnam, P.C. (1948). "Power from the Wind." Van Nostrand-Reinhold, Princeton, New Jersey.
[22] United Nations (1963). "New Sources of Energy: Solar Energy, Wind Power, and Geothermal Power," Vols. 1-7. UN Rept., New York.
[23] Spanides, H.G., and Hatzikakidis, A.D., eds. (1964). "Solar and Aeolian Energy," Proc. Internat. Seminar on Solar and Aeolian Energy, Sounion, Greece, 1961. Plenum, New York.
[24] Lachenbruch, H.H. (1970). "Crustal Temperature and Heat Production." J. Geophys. Res. Vol. 75, pp. 3291-3300.
[25] Kruger, P., and Otte, C.A., eds. (1973). "Geothermal Energy: Resources, Production, and Stimulation." Stanford Univ. Press, Stanford, California.
[26] New York Times (1972). June 17.

[27] Atomic Energy Commission (AEC) (1971). "A Feasibility Study of a Plowshare Geothermal Plant." AEC Rept. PNE 1550.

[28] Hubbert, M.K., ed. (1969). In "Resources and Man." Freeman, San Francisco, California.

[29] Barnes, J. (1972). Scientific American Vol. 226, p. 70.

[30] Rex, R.W. (1971). Bull. At. Sci. Vol. 27, p. 52.

[31] McMillan, D.A., Jr., ed. (1970). UN Symp. on Development and Utilization of Geothermal Resources, Pisa.

[32] Zapp, A.D. (1962). "Future Petroleum Producing Capacity of the US." US Geol. Surv. Bull. 1142 H.

[33] Hubbert, M.K. (1969). Op. cit.

[34] Hubbert, M.K. (1971a). "Energy Resources for Power Production," IAEA-SM-146/1. In Symp. on Environmental Aspects of Nuclear Power Stations, 1970. IAEA, Vienna; (1971b). Scientific American, September.

[35] Averitt, P. (1969). "Coal Reserves of the United States." US Geol. Surv. Bull. 1275.

[36] Faulkner, R.L. (1971). "Official Uranium Reserves." AEC Rept. WASH-1098.

[37] Adams, J., Kline, M.C., Richardson, K.A., and Rogers, J.J.K. (1962). Proc. Natl. Acad. Sci. Vol. 48, p. 1898.

[38] Hubbert, M.K. (1962). Op. cit.

[39] Starr, C. (1971). "Energy and Power." Scientific American, September, pp. 37-69.

[40] United Nations (1970). "World Energy Supplies 1965-1968." Statistical Paper Ser. J., No. 13, UN, New York.

[41] McKelvey, V.E. (1972). Amer. Sci. Vol. 60, p. 32.

[42] Starr, C. (1971). Op. cit.

[43] US Dept. of Interior (1973). "International Petroleum Annual 1971." Bureau of Mines, USGPO.

General References

Akins, J.E. (1973). "The Oil Crisis: This Time the Wolf Is Here." Foreign Affairs, April.

American Petroleum Institute. "Petroleum Facts and Figures." Bimonthly pamphlet available from API, Washington, D.C.

Fischer, J.C. (1973). "Energy Crisis in Perspective." Wiley, New York.

Independent Petroleum Association of America (frequently updated). "US Petroleum Statistics." Available from IPAA, Washington, D.C.

National Coal Association (annual). "Bituminous Coal Data." National Coal Association, Washington, D.C.

National Petroleum Council (1973). "Report on US Energy Outlook." Available from NPC, Washington, D.C.

Putnam, P.C. (1953). "Energy in the Future." Van Nostrand-Reinhold, Princeton, New Jersey.

Shell Oil Co. (1973). "The National Energy Problem." Available on request from Shell Oil Co.

Problems

Theobald, P.K., Schweinfurth, S.P., and Duncan, D.C. (1972). "Energy
   Resources of the United States." Circular 650, US Geol. Surv.,
   Washington, D.C.
Tompkins, D.C. (1972). "Power from the Earth." Public Policy Bibliog-
   raphies 3, Institute of Governmental Studies, Univ. of California,
   Berkeley, California.
Tugendhat, C. (1965). "Oil: The Biggest Business." Putnam, New York.
United Nations (1962). "New Energy Sources and Energy Developments."
   UN Rept., UN, New York.
US Congress (1972). "Natural Gas Regulation and the Trans-Alaska
   Pipeline." Hearings before the Joint Economic Committee, June 7, 9,
   22. USGPO.

PROBLEMS

1. From the various sources in this chapter, compile a list of countries in order of their fuel reserves per capita (kWh/person). If you were the political leader of each country, outline the way these numbers would influence your policy.

2. Convert 68° F, room temperature, to (a) ° C, and (b) ° K.

3. Sketch how the conservation of energy applies in each step discussed in this chapter for the birth of the sun.

4. Discuss the nature of the dominant conversion processes that convert solar energy to other forms of energy in the following geographic areas: the North Pole, the Sahara Desert, the region of the Nile River, the Alps, the Equator, the Great Lakes, and the Atlantic Ocean.

5. Discuss what 10 Hz means in terms of:

   (a) A wave such as discussed in Technical Notes 2-2 and 2-5;
   (b) A weight hanging from a string swinging back and forth
        (pendulum).

6. Estimate the area of your roof and assume it to be covered with photocells. Estimate too the average number of hours of sunlight on your house during the year, and calculate how much energy you can harvest from your personal solar farm, assuming that the sun arrives perpendicular to the roof. How does this compare to your own uses of electricity, gas, oil, and coal?

7. One scheme for solar heating of houses is to allow water to

drip slowly down a black solar-heat collector, protected from the out-side by interference filters (Technical Note 2-5). The water, if we are lucky, is hot enough to circulate in a hot-water heating system.

Sketch such a system. Consider also using water, even when tepid, as a "heat source" for a heat pump. If the temperature of the inside air is 68° F, that of the outside 38° F, and of the tepid-water tank 53° F, what advantage does the partial solar heating provide?

8. (a) Discuss the units for η in Carnot's formula.

(b) What determines T_c of the working fluid in an electrical generating facility?

(c) What factor might cause η to vary for plants located in various parts of the world, all other factors being the same?

9. A coal-fired power station to produce 1000 MW_e requires 3000 MW of heat, i.e., thermal input (MW_t). From Table 2-8, how many tons of coal would be involved in producing this 3000 MW_e?

10. Most of the problems in this book only need rough estimates to give a grasp of the situation. A freight car in the U.S. takes about 100 tons of coal. Normal train sizes are about 100 cars long. How many trainloads are needed each *day* to keep the power station above running? Coal weighs about 100 lb/ft^3. If coal runs in seams 10 ft thick, how much area must be strip-mined each day, each week, each year? What fraction of the state of Wyoming is needed for this one power station? What fraction for 1000 power stations?

11. The 1980 projected demand for electricity in the New England area (Maine, New Hampshire, Vermont, Massachusetts, Connecticut, and Rhode Island) is 25,000 MW [Zinder, H. (1970). "A Study of the Electric Power Situation in New England." Prepared for the New England Regional Commission].

Assume that the peak-demand rate is twice the average rate; that power stations are unavailable, due to breakdowns and maintenance, 30% of the desired time; and that the average efficiency of electricity generation is 30%. Estimate as follows:

(a) If the electricity is generated by oil, how much oil is consumed in the year? If it comes from the Middle East and $1.00/bbl is paid to the producing countries, what effect is there on the U.S. balance of payments? How many oil-tanker trips at 100,000 tons/trip? How much revenue would a $0.05/gal tax bring in?

(b) If the electricity were generated by natural gas, how much gas?

(c) If the electricity were generated by coal, how much coal is needed? How many trainloads per day at 40 tons per hopper car? If the coal gives off 1% of its weight in fly ash, how much fly ash is produced? If coal gives off 2% of its weight in sulfur dioxide, how much sulfur dioxide?

(d) Consider whether all the electricity could be produced by one big hydroelectric station. If the water level in the reservoir is allowed to fall 10 ft in a 6-month relatively dry summer, and the water falls 100 ft to generate electricity, how many square miles must the reservoir cover?

(e) Consider producing the electricity by solar power, using photoelectric cells of 10% efficiency. If the sun shines, on the average, 4 hr/day, how large an area is needed?

(f) Consider using nuclear power alone, with light-water reactors. How much uranium is needed? How much land for power generators? Is this smaller or larger than for fossil-fuel power stations?

(g) Remembering that the total energy demand is about 3 times the electricity demand, consider which of the above are applicable to transportation and heating needs.

(h) Have you any policy recommendations for the Governors of these New England states?

12. We have discussed in the text the possibility of extracting shale oil at a high cost to substitute for dwindling oil reserves. Shale oil is oil embedded in rock and present 1 part in 10 by weight (at best). An examination of the conversion of Table 2-8 shows that oil and coal, weight for weight, give similar amounts of energy.

Repeat the problem above about the area needed for strip-mining coal for strip-mining the shale for shale oil.

How much area do we need to strip-mine each year if all the U.S. energy demand by the year 2000 is to be met by using shale oil?

13. In pumping oil up from the earth, energy must be expended to raise the oil against the force of gravity. At what depth is this energy exactly equal to the energy content of the oil?

14. Assume that nuclear power has developed fast so that we are using uranium at a price of $50/lb. This is the cost of extraction from rock containing only 50 parts per million of uranium by weight. How much strip-mining will be needed for the 1000-MW$_e$ power station to get this uranium and how does it compare with coal?

3

Energy Demand
and Cost

THE CONSUMPTION OF ENERGY

The amount of energy used throughout the world is increasing
quite rapidly. In America, a high per capita consumption of energy
has always been a way of life.

Three hundred years ago, it was said that every American family
needed half an acre of woodland in order to have enough wood for fuel.
Yet the per capita consumption of fuels in this country has increased
by only a factor of 2.3 in the last 150 years; that fuel consumption
has little more than doubled in a century and a half can be attributed
to the more efficient ways in which fuels are now converted into usable
energy.

A striking example of improved efficiency, although not directly
pertinent to fuel consumption, is the increase in efficiency by a factor of ten of the tractor over the horse. A most pertinent example
is found in generating electricity. The thermal efficiency of power
stations in 1890 was 4%; today power stations can have an efficiency of
40%. [Technical Note 2-4.]* A change from wood to oil for home heating

_____

* There is a current tendency towards referring to the efficiency
of a thermal power plant in terms of Btu/kWh: the "heat rate." One

gives an improvement in efficiency from 8% to more than 50%. Efficiencies cannot be increased much over what they now are, as they already approach theoretically established limits. Because future improvements in the standard of living depend on a greater use of energy, these improvements can only come about through an increase in power consumption, not through improved efficiencies.

The widespread use of energy in the United States and the present great growth in its use throughout the rest of the world may be attributed to its being a relatively cheap commodity. The energy resources of the United States were always ready to be harnessed inexpensively, and now this is also true in most other countries.

Compare the cost of energy used in your home to the cost of food. Converting the food to its energy value in the body, the average person in the United States uses an amount of energy equivalent to one hundred times his average food consumption. It is a lot cheaper to consume energy than to eat. [See Worksheet 3-1.]

It is, in fact, interesting to see how energy consumption has changed in amount and distribution with time. Figure 3-1 concisely presents this information, comparing energy use in the U.S., India, and "the rest of the world" in 1900 and 1970. As a point of reference, the use of energy by primitive man is included. To bring the data into perspective, the per capita energy use is plotted. Figure 3-2 shows the growth of energy use in the United States from 1900 onward.

The per capita energy demand in the rest of the world is lower than that of the United States on an average by a factor of 6; for India, it is lower by a factor of 30. India uses only three times the per capita energy used by primitive man. Clearly, it should be our aim to increase the standard of living in poor countries, and insofar as energy contributes to our standard of living, the energy demand must increase.

---

kWh is equal to 3410 Btu. Therefore, if a fossil-fuel (or any other type) electric-power plant consumes 9800 Btu to produce 1 kWh of electrical energy, the conversion efficiency is 34.8%. It is always advisable to inquire if the number 9800 includes all energy consumed by the plant. The electricity required to operate pumps, heaters, lights, ventilating fans, etc. in the plant cannot be delivered to the outgoing transmission lines. That portion of generated electricity (or any other energy form) delivered to the plant and consumed within the plant must be taken into account to give a true efficiency figure.

Suppose the auxiliary energy required to keep the plant amounts to about 1039 Btu/kWh of electricity delivered to the transmission line. The true Btu/kWh "heat rate" is, then, 10,839 Btu. The net efficiency of the plant is 31.5%.

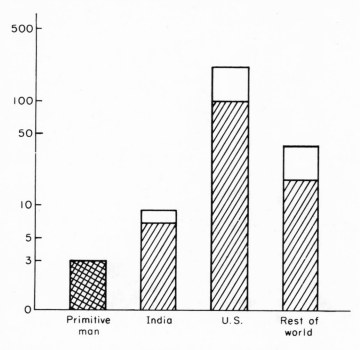

Fig. 3-1. Growth of energy demand. Shaded area, to 1900; unshaded area, 1900-1970.

The following quotation from the Joint Economic Committee of the Congress of the United States expresses the issue very well:

The economy of the United States and the technologically advanced nations is based on energy. Energy is the ultimate raw material which permits the continued recycle of resources into most of man's requirements for food, clothing, and shelter. The productivity (and consumption) of society is directly related to the per capita energy available [1].

To add an additional consideration to our discussion, we note that the population of the world is increasing. It is now about 3.5 billion (3.5×10^9) people. How much will the population increase? And how much can we allow the energy demand to increase? One optimistic view of the future impact of technology on the environment [2] argues that the world's resources could support indefinitely a population of 20 billion (2×10^{10}) people, with considerable recycling of raw materials. Recycling of raw materials requires energy, and this therefore assumes that energy consumption must rise to 20 kW per capita without any change in standard of living above the present U.S. average.

WORKSHEET 3-1

The Cost of Food Energy

The unit of energy known as the calorie is defined as the amount of heat required to raise 1 g of water from 15 to 16° C. The caloric value of food is given in Calories (note the capital C) and each food Calorie is equivalent to 1000 cal. Therefore, the Calorie is what we in this book refer to as the kilocalorie. Such differences in nomenclature between different branches of science and engineering is not unusual.

The food we eat, which is the fuel that drives us, is ultimately "burned" (combined with oxygen) within our system with a release of its chemical potential energy so that we may do work (in the strictly scientific sense of the word).

A cup of hot water will not provide energy to do work, as the body does not process heat energy from our intake, but rather chemical energy. However, on a cold day a hot drink might have some value, and you should be able to deduce why.

(a) We consume about 2000 kcal of food daily (1 kcal = 4185 j). List as many fossil-fuel energy-consuming steps as you can think of that precede the food reaching your table. This should include farm equipment, shipping, and preparation:

(b) Using the population of your city, the type of foods you eat, etc., work out a rough estimate of how much fossil fuel is consumed daily to keep you fed. (Use the Statistical Abstract of the United States and tables in this book for fuel-energy values.)

76a

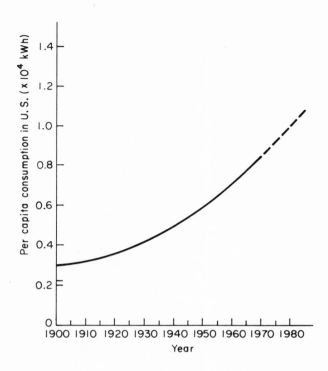

Fig. 3-2. Growth of energy demand in U.S. from 1900 onward.

   These predictions and calculations are regarded as excessive by
many environmentalists, but we note here that keeping use down even
to this level demands either great self-control in the U.S., or a continued lower standard of living elsewhere, particularly in the Asian
nations. For the sake of having some working numbers, we will take
the above estimate as a convenient optimistic goal; thus the world
energy consumption would rise 100-fold over present figures. This
rise in energy consumption must not bring with it any worsening in
the environmental effects of the necessary power production; preferably,
such environmental effects should be reduced. Whether or not we will
in fact use so much energy, this goal of a 100-fold reduction in average
adverse environmental impact is clear.
   From Fig. 3-2 we see that in the United States our standard of
living in 1970 carried with it a per capita energy consumption of about
9×10^4 kWh, or an average power consumption of 10 kW per person.
This is a huge figure. Ten kW corresponds to 100 light bulbs continuously operating.
   Study Table 3-1, which gives the distribution of per capita energy
use in the United States in 1970. We see that use in households is
considerable and so also in transportation; the largest use, however,
is in process heat in industry (aluminum processing, etc.). The relation of each of these entries to our standard of living is almost
self-apparent. [See Worksheet 3-2.]

TABLE 3-1

U.S. Per Capita Energy Use, kW [2]*

	Household	Commercial	Transport	Industry	Other	Total
Space heating	1.14	0.13	0.03	0.14	0.07	1.51
Other heat	0.33	0.4	–	2.0	0.6	3.33
Motive	–	–	2.0	–	–	2.0
Electricity (including power station loss)	0.5	0.3	–	1.0	0.3	2.1
Nonenergy	–	–	–	0.41	0.7	1.11
Total	1.97	0.83	2.03	3.55	1.67	10.05

* Man uses 0.1 kW from food, which was the only energy resource of primitive man.

TABLE 3-2

Annual Energy Use by Resource, 1971 [3]*

Resource	In usual units	kWh/yr	kWh/person/yr	kW/person (avg)	Our suggested use, year 2000
Fossil fuels					
Coal	4.95×10^8 tons/yr	4.3×10^{12}	2.2×10^4	2.2	Chemicals, electricity
Oil (including imports)	5.55×10^9 bbl/yr	9.4×10^{12}	4.6×10^4	5.2	Mobile: cars, airplanes
Gas	2.21×10^{13} ft^3/yr	6.7×10^{12}	3.2×10^4	3.7	Domestic: cooking, heating
Hydroelectric	–	2.66×10^{11}	1.3×10^3	0.15	Electricity
Geothermal	–	2.0×10^9	6	0.001	Electricity
Tidal	–	–	–	–	Electricity
Solar	–	–	–	–	Direct heat
Nuclear fission	–	3.8×10^{10}	184	0.021	Electricity
Nuclear fusion	–	–	–	–	Electricity
Total		2.07×10^{13}	1.13×10^4	10.1	

* These figures include industrial use and power-station losses.

79

3. Energy Demand and Cost

In Table 3-2 we show the total energy used in the United States in 1965, which gives a fair idea of what the trends were before the present sudden shortages, and the sources of that energy.

The question of *energy conservation* is being much discussed. This has nothing to do with the physical law that energy is conserved as it changes form; a better title would be *fuel conservation*, *wise use of energy*, or *increased energy productivity*.

What is the potential for using our energy more wisely? This is no longer an academic concern. Obviously, we want to spend our efforts on the largest entries in Table 3-1: industrial (process) heat, transportation, and household space heat. In all of these, the low cost of oil and gas until 1973 has reduced the incentive for conservation. We assign some problems to enable you to understand some of these issues directly. Energy utilization measures that are possible in the U.S. are discussed in [4-8].

Recycling is often proposed, both to save raw materials and, in some cases, to save energy. In Table 3-3 we show the approximate amounts of energy used to fabricate 1 kg (2.2 lb) of material from ore and recycled scrap, respectively, without taking into account the energy for collecting the scrap. It is clear that the energy gain for steel, aluminum, and copper may make recycling economically attractive. The advantages of recycling glass are, however, not clear at this time, particularly since the raw material, sand, is common. Environmental efforts should, therefore, be directed to metal scrap collection rather than bottle collection: the reverse of the usual (and easy) course.

TABLE 3-3

Energy Required to Produce Various Materials (kWh/g)

	From ore	From scrap
Steel	10	2
Aluminum	50	2
Copper	17	1
Glass	3	3

THE COST OF ENERGY

It is also important to discuss whether, how, and when to halt the escalating demand for energy. Barry Commoner [9] eloquently argues that the time is now. It is worth reading Commoner to help you make up your own mind on the matter.

Personal Energy Resource Consumption

Refer to Table 3-2 to determine the 1971 per capita consumption of coal, oil, and gas in the United States. You should keep in mind that this is approximately the amount of the Earth's nonreplaceable natural resources that you were responsible for depleting in that year:

(a) Calculate the population of the U.S. in 1971: _____ people.

(b) Coal used per person: _____ tons.

(c) Oil used per person: _____ barrels.

(d) Gas used per person: _____ cubic feet.

The coal and oil that each of us were responsible for consuming were not used solely for energy purposes. List a number of products for which coal or petroleum is used as a raw material or processes which require petroleum or coal (or a byproduct) for other than an energy source:

<u>Coal</u>   <u>Petroleum</u>

Theoretically, to reduce the demand for anything, one increases its cost. That the cost increase may have to be a drastic one is exemplified by very high cigarette taxes in some states which have produced no noticeable reduction of smoking. Or, notwithstanding the very high price of automobile fuel in Europe, coupled with wages that in some of these European countries are much lower than those in the United States, there still exists a large automobile population, traffic jams, and much highway driving.

In the United States, a gallon of gasoline at the pump varies from $0.35 to $0.85 (about 160 kWh/$), including tax. While more expensive than the crude oil from which it is derived, it is still only 15% of the cost of running an automobile. With a doubling in fuel cost, it is hard to see how automobile travel would be reduced. The suburbs are a function of the automobile. At best, some people might start to run a more efficient automobile. But all matters considered, one must regard gasoline as an inexpensive item. Hence, only an out-and-out reduction in supply or rationing will curtail its use.

Likewise, we see that the cost of electricity generation is very cheap. Most consumers in the United States pay about $0.04-0.05/kWh. The rough derivation of this amount, based on the Boston Edison Company figures of March, 1972, is shown in Table 3-4. In this table we see that the cost of the environmentally more favorable low-sulfur fuel

TABLE 3-4

Cost of Electricity, 1972 Prices*

	mils/kWh ($0.001/kWh)
Low-sulfur (0.5%) oil (35% efficiency)	8.8
High-sulfur (2.5%) oil	6.0
Uranium	2.0
14% interest on 1000-MW$_e$ oil station operative for 6000 hr ($270 million capital cost)	6.3
14% interest on 1000-MW$_e$ nuclear station operative for 6000 hr ($330 million capital cost)	7.5
Cost to authors as residential consumer (average)	33 ($0.03/kWh)

* Based on costs to Boston Edison Company (Pursel 1972) in March, 1972. The cost of the power stations is based on new capacity operated as base load; older power stations, built with "cheap money," cost less.

is a difference in cost of $0.0028 mils/kWh, 10% of the cost of electricity, and the total generating cost is less than half the charge to the consumer. The cost of the energy itself is only 25% of the cost to the customer! The greater part of the cost is in the generator, transmission lines, distribution, etc.

This conclusion, that energy is cheap, is at variance with that of some nonconservationist conservatives who argue that it is too expensive to halt pollution and the bill is too great for society to pay. However, our simple ideas are confirmed by a detailed calculation by Ford and Leontief [10], using the sophisticated economic techniques of input-output analysis. In this calculation Ford and Leontief traced the effects on every part of the economy of an increase of fuel prices. In particular, they found that a switch from high- to low-sulfur fuels would change the price of no item more than 1%. This should be increased to 2%, since the cost of fuel oil with low-sulfur content has increased dramatically from the time of Ford and Leontief's study. It is likely to increase more in the coming years. Ford and Leontief claim that there would be no tendency for one segment of the economy to suffer more than another, although it seems that the indirect cost of the low-sulfur fuel is to be spread equally.

The direct cost will bear *more* heavily on the poor than on the rich, since the poor pay a larger fraction of their very limited income on energy sources. This increase of cost therefore resembles a sales tax in its regressive nature (regressive, of course, solely by comparison with a graduated income tax). Still more important is the cost of energy in a poor country like India. However, the U.S. can and should clearly pay the price of pollution control.

Much confusion has resulted from an increase in world oil prices simultaneously with the introduction of low-sulfur fuels. Low-sulfur fuels from natural sources can be found in Nigeria and Libya. Until the sudden demand for low-sulfur fuels, few refineries extracted sulfur. With this demand came an increase in price, comparable to the cost of extracting the sulfur in a refinery.

The impact of these changes can be illustrated by their effect on the Boston Edison Company. In 1970, Boston Edison bought oil under a long-term contract at $1.75/bbl; the price paid in 1973 for low-sulfur oil is $4.75/bbl. Only a part of this increase can be truly attributed to the environmental requirement itself. Part is due to a natural increase in price, and part to a hasty insistence on the low-sulfur requirement, which led to the dropping of an advantageous long-term contract.

On the other hand, there are "energy enthusiasts" who feel we should not limit the production of energy. In their view, unlimited cheap energy will make possible many technological things that are not possible today. They argue, for example [11], that with cheaper energy we might reclaim the Sahara Desert for agriculture. But is it the unavailability of cheap energy that hinders the development of the desert, or is the lack of a technology to use this energy? What do you do with this energy once you have it? On the other hand, in 1973/74 we see what a cutback in the energy supply can do to highly developed countries.

Why the difference in views? We can easily afford to pay for a plentiful supply of reliable, nonpolluting electricity. However, we probably cannot afford an expansion of an electrical supply system that is unreliable and has adverse side effects. Perhaps there is a lesson to be learned from history. Common salt is vital to good cooking and good health. A thousand years ago wars were fought over salt monopolies. Although a plentiful supply of salt is essential, the cost of this commodity is very small. Will the same be true some day of electricity?

Given our present means of obtaining energy, we should be concerned with ways of limiting its consumption. At first glance, taxation might be the best method to do this. It is certainly better than allowing prices to rise, thus enabling the few rich people in the energy industry to become relatively richer. But is this so, and would it be effective [see Problems]?

It would appear to be hypocritical to urge that this energy demand be reduced until one's own demand is reduced. For this reason we have calculated our own personal demand and that of our families. As shown in Table 3-5, we use the average U.S. amount of energy and would be reluctant to see our consumption forcibly decreased.

TABLE 3-5

Comparison of Authors' Power Use to U.S. Average, 1971 (kW per capita)

	U.S. average [2]	Wilson's house	Jones' house
Electricity (including generating losses)	0.5	0.53	1.9
Gas (heat and cooking)	1.47	1.6	none
Car travel		0.25	0.32
Air travel (mainly work)	2 (including industrial)	1.6	1.0

3. Energy Demand and Cost

ELECTRICITY: DEMAND VERSUS TIME

The demand for electricity in a big city follows a graph as shown in Fig. 3-3 [12]. The lowest load level, at night, is about one-half the daytime load. The peak appears in late afternoon during the summer, due to air conditioning, but it may appear at other times of day in the winter, due to heating.

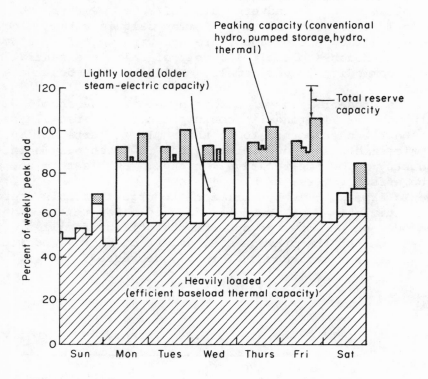

Fig. 3-3. Typical weekly load curve for a city electrical utility company.

The electric companies like to divide their generating facilities into three categories:

1. *Base load:* Plants that run all day and all night;
2. *Cycling:* Plants that run between dawn and midnight;
3. *Peaking:* Plants that run in the late afternoon only.

A power station with a low running cost is ideal for a base load. Such a station can write off the high capital cost of construction over a long period. On the East Coast of the United States, this base

84

load is handled more and more by nuclear plants; on the West Coast, coal is still the preferred base-load plant.

Oil-fired fossil fuel is often used in cycling plants.

Peaking plants are hydroelectric stations, pumped-storage generator systems, and gas turbines. The gas turbines, for example, have a high fuel cost, but low capital cost.

Since they operate for only a fraction of the day, peaking or cycling plants might be located within the city to save transmission-lines costs. However, for the short period that they operate, the amount of pollution they generate is greater than that produced by a base-load plant generating the same amount of electricity. The fact that this pollution might be generated within the city limits makes the problem even more complex. Of course, these last comments exclude those peaking plants that are run by water power.

Energy Storage Devices

Ideally, we would like to produce energy at a steady rate and during periods of low demand store the extra energy for use when needed. The technology for efficient storage of energy in large quantities is not yet with us. As we have seen in connection with solar energy, we have no means of storing large amounts of heat that could later be used to make steam. We have not yet developed a capacity for storing large quantities of electrical energy in giant storage batteries, or perhaps superconducting coils, so that we could immediately tap them when needed. We can, however, harness gravitational potential energy by using electrical energy generated in the "off hours" to pump water up to a man-made reservoir built on high ground. [See Technical Notes 3-1 and 3-2.]

TECHNICAL NOTE 3-1

The Galvanic Cells: Electrical Storage Devices

The three major devices for storing electrical energy are the dry cell (such as used in flashlights, Fig. 3-4), the wet cell (such as used in cars, Fig. 3-5), and the fuel cell (Fig. 3-6)*.

---

* Figures 3-4, 3-5, and 3-6 adapted from Brescia, F., Arents, J., Meislich, H., and Turk, A., "Fundamentals of Chemistry," 2nd Edition. Academic Press, New York and London, 1970.

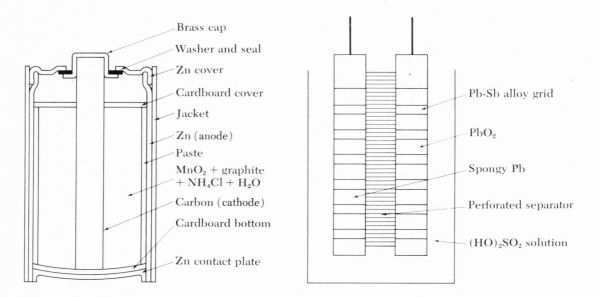

Fig. 3-4. A dry cell
as used in flashlights.

Fig. 3-5. A lead-acid
storage cell.

In all cases chemical potential energy will be released as electrical energy. The dry cell is "dry" only in the sense that it contains a paste rather than a liquid; it could not function if water were absent. The electrode reactions are complex and subject to some controversy. In brief, the zinc reacts to give up two of its electrons (making it positive). Through a reaction in the paste between the ammonia (NH_4) and the magnesium dioxide (MnO_2), the electrons collect on the carbon rod. In the process Mn_2O_3, NH_3, and H_2O are produced. The cell dies when nearly all of the Mn_2O_3 and NH_4 is used up.

The lead-acid storage cell, in its charged state, consists of an electrode of spongy lead and an electrode of finely divided solid lead oxide, supported by a grid of lead and antimony (which is stronger and more resistant to corrosion than pure lead). A solution of sulfuric acid serves as the electrolyte; the sulfuric acid is consumed during discharge and regenerated upon charging. Please note that there are other types of wet cells that use different metals and electrolytes.

A simplified diagram of a fuel cell is shown in Fig. 3-6, similar to ones used in spacecraft. It achieves its unique position in that reactants are continuously fed into the cell and the products are continuously removed. This type of fuel cell, since it requires hydrogen as a fuel, is expensive and cumbersome. The potential for fuel cells is great. Fuel cells that would burn compounds of hydrogen and carbon instead of hydrogen might cause the internal combustion engine to be superseded by electrical engines. Such hydrocarbon cells have been built, but they need high-temperature operation and have resulting short lifetimes.

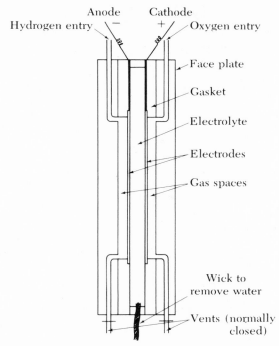

Anode Cathode
Hydrogen entry — + Oxygen entry
Face plate
Gasket
Electrolyte
Electrodes
Gas spaces
Wick to remove water
Vents (normally closed)

Fig. 3-6. A hydrogen-oxygen fuel cell.

    The only product discharged by the hydrogen fuel cells is pure water. Natural gas fuel cells discharge carbon dioxide and water. In the hydrogen fuel cell the electrodes are thin coatings of porous platinum. The electrolyte is a solid membrane of a material that causes an exchange of ions in the liquid flowing through it with ions that are in the material. For example, hard water contains calcium ions. When made to flow through an exchanger containing sodium ions, the calcium ions stay in the material, and the sodium ions go into the water and "soften" it. These are called ion-exchange materials and form the heart of the fuel cell. In the cell, the exchange material contains H_3O^+ ions.

TECHNICAL NOTE 3-2

Mechanical-Energy Storage, the Flywheel

    A heavy disk spinning at a high speed possesses a great deal of kinetic energy. A disk brought up to high speed could drive an electric generator within a vehicle to power an electric motor. The obvious question is how much could we "charge" up such a disk? How long before it would run down?

87

3. Energy Demand and Cost

The Oerlikon Electrogyro bus used in parts of Europe and Africa during the 1950's and 1960's employed a 3300-lb flywheel spinning at 3000 revolutions per minute (rpm). A fully "charged" wheel could drive the bus 3/4 mile, at which point a trolley on top of the bus was raised to a cable for 40 sec to recharge the wheel (see Fig. 3-7).

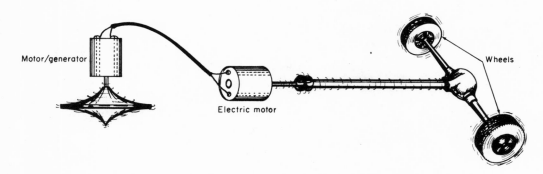

Fig. 3-7. A flywheel system.

Lockheed Missiles and Space Company has developed a flywheel of new design and material that is now to be tested in a bus in San Francisco. The wheel is 3-1/2 ft in diameter and weighs only 600 lb, but it is designed to spin at 18,000 rpm. A computer was used to determine the optimum shape of the wheel; it is thicker at the center than at the edges, and new materials technology was employed to fabricate a wheel that would not spin itself apart at these speeds.

The flywheel can generate 200,000 W, and it will drive the bus for 6 miles. Recharging from 9000 rpm takes 2 min. The flywheel is housed in a vacuum. The motor that turns the wheel is switched into a generator mode when the wheel is fully charged.

If such vehicles prove safe and durable, within the bounds of a city they will provide quiet and pollution-free transportation. Refer to Problem 3-13 for possible negative aspects of this type of vehicle.

In the pumped-storage plant, water is pumped uphill from a lower reservoir, usually a river, to a reservoir at the top of a hill. When needed, the water is allowed to return through the same pump which pushed it up. However, with the falling water spinning the pump around, the pump becomes a turbine that drives a generator. This same generator, during the pumping process, serves as a motor to power the pump (Fig. 3-8). [See Worksheet 3-3.]

WORKSHEET 3-3

The Pumped-Storage Generating Plant

In Bear Swamp, Massachusetts, an upper lake is used as a pumped-storage reservoir. The dimensions of the lake are assumed to be:

$$0.7 \ km \times 0.5 \ km \times 15 \ km.$$

Fact: $1 \ m^3$ of water weighs 9.8×10^6 N. (It is left to the reader to relate these numbers to the British system of units.)

(a) What is the gravitational potential energy stored in this water with respect to the 200-m drop to the lower-lake reservoir where the turbine blades are located?

The weight of the water in the lake is _____.

The potential energy = weight × height

$$= \underline{\hspace{1cm}}$$

$$= \underline{\hspace{1cm}} \ j.$$

(b) Convert this figure to kilowatt-hours. Recall the definition of a watt as the rate of flow of energy at 1 j/sec. (Solve first for the number of joules in a kilowatt.)

At an efficiency of energy conversion of 30%, how much electrical power would the reservoir supply?

Given that the efficiency of the original generating plant was 33%, that pumping the water into the reservoir the energy loss was 15%, and the final efficiency of converting the stored water to electricity is 85%, how many tons of coal were required to obtain this electrical energy? How many tons of coal are required to obtain this amount of electricity from the primary generating plant?

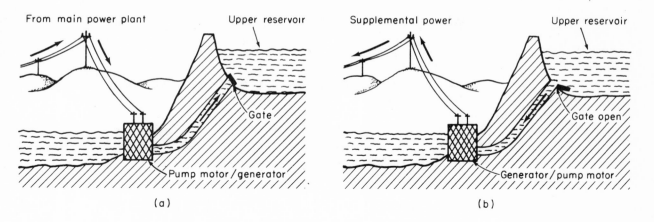

Fig. 3-8. A pumped-storage system: (a) with current from base-load plant, generators used to drive pumps and load upper reservoir; (b) when peaking power is needed, gate is open and water drives generator.

The pumped-storage unit has its environmental hazards; it uses land that is often in a wildlife area (although not as much as a comparable hydroelectric station), and the reservoir level goes up and down with usage so that fish may be pulled through the turbines and killed.

Moreover, there is a 30% energy loss in this overall process which adds to thermal pollution, although part of this thermal pollution may be compensated for by evaporation from the upper reservoir surface.

The most serious aspect of environmental effects from a pumped-storage facility appears not at the site of the facility, but at the base-load plant, where the 30% loss figure becomes particularly meaningful.

To pump the water into the reservoir, the pump motors are powered by electricity from the base-load plant. In New York City, for example, this would be electricity generated in the low-demand, early morning hours. Often, these are the hours that the winds partially cleanse the air of the previous day's debris. With a pumped-storage facility, the base-load plant would be operating at full capacity during these hours.

The administration of New York City opposes Consolidated Edison's plans for a pumped-storage facility on the grounds that it will be too close to a water aqueduct supply line. Environmentalists oppose the plant because of its infringement on the scenic beauty of the Hudson River shoreline. However, the power company contends that this plant is the least expensive and least environmentally detrimental step it can take to prevent blackouts due to the sudden overloading of their generators.

A possible future method of storing energy is by electrolysis of water, that is, by separating each molecule of water into its constituent atoms of hydrogen and oxygen. These gases can then be transported by pipeline to another site for later burning. This is analogous to the obvious method of refraining from burning a fossil fuel until it is needed, a procedure that the utility companies dislike because of wasted usable space.

The use of hydrogen in fuel cells, which we will discuss in Chapter 12, would allow a much higher efficiency in the production of electricity and is a very attractive possibility.

Power Sources for Peaking Plants

Both the conventional hydroelectric plant and the pumped-storage unit admirably fill the specific needs of peaking plants. The peak demand for electricity is twice the average demand (refer again to Fig. 3-3). Hydroelectric power can be turned on instantly, so to speak. Hydroelectric-driven turbines can go from 20 to 100% of full power in one minute. They can therefore take a load while another overloaded generator is slowing down.

A recent, and now rather common, method of producing peaking power is by use of the gas turbine. This method began as little more than a jet engine blowing against a windmill. Gas turbines are still in an early stage of development but will be used more and more. At the moment the capital cost is low, although the fuel cost is high. The thermal efficiency of gas turbines is low, but the waste heat goes into air and not into water and is spread out over many small units. An environmental advantage of gas turbine units derives from their small size and the fact that they can be placed where they are needed, thereby saving transmission line costs. New York's Consolidated Edison Company has used turbines floating on a barge in the East River. The hazards are the usual ones of fossil fuels: CO_2 and NO_2 production and noise.

A gas turbine can start and take a load in 7 min. This is not quite quick enough in the event of a sudden power failure. However, if the turbines are kept spinning during peak periods in anticipation of possible failure somewhere in the system, they can do the job.

The traditional diesel engine used by trucks and trains is also used to drive generators to produce peaking power. Small diesel engines are used to produce electrical power on farms that are not tied into main systems. They also serve as backup systems at airports and hospitals.

Four minutes are required to start and bring a diesel-driven generator to full power. As with the turbine, the diesel generator has the advantage of mobility because of its small size. If operated for short periods, the total pollution output is low.

One of the functions of the peaking plant is to prevent a blackout due to the sudden failure of one of the supply units. It might be worthwhile to note that there can be more than one cause of a blackout. Too long a time lag in starting electrical generating capacity accounted for the famous Northeast blackout of 1965. However, local blackouts often result from the failure of distribution equipment, such as the transformers or safety relays that service a given area. Hot weather, with the high-power demands to operate air conditioning equipment that it brings, leads to overloading and overheating of equipment. Whether there are reasonable limits on the reserve capacity of any piece of equipment or whether the utility companies are guilty of poor planning, poor maintenance, or not properly upgrading their equipment with increased power demands, are questions that must be asked and answered separately in every case.

LONG-TERM ENERGY POLICY

We already see that we will not be able to use natural gas and oil as freely as in the recent past. Oil may ultimately be reserved by law for mobile use, since no one has come up with an aircraft engine, or even a good automobile engine, that runs on as cheap a fuel. Natural gas is ideal for small burners, kitchen stoves, and so on, and may be reserved for domestic use (in spite of the nitrogen oxides produced by its use). Thus for large uses - electric utilities, hospitals, and industry - we must revert to coal, liquify or gasify coal, or use nuclear fuels. The choice may be made on either economic or environmental grounds.

Two extreme positions are presently being argued in the U.S. The first is that coal is a dirty fuel both in mining and in use, and to make it clean is impractical and improbable; therefore, we must switch to nuclear fuels as soon as possible. If we use only U^{235}, we will run out of cheap uranium by the year 2000, and out of all \$100/lb uranium by 2150. Associated with this position is the idea that we must, then, develop breeder reactors as soon as possible and by no later than the year 2000. If we put priority on this now, we might have breeders going by 1985, allowing 15 years for slippage. This is the Administration or "establishment" position.

Simultaneously, the Administration is urging gasification of coal as the cleanest way of burning this fuel, and long-term research on nuclear fusion and solar power, both of which are likely to be cleaner than either coal or nuclear fission.

This official view was clearly stated on July 27, 1971, by Dr. Glenn Seaborg, then Chairman of the AEC:

Hydro power today gives us less than 5% of our total electricity, and will continue to provide only a small fraction of our power because we have already developed most of our natural hydro power locations to their fullest capacities...

   Geothermal energy, tapping the heat released deep within the earth, is another source. But even with the fullest development of such a source, it is doubtful that geothermal steam could fill but a small fraction of our total electricity needs in the future... Future technologies may be developed to concentrate, collect, and store the enormous but low-intensity energy of the sun in certain relatively cloudless areas of the country, or even on solar cells *orbiting in space,* but it seems doubtful that we will see such technologies in large-scale use in this century...

   Likewise, it would not be wise to set stock in the full-scale, widespread use of controlled fusion as a *major* source of electric power for the coming decades, perhaps not until well into the 21st century...

Bearing this in mind, President Nixon stated in his July, 1971 Message to Congress on Energy:

Our best hope today for meeting the Nation's growing demand for economical clean energy lies with the fast breeder reactor. Because of its highly efficient use of nuclear fuel, the breeder reactor could extend the life of our natural uranium fuel supply from decades to centuries, with far less impact on the environment than the power plants which are operating today.

But he also said: "The sun offers an almost unlimited supply of energy if we can learn to use it economically." Yet hardly any money has been allocated for solar research.

   A second position is taken by George L. Weil [13], one-time Chief of the Civilian Power Branch of the AEC, who personally pulled out the control rod starting the first nuclear chain reaction, in Chicago:

Even if the AEC, utilities, reactor designers, and manufacturers are doing everything they can think of to avoid a major accident in a nuclear plant, it would indeed be surprising if the nuclear industry can long escape the relentless truth of Murphy's law, proven time and again: "If something can go wrong, it will!" Though the possibility of a major accident may be very

low, without the precaution of underground plant construction the risk to the public is staggering.

A crash program to clean up coal would assure
a resource of energy, as many reliable sources have
indicated, for 100 years or longer without the help
of a single nuclear power plant. Such a cleanup
program should buy us enough time to develop a limit-
less energy alternative, for example, fusion or solar,
that is superior to both coal and fission.

As for the promise of nuclear energy, whatever
benefits we may eventually reap from it will hardly
come from the low-performance nuclear plants now being
sold to U.S. utilities and to the American public.
They are just a nuclear flash in the energy pan!
Moreover, no one claims that the technology and experience from these plants are necessary preludes to
developing breeders. Today's nuclear power plants
are a dead-end street in this respect. They are ...
too many, too large, too soon, too inefficient; in
short, they offer too little in exchange for too
many risks.

Still a third is the official Canadian position: Although they
do not doubt that breeders could be built safely, they doubt the economy
of building them. A *converter* (near breeder) working on a uranium-
thorium cycle in a Canadian-type heavy-water reactor, or a Gulf-Atomic
high-temperature gas-cooled reactor, can, on the other hand, increase
by a factor of 10 the fuel utilization to stretch fuel reserves for
centuries.

Most industrial countries (England, France, Germany, U.S.S.R.,
Italy, and Japan) are pushing ahead with the Liquid-Metal Fast Breeder
Reactor (LMFBR) and are even ahead of the U.S. in this development.
Some suggest that the Administration's enthusiasm for the fast breeder
may, in part, be due to the fear of having to import a breeder reactor
from Europe.

The choice between these positions is difficult but important;
it will determine not only the cost of energy, but also some of our
options in foreign policy. When it is necessary in the following pages
to make an assumption about the future, we will assume that, as usual,
the U.S. will decide in all directions at once. Thus *our* projection
in Fig. 3-9 shows less electricity than do projections of the Federal
Power Commission [14, 15] or the AEC [16]. But we believe the breeder
reactor will be developed, and we share the hope that within a century
it will either be proven obviously safe or replaced permanently by one
of those sources of energy that are still just beyond the horizon.

Our predicted capacity increases by a factor of 4 over 1970, compared to the "official" estimated factor of 6. We anticipate that the
price increase, environmental effects, and fuel shortages will combine

to reduce demand below the official estimates. We expect that all presently ordered nuclear power stations will operate, but with an average of one year's delay, and subsequent expansion will be slower. The High-Temperature Gas-Cooled Reactor (HTGR) and the Liquid-Metal Fast Breeder Reactor (LMFBR) will, as new types, be taking on much of the demand.

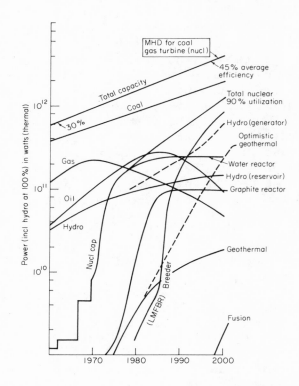

Fig. 3-9. Electrical generating capacity projection, conservative consumption, optimistic efficiency (data to 1970, projections beyond).

The effect that these projections must have on the coal industry is not so well known. In Fig. 3-9 we show coal output increasing. An alternative would be to import increasing amounts of oil and gas in the next ten years, and to use more coal after 1980. This would allow time for development of better methods of burning coal.

We assume that oil and gas consumption will be reduced as their supply decreases; geothermal power and hydropower will reach their full potential by 2000, and fusion will (maybe) begin to produce power by 2000.

Other useful general references for this chapter are given in [17-26].

94

REFERENCES

[1] US Congress (1970). "The Economy, Energy, and the Environment." Prepared for Joint Economic Committee, USGPO (September).

[2] Weinberg, A.M. (1970). "Nuclear Energy and the Environment." Bull. At. Sci. Vol. 26, p. 69; "Limits to the Use of Energy." American Scientist Vol. 58, p. 413.

[3] US Govt. (1971). "Statistical Abstract of the United States." USGPO.

[4] US Govt. (1972). "The Potential for Energy Conservation." US Executive Office, USGPO (October).

[5] Symp. on Effective Energy Utilization (1972). Drexel Institute of Technology, June 8-9, Philadelphia, Pennsylvania.

[6] US Congress (1973). "Individual Action for Energy Conservation." Prepared for Committee on Science and Astronautics, Subcommittee on Energy, USGPO (June).

[7] US Senate (1973). Print 73-7. Prepared for Committee on Interior and Insular Affairs, USGPO.

[8] Commonwealth of Massachusetts (1973). "Energy Conservation." Pamphlet by Office of Consumer Affairs, Boston, Massachusetts (December).

[9] Commoner, B. (1971). "The Closing Circle." Knopf, New York.

[10] Ford, D., and Leontief, W. (1970). Scientific American.

[11] Seaborg, G.T., and Bloom, J.L. (1970). "Fast Breeder Reactors." Scientific American Vol. 223, p. 13.

[12] Thompson, T.J. (1971). "The Role of Nuclear Power in the United States of America," IAEA-SM-146/4. In Symp. on Environmental Aspects of Nuclear Power Stations 1970, IAEA, Vienna.

[13] Weil, G.L. (1971). "Nuclear Energy: Promises, Promises." Privately circulated booklet (1st printing).

[14] Federal Power Commission (FPC) (1964). "1964 National Power Survey," Parts I, II. USGPO.

[15] FPC (1970). "1970 National Power Survey," Parts I-IV. USGPO.

[16] Battelle Memorial Institute (1969). "Pacific NW Laboratories: A Review and Comparison of Selected U.S. Energy Forecasts." Battelle Memorial Institute, Seattle, Washington.

[17] Schurr, S.H., et al. (1960). "Energy in the Atomic Economy 1850-1975." Johns Hopkins Univ. Press, Baltimore, Maryland.

[18] Ayres, E., and Scarlett, C.A. (1952). "Energy Sources." McGraw-Hill, New York.

[19] Fabricant, N., and Hallman, R.M. (1972). "Toward a Rational Power Policy." Braziller, New York.

[20] IAEA (1971). Proc. Symp. on Environmental Aspects of Nuclear Power Stations." IAEA in cooperation with USAEC, New York, August 10-14, 1970. IAEA, Vienna.

[21] US Govt. (1970). "Electric Power and the Environment." Prepared by Office of Science and Technology, USGPO.

[22] Metcalf, L., and Reinemer, V. (1967). "Overcharge." McKay, New York.

[23] Hanon, B. (1972). "Bottles, Cans, Energy." Environment Vol. 14, p. 11.

[24] Hirst, E., and Moyers, J. (1973). "Efficiency of Energy Use in the USA." Science Vol. 179, p. 1299.

[25] Makhijani, A.B., and Lichtenberg, A.J. (1972). "Energy and Well Being." Environment Vol. 14, p. 10.

[26] Moyers, J. (1971). "The Value of Thermal Insulation in Residential Construction." Oak Ridge Natl. Lab. Rept. ORNL-NSF-EP-9, Oak Ridge, Tennessee.

General References

Fisher, H. (1973). "Energy Crisis in Perspective." Wiley, New York.

Meadows, D.H., Meadows, D.L., Randers, J., and Behrens, W. (1972). "The Limits to Growth." Universe, New York.

Susskind, H., and Raseman, C.J. (1970). "Combined Hydroelectric Pumped-Storage and Nuclear Power Operation." Brookhaven Natl. Lab. Rept. BNL 50238, Brookhaven, New York.

Special Set of References on the Origin of the 1973 US Energy Crisis

    Some experts foresaw the crisis and urged that the U.S. plan for it ...

Akins, J.E. (1973). "The Oil Crisis: This Time the Wolf Is Here." Foreign Affairs, April; reprinted in Petroleum Intelligence Weekly, March 26.

Amuzegar, J. (1973). "The Oil Story: Facts, Fiction, and Fair Play." Foreign Affairs, July.

Griffith, W. (1974). "The Middle East, the Energy Crisis, and US Policy." Reader's Digest, January.

Meyer, A.J. (1973). Testimony to US Senate Committee on Interior and Insular Affairs, November. USGPO.

... but others thought that the problem could be avoided or had different causes.

Adelman, M.A. (1973). "How Real Is the Oil Shortage?" Wall Street Journal, Feb. 9.

Adelman, M.A. (1973). "Is the Oil Shortage Real? Oil Companies as OPEC Tax Collectors." Foreign Policy, Vol. 9, Winter.

Arrow, K.J., Fisher, F.M., Galbraith, J.K., Kuznets, S., Leontief, W., Peck, M.J., Samuelson, P.A., and Solow, R.M. (1973). "Oil and Politics in the Middle East." Press Release, Cambridge, Massachusetts, Oct. 10.

PROBLEMS

1. Work out a personal table of energy consumption for gas,
electricity, heating oil, and other items. Calculate your average
energy use. In the case of electricity, allow for the power-station
efficiency of 30%, oil 70%, and gas 80% for heating. For example,

(a) Take the readings of the house electricity and gas from one
year's bills, and divide.
(b) Measure the mileage of your car and calculate gasoline used
at 15 miles/gal, and assume that the energy content of gasoline is
similar to oil.
(c) Calculate miles traveled on a bus that runs at 7 miles/gal
and the average number of passengers per trip at 15. (Calculations
can be made from figures in the Statistical Abstract of the United
States and other references.)

2. Outline a procedure for reducing your own energy consumption
by 25% without appreciably reducing your standard of living. Note
particularly why you have not taken these steps.

3. Refer to Table 3-1. In terms of a reduction in energy supplies,
discuss the effect on our standard of living that a curtailment of
energy consumption has on each of the items listed in the table.

4. From tables in the Statistical Abstract of the United States
(or other tables), determine:

√The total amount of petroleum fuel used by buses and the total
number of passenger miles traveled by buses. Hence, derive the
number of passenger miles per gallon of petroleum fuel.

√Make a similar calculation for passenger train travel, travel
by private automobile, and travel by jet airplane. Also calculate the same thing for the proposed SST or Concorde Supersonic
airplane by using company projections, or other data. Tabulate
these data for ease of comparison.

5. Plot the consumption of some interesting use of energy against
time. Use, for example, the Statistical Abstract of the United States
or United Nations Surveys (for the world). Plot both the total and
per capita amounts, and put in units of kilowatts average per capita.
(Use a logarithmic plot and extrapolate both curves to the year 2000.
Are these extrapolations reasonable?)

(1) Commercial air travel in U.S.

(2) Commercial air travel in world.
(3) Ocean freight travel.
(4) Truck-loaded freight.
(5) Personal automobile travel.
(6) Total oil consumption in U.S.
   Total oil consumption in world.
   Total oil production in U.S.
(7) Food per capita in U.S. in calories per capita.
   Same for world.

6. Losses of heat from hot bodies to colder ones vary as the difference in temperature. Calculate the fuel savings, averaged over winter days from November through March, of reducing house temperatures in New England from 74 to 68° F. What other information do you need to know? Look it up or estimate it.

7. Calculate the effect of reducing the house temperatures from 68 to 58° F from 11 p.m. to 8 a.m. Comment on widespread statements (prior to 1973) that this is not helpful.

8. Consider a house in summertime. The outside temperature rises to 95° F from 10 a.m. to 6 p.m. and falls to 65° F from 8 p.m. to 6 a.m. How can the house best be kept at a comfortable temperature without air conditioning? Outline and compare the use of the following aids:

(1) Opening and closing windows,
(2) Window awnings and shutters outside the house,
(3) Curtains and blinds inside the house,
(4) Color of paint on the house,
(5) Use of attic insulating fiberglass,
(6) Use of aluminum foil for attic insulation,
(7) Use of an attic fan or window fan.

9. Refer to the projection of coal use as shown in Fig. 3-9. Assume that all the increase in coal mining comes from strip mines in Montana and Wyoming. Calculate the number of unit trains necessary per day to transport this coal. By examining a railroad map of the U.S., estimate the ability of the U.S. railroads to handle this traffic.

10. In the U.S. the production of *food energy* involves fertilizers (artificial) and mechanized equipment as well as long-distance transportation systems. Draw up some sort of a flow chart that shows the various forms of energy that are introduced into the cycle before the food product reaches the consumer. The flow chart will vary for different agricultural products and meats; therefore, select a class of product of interest to you.

Problems

11. The aluminum industry is one of the great industrial consumers of electricity. Much energy is needed to separate the aluminum from its state in the ore. (a) Assume that we tax heavily large users of electricity, and, in all too typical fashion, the costs are passed along to the consumer. Work out a table of price versus percentage tax increase for some typical aluminum consumer products, and see at what point the tax will clearly affect sales and use of each product. (b) Assume instead that the government orders the industry to discontinue the manufacture of nonessential aluminum products. What products would you put in this classification? How would it affect the way you live?

12. Including private cars, how many applications can you think of for the flywheel, if in its new mode it proves successful and subject to still further improvement? Does the flywheel really do away with pollution?

13. Assume that at some time in the near future, electrical energy becomes cheap and plentiful, say, through fusion power. List a number of fossil-fuel systems that could run on electricity, that do not do so now, e.g., the automobile. Describe how the system would have to be modified, such as an automobile running on a fuel cell and electric motor, or a flywheel charged by an electric motor and driving an electric motor.

14. Sketch the system necessary for each of the following methods of house heating:

    (1) Gas-fired hot-air furnace,
    (2) Oil-fired hot-water furnace,
    (3) Electric-resistance heating,
    (4) Heat pump.

Discuss the reliability of the components in each case and any steps you can think of to improve the heat pump. Consult with your local utility companies when necessary.

4

Thermal Pollution

GLOBAL ENERGY BALANCE

When we collect and use the heat coming from the sun, drive turbines with hydroelectric power, or harness the tides, we use energy which will ultimately be dissipated as heat. Were we not to tap these energy sources, the energy would dissipate in natural ways as heat. Surely the harnessing of nature's daily released energy must be considered among the highest accomplishments of man's intelligence.

On the other hand, when we use coal, gas or oil, or utilize nuclear fission or fusion, we use up irreplaceable resources, and, indeed, in the end, we also generate waste heat. But, this heat would not have been created had we left nature alone.

If our actions were on a small scale, we could afford to ignore the question of waste heat. However, our use of energy is increasing at such a rate that we must be concerned with possible major changes in the Earth's temperature, both at specific locations as well as an overall average, within the next several years.

To understand this overall problem, let us look briefly at what is called the energy balance picture between the Earth and the sun. In Chapter 2 we looked at how the energy coming from the sun to the Earth is absorbed and reflected. We also looked at the energy radiated by the Earth itself (refer to Fig. 2-2). To study this picture in more detail, let us assume the Earth is transported away from the sun, so that it stands alone in the darkness of space. Inevitably, the Earth would cool as its heat energy was radiated into space. Similarly, if we transport the Earth to an orbit somewhat closer to the sun, the Earth would become warmer, absorbing and radiating more energy than it does now.

With the Earth in its normal orbit, it should be apparent, therefore, that there is an energy balance between the amount of radiant energy the Earth absorbs and the amount it radiates outward, so that the temperature of the Earth stays constant.

Scientists calculate the radiation of the Earth in a rather interesting way. They say the Earth behaves pretty much as if it is a *black body*. The concept of a black body can be explained as follows: Assume a material absorbs all of the light that falls on it. Place a sheet of this material on the ground in bright sunlight. How much light will be reflected from the material to your eye? None, if we are dealing with a perfect black body. If no light reaches your eye from the body you are looking at, you see pitch black. (Similarly, a perfectly white body reflects all of the light that falls on it.)

No material exists that is perfectly black; you have only to look over fine-quality black sheets in an art supply store to see that they vary in blackness, that is, some sheets absorb more of the light that falls on them than do others.

An important characteristic of black bodies, but not an obvious one, is that they are also perfect radiators of energy. Therefore, if you heat up a black body and a similar nonblack body to the same temperature, the black body will radiate more energy. (Now don't go thinking of a black body as a sheet of paper, there is more to black bodies than that.)

In the context of our discussion, the Earth behaves as if it is a black body: it is a very good absorber and a very efficient radiator of energy. The trees, the oceans, etc., all absorb the sun's energy very effectively, giving the Earth its characteristic black-body properties. And since much is known about the way black bodies "behave," to use the phrase physicists use, we can pretty well predict how the radiation balance between the sun and the Earth will be affected if the temperature of the Earth increases.

Look then at Table 4-1, and as a specific example, the third line of the table. The projection is made that in the year 2060, the world's power consumption will be 2200×10^{12} W, and there will be that much extra heat energy on the Earth. To radiate this extra energy away, that is, to maintain the balance of sun-Earth energy, the Earth will become warmer, for only by becoming warmer can a black body radiate more energy. In this case the Earth will become 2.3° F warmer. [Refer to Worksheet 4-1.]

TABLE 4-1

Average Heating of the Earth by Use of Power

Year	Power consumption in world ($\times 10^{12}$ W)	Average temperature increase	
		(°C)	(°F)
1970	4.5	0.003	0.005
2000	35	0.02	0.04
2060*	2200	1.5	2.3
2100**	400	0.3	0.5

  * If exponential increase, "Ehrlich's pessimism" [1].
 ** Weinberg's "reasonable limit" [2].

TECHNICAL NOTE 4-1

Black Bodies and Absolute Zero

A black body is a perfect absorber of energy. If radiant energy in the form of light were to fall on a black body, because it would be fully absorbed, none would be left to be reflected to the eye. The body would therefore appear perfectly black, and hence its name. (In practice, the eye alone would be a pretty poor judge of what was perfectly black.)

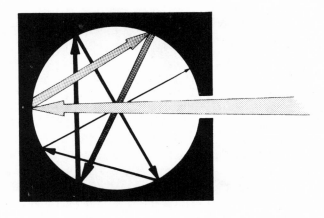

Fig. 4-1.

WORKSHEET 4-1

The Earth as a Black Body

Let us look at the radiation balance between the sun and Earth. The radiation striking the Earth's atmosphere is $1.395 \ W/m^2$. We do not multiply this by the Earth's surface area $(4\pi R^2)$.* The projected area of the half of the Earth receiving the sun's radiation is:

$$\pi R^2, \quad \text{where } R \text{ is } 6378.4 \text{ km}$$

The total radiation reaching the Earth is _____ .

To calculate the energy radiating away from the Earth, we take the Earth's average temperature to be 50° F or 10° C. Referring to Technical Note 4-1,

$$\text{Energy/second} = 5.67 \times 10^8 \times T^4, \quad \text{where } T \text{ must be in } °K.$$

$$= \text{_____} .$$

How much of the incoming sun's radiation must be reflected from the upper atmosphere in order for the absorbed and emitted radiation to be equal?

_____

If the Earth produces an additional amount of heat energy due to power consumption of $400 \times 10^{12} \ W$, how much must the temperature of the Earth increase so that this extra heat energy will be radiated away?

_____

_____

    * The sun "sees" the Earth as a disk or circle, not as half a sphere. Hence the area we use is that of a circle, πR^2.

102a

102b

Global Energy Balance

In the laboratory, one can make a good approximation to a black body by using a cavity which is connected to the outside world only by a small hole. Energy passing through this opening would strike the cavity walls many times, and in each case be partially absorbed and partially reflected. Very little energy would find its way back out the opening (see Fig. 4-1).

In the late 1800's and the turn of this century, the black body was a subject of intense study. One can show that a black body is not only a perfect absorber of energy, but a perfect emitter of energy. When heated, a black body will, in turn, radiate energy most efficiently. However, not until the 1900's were physicists able to predict the relation between the radiation from the body and its temperature. The theoretical resolution of this difficulty ultimately gave birth to quantum mechanics.

We will need for our work only one of the several expressions related to black-body phenomena, that the energy goes as the fourth power of the temperature:

$$E = 5.67 \ T^4 \times 10^{-8} \ (°K)^4 \ W/m^2$$

Seeing watts in the units of energy should lead us to conclude that the temperature is to be measured in centigrade and not Fahrenheit. But that is not quite the case.

The zero point of the centigrade scale is taken as the freezing point of water. That is not what nature means by zero. Absolute zero is where every subatomic particle in the atom is in its lowest energy state: On the centigrade scale, this is -273.15° C.

The temperature scale whose degrees are the same size as centigrade degree but whose zero point is set at absolute zero is called the Kelvin scale:

$$0° \ K = -273° \ C$$

$$273° \ K = 0° \ C$$

(where we have rounded the number off). We have here repeated a bit of what was stated in Technical Note 2-1.

A mean temperature rise of 1° F over the earth is probably tolerable, since 2° F changes have been noticed in geologic time, but 5° F might have serious consequences. This argument has been put forward by Ehrlich [1] to show that we cannot go on increasing our consumption of energy. Weinberg [2] has argued that we can comfortably go on to a consumption 100 times greater than our present consumption.

Of course, our elementary calculation assumes that other readjusting or other amplifying forces do not take over. As we burn fossil fuels, CO_2 is produced. About one-half of this stays in the atmosphere and increases the concentration of CO_2 in the air, which has therefore gone up 15% since 1850. This creates a "greenhouse effect" as the CO_2 absorbs the infrared emitted by the Earth, and allows the direct sunlight to pass; the temperature rise of the Earth between 1845 and 1945 was about 0.8° F. Since 1945, *particulates,* partially from burning of fossil fuels (Chapter 8), have increased in number and the temperature has dropped about 0.3° F as the sunlight is absorbed (a dirty greenhouse effect). If we were really sophisticated, we could control and balance the two effects, but no doubt there are other effects which are just as important.

We do not wish to go into detail about the maximum tolerable world temperature increase. Changes of 1° F from place to place and season to season are common. It seems wise to consider 1° F an upper limit to ensure against drastic global changes. This limit allows plenty of scope, but the distribution of temperature increase must be considered.

For the next 100 years, our problem is a local one, namely, how to spread around the extra heat. This problem is, of course, reduced a little if we manage to use our energy efficiently (see Table 4-2). For example, on heating a house, some heat may go up the chimney; a natural-gas burner wastes only 20% of the energy content of the gas, while an oil burner wastes perhaps 30 to 40%. Although no electric heat goes up the chimney, heat is wasted at the power station in converting heat into electricity.

As we use more and more electricity, the best fuel-burning devices, fossil or nuclear, may be installed in large power stations remote from our cities. Nevertheless, we will find that there is a concentration of waste heat at the power stations. This is a matter of concern.

We have already seen that there are *theoretical* limits to the efficiency our generating plants can achieve. [See Technical Note 2-4 and Worksheet 2-2.] Thus we must seek other solutions to this problem.

COOLING BY RIVER WATER

Until recently, all power stations were built at the most convenient geographical location, usually on a river. Vast quantities of river water are taken into the power station, used to cool the condenser, and discharged as heated water. For obvious reasons, this system is called "once-through cooling." Refer to Fig. 4-2 for a schematic of this system.

TABLE 4-2

Electric Power Generating Efficiencies*

Type of electricity generator	Efficiency (η) (%)
Gas turbine (used for peaking power)	15-20
Diesel generator	20
Light water-cooled nuclear reactors; PWR, BWR (with once-through cooling)	33
Light water-cooled nuclear reactors; PWR, BWR (with forced-air cooling towers)	30
Early British graphite Magnox reactors (CO_2 cooled)	34
Oil- or coal-burning plant suitable for cycling	35
Oil- or coal-burning plant suitable for cycling (with SO_2 suppression in flue gas)	33
British advanced gas-cooled reactors (AGR); Gulf Atomic (HTGR)	41
Liquid metal-cooled fast breeder reactor (LMFBR)	41
Best fossil-fuel plants, suitable only for base load	40
Best fossil-fuel plants, suitable only for base load (with SO_2 suppression in flue gas)	37

Hypothetical Cases

Fossil-fuel plant with magnetohydrodynamic (MHD) generator	50
Helium-cooled fast breeder with helium turbine	50
Combined-cycle gas turbine, 3rd generation [3]	57
Combined-cycle gas turbine (overall efficiency coal to electricity)	49

* Most of the waste heat must come out by the heating up of cooling water, although some of the waste heat for fossil-fuel plants comes out through the smokestack.

4. Thermal Pollution

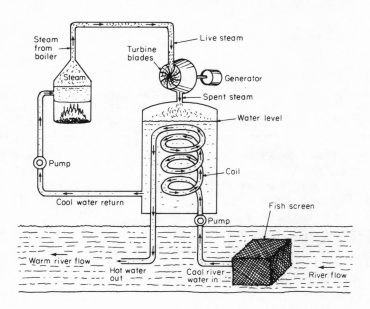

Fig. 4-2. Schematic diagram of steam-turbine system with "once-through" cooling, using river water. Note the separation of primary and secondary flow.

Near their sources most rivers are cooler than the environment, and they become warmer, as they flow to the sea, by mixing with the air mass above them. At first sight it seems that a power station located at a river source will cause no ecological damage but will merely accelerate a natural trend. This is certainly not true in trout streams. Figure 4-3 shows the well-being of several species of fish as a function of temperature. For example, trout cannot live at 70° F, and the middle reaches of the river would become uninhabitable for them.

We might then argue that we could replace the trout by the northern pike, which likes a higher temperature. But this will work only if the temperature is raised permanently. Fish are intelligent and can accommodate to seasonal changes by changing the habitat, but they may not be able to accommodate such sudden changes as can be caused by the switching on and off of a power station.

In spring, 1972, for example, an unusual quantity of dead fish was found near Oyster Creek power station (New Jersey) just after the station switched off for scheduled maintenance.

Hopefully the temperature changes will not extend all the way across a river, or to all depths. The temperature distribution for a TVA station is shown in Fig. 4-4. Therefore, any fish that desires

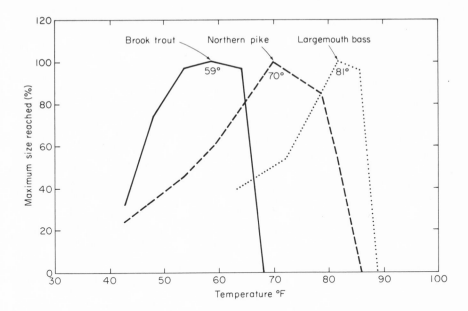

Fig. 4-3. Shift in species well-being with temperature increase (growth rate) [4, Part 1, p. 362].

to bypass the hot water, such as a salmon going to its spawning grounds, could find a way around. Merriman [6] has shown that this indeed occurs in a typical situation. The regulatory agencies therefore allow some heating of a river or lake, but only inside a mixing zone, outside of which there should be little change. The complete heating up of a reservoir or small lake, a riverbed, or estuary, could be very bad.

If we ignore these problems, or if we find a way of surmounting them, we could mount several power stations on one river; after 20 to 30 miles, the river water will have achieved thermal equilibrium with the surroundings, and another power station can be located. A simulated temperature profile for the Illinois River has been drawn (Fig. 4-5), accommodating 10,000 MW of capacity. We see that the river temperature can indeed return to the ambient temperature between power stations.

In Fig. 4-6 we show a map illustrating the average flow in the major streams in the U.S. The Illinois River is indicated by the letter I; the flow is less than 5000 ft^3/sec. On this basis some people argue that we could accommodate over 2,000,000 MW of power stations on the rivers of the U.S., which would supply almost the whole electricity demand in the year 2000, and without cooling towers. But fortunately we do not have to do this, as there are other methods of cooling. Fish are some of the organisms which cleanse the rivers of our industrial wastes, and we should not risk destroying them.

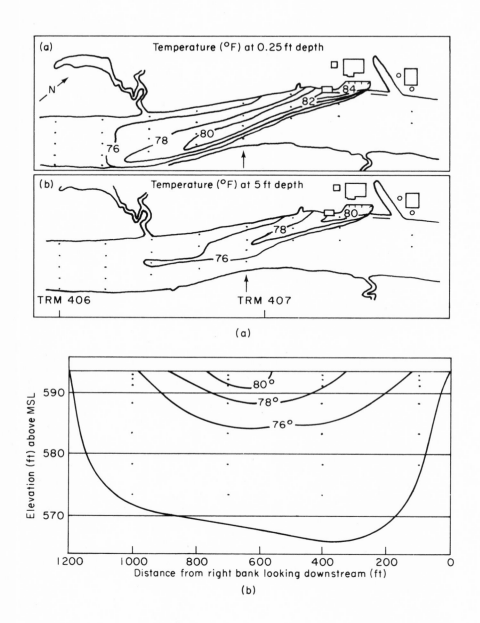

Fig. 4-4. Temperature distribution of water below Widow's Creek Steam Generating Power Station (TVA), August 30, 1967. (a) Horizontal section at various depths, (b) vertical section 2400 ft below power station at Tennessee River Mile 406.9 [5].

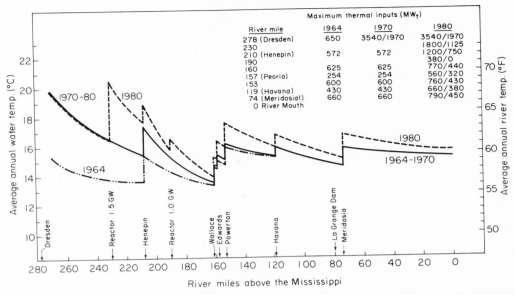

Fig. 4-5. Simulated temperature profile for the Illinois Waterway, 1964-1980 (no cooling towers) [5].

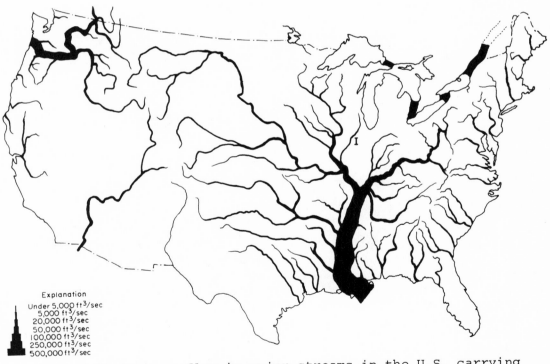

Fig. 4-6. Average flow in major streams in the U.S. carrying 5000 ft³/sec or more.

4. Thermal Pollution

TECHNICAL NOTE 4-2 & WORKSHEET 4-2

Specific Heat

Specific heat is a concept that the reader already has in his repertoire of experience. It is the heat energy needed to change the temperature of an amount of material by one degree.

Measuring the heat energy in calories instead of joules, the specific heats (kcal/kg-°C) of some common substances are:

aluminum	0.22
iron	0.11
water	1.00
copper	0.093

The units themselves spell out the definition of specific heat: 1 kg of aluminum requires 0.22 kcal of energy to increase its temperature by 1° C.

(a) How much heat is required to raise by 3° C the temperature of 2 kg of aluminum?

_____

(b) Use Q as the symbol for heat energy and c for specific heat. Write out a formula for Q in terms of the specific heat. (Check for dimensional accuracy.)

$$Q = \underline{}$$

Here are two examples of the role of specific heat: The oil in a thin frying pan heats faster than in a heavier iron pan, but the iron pan will do the better cooking job. As soon as the food is placed in the thin pan, it will lower the temperature of the pan and oil. The lower temperature will keep the oil from searing the food (and thereby it will absorb more oil) and may permit moisture to come out, thus causing the food to stick to the pan.

An iron radiator in a room will continue to heat a room after the furnace has completed its cycle and shut down. A baseboard radiator with fins will not.

(c) Account for both of these effects in terms of the specific heat of materials.

Another law of nature, one that we have all observed in action, is that bodies at different temperatures, in contact, will eventually reach the same temperature. Many people cool coffee by the addition of cold milk: the temperature of the coffee lowers, that of the milk rises, and when both reach some intermediate temperature, a state of thermal equilibrium will have been established. Formal definitions require that we state that the coffee/milk system is isolated and does not give up or absorb heat from its surroundings. We will tacitly recognize this qualification but idealize our examples and concentrate on the basic principles.

We are dealing with the conservation of energy in the form of heat energy: the coffee gives up to the milk a certain amount of energy Q, and in the process its temperature lowers. The milk increases in thermal energy by an amount Q, and its temperature rises.

(d) We will first ask that you work out a formula for heat transfer and then solve a problem. Return to your solution for (b). Two materials, one of mass m_1 and temperature T_1, the other of mass m_2 and temperature T_2, are placed in contact. They reach a final temperature T_f. Take the specific heats to be c_1 and c_2. Use the conservation of energy as stated in the preceding paragraph, and set up a relation that will allow you to solve for T_f.

(e) A 0.5-kg slug of iron at 90° C is placed in 2 kg of water at 30° C. (We neglect the effect of the container and surrounding air.) What will be the final temperature of the water and iron?

————

FISH-KILLS

One of the problems with any water-circulation system that draws water from a natural body of water is that fish, particularly slow-swimming fish such as flounder, get entrapped in the cooling water. Some aquatic life does not "swim" but drifts with the flow. Every power station employs a complicated system of screens to stop fish (and the flotsam and jetsam of river water) from entering the condensers (cooling coils). These screens must be continuously cleaned, and huge quantities of dead fish are found in them. Usually the fish are buried on site to prevent the problems that might arise upon their being seen by local environmentalists.

Well-designed screens are located far enough out in the stream, and most fish can swim away and avoid entrapment. Under these circumstances, the fish-kill from a power station is smaller than the number of unwanted fish thrown back into the water by a fishing vessel, but care must be exercised in operation, for the weak swimmers and non-swimmers will be caught anyway. Many fish species will deliberately come to the outflow of a power station because it is warm, and a sudden change of temperature can kill them; thus, some control of the rate of change of temperature seems necessary. Moreover, the condenser pipes must be cleaned periodically. This is usually done by passing through chlorine, which can then kill all the fish collected in the outflow. A more modern, environmentally superior, but more expensive method, which is more common in Europe than in the U.S., is to pass through rubber balls which closely fit the pipes. In one planned sea-water cooling system (Maine Yankee Atomic Power Station), the main problem expected will be the growth of mussels in the condenser pipes. The plan is to persuade the mussels to loosen their grip by periodic flushings with unusually hot water.

There is a possible serious long-term effect in the entrapment and killing of fish larvae. The life cycle of fish is far from being fully understood; tens of thousands of eggs are produced by every fish, and only one or two need survive to maintain the species. The rest may, and do, get killed by physical conditions or eaten by other fish or animals. But we do not know how delicate this balance may be, or how a power station may upset it. The larvae will pass all the screens and be pulled into the condenser, where the sudden temperature change may kill them. If we reduce the temperature rise of the cooling water, to mitigate other effects, we must double the flow and hence double the fish larva problem. Estuaries, in particular, are birthplaces for fish. It is for this reason that the Environmental Protection Agency (EPA) suggests very strict standards for temperature rise of water in estuaries (1.5° F in summer, 4° F in winter).

Since this and other long-term effects may not be serious, it seems that the best procedure is to watch it *very* carefully while going ahead. We must also beware of assigning all fish-kill problems to power stations. Chemical plants are usually worse in this regard. However, the natural tendency to blame the "big guy" may not be bad, because the power company, in a defensive public relations move, must locate the real offender.

The uncertainties in understanding the fate of fish eggs, larvae, and young fish are exemplified by the case of the Hudson River. Figure 4-7 is a map of energy facilities projected in 1972 on the Hudson River. The amount of water that is planned to be circulated through each power station is huge. The region from Haverstraw Bay in the south to Marlboro in the north is a spawning region for striped bass, a fish loved by sportsmen and others. Each fish lays about 100,000 eggs, and eventually one or two survive to complete the life cycle. Optimists say that the Hudson is only a minor breeding ground and that Chesapeake Bay and the James River are more important. Pessimists maintain that the Hudson is the primary breeding ground on the East Coast. We outline two alternative possibilities.

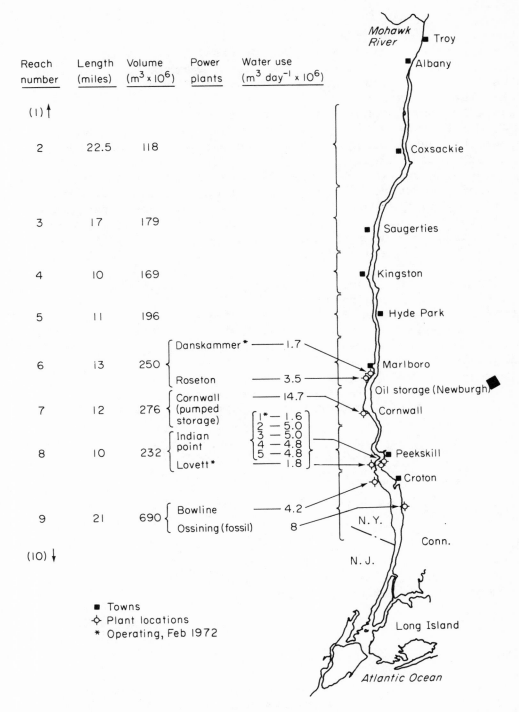

Fig. 4-7. Present and projected energy facilities on the Hudson River.

4. Thermal Pollution

According to the pessimistic approach [7], we assume that all fish eggs, larvae, and fish less than 2 in. in length will pass through any screen and be killed either by the rise in temperature or pressure. These fish larvae will float up and down the river with the tide. Eventually the live fish will swim down, at a size of 1 to 2 in., to the open sea. In summertime, the mean river flow (averaged over tides) is reduced to only about 2-1/2 times the total water requirements of the power stations, so 40% of the upstream eggs, larvae, and fish will be drawn through and killed. Again, we assume this means that the overall survival fraction is not 1 in 100,000 but 0.4 out of 100,000, or perhaps even smaller, because of a greater influence of predatory fish. The replacement of fish by fish from a hatchery may not prove possible. Since fish want to spawn in the river where they were hatched, the replacement of destroyed fish may not be simple.

According to a more optimistic approach, only the fish eggs and larvae in the immediate vicinity of the power station will be sucked into the condensers. Once the fish go downstream to the sea, they will travel with the tide, and the fraction trapped will be the ratio of the total water requirements to the tidal flow (about 4%) and mortality will be less than 100% of this. Moreover, since only one or two fish need survive out of 100,000 larvae, the loss of even 90% of the larvae will leave plenty to survive. Even if some accident (such as an oil spill, not considered in either argument) were to kill all the fish, a fish hatchery could be used to replace the fish.

The data on which decisions must be based were collected in a Hudson River Fisheries survey [8] financed but not conducted by the power company, Consolidated Edison Company of New York. The Atomic Energy Commission, like the authors of this book, do not distinguish between these two alternatives. The AEC recommends a closed-cycle cooling system for Indian Point 2 power station [9]. Such an alternative would not seem possible for the proposed pumped-storage plant at Cornwall. This has been used as one of the arguments for rejection of this plant [7], but this argument was rejected by the Federal Power Commission [10] and the courts (see also Chapter 12). Of course, there are other fish than striped bass; but sport fishermen have been particularly active in conservation causes (through the Izaak Walton League, among others), and they obviously stress those issues about which they have particular knowledge and concern.

COOLING TOWERS AND PONDS

The easiest way to circumvent public concern about thermal pollution is to construct a cooling tower, and all over the U.S. utility companies are planning to do just this. There are three types of cooling towers:

mechanical-draft wet-cooling towers, natural-draft wet-cooling towers, and dry-cooling towers. Figure 4-8 shows how a cooling tower can be connected to the system. Most of the waste heat leaves the cooling tower as heated air. A very small fraction of the waste heat enters the river. This figure illustrates wet-cooling towers. The addition of fans to aid the flow of air distinguishes the mechanical-draft type of tower from others.

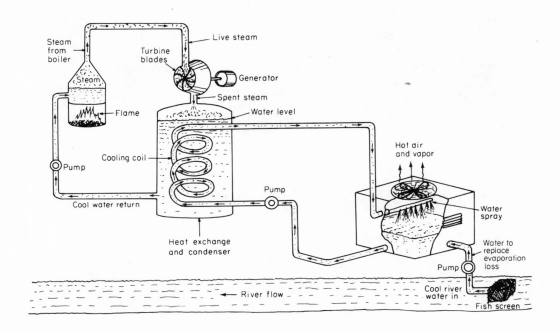

Fig. 4-8. Closed-circuit cooling-tower system.

In the first two types of towers, the water is cooled by evaporating a portion of it. The problem with this method is that the cooling is slowest on a hot, humid summer day when electricity demand for air conditioning and the need for thermal efficiency at the power stations are greatest. The mechanical-draft towers (Fig. 4-9) are cheapest to install but need maintenance and electricity to run and are noisy. The natural-draft cooling towers (Figs. 4-10 and 4-11), and to an even greater extent the dry cooling towers, are large and unsightly. The evaporative cooling towers cause a good deal of local condensation that can be unpleasant. This can be seen in Fig. 4-12, which shows

Fig. 4-9. Induced mechanical-draft cooling tower.

Fig. 4-10. A natural-draft cooling tower dwarfs the 1100-MW_e (3400 MW_t) nuclear power station it cools. The visual impact is obvious. [Courtesy Portland General Electric Power Co., Portland, Oregon.]

Fig. 4-11. Hyperbolic natural-draft cooling towers, fossil-fuel plant.

Fig. 4-12. Mechanical-draft cooling towers at a geothermal generating plant. (The Geysers, California, courtesy of Pacific Gas & Electric Co.)

4. Thermal Pollution

TECHNICAL NOTE 4-3 & WORKSHEET 4-3

Latent Heats

This concept is somewhat more subtle than that of specific heats. It will be most easily understood if we first look at what is going on at the molecular level. Let us use water as the subject of our investigation.

As we increase the temperature of the water, we observe that the water molecules increase in kinetic energy, and we observe them in an increased state of random agitation. As we continue to heat the water, we observe that its temperature rises further, and the molecules move about still more quickly. But at 100° C, the picture begins to change. Now as we put more heat into our substance, we see that the molecules are breaking apart into separate atoms. The additional heat energy is doing work to overcome the force of attraction between the molecules that kept H_2O in the liquid state. The kinetic energy of the molecules is no longer increasing (the temperature remains constant), but the liquid is becoming a gas.

When all of the liquid has become a gas, as we continue to apply heat, the kinetic energy of the gas molecules will again increase, and the temperature of the steam will rise above 100° C.

It requires 540 kcal of heat energy to convert 1 kg of water already at 100° C into steam at 100° C. This figure of 540 kcal/kg is called the heat of vaporization of water. [Alcohol (ethyl) has a boiling point of 78° C and a latent heat of vaporization less than half that of water, 204 kcal/kg.]

How much heat is required to boil 0.4 kg of water at 20° C and to raise the resulting steam temperature to 120° C?
The heat to raise the water to 100° C is:

$$Q_1 = \underline{\hspace{2cm}}$$

The heat to boil this water is:

$$Q_2 = \underline{\hspace{2cm}}$$

What is the heat needed to raise the temperature of the steam to 120° C? (The specific heat of steam is 0.48 kcal/kg-°C.)

_____

The total heat energy involved in this three-stage process is:

_____

The change of state from a solid to a liquid follows along similar lines. In the case of the ice/water transition, which, as you know, takes place at 0° C, the heat necessary to bring about the change of state is 80 kcal/kg. This quantity is called the heat of fusion. To freeze 1 kg of water, 80 kcal of heat energy must be removed from the water. To melt 1 kg of ice, 80 kcal of heat must be supplied.

Fig. 4-13. The cooling lake, made artificially, for the Robinson Power Station of the Carolina Power and Light Co. at Hartsville, S.C. The power station on the left is a moderate-sized coal-fired unit (Robinson No. 1). The one on the right is a pressurized cooler reactor (PWR) of Westinghouse, capacity 700 MW_e. Lake Robinson occupies 2250 acres (over 3 square miles) and also has recreational uses. (Courtesy of Westinghouse Electric Corp.)

the cooling tower at The Geysers geothermal field. The cooling towers at this location look like geysers themselves. (For a general reference see Woodson's article in Scientific American [11].)

In dry-cooling towers, the water is not allowed to evaporate but is cooled by conduction of heat to the air. This is less efficient and uses a lot of space.

Cooling ponds operate in the same way as cooling towers but are spread out horizontally and thereby spread the evaporation over a large area, with less deleterious effect on cloud formation. But they require space. At first sight, it seems logical to try to use these ponds for recreation or fish; however, the water-temperature change caused by shutting the power station on and off (for economy) is large. Multiple usage of a cooling pond has, therefore, never been completely successful.

In Fig. 4-13 we show a cooling pond for the two "Robinson" stations, one fossil, one nuclear, of the Carolina Light and Power Co.; the pond is also used for recreation.

We must therefore come to face the basic problem of land and water use. Twenty years ago we were filling in estuaries and swamps to get more land: now we are digging it out to get cooling ponds! Cannot the two be combined? We could ask a power company to buy a section of waterway for use as a cooling pond, and we could buy an equivalent area of land to put back into the public domain.

LAKE COOLING

It seems that lakes would make excellent cooling ponds, but in view of the comments about multiple use in the last section, they must be used with caution. A major problem that arises is that water is usually withdrawn from and discharged into only the in-shore portion of the lake. It is in this in-shore section that most of the fish live; for example, Green Bay, Michigan has 16% of the area of Lake Michigan, but accounts for 65% of the fish catch.

It might seem at first sight that the heated effluent can be sent into the middle of the lake by projecting it fast enough, but the Coriolis force, an effect due to the Earth's rotation, would prevent this. Because of this force, water coming from a river or a power station turns as it enters a second body of water; it turns right in the Northern Hemisphere, and left in the Southern Hemisphere. This tends to prevent the warm water from reaching the center of the lake. The extent of this effect is visible from the air, where the plume of polluted river water can easily be seen to turn. [See Technical Note 4-4.]

TECHNICAL NOTE 4-4

The Coriolis Force

In its most common manifestation, the effect of the Coriolis force is seen when water approaches a drain. The water does not flow "straight" down the drain; it circles around the drain following a spiral path. In the Northern Hemisphere the spiral is to the right, and in the Southern Hemisphere, to the left. Only at the equator is this effect not observed.

The Coriolis force results from the rotation of the Earth. It affects the winds, ocean currents (deviation of the Gulf Stream and tidal currents of the Northern Hemisphere to the right), and the path of ballistic missiles.

We can develop the origins of this force in an intuitive manner, and to do so we start with two simple examples. The two circles in Fig. 4-14 represent the paths of identical weights being whirled at the end of strings. We impose the condition that the time for one revolution of each weight around its circle be the same. Quite obviously, the weight must move faster around the larger circle to cover the extra distance in the same time as the weight going around the

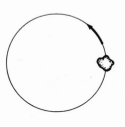
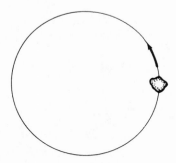

Fig. 4-14.

4. Thermal Pollution

smaller circle. Now we must call on our intuition. Assume you are
holding the string in both cases. In which case would you feel the
weight pulling on your hand with the greater force? The faster-moving
weight would exert the greater force.

If the string were let loose, the weight would fly off tangentially
as shown in Fig. 4-15. Thus to keep the weight from flying off tangentially, the string must pull the stone inward.

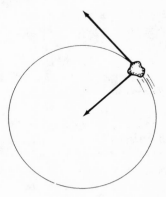

Fig. 4-15.

Let us relate these facts to bodies on Earth. Visualize two
identical bodies at two latitudes. Their paths as the Earth rotates
correspond to the two circles in Fig. 4-16. Both make one revolution
in the same time; Body A has a greater velocity than Body B.

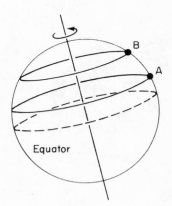

Fig. 4-16.

   *Gravity holds both bodies on the Earth (pulling inward just as
the string did). Now let us take a look at how gravity acts on a body.
It is not simply inward as shown in Fig. 4-17. Gravity pulls a body*

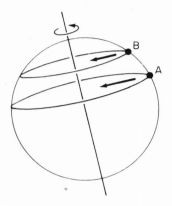

Fig. 4-17.

*toward the center of the Earth (Fig. 4-18). But the force needed to
hold bodies on the Earth is pointed directly toward the axis (just as
was the string). Is this a problem? Not at all. Call upon your intuition again. Have you ever seen a box or sled pulled with a rope at an
angle (Fig. 4-19)? The sled moves forward (Fig. 4-19b); therefore,
there must be a force in the forward direction. However, the sled is
also lifted slightly; therefore, there is an upward component. In
short, the diagonal force on the rope can be thought of as the sum of
two forces, one forward and one upward. And the same is true with the*

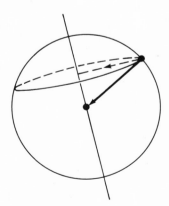

Fig. 4-18.

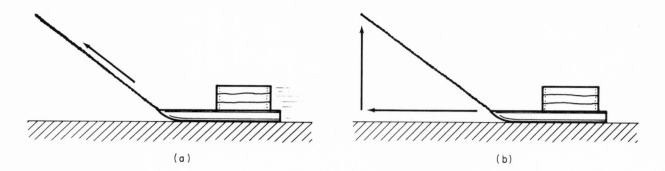

(a)

(b)

Fig. 4-19.

*inward gravitational force: it can be thought of as the sum of two
forces, one inward and one downward (Fig. 4-20). This downward force
tends to move bodies toward the equator (in the Northern Hemisphere).
The force tending to move the body (or river currents) toward the
equator is greater at B than at A and produces the curved paths we
spoke of in the opening paragraphs.*

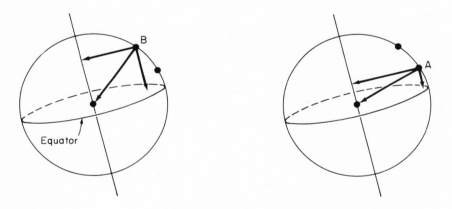

Fig. 4-20.

The Coriolis force is important only in large lakes, but it tran-
spires that currents set up by winds *also* cause the water to circulate
primarily along the shore [12].

In order to use the central region of the lake for cooling, we
must construct long, large pipes. Figure 4-21 shows the temperature
profile across Lake Michigan for the month of August. Surely we could
take water from 5 miles out and 80 ft down at about 40° F (about 7° C)
and expel it to the surface of the lake at 60° F with little deleterious
effect. The surface temperature varies from 50 to 70° F, and the
average would fall slightly.

124

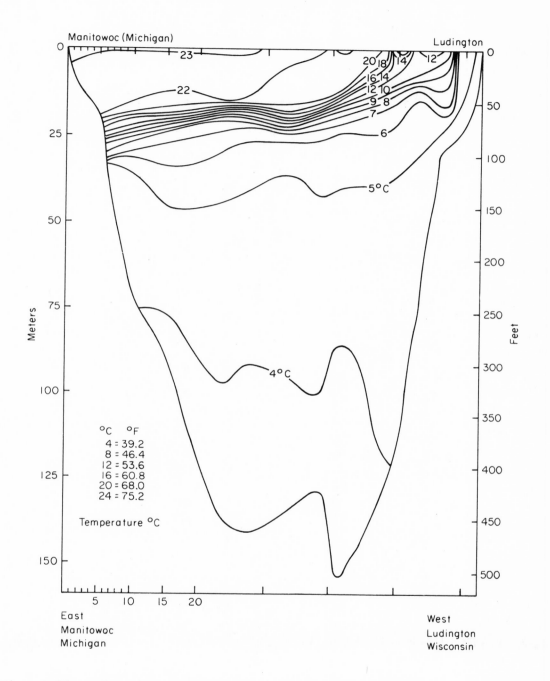

Fig. 4-21. Lake Michigan vertical temperature profile in mid-August, showing thermocline and a seiche-induced upwelling of cold water along the east shore [13].

4. Thermal Pollution

The average surface-temperature rise (from industrial cooling-water effluent) for this lake and some others has been calculated [14, 15] using all known data. Heat is lost from the surface by evaporation and convection and by reflection (instead of absorption) of sunlight. In Table 4-3 you can see the *average* surface-temperature increase of Lake Michigan and other lakes for all present power stations and for those projected up to the year 2000.

TABLE 4-3

Effects of Utility Discharges on the Great Lakes,
Present and Projected [14]

Lake	Year	Utility discharges (MW)	Average heat flow ($\times 10^{-2}$ W/ft^2-hr)	Average temperature rise (°F)
Superior	1970	720	0.08	0.0008
	2000	4,800	0.53	0.0053
Michigan	1970	7,000	1.11	0.0098
	2000	90,000	14.4	0.126
Huron	1970	1,250	0.019	0.0017
	2000	54,000	8.2	0.076
Erie	1970	7,000	2.6	0.022
	2000	95,000	34.8	0.29
Ontario	1970	5,200	1.8	0.022
	2000	70,000	32.5	0.29

In the above scheme, the surface temperature in summer would not seem to rise at all. There is a compensating effect; the average temperature rise in winter will be greater, extending slightly the Great Lakes shipping season!

This sounds ideal. The usual 20° F rise across the cooling condenser will give an effluent temperature less than the August on-shore surface temperature, and we might even reconsider allowing the effluent to be released close to shore. The low temperature of the cooling water will ensure a high thermal efficiency of the plant even in August, when efficiency is most needed.

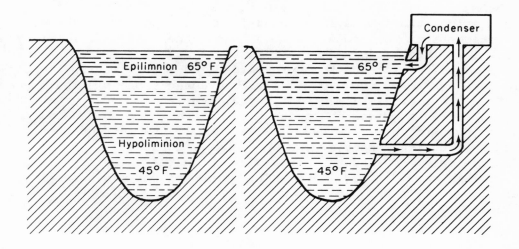

Fig. 4-22. Cayuga Lake, as it is now and as it would be if used for power-station cooling.

This is shown in Fig. 4-22 for Lake Cayuga in New York State, where a power station is projected by New York State Gas & Electric Co. In terms of this diagram, the following positive ecological consequences are projected [15]:

1. The thermal layers will define themselves earlier in the spring than they now do. Because the volume of the epilimnion will be further increased beyond its natural size during the course of the summer, these thermal stratification layers will last for a longer time in the fall.
2. The growing season for plants and animals in the upper layer will therefore be extended.
3. The water brought up from the lower layer will contain nutrients previously unavailable to plants in the lighted portion of the upper layer. It is in the upper layer where most of the biological production - growth and reproduction of plants and animals - takes place.
4. The longer growing season and the additional nutrients will result in a greater capacity for biological reproduction.

This glowing view is countered by the following conjecture [16]:
The prolonged stratification period will extend the period of oxygen depletion in the large underlying layer of cooler water where trout live during the summer. Thus, oxygen levels will become lower than they do at present before being replenished by the delayed mixing of upper and lower layers.

127

4. Thermal Pollution

Using the deep water of a lake involves, for a 1000-MW electrical power station, two 5-mile lines of 4-ft diam. pipe. The expense may well be less than for cooling towers, since the intake is lower than the level at which fish and fish larvae are found, and they will not be trapped on the screens that prevent solids from entering the condensers. Therefore, the ecological disadvantages of this would seem to be the least of all (inland) alternatives, and there may be advantages in a slight extension of the Great Lakes shipping season, and in bringing nutrients from deep in the lake to the surface to help replenish the fish supply, which we steadily deplete.

A typical "once-through" installation on the shore of a lake (Ontario) is shown in Fig. 4-23. The warm effluent discharge is clearly visible in the picture.

Fig. 4-23. Aerial view of Ontario Hydro's new Pickering Nuclear Power (heavy-water moderated) Station. Note the plume of hot water which comes from only one of the four 540-MW$_e$ units.

OCEAN COOLING

In the last ten years, materials have been developed which allow salt water to be used for cooling without danger of corroding the condenser. The problems of using ocean water for cooling are extensions of those for lake water just mentioned. Long Island Sound, for example, has very little flow to the ocean itself (roughly twice the flow of the Connecticut River); tides make the water go to and fro, but without much flow. The main effect of using Long Island Sound for cooling is the pond effect as noted above for Lake Michigan. Again, increasing the length of long pipes will reduce the environmental effect. Power-station sites on the ocean side of sounds are harder to find. The ocean shore is used for recreation, and the sea is rough. A new island may have to be made; a power station could be built on a barge anchored 3 miles out, or on the edge of the continental shelf. Such a power station would avoid many cooling and siting problems, but the accessory underground transmission lines make this solution prohibitive for all but the metropolitan areas, where any other solution is worse. The Public Service Corp. of New Jersey, General Electric Co., and Westinghouse Electric Co. are preparing designs of nuclear power stations on barges. The estimated cost is $450 million for a 1200-MW$_e$ plant, about 20% more than the 1971 figures for a land-based power station.

TECHNICAL NOTE 4-5 & WORKSHEET 4-4

The Laws of Thermodynamics

Thermodynamics in itself is a fascinating subject, relating phenomena dealing with heat with those dealing with mechanical motion. For our purposes, let us take the most general statement of the first law:

> *The total energy of the universe is a constant.*

On a restricted scale it might be said to be a restatement of the conservation of energy as it applies to specific problems. We can reword the first law in terms of the atomic picture that we have already discussed,

heat added to a system} appears as {a change in the internal energy} and/or {is used to do work

4. Thermal Pollution

The first law is intimately related to the fact that a perpetual motion machine cannot be made. Those perpetual motion machines that would violate the first law and would produce more energy than they consume are called perpetual motion machines of the first kind. Two examples of such machines are given below. See if you can determine why they will not work.

It is one thing to glibly pronounce that a perpetual motion machine will not work because it violates the first law of thermodynamics. It is quite another matter to understand precisely where a scheme goes wrong. Two proposed perpetual motion machines of the first kind are shown in Fig. 4-24. Give a qualitative explanation of why they will not operate as suggested below. In other words, find the "fly in the ointment."

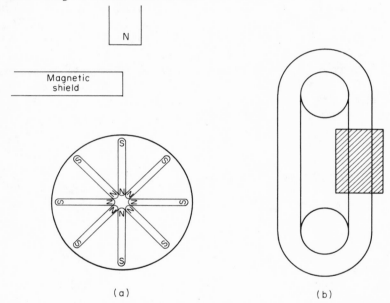

(a)   (b)

Fig. 4-24. Two perpetual motion machines of the first kind:
(a) magnetic wheel, and (b) airtight tube.

The machine in part (a) consists of a wheel whose axle is to act as the driveshaft of a vehicle. The spokes of the wheel are permanent magnets. The magnets are mounted so that their south poles all lie on the periphery of the wheel. Mounted above the center of the wheel is another permanent magnet. Symmetry considerations show that the net torque on the wheel is zero. To change this balance of torques, a magnetic shield is erected, so as to eliminate the magnetic forces (and the torques) on the left side of the wheel. (A very crude magnetic shield might be simply a piece of soft iron. More elaborate magnetic shielding is used

130

regularly, for example, to cancel the magnetic field of the earth in certain precision experiments.) With the shielding in position the net torque on the unshielded right side of the wheel should produce a counterclockwise rotation of the wheel.

The second device in part (b) consists of a flexible airtight tube designed to rotate around two pulley hubs. The axle of the lower hub serves as the driveshaft of a vehicle. Standing alone the gravitational force on the left side of the tube balances the force on the right, that is, there is no net torque and no rotation. By surrounding the right side of the tube with a "silo" filled with water, a buoyant force is brought into play, that is, the portion of the tube inside the silo displaces water and is buoyed up by a force equal to the weight of the water displaced. With the buoyant force acting upward, the right side of the tube moves upward. Because of its continuous loop construction, a fixed volume of tubing is always submerged and the hubs rotate continuously, delivering power to the driveshaft [17, pp. 38-39].

The second law may be stated as:

It is impossible to devise a process whose only result is to extract heat from a heat reservoir and transfer it to a reservoir at a higher temperature.

Give examples of how a violation of this law could be a boon to mankind.

PONDS, LAKES, AND LAND USE

If we use 1600 acres of land for a cooling pond, that land cannot be used for many other purposes. It can be used for sailing or for aquaculture.

On the coast, it seems sensible to allocate areas of water for cooling ponds and, if possible, aquaculture. Inland, large areas are being cut out as ponds, while, near many of our cities, waterways have been reduced to make salable land. The assignment of water as a cooling pond is clearly no worse.

This question of land use for cooling ponds is very similar to the question of land use that arises in connection with hydroelectric power stations. A large area of land is used for every hydroelectric dam; and, being near a river, it is often some of the most fertile land in the area. Dams occupy 25 square miles per 1000 MW_e, and the large dams in the western U.S. are particularly bad in this regard [18]. A typical reservoir is much larger than 1000 acres (1.3 square miles, or 4 km^2). Thus it becomes apparent, if we worry (as we do and should) about the land area taken up by cooling ponds and by the mixing zones in lakes or sea necessary for once-through cooling of a power station, how much *more* we should worry about hydroelectric dams!

At natural waterfalls power can be produced with the primary concern the alteration in the scenic beauty of the falls. Niagara Falls, shared between the U.S. and Canada, produces over 4000 MW$_e$. Dams clearly dislocate many people and much land, but this dislocation is often intended to be advantageous, in terms of downstream irrigation or flood control. But alterations in the ecology can be serious, as is shown most clearly by the Aswan Dam in Egypt.

Biological effects of the Aswan Dam are so numerous that its very existence tends towards disaster. The flooding of the Nile Valley has produced larger numbers of snails than before. These snails are carriers of a very serious disease, Schistosomiasis, which is second only to malaria in its severity to mankind.

The sardine catch in the Mediterranean at the mouth of the Nile declined from 18,000 tons in one year to 500 tons/yr since the filling of the Aswan Dam began (1970). While this may be partially compensated by an increased abundance of freshwater fish in Lake Nasser above the dam, such increases are usually transitory. The predatory fish that reduce the overall fish population do not arrive in numbers until some time after the dam is filled.

The Kariba Dam in Central Africa also brought problems in its wake. Fifty-thousand people, including whole tribes, were displaced and many animals wiped out. Clearly, also, the great mass of water can, particularly if accompanied by seepage, change the seismological activity in the area.

When a dam has been built, most of the implicit environmental damage has been done (apart from the accident questions we will bring up later). This suggests that we could use any reservoir as a cooling pond for one or more large power stations. This can introduce heat to compensate that energy withdrawn by the hydroelectric turbines. But we must be aware that the sign of the thermal-pollution effects of hydropower is not certain. Without the turbine the water will certainly generate heat in falling; yet, falling water sprays and causes evaporation. Moreover, the lake may absorb more of the sun's heat. The sign of the effect is probably unknown. This emphasizes the need for research.

In Table 4-4 we summarize costs for various types of cooling systems. Finally, we note that there are larger-scale environmental effects than noted here, as the following quotation suggests:

> Not all the thermal problems are obvious. Local increases in power-station heat releases can aggravate the problems associated with "urban heat domes." This type of heat pollution occurs when rising warm and dry air diverts regional winds upward over

TABLE 4-4

Comparative Costs of Cooling Systems for Steam-Electric Plants [20]

Type	Investment Cost*		Space needed (acres)	Environmental Cost
	40% efficient plant (HTGR, LMFBR, fossil)	30% efficient plant (LWR)		
Once through (almost independent of fresh or salt water)	3	5	0	Kills fish
Cooling pond	6	9	1000	Use of land
Wet cooling towers				
Mechanical draft	8	11	1.5	Fog, noise
Natural draft	9	13	15	Fog, ugliness
Dry cooling tower	21	32	15	Ugliness, noise
Once through (with 5-mile long pipes)	20 (our estimate)	30 (our estimate)	0	?

* In millions of dollars, for a 1000-MW$_e$ plant. For comparison, the power station itself costs about $200 million (ordered in 1969).

133

the city, isolating the polluted urban air. Thus, an unplanned perimeter of large heat sources around a city of the future, placed to give the cheapest transmission costs to urban load centers, can create conditions that would increase all types of air pollution [19].

AQUACULTURE

Not all environmental effects of heat are bad. We have already noted that a power station, by circulating water, can replenish oxygen or nutrients. The heat itself can be used to grow fish for food.

The quantity of fish consumed in the U.S. is not large, but Japan and Great Britain are not self-sufficient in food and have studied aquaculture. It has been noticed, for example, that shrimp are more plentiful near the Berkeley Nuclear Power Station on the Severn Estuary in England.

These studies are still in their infancy; we refer here to a fine collection of papers from an international conference [21], which summarizes the recent experiments.

HEAT PUMPS

There is a method of using heat more efficiently that deserves much attention. In the discussions in Technical Note 2-4 and Worksheet 2-2, we found a maximum efficiency for a heat engine of $\eta = (T_{hot} - T_{cold})/T_{hot}$. This maximum efficiency is achieved with a reversible heat engine, that is, an engine which can be reversed at any stage.

An example of a heat engine working backwards is the domestic refrigerator. Heat is taken from inside the refrigerator and placed outside; in addition, the electricity to operate the refrigerator heats up the outside. We could use a domestic refrigerator to warm the cold winter air and heat up the inside of a house. There will then be *more* heat than provided by the electricity. The maximum possible increase (gain) is the factor $T_{hot}/(T_{hot} - T_{cold})$, where T is measured in ° K. Typically this is a factor of 10. In practice, a factor of 2 to 6 is obtained, still a very valuable factor that can compensate for the heat wanted at the electricity generating station.

A refrigerator is a more complex device than a simple resistance-wire electric heater. It therefore has a high capital cost and high maintenance costs. These have prevented public acceptance until recently. However, the use of heat pumps is now widespread in Ohio, where competent suppliers and servicemen are being trained. The capital cost is reduced when we realize that the same equipment can double in the summertime as an air conditioner, simply by reversing it.

134

Although heat pumps, like refrigerators, can in principle operate on gas or fossil fuels, only electric devices are presently economically practicable. The use of heat pumps will therefore make the use of electricity for house heating much less wasteful of energy than direct use of fossil fuels, contrary to popular belief. Heat pumps are also useful auxiliaries to solar heating systems [see Problems 6 and 7 in Chapter 2].

REFERENCES

[1] Ehrlich, P.R., and Ehrlich, A.H. (1970). "Population Resources and the Environment." Freeman, San Francisco; Ehrlich, P.R., and Holdren, J.P. (1971). Saturday Review, April 3.

[2] Weinberg, A.M. (1970). "Nuclear Energy and the Environment." Bull. At. Sci. Vol. 26, p. 69; also Weinberg, A.M., and Hammond, R.P. (1970). American Scientist Vol. 58, p. 419.

[3] Hottel, H.C., and Howard, J.B. (1971). "New Energy Technology." MIT Press, Cambridge, Massachusetts.

[4] US Congress (1970). "The Environmental Effects of Producing Electric Power," Vol. 1, Parts 1, 2; Vol. 2, Part 2; combined index Vol. 2, Part 2. Hearings before the Joint Committee on Atomic Energy, October, November, 1969. USGPO.

[5] US Congress (1971). "AEC Authorizing Legislation for Fiscal Year 1972," Parts 1, 2. Hearings before the JCAE. USGPO.

[6] Merriman, A.M. (1970). "The Calefaction of a River." Scientific American Vol. 222.

[7] Scenic Hudson Preservation Conference (1971). Scenic Hudson Preservation Conference, et al. vs. Federal Power Commission's US Petition for a Writ of Appeals Docket. Certiorari US Supreme Court Docket Nos. 71-1219, 71-1220, 71-1221. See also Talbot, A.R. (1972). "The Storm King Case and the Birth of Environmentalism." Dutton, New York.

[8] New York State (1970). "Hudson River Fisheries Investigation 1965-1968." NYS Conservation Dept., Div. of Fish and Wildlife Rept., Albany. (See also [9], which refers to this extensively.)

[9] Atomic Energy Commission (1972). Final Environmental Statement Indian Point 2 Power Station (including comments on preliminary statement). USGPO (November).

[10] Federal Power Commission (1970). "Order and License to Consolidated Edison Co. of New York on the Pumped-Storage Plant at Cornwall (Storm King Reservoir)." Opinion 584, August 19, USGPO.

[11] Woodson, R.D. (1971). "Cooling Towers." Scientific American Vol. 224, No. 5, p. 70.

[12] Rossby, C.G. (1937). "On the Mutual Adjustment of Pressure and Velocity Distributions in Certain Simple Current Systems." MIT Rept., Cambridge, Massachusetts.

4. Thermal Pollution

[13] US Govt. (1970). "Physical and Ecological Effects of Waste Heat in Lake Michigan." Prepared by Dept. of Interior, Fish and Wildlife Service. USGPO (September).

[14] Asbury, J.G. (1970). "Effect of Thermal Energy Discharges on the Mass/Energy Balance of Lake Michigan." Argonne Natl. Lab. Rept. ANL/ES-1, Argonne, Illinois.

[15] Asbury, J.G., and Frigo, A.A. (1971). "A Phenomenological Relationship for Predicting the Surface Areas of Thermal Plumes in Lakes." Argonne Natl. Lab. Rept. ANL/ESS, Argonne, Illinois.

[16] Harte, J., and Socolow, R.H. (1971). "Patient Earth." Holt, New York.

[17] Kelly, D.C. (1973). "Thermodynamics and Statistical Physics." Academic Press, New York and London.

[18] New York Times (1970). "New York Times Encyclopedic Almanac." New York Times Books, New York (any year will do).

[19] Culler, F., and Harms, J. (1972). "Fast Breeder Reactors." Physics Today Vol. 24, No. 5, May.

[20] Belter, W.G. (1969). Proc. Meeting of the Amer. Assoc. Advan. Sci., Boston, Massachusetts (December).

[21] Mathur, E.D. (ed.) (1972). NYS Dept. of Environmental Conservation Conf. Rept. (August, 1971).

[22] Parsegian, V.L. (1968). "Introduction to Natural Science," Vols. I, II. Academic Press, New York and London.

General References

American Institute of Chemical Engineers (1972). "Chemical Engineering Progress Technical Report on Cooling Towers." AIC, New York.

Kinne, O. (ed.) (1972). "Marine Ecology." Wiley, New York (see particularly Vol. 1, "Environmental Effects").

Likens, G.E., Bormann, F.H., and Johnson, M.H. (1972). "Acid Rain." Environment Vol. 14, p. 33.

New York State (1965-1968). Hudson River Fisheries Investigations, 1965-1968. Available NYS Conservation Dept., Div. of Fish and Wildlife, Albany, or Con. Ed., New York.

PROBLEMS

1. Discuss projected global consequences of a temperature rise on the Earth of more than 2° C (see, for example, [22, Vol. I, p. 488]).

2. If the average temperature of the Earth dropped by 5° C, what would be the effects on plants and people living in the present temperate zones and in the torrid zone?

Problems

3. (a) Discuss why the hypolimnion (Figs. 4-21 and 4-22) become depleted in oxygen over the course of a summer season.

(b) Explain why warmer water floats over cooler water.

4. How much will minimum river flow be less than the average flow shown in Fig. 4-6?

Assume that after 30 miles the temperature of a river has regained the temperature of the surrounding air, so that a new power station is possible. How many power stations, with once-through cooling, are now possible in the U.S.?

5. Assume a 1000-MW$_e$ power plant operating at 33% efficiency. What energy has to be taken away by the cooling water?

Assuming a once-through cooling system and a rise in temperature of the cooling water of 18° F (= ? ° C), how much cooling water must be taken from and returned to the river per hour?

If the average river temperature is allowed to rise 1° F, due to the power station, in late summer what must the minimum river flow be?

A fish can swim away from the cooling water intake at 1 mph. What must the size of the water intake be at the location of the fish screen?

Assume that once a river is heated by a power plant, it stays heated. From Fig. 4-6 calculate the total number of power stations possible on the rivers of the U.S., with a 1° F temperature.

6. For the same 1000-MW$_e$ power station, calculate the amount of water evaporated in an evaporative cooling tower, assuming that *all* the heat is taken away by the latent heat of evaporation of water.

What fraction is that of the once-through cooling flow in the previous problem?

7. Make a plan for a large (3000-MW$_e$) power plant and industrial complex, including use of the warm effluent for aquaculture.

8. What societal problems do you anticipate in building the power complex designed in Problem 7, and how would you address them?

5

Nuclear Fission
and Fusion

INTRODUCTION

Thus far we have discussed the conversion of *chemical energy* in
common fuels: wood, gas, oil, or coal to heat. Then the heat can be
used directly for comfort, for industrial processes such as blast fur-
naces, or to make steam to run a steam engine to generate electricity.
The conversion sequence proceeds, as we know well, from chemical energy
to heat, to mechanical energy, and to electrical energy.

In using nuclear energy we will again generate heat to produce
steam to drive a steam turbine to generate electricity. But the process
of producing heat from nuclear fuels is very different from the burning
process of an ordinary fuel, and it is not so commonplace. We must
therefore grasp the basic principles of nuclear energy before we can
understand its unique potential and its unique dangers.

We will see that the size and complexity of "burners" for either
nuclear fission or nuclear fusion are such that they can only be used
in the largest factories or for electricity generation. This is one
of the reasons why we pay so much attention to electricity generation
in this book, and why the trend towards the use of electricity to
replace other fuels is a trend towards the future.

As the world's supply of natural gas diminishes and petroleum
becomes more difficult to extract from the earth without serious environmental damage, the tendency will be to reserve these supplies for applications where electricity is not suitable, as, for example, in the
propulsion of aircraft.

THE ATOM

We will start by considering the structure of an atom. Our picture of the atom will cover only the details that we need for this discussion.

(1) The atom, of course, has mass, but most of the mass is found in a small central core, the *nucleus*. The nucleus is found to have a positive electrical charge.

(2) The nucleus is surrounded by particles known as electrons, each of which has a negative charge. Because of the way the atom is now pictured, physicists say the nucleus is surrounded by "a cloud of electrons."

(3) There are two types of particles in the nucleus: A proton, which has an electrical charge of $+1.6 \times 10^{-19}$ C (coulombs [see Technical Note 5-1]) and a mass of 1.6726×10^{-27} kg, and a neutron, which has no electric charge and a mass of 1.6749×10^{-27} kg, just slightly greater than that of the proton.

(4) The electron has a negative electric charge of magnitude *exactly* the same as that of the proton, -1.6×10^{-19} C and a mass of 9.1×10^{-31} kg, 1/1836 of the mass of a proton or neutron.

We emphasize here that mass and charge are different concepts and are no more related than size and color of an automobile. The electron charge and proton charge exactly cancel, but the masses are unequal.

TECHNICAL NOTE 5-1

The Concept of Charge

Each of the fundamental particles that occupies the subatomic world of the atom and nucleus is identified by its characteristic electrical charge; it is either the type that is found on an electron, which is said to be negative (-), or the type that is found on a proton, which is said to be positive (+). Some particles have no charge and are said to be electrically neutral.

If a proton and electron are brought together, the effect of their charges cancels. We thus conclude that each has a charge of the same size. No charge has ever been found that is one-half, one-quarter, or any fraction of the charge on the electron or proton. It is believed, therefore, that this is probably nature's fundamental unit of charge, that is, the smallest quantity of charge to be found.

Particles do not change the sign of their charge (electrons, for example, are always negatively charged), and charge is neither created or destroyed.

5. Nuclear Fission and Fusion

In nuclear reactions, as we shall see, even "fundamental" particles, such as protons, can be changed into a pair of other particles, but charge is conserved (one particle coming off will have a positive charge and the other no charge).

Just as there exists a gravitational force that attracts bodies to each other although they may be great distances apart, so are there electrical forces that also act over a distance. Whereas gravity is an attractive force between two masses, in electrical phenomena, particles having the same charge repel each other, while particles having opposite charges attract.

The forces that hold atoms together to make molecules are electrical in nature and come about by a sharing of electrons between groups of atoms. Molecules in solids and liquids are bound together by electrical forces.

We state as a point of general information, that for historical reasons electrical charges are measured in units named after an early experimenter in the field, the French physicist, Charles Coulomb (1736-1806). The electron has a charge of -1.6×10^{-19} C. This small number shows that the electron was studied well after the coulomb itself had been defined.

TECHNICAL NOTE 5-2

Electric Current, Conductivity, and Resistance

A simple picture of an electric current is that electrons flow through a wire. (This picture is no longer considered precise, but it is adequate for our purposes.) In passing through a wire, the electrons meet resistance by hitting other electrons and nuclei, in the same way that water meets resistance in running through a pipe. The electrons are pulled through the wire by the attraction of electrical forces. Just as we can view bodies under the influence of gravity as being subjected to gravitational forces or having gravitational potential energy, whichever view is more convenient to us, so can we view these electrons as being subjected to electrical forces or as having electrical potential energy.

You will recall that power is the energy flow per unit time, that is,

$$power = energy/time$$

Electrical energy is given by voltage (volts) × charge (q):

$$energy = volts \times q$$

140

and power by

$$power = volts \times q/t$$

We now define a term which you have many times heard about: current. Current is the rate at which charge flows past any point in a wire, or, using the symbol i for current,

$$i = q/t$$

(We see here an analogy with the flow of water passing through a pipe.) From this definition you should be able to see that power can be found by multiplying the voltage across an appliance by the current it draws:

$$power = volts \times i$$

Finally, the units of i are given as amperes. Of course, power, as we saw in the earlier chapters, is measured in watts.

The electrical resistance (R) of a wire is measured in ohms. If we were to compare wires of different resistance and put the same voltage across each, the wire with the lowest resistance would have the largest current, and vice versa. These three quantities are related by the formula:

$$V = iR \quad (Ohm's \ law)$$

At very low temperatures (in the neighborhood of absolute zero), some metals have no resistance to electrical currents and are called superconductors. This phenomenon was discovered by Kammerlingh Onnes in 1911.

A theory of superconductors was developed in 1956 by Bardeen, Cooper, and Schrieffer, who were awarded the Nobel prize in 1972. Since then many alloys (mixtures of elements) have been produced which are good superconductors. As we shall see later, there is a great stake in developing superconductors that work at high temperatures and can be cheaply used for the transmission of electricity.

The Chemistry of Atoms

The chemical properties of an atom are determined by the number of protons in its nucleus (or alternatively, by the number of electrons in the surrounding cloud). An atom of iron has 26 protons and 26 electrons; an atom of copper has 29 protons and 29 electrons. The science of chemistry deals with the interchanges of the outer electrons surrounding the nuclei.

Ninety percent of the iron atoms found in nature have 30 neutrons in their nuclei. Others have 29, 31, or 32 neutrons. All these atoms, although different, behave the same chemically, and all have the family name "iron." Those atoms that have the same chemical properties but different numbers of neutrons are called *isotopes*. Iron with 30 neutrons is the common isotope; iron with 29, 31, or 32 neutrons is less common (see Fig. 5-1).

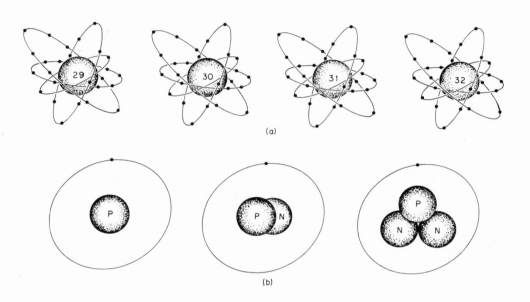

Fig. 5-1. (a) The isotopes of iron; (b) the isotopes of hydrogen.

For each chemical element we can imagine elements with any number of neutrons we choose, but only a few of these occur naturally. For the light nuclei, the number of neutrons is nearly equal to the number of protons, but the number is greater for heavy nuclei.

In our discussions we will be dealing with many more isotopes of chemical elements than those that occur naturally. Some are created in the process of fission. Many hundreds of isotopes are now known, and their properties listed [1].

The Role of the Electron

Electrons play an important role in an atom. As we discussed, under normal circumstances atoms are electrically neutral: each atom has an equal number of protons and electrons. The combined charge of the electrons cancels out the effect of the combined charge of the protons in the nucleus.

When an electron is removed from an atom, the atom becomes positively charged. When an extra electron is added to an atom, it becomes negatively charged. If a sodium atom loses an electron, and a chlorine atom gains one, they attract each other and form the chemical compound sodium chloride (common salt).

This is an oversimplified view of a particularly simple chemical reaction. Chemistry is the study of the joining of atoms, by the exchange of electrons, to form compounds and molecules. The nucleus remains unaltered in these chemical reactions (see Fig. 5-2).

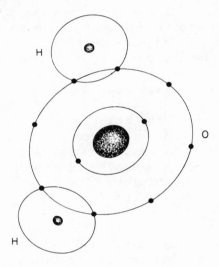

Fig. 5-2. Schematic representation of hydrogen (H) and oxygen (O) combined to form water (H_2O).

The Energy Formula of Einstein

In 1905 Albert Einstein published an epoch-making paper on what is now described as the special theory of relativity [2]. One of the predictions of this theory was that the laws of conservation of energy and conservation of mass are connected, and that the *sum* of energy and mass are conserved. The equation of transformation from energy units to mass units is Einstein's famous energy formula $E = Mc^2$, where c is the velocity of light in vacuum.

This formula does not, in itself, tell us how to transform mass into useful energy, but it does tell us, for example, that 1 g of coal, if it could be converted to energy, would give 10^{10} times the amount of energy as burning it. However, 34 years passed before the discovery of uranium fission and the immediate realization by physicists all over the world that a fraction, 0.1%, of the mass of a uranium atom can be converted into energy. Nonetheless, this dramatic extension of physical theory stimulated the search.

5. Nuclear Fission and Fusion

As an aside, therefore, we mention this outstanding achievement of Einstein. There existed, at the turn of the century, some unresolved questions in electromagnetic theory. Einstein set out to resolve these problems by making two simple postulates:

(1) The laws of physics remain the same for an observer moving with a constant velocity as for a stationary observer. (This was already a postulate before Einstein; the new assumption is the second.)

(2) The velocity of light is the same when measured by an observer moving with constant velocity and measured by a stationary observer. This is a new postulate, surprising to anyone schooled in the mechanics of Newton, under which the velocity of sound as measured by the moving observer is certainly not the same as that measured by a stationary observer, and their relative velocities play an important role.

The law of conservation of mass must be one of the physical laws that satisfy the first postulate. Einstein found that it had to be modified in such a way as to suggest the relation $E = Mc^2$.

The detailed derivation from these postulates is too complex for this book and we refer to elementary physics texts for it [3].

This is one of the best examples of important practical results coming from fundamental principles.

Binding Energy

We shall define binding energy and illustrate the use of $E = Mc^2$. To do so, we shall look at an isotope of hydrogen.

The most common isotope of hydrogen is the simplest of all atoms. Ordinary hydrogen consists of a single proton around which orbits one electron. Far more rare is the isotope of hydrogen (deuterium) that has a nucleus of one proton and one neutron, and still more rare the isotope that has one proton and two neutrons (tritium) (Fig. 5-1). We shall look at the nucleus of deuterium. This nucleus is common enough to have a name of its own, the deuteron.

The deuteron, made up of a neutron and a proton, has a mass less than the total of a separate neutron and proton:

$$\text{mass of proton:} \quad 1.67261 \times 10^{-27} \text{ kg}$$

$$\text{+ mass of neutron:} \quad 1.67492 \times 10^{-27} \text{ kg}$$

$$\text{total:} \quad 3.34753 \times 10^{-27} \text{ kg}$$

$$\text{- mass of deuteron:} \quad 3.34357 \times 10^{-27} \text{ kg}$$

$$\text{difference:} \quad 0.00396 \times 10^{-27} \text{ kg}$$

If we bring a proton and neutron together to form a deuteron, the mass difference goes off in the form of energy. Applying $E = Mc^2$ where M is the mass difference and c the velocity of light (3×10^8 m/sec or 186,000 miles/sec), this mass is equivalent to an energy of 3.6×10^{-13} j. [See Worksheet 5-1.] Experimentally it is found that an energy of 3.6×10^{-13} j is needed to separate the nucleus into a proton and a neutron.

We are setting forth two important concepts:

(1) The mass of a nucleus is less than the mass of its separate constituent particles.

(2) If mass is "lost" in forming a nucleus, it appears as energy. In this case, where a neutron and a proton form a deuteron, most of the energy goes off as a gamma (γ) ray, and a little as the kinetic energy of recoil of the deuteron. The sum of these two is called the *binding energy* of the nucleus.

An analogy may be useful. We have just discussed the release of energy as a proton and neutron attract each other and form a deuteron. When an orbiting spaceship finally falls to earth, it liberates gravitational energy in the form of heat, and it is finally "bound" to the earth by the gravitational forces.

NUCLEAR FISSION

The masses of the nuclei, as well as the binding energy, can be measured and tabulated. We will now see how with this information we can tell whether energy can be produced in a nuclear fission (the separation of a nucleus into two or more other nuclei), and how therefore we can predict the conditions for releasing nuclear energy.

For this purpose we refer to Fig. 5-3. In this graph of stable nuclei, we have plotted along the abscissa (or horizontal axis) the number of particles in the nucleus ($=A$, the atomic number [see Technical Note 6-4]), and along the ordinate (or vertical axis) the binding energy divided by the number of particles.

The binding energy is given in millions of electron volts (MeV), a unit of energy more convenient to nuclear reactions than the joule. The electron volt is related to the joule by

$$1 \text{ eV} = 1.60 \times 10^{-19} \text{ j}$$

$$1 \text{ MeV} = 1.60 \times 10^{-13} \text{ j}$$

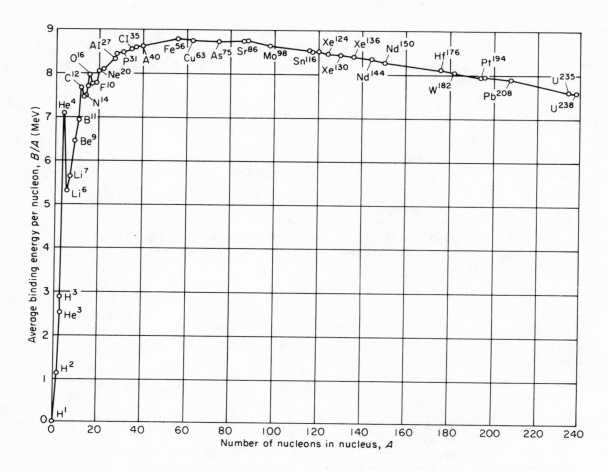

Fig. 5-3. Average binding energy per nucleon as a function of the number of nucleons, *A*.

The curve of Fig. 5-3 shows that the binding energy per nucleon reaches a maximum near the nucleus of iron (*A* = 56). The nuclei in this region are the most strongly bound of all, or, in nuclear terminology, the most stable. It is this fact that makes iron one of the elements most commonly found in nature.

We can now also see why we are plotting binding energy per particle rather than the total binding energy of each nucleus. Obviously, a nucleus with 200 particles will have a greater total binding energy than one with 60. But the binding energy per particle may be less for the heavier nucleus, and it may therefore be less strongly bound. As drawn, this graph gives a quick view of the relative binding strengths of the various nuclei.

Binding Energy

Let us apply the formula $E = mc^2$ to the case of the deuterium nucleus and determine its binding energy.

c is the conventional symbol for the speed of light, 3×10^8 m/sec (approximately 186,000 miles/sec). m is the mass of material whose energy equivalent we seek. In this case it is the mass difference between the nucleus and the separate particles, 0.00396×10^{-27} kg.

(1) Carry through the calculation:

$$E = \underline{\hspace{1cm}} \text{ kg} \times \underline{\hspace{1cm}} \text{ (m/sec)}^2$$

$$= \underline{\hspace{1cm}}$$

$$= \underline{\hspace{1cm}} \text{ j}$$

(2) Use the definition of kinetic energy to show that E here has the units of joules.

(3) If one was able to extract this energy from each atom of 1 kg of deuterium, how much energy would be given off?
(a) The conversion factor for 1 kg is found from:

$$3.34355 \times 10^{-27} \text{kg} \times \underline{\hspace{1cm}} = 1 \text{ kg}$$

(b) Applying this conversion factor to the energy/atom:

$$\underline{\hspace{1cm}} \text{ j} \times \underline{\hspace{1cm}} = \underline{\hspace{1cm}} \text{ j}$$

(4) Convert 3(b) to watt-hours and then kilowatt-hours:

$$\underline{\hspace{1cm}} \text{ j/sec} = \underline{\hspace{1cm}} \text{ W-hr}$$

$$= \underline{\hspace{1cm}} \text{ kWh}$$

Compare this to the value given in the energy conversion table in Chapter 1.

146b

Nuclear Fission

Nuclear fission, often called "splitting the atom," refers to dividing the nucleus into two or more parts. It is the process used in the atomic bomb and nuclear reactors.

Let us assume that we can split the nucleus $A = 238$ into two other nuclei, say, $A = 148$ and $A = 90$. From the graph, we compare the binding energy per particle for each of these three nuclei. We start with a binding energy of 7.6 MeV/particle and end with a net of 8.5 MeV/particle. The energy liberated in this splitting is

$$238 \text{ (particles)} \times [8.5 - 7.6] \text{ (MeV/particle)} = 215 \text{ MeV}$$

In summary, the heavy nucleus splits and gives off two lighter nuclei (fission fragments), each of which binds its nucleons more tightly than the uranium. The energy then becomes available, some directly, and some from decay products. A listing of the energy in the fission of U^{235} is given in Table 5-1.

TABLE 5-1

The Average Amount of Energy Released in the Fission of U^{235} (MeV)

Kinetic energy of the fission fragments	168
Prompt γ-rays	7
Fission neutrons	5
γ-rays produced by neutron capture*	3–12
Energy of decay products of fission fragments	
γ-rays	7
β-rays	8
Neutrinos*	12
Total	210–219

*The elusive neutrinos pass out of the reactor and even through the earth. The energy of the neutron capture γ-rays depends on the capturing material.

The question then arises, how can we make the nuclei split at will, and often enough to produce energy?

Subsequent to the discovery of uranium fission by Hahn and Strassman in 1939, theoretical and experimental research has shown the following about heavy nuclei (in the $A = 200$ range). If A is a multiple of four, the nucleus will split into two slightly uneven parts within a fraction of a second. The reasons are too complex to go into here; all that matters, for our purposes, is that it is an experimental fact. [See Worksheet 5-2.]

5. Nuclear Fission and Fusion

We shall look at two such nuclei, uranium ($A = 236$) and plutonium ($A = 240$). The shorthand notation for these nuclei are $_{92}U^{236}$ and $_{94}Pu^{240}$. We must first form these unstable nuclei, as because of their short lifetimes they are not found in nature.

TECHNICAL NOTE 5-3

Notation for Nuclear Reactions

An atomic nucleus can be characterized by two numbers: Z is the atomic number, or the number of protons in the nucleus. The total charge of the nucleus is exactly Z multiplied by the proton charge.

A is the mass number. This is defined as the number of protons in the nucleus plus the number of neutrons. The total mass of the atom is approximately A multiplied by the mass of a proton. It is actually a little less than this because of the binding of the nuclei.

An atom that is electrically uncharged (neutral) will have exactly Z electrons to balance the charge of the protons.

An atom is then represented by a symbol

$$_Z Symbol^A$$

For example, a hydrogen atom is described as $_1H^1$, which says that it has one proton, no neutrons, and one electron surrounding the nucleus.

The usual iron atom is described as $_{26}Fe^{56}$ (from Latin Ferrum, iron), which says there are 26 protons and (56-26)=30 neutrons in the nucleus.

The other isotopes of iron, to which we referred in the text, are $_{26}Fe^{55}$, $_{26}Fe^{57}$, $_{26}Fe^{58}$. Since all iron atoms have Z=26 (26 protons), the symbol Fe and the number 26 are redundant. Sometimes the atomic number is omitted and only the name is used with one number to describe the mass number (e.g., iron 55, iron 57, iron 58). In these cases the number of neutrons is 29, 31, and 32, respectively.

A nuclear reaction can take place when two atomic nuclei combine (fusion), or when one splits (fission) into new products. For example, a proton and neutron can come together to form a heavy hydrogen nucleus (deuterium) and release energy in the form of a gamma ray.

The shorthand notation becomes

$$_0N^1 + _1H^1 \longrightarrow _1H^2 + \gamma$$

The isotopes of hydrogen are so common that they have special names and symbols: deuterium, $_1H^2$ or D (nucleus, deuteron); and tritium, $_1H^3$ or T (nucleus, triton).

WORKSHEET 5-2

The Energy in a Pound of Uranium

As shown in Table 5-1, 200 MeV is released in the fission of one nucleus of U^{235}. Let us use this datum to relate those numbers to our common power needs. To do so, we will need the following conversion factors:

$$1 \text{ MeV} = 1.6 \times 10^{-13} \text{ j}$$
$$1 \text{ kg corresponds to } 2.2 \text{ lb weight on Earth}$$

You will also need to know that the mass of an atom of U^{235} is roughly 39×10^{-27} kg.

How much energy can we get from this pound of uranium?

(a) Energy per atom _____

(b) Number of atoms per pound _____

(c) Energy per pound _____

(d) How long would this pound of uranium last if it had to supply 1 MW of energy?

_____

(e) Compare the result to the number given in the energy conversion table in Chapter 1.

These nuclei are formed by adding a neutron to more stable isotopes of these elements. Using a nomenclature that does away with the clumsiness of words, we see *the before* (a neutron being added to the more stable nuclei) and *the after* of the reaction at a glance:

$$_0N^1 + {_{92}}U^{235} \longrightarrow {_{92}}U^{236} \longrightarrow \text{two parts (fission fragments)}$$
$$+ \text{extra free neutrons}$$

$$_0N^1 + {_{94}}Pu^{239} \longrightarrow {_{94}}Pu^{240} \longrightarrow \text{two parts (fission fragments)}$$
$$+ \text{extra free neutrons}$$

The elements $_{92}U^{235}$ and $_{94}Pu^{239}$ are called "fissile" elements because they may be easily "fissioned" by the addition of a neutron. (See Table 5-1 and Fig. 5-4.)

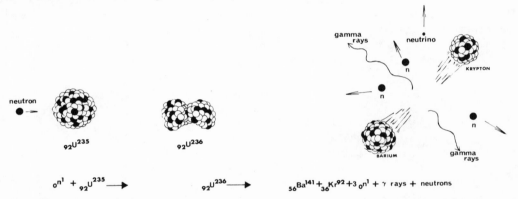

Fig. 5-4. An example of how uranium experiences fission (from V.L. Parsegian, *et al.*, "Introduction to Natural Science." Academic Press, New York and London, 1968.

Radioactivity

As we have now seen, not every combination of protons and neutrons makes up a stable nucleus. The above nuclei split immediately, in fractions of a second. Other unstable nuclei decay more slowly and seek a stable configuration for their constituent particles by means other than splitting. Radium is the best-known example of this type of nucleus.

The term used to measure the rate of radioactive decay is the half-life; the half-life of radium is 1622 yr. Starting with 1 g of radium today, in 1622 yr only 1/2 g would remain, and in another 1622 yr (one-half of the one-half), only 1/4 g would be left.

5. Nuclear Fission and Fusion

Radium decays by emitting a tightly bound cluster of two neutrons and two protons. This is, in fact, the nucleus of helium. This nucleus usually picks up two electrons from the air to become a helium atom. When radium was first studied, one of its mysteries was why helium was always found in its presence.

If we write down the equation for this decay, we have

$$_{88}Ra^{226} \longrightarrow \ _{86}Rn^{222} + \ _{2}He^{4}$$

where Rn is the symbol for the element radon, the nucleus that is left after the radium decays. Radon itself is unstable and decays further. This decay continues through several intermediate nuclei until a stable isotope of lead (Pb^{206}) is reached. In lead the number of neutrons and protons is nearly equal.

Radioactivity accompanies this decay. The ejected helium nucleus is part of the radioactivity. Electrons and high-energy γ-rays can also be released in the process of decay. The γ-ray is energy in the form of electromagnetic radiation. It results from part of the mass being converted into energy because of the higher binding energy per particle of the lighter nuclei. This hazardous radiation and its effects on biological systems will be discussed in Chapter 9.

TECHNICAL NOTE 5-4

Radioactivity and Half-Life

A radioactive element emits radiation spontaneously. The rate of emission is not affected by external circumstances such as temperature, pressure, or even chemical combination.

If we start with a certain amount of a radioactive element and arrange to measure its activity as a function of time, we find the activity is steadily diminishing. The quality of the radiation, that is, the energy of each α-, β-, or γ-ray does not change, but the quantity decreases.

Figure 5-5 shows the activity of a sample of strontium 90 measured in some arbitrary units, as a function of time. Strontium 90 emits β-rays, or electrons, with varying energies up to 540,000 eV. The ordinate I is proportional to the number of β-rays emitted per second.

After 28 years, the activity has decreased to half its initial value I_0, by the 56th year it is down to one-quarter, and so on. The time during which the activity drops to half its value is called the half-life of the substance and is a characteristic of the particular radioactive nucleus. (Note that we can begin at any time in the figure and still reach the same answer.)

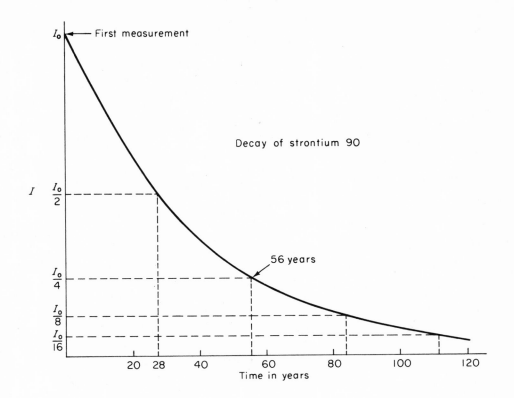

Fig. 5-5. Decay activity of strontium 90 as a function of time.

It is interesting to note the similarity of the concept of the half-life to the less exact concept of doubling time noted in Chapter 1. The half-lives of some interesting elements are given below:

Strontium 90 ($_{38}Sr^{90}$):   28 years

Radium ($_{88}Ra^{226}$):   1622 years

Plutonium ($_{94}Pu^{239}$):   24,360 years

Iodine ($_{53}I^{131}$):   8.05 days

($_{53}I^{129}$):   17.2 million years

Krypton ($_{36}Kr^{85}$):   10.4 years

($_{36}Kr^{88}$):   2.8 hours

151

5. *Nuclear Fission and Fusion*

One of the interesting applications of radioactivity is its use in dating techniques. Carbon 14 is used in dating the age of carbon-bearing specimens that were at one time parts of living organisms. Carbon 14 is produced in the air constantly by cosmic radiation. It enters living tissue during breathing with the intake of breath, and therefore all carbon in living organisms must have the same activity per unit weight. After the tissue dies, carbon 14 no longer enters, and that already there decays. Thus by knowing the half-life of carbon 14 and the measurement of carbon 14 activity per unit weight of the specimen, one can arrive at the age of the specimen [4].

The Chain Reaction

If we look at a list of stable nuclei, we find that light nuclei have approximately equal numbers of protons and neutrons. Examples are carbon $_6C^{12}$ and oxygen $_8O^{16}$. On the other hand, stable heavy nuclei have more neutrons than protons, e.g., uranium $_{92}U^{238}$ has 92 protons and 146 neutrons.

The reason for this has to do with the electrostatic repulsion between the positive charges on the protons, but the details need not concern us.

Isotopes of nuclei that have more neutrons than the stable isotope are called *neutron rich* and decay by emission of electrons. For example, the neutron-rich isotope $_6C^{13}$ decays according to the reaction:

$$_6C^{13} \longrightarrow {}_7N^{13} + e^- + \nu^-$$

What happens when a uranium nucleus, with more neutrons than protons, splits into two lighter nuclei? These lighter nuclei are neutron rich and radioactive. In addition, one or more neutrons may be emitted in the initial fission.

As we shall see, the average number of extra neutrons is a very important and exciting number if it is greater than one. In two dramatic experiments performed almost simultaneously in 1939, by Joliot, Halban, and Kovarski in Paris and by Dunning and others in New York, the average number of extra neutrons for fission of uranium 235 was shown to be 2.07.

A continuous process of fission becomes theoretically possible because of these extra neutrons given off when each U^{235} nucleus divides. If these extra neutrons are captured by other U^{235} nuclei, they in turn will split and give off further neutrons, which in turn will carry the process on (see Fig. 5-6).

If only one extra neutron is produced per fission, only one more nucleus can be split in the next stage; if more than one, the reaction can multiply. In a bomb, this chain reaction is completed in one-millionth of a second; in a reactor it must be controlled so that the energy is released over a long period of time.

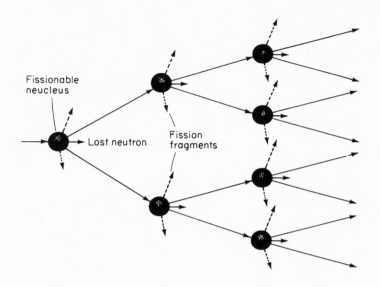

Fig. 5-6. Schematic diagram of chain reaction.

In a bomb, pure plutonium 239 or uranium 235 (i.e., the pure fissile isotope) is suddenly assembled into a critical mass (by firing from a gun!). A neutron from a radioactive source then detonates the explosion.

If uranium 238 is mixed with the uranium 235 (up to 50%), the U^{238} absorbs enough neutrons to prevent a chain reaction so that the bomb cannot be detonated, even if the size of the bomb is made larger. If the neutrons are slowed down, however, then more of the available neutrons are likely to be captured by the U^{235} (the slower a neutron is moving, the longer it remains close to a nucleus and the greater the chance that it can be captured), and a chain reaction can once more occur.

Neutrons are slowed down by collisions with other nuclei of similar mass. Protons (hydrogen nuclei, H) are of the same mass, deuterium (heavy hydrogen nuclei, D) twice the mass, carbon (C) atoms 10 times the mass, and oxygen (O) atoms 16 times the mass. We must choose materials that do not capture the neutrons themselves; of the above, only hydrogen captures neutrons appreciably, but even then not as much as many other elements.

The slowing-down material, or *moderator*, can then be water (H_2O), heavy water (D_2O), or graphite (C).

Most of the reactors used in the U.S. have ordinary water (H_2O) as a moderator. In these, the hydrogen captures enough neutrons so that the uranium cannot be used in its natural state (0.71% U^{235} and 99.29% U^{238}) but must be enriched with the "fissile" isotope U^{235}, until there is 3% U^{235} in the sample of uranium. Canada uses heavy-water reactors, while England has concentrated on graphite reactors, which do not capture neutrons. With both these types of reactors natural uranium can be used.

THE NUCLEAR REACTOR

In a rather brief overview, we will cover the technology of the nuclear reactor here. In Chapter 10, where we deal with accidents and sabotage, we will return to the reactor and study some aspects of it in further detail.

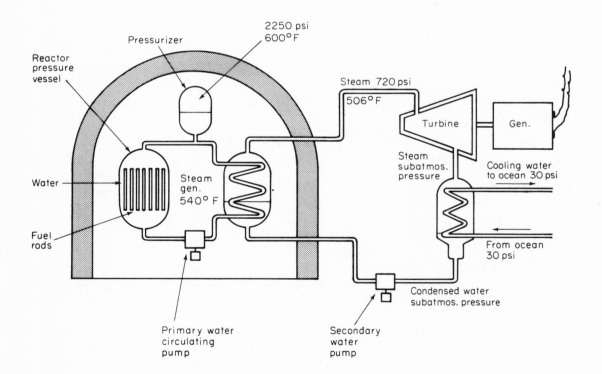

Fig. 5-7. Schematic diagram of pressurized-water nuclear-power plant.

The Nuclear Reactor

In Fig. 5-7 we show how a nuclear reactor is used in a power station. The reactor itself consists of a number of metal tubes containing uranium-oxide pellets. These tubes are immersed in water; the hydrogen in the water slows the neutrons down.

The tubes are contained in a strong steel boiler under pressure. This water is heated by the nuclear reaction. In some types of reactors, for example, the boiling-water reactor (BWR), steam is directly produced, and this boiler takes the place of a coal-, oil-, or gas-fired boiler in a power station. This is easily seen by comparing Fig. 5-7 and the equivalent fossil-fuel system of Fig. 4-2. We will discuss in Chapter 9 how the radioactivity is contained within the reactor.

In the reactor of Fig. 5-7, we prevent the water from boiling by keeping it at a high pressure. This water then passes to a heat exchanger where the water (at a lower pressure) is converted into steam to run the steam turbine. This is called a pressurized-water reactor (PWR), and reactors of this type are used in every nuclear submarine and aircraft carrier.

Control of a Reactor

This looks simple, and so far it is. The complications come with the control devices. The reactor is controlled by adding materials that absorb (capture) neutrons and prevent more than one neutron per fission from causing further fissions. Such a material is boron (A = 11), a convenient solid that can be placed on a control rod and lowered into the reactor; also, borax (a household chemical containing boron) can be added to the water. As a boron-control rod is removed, the reactor will "go critical." More than one of the neutrons produced in each fission will give further fissions.

For a reactor at constant power, the rate of birth of neutrons must equal the rate of death (absorption, loss, inability to be captured by a fissile nucleus). We say then that the *reactivity* is zero. If the reactivity is positive, the number of neutrons, and hence the power, is increasing.

There are two factors that make reactor control possible. First, some of the subsequent fissions do not immediately follow the first fission but have a small time delay; second, we can arrange matters so that if the reactor heats up, the reactivity goes down. The time delay enables this control to occur.

The most important time delay is given by the existence of delayed neutrons. 0.65% of the neutrons from fission of U^{236} (n + U^{235}) are delayed. [See Technical Note 5-5.] If a spontaneous fluctuation, or accidental removal of a control rod, changes the reactivity less than 0.65%, the rate of increase of reactor power is limited by these delayed neutrons. Another cause of delay is the slowing down of the neutrons.

5. Nuclear Fission and Fusion

This is about 1/1000 sec (1 msec). Unless the change is more than 0.65%, this is unimportant. The important design feature is to ensure that no change in reactivity greater than 0.65% can quickly occur. This can be done by ensuring that only one of several control rods may be withdrawn at a time and that it can only be withdrawn slowly.

TECHNICAL NOTE 5-5

Delayed Neutrons

These neutrons are not emitted in the fission process itself but arise as the result of decay by neutron emission of a particular fission product. An example is the decay of the fission fragment of iodine:

$$_{53}I^{137} \xrightarrow[\text{(22 sec)}]{\beta} {}_{54}Xe^{137} \xrightarrow[\text{(instantaneous)}]{n} {}_{54}Xe^{136}$$

The neutron emission by xenon 137 is instantaneous, so these neutrons appear to decrease with a half-life of 22 sec.

There are 6 groups of delayed neutrons, from 6 different fission products, with lifetimes from 0.22 to 54 sec. 0.65% of the neutrons from thermal fission of U^{236} are delayed, but only 0.3% of the neutrons from fission of Pu^{240}. This gives a reactor using plutonium a slightly smaller safety margin than one using uranium.

This delay time of about a second is still short, so there must be an automatic mechanism that can act faster than a human operator and faster than the mechanical task of moving a control rod. This is done by designing the reactor so that, as the reactivity and the temperature increase, the reactivity tends to reduce again.

Two physical factors assure this: First, as the temperature of the reactor increases, the absorption of neutrons by the U^{238} increases, reducing the number available for further fission. The U^{238} actually absorbs all neutrons of a particular (resonant) energy; as the temperature increases, the uranium molecules move in random directions, and the resonant energy becomes broadened into a band of energies by the Doppler effect (the same effect that changes the resonant whistle of a railroad engine when the engine is moving).

In the second process, the moderator expands as it is heated, thereby providing more space for the neutrons to pass through it without collision and allowing fewer neutrons to slow down adequately.

Both these processes make a nuclear reactor stable against undesired changes of power. In fact, a smoothly running nuclear power station is easier to operate than any fossil-fuel power station: about as easy as a hydroelectric station. It only needs refueling once a year, and between fuelings the control rods need only be slowly withdrawn to maintain reactivity.

The high-energy density of the uranium fuel brings the advantage of a relatively small power station with small facilities. But this high density brings with it the problems of stored energy, with an accident potential and a waste problem, which we will be discussing in a later chapter.

Types of Reactors

In addition to the pressurized-water reactor (PWR), there are several other reactor types. In the boiling-water reactor (BWR) (Fig. 5-8), water is also used as a moderator, but the water is boiled directly in the reactor vessel without the intervening heat exchanger (steam generator). Canada has specialized in reactors moderated with heavy water (D_2O), CANDU reactors, in which unenriched uranium can be used as fuel, since deuterium does not capture the neutrons. Great Britain, which pioneered electricity generation with nuclear power, uses carbon in the form of graphite as the moderator and carbon dioxide (CO_2) gas as the heat-transfer fluid. Since CO_2 is gaseous, it is less efficient than water at transferring heat, and the reactor of necessity becomes larger and more costly. Shell-Gulf Atomic in the U.S. makes graphite reactors with helium as a coolant.

Each of these types of reactor has its advantages and disadvantages in operation, cost, and safety features; all have been made to operate reliably at a cost competitive with fossil-fuel power plants. Details can be obtained from the manufacturers in each case.

Converters

The heavy-water and graphite reactors have an advantage called "neutron economy." None of the neutrons produced in a fission of the isotope U^{235} are captured in the moderator. They will either be re-captured by more U^{235} atoms (and produce further fissions) or U^{238} atoms, or they will escape from the reactor. The capture of neutrons by U^{238} leads through several steps to production of another fissile material, plutonium (Pu^{239}). These decays take place with a half-life of 2-1/2 days.

As we discussed earlier, Pu^{239} is a good reactor fuel. Thus if we design a reactor so that few neutrons are captured by surrounding material, some of the plentiful isotope U^{238} is converted into a usable fuel. Such a reactor is said to have good neutron economy.

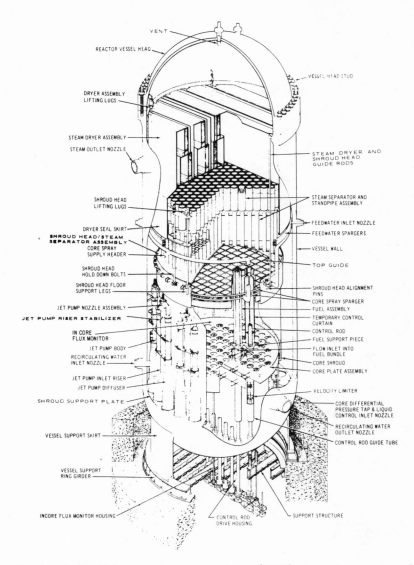

Labels in figure (clockwise / as positioned):

VENT
REACTOR VESSEL HEAD
VESSEL HEAD STUD
DRYER ASSEMBLY LIFTING LUGS
STEAM DRYER AND SHROUD HEAD GUIDE RODS
STEAM DRYER ASSEMBLY
STEAM OUTLET NOZZLE
STEAM SEPARATOR AND STANDPIPE ASSEMBLY
SHROUD HEAD LIFTING LUGS
FEEDWATER INLET NOZZLE
FEEDWATER SPARGERS
DRYER SEAL SKIRT
VESSEL WALL
SHROUD HEAD/STEAM SEPARATOR ASSEMBLY
CORE SPRAY SUPPLY HEADER
TOP GUIDE
SHROUD HEAD HOLD DOWN BOLTS
SHROUD HEAD ALIGNMENT PINS
SHROUD HEAD FLOOR SUPPORT LEGS
CORE SPRAY SPARGER
JET PUMP NOZZLE ASSEMBLY
FUEL ASSEMBLY
JET PUMP RISER STABILIZER
TEMPORARY CONTROL CURTAIN
IN CORE FLUX MONITOR
CONTROL ROD
JET PUMP BODY
FUEL SUPPORT PIECE
RECIRCULATING WATER INLET NOZZLE
FLOW INLET INTO FUEL BUNDLE
JET PUMP INLET RISER
CORE SHROUD
JET PUMP DIFFUSER
CORE PLATE ASSEMBLY
SHROUD SUPPORT PLATE
VELOCITY LIMITER
CORE DIFFERENTIAL PRESSURE TAP & LIQUID CONTROL INLET NOZZLE
VESSEL SUPPORT SKIRT
RECIRCULATING WATER OUTLET NOZZLE
CONTROL ROD GUIDE TUBE
VESSEL SUPPORT RING GIRDER
INCORE FLUX MONITOR HOUSING
CONTROL ROD DRIVE HOUSING
SUPPORT STRUCTURE

Fig. 5-8. Typical boiling-water reactor (BWR) reactor vessel, showing detail of all the devices for correct operation. (Source: Vermont Yankee Nuclear Power Co.)

Another source of fuel results from thorium ($_{90}Th^{233}$) absorbing a neutron and, again through several stages, becoming U^{234}. Uranium 234 is a useful fuel for fission. Thorium is a much more plentiful fuel than uranium.

A reactor which produces useful fuel from the nonfissile elements in the core is called a *converter*.

In a light-water reactor, there is about one plutonium (Pu^{239}) atom produced for every three fissions of U^{235} (1:3). In a heavy-water reactor this ratio can go as high as four Pu^{239} atoms for every five U^{235} atoms (4:5). In the graphite reactor of Shell-Gulf, a uranium/

thorium fuel is used for which this number is about 3:4. There will
be fission of the plutonium itself producing more plutonium atoms;
for every U^{235} atom originally present, three other fissile atoms are
eventually produced and consumed. The ratio of the number of fissile
nuclei produced to the number consumed is called the *breeding ratio*.
For the light-water reactor it is 0.33; for the heavy-water reactor,
0.8; for the Shell-Gulf, 0.8.

TECHNICAL NOTE 5-6

*We can easily calculate the total number of fissile atoms used
for each one initially present. If the breeding ratio has the alge-
braic symbol η, we add the number of atoms produced in each stage:*

$$1 + η + η^2 + \cdots + \text{(to infinity)} = \frac{1}{1-η} = 1\text{-}1/2 \text{ for light-water reactor}$$

$$= 5 \text{ for the Shell-Gulf reactor}$$

*When the breeding ratio η becomes greater than 1, the number becomes
infinitely large and we have a breeder reactor, which makes more fissile fuel than it consumes.*
*In view of the shortages of the uranium isotope U^{235} (Chapter 2),
it is highly desirable to stretch the reserves by a convector or a
breeder.*

Breeder Reactors

A breeder reactor usually uses fast neutrons, so that first, fewer
neutrons are captured by surrounding materials (capture, as mentioned
earlier, is easier with slow neutrons), and, second, the number of neutrons per fission is greater.
The heat-transfer material in a fast-neutron reactor cannot be
water, for that would slow the neutrons down. It must therefore be
either a gas or another liquid: molten sodium is usually chosen.
Sodium remains liquid at quite high temperatures (boiling point 892° C
= 1638° F), so that pressure vessels are not needed to keep it liquid;
moreover, high temperatures allow high thermal efficiencies. It must,
however, be kept away from water and air to prevent chemical interaction.
Because it absorbs slow neutrons as much as does hydrogen, it is not
particularly advantageous for a slow-neutron reactor. Liquid sodium
is also opaque, so that if anything goes wrong, the reactor must be
fixed without seeing the parts.

5. *Nuclear Fission and Fusion*

The inherent stability found in almost any slow-reactor design is true for fast reactors, except that there is no moderator to give a further safety factor for large changes. To complicate matters further, the liquid-metal (sodium)-cooled fast-breeder reactor (LMFBR) has a possible instability: If a bubble is produced in the boiling sodium, fewer neutrons will be captured, and the reactivity will go *up*. Fortunately, this can happen only in a very small volume, so this "sodium-void coefficient" is believed to be unimportant in present reactor designs.

These disadvantages have made LMFBR's complicated and, so far, expensive. However, the first reactor to produce electricity was a breeder (EBR I), and large prototype fast-breeders of 300-MW$_e$ size became operational during 1973 in the U.S.S.R., Great Britain, and France. Breeder reactors of 1000 MW$_e$ are being designed and are expected to be commercially competitive in Great Britain by 1980.

It is hoped that the fast-breeder reactor, when fully developed, will be safe and cheap. It promises to provide economically enough electricity to last 100,000 years, as the cost of uranium becomes too expensive to use in slow reactors, and using thorium ores after conversion to U^{233}. (Refer to Table 2-3.)

Although we have discussed the liquid-metal-cooled fast breeder, some work is proceeding on a gas-cooled fast breeder, a development from the Shell-Gulf gas-cooled thermal reactor, and a slow breeder using a molten uranium salt has been suggested.

Reviews of breeder-reactor technology may be found in references [4-12].

The environmental problems of breeder reactors are similar to those of other fission reactors: the large quantity of radioactivity must be kept under control. The safety issue arising from abnormal operation is different for a breeder than for other types of reactor, but not necessarily more serious. The disposal of radioactive wastes poses the same problems in both cases (Chapter 13). However, the production and transportation of large quantities of plutonium present unique problems both of spillage and of theft for subsequent military use (Chapter 14).

NUCLEAR FUSION

Let us not lose perspective on what we are doing: We are looking for an energy source to generate heat. Once we have sufficient heat energy, we will use it in conventional ways. With this in mind, we now look to another source of energy.

If we look again at the graph of Fig. 5-3, we see that if two nuclei combine together (fuse) to make a heavier nucleus but one that is still lighter than iron, there will be a release of energy. The problem arises of how to encourage this fusion.

160

Nuclear Fusion

The Stellar Fusion Reaction

The sun obtains its energy from nuclear fusion. Let us see how
that happens and whether that method can be controlled and used on
earth.

It is believed that hydrogen is the major part, if not all, of
the initial matter in the universe. As we have mentioned, gravitational attraction makes clouds of hydrogen form, which then condense
into large stars. The gravitational attraction gets stronger as the
particles get close together. Two protons in the cloud then can be
close enough to combine. The two protons have more mass than a deuteron, so that if they combine, energy will be released. The release
of energy is clearly a *sine qua non* of a reaction, but it is not enough;
a deuteron consists of a proton and neutron bound together, not two
protons. Therefore, a proton must, somehow, turn into a neutron.

This can happen, according to the rules of radioactive decay,
which are governed by what is called the weak interaction: a force
which changes neutrons to protons or vice versa (and other things not
relevant here). It is called weak, as the force is too weak to act
quickly. The spontaneous decay of the neutron is slow: a half-life
of 12 min. The reaction for the sun's heat is therefore slow. We
write it, in shorthand form, as

$$_1P^1 + {}_1P^1 \longrightarrow {}_1D^2 + \text{electron} + \text{neutrino}$$

The electron is necessary to balance the charge (or atomic number)
on both sides of the equation and the neutrino (whose properties need
not otherwise concern us) to uphold another of physics' conservation
principles, the conservation of angular momentum.

Within the sun, the heat generated by this reaction builds up an
outward pressure balancing the internal gravitational pull that would
otherwise cause the sun to collapse on itself into a superdense sphere.
This balance ensures that the reaction will go on until all the hydrogen
is consumed. If the reaction slows down, the internal pressure drops,
and gravitational attraction once again brings the particles close
together.

Terrestrial Fusion Reactions

The reactions that take place in the sun cannot take place on the
Earth. To hold the hydrogen cloud together by gravitation until the
slow interaction takes place requires a mass of material equivalent
to that in a star. With a small size there is no way of holding the
hydrogen together by gravitation until the slow interaction takes
place.

5. *Nuclear Fission and Fusion*

There are, however, faster reactions. The "ordinary" nuclear force is called the strong interaction and is about 10 million times stronger. This force *cannot* change protons to neutrons, but there are processes that can take place without changing protons to neutrons. An examination of an isotope table shows, in fact, that there are several.

Here, we mention only two, which involve the rarer forms (isotopes) of hydrogen, deuterium (D), and tritium (T):

(5-1)
$$_1D^2 + {}_1D^2 \longrightarrow \begin{cases} _2He^3 + {}_0N^1 + 3.3 \text{ MeV} \\ \\ _1T^3 + {}_1P^1 + 4 \text{ MeV} \end{cases}$$

(5-2)
$$_1D^2 + {}_1T^3 \longrightarrow {}_2He^4 + {}_0N^1 + 17.6 \text{ MeV}$$

These reactions proceed by the "strong interaction" and are rapid (10^{-27} sec). They have been much studied in the laboratory, but in order to make them a useful source of power many nuclei must so interact. They are illustrated in Fig. 5-9.

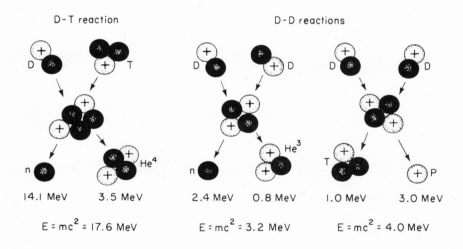

Fig. 5-9. Fusion reactions of D-T. Also possible is a D-He^3 reaction, producing He^4+H+18.3 MeV.

As we bring a deuterium nucleus (deuteron) close to a tritium nucleus (triton), the first notice one nucleus takes of the other is a repulsion between the two positive charges. This will prevent the two nuclei ever being close enough to each other to interact by the strong interaction. In the laboratory we overcome this by accelerating these particles very fast, but we can only accelerate a few particles at a time, typically 6×10^{12} particles/sec, whereas just 1 cm^3 of water contains 7×10^{22} hydrogen atoms. This will not do for power production.

We must increase the energy of many nuclei. When we have all the nuclei at a high energy, the material is said to be *heated*. (In fact, on a molecular basis, this is what heat is all about. Therefore, we must raise the temperature of the object.

Calculations show that it appears we would need a temperature of 10 billion degrees centigrade (10^{10} °C) to give the energy where the electrostatic (coulomb) force is just balanced by the nuclear force.

While, according to quantum theory, there is some probability of interaction even at lower temperatures, these lower temperatures are still in the range of 100 million degrees.

Such high temperatures are found in nature. The insides of stars are at temperatures of millions of degrees. On Earth, in certain electrical discharges in gases and when a fission bomb is exploded, these temperatures are reached. If a fission bomb is surrounded by materials containing deuterium or tritium, a hydrogen bomb is produced. However, the energy in the bomb is not controllable enough to produce continuous power.

When any material is heated to a high temperature, the energy is quickly transferred to cool walls on the sides, even for an insulator where the thermal conductivity is lower than for a conductor. So we are led to two basic possibilities for fusion.

First, raise the temperature so fast that the fuel is all consumed *before* heat escapes, or second, discover some container which does not conduct heat. Let us discuss the second way first.

Let us look at the possible techniques that are used to constrain a high-temperature gas so that it will not come into contact with the walls of the vessel. First of all, we will deal with a gas that is electrically charged because most of its atoms are stripped of one electron. Then we use a fundamental property of moving charged particles [Technical Note 5-7].

When an electrically charged particle is in motion, it generates a magnetic field. A wire carrying an electric current similarly generates a magnetic field. Conversely, when an electrically charged particle moves through a magnetic field, it experiences a force. Unlike the electrostatic (coulomb) force, it is not a direct attraction or repulsion, but a sideways push. An electrostatic force could prevent particles of one charge reaching the walls, but would attract particles of another charge; a magnetic field can prevent particles of both charges reaching the walls.

5. Nuclear Fission and Fusion

TECHNICAL NOTE 5-7

Ionization and Ionizing Radiation

Atoms have a central positively charged core and a surrounding negatively charged electron cloud, so that the charge on the whole atom totals zero. When a charged particle travels through matter rapidly, it can by collision separate an electron from the atom, leaving a net charge. The atom is then said to be ionized. *The atom is a positive ion and the electron a negative ion.*

An electron traveling at half the speed of light through normal air makes 2000 such ion pairs. The amount of energy expended to create one ion pair in air is 33 eV. A particle whose initial energy is 1 MeV can produce 30,000 ion pairs before it stops.

Radiation which produces these ions is called ionizing radiation. Alpha particles (charged helium nuclei) and beta rays (free electrons) ionize directly. Gamma rays (electromagnetic radiation like light or X rays but with a shorter wavelength) ionize indirectly by producing electrons.

Excessive ionization, when it occurs in human tissue can destroy it, and this is the hazard of radiation. When ionization occurs in air or a gas, the electrically charged ions can be detected and be a detector of this radiation.

In Fig. 5-10, we show how various arrangements of magnetic fields can contain particles. Generally a *toroidal* magnet is used, where the charged particles execute tight spirals and never strike the walls.

A number of approaches are being followed to develop an effective system for containment. Numerous criteria must be met to achieve success. There is a break-even point where the temperature will sustain itself by a nuclear reaction. Nuclei must hit each other often enough and at high enough an energy to produce energy. They must produce energy faster than it leaks away to the container. There are various approaches for reaching this break-even point. We can start with a denser gas, or a higher temperature, or try to keep it contained for a longer time. The different devices so far built are approaching the break-even point from different directions.

In addition to the break-even point for the reaction itself, we want some energy left over to supply the power for the magnet we use to establish the containment.

As the size of a fusion reactor is increased, the surface area only increases as $V^{2/3}$. Losses of heat to the surface become then relatively less important. It is now estimated that feasible fusion reactors will have a size of 5000 MW_e or more and be very expensive

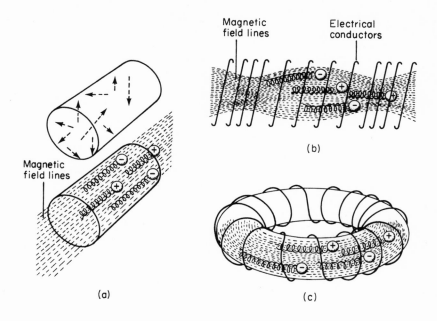

Fig. 5-10. Various arrangements of magnetic fields: (a) Particle trajectories without (upper) and with (lower) magnetic field; (b) linear magnetic confinement; (c) toroidal magnetic confinement.

($3 billion). To build many large devices before a feasible one is built is unattractive; therefore, intermediate size devices are being built, and the characteristics measured, to discover the best parameters.

We see also from Eqs. 5-1 and 5-2 that the D-T reaction liberates more energy than the D-D reaction. If we can demonstrate feasibility at all, we will first do so with the D-T reaction.

Advanced Details

There is a further problem with the D-T reaction; tritium is a radioactive material and does not occur naturally in large quantities. Any reactor must, therefore, regenerate tritium. This can be done by surrounding the reactor with a blanket of lithium of isotope 6 (Li^6). The plasma will lose energy by neutron emission from the fusion reaction itself. These neutrons will interact with the lithium:

$$_0n^1 + {_3}Li^6 \longrightarrow {_2}He^4 + 3({_1}T^3) + 4.8 \text{ MeV}$$

If we combine this with the D-T reaction, we effectively reach

$$_1D^2 + {_3}Li^6 \longrightarrow 2({_2}He^4) + 22.4 \text{ MeV}$$

Thus this combined reaction burns deuterium (which is plentiful) and lithium (which is not so plentiful). It is for this reason that in Chapter 2 lithium is included among the world's energy resources.

Neutron "multiplication" can be achieved by some capture on $_3Li^7$ according to the reaction

$$_0n^1 + {}_3Li^7 \longrightarrow {}_2He^4 + {}_1T^3 + {}_0n^1 - 2.5 \text{ GeV}$$

which is endothermic (meaning that it absorbs energy) and only works for fast neutrons. Another "multiplier" is the reaction

$$_0n^1 + {}_4Be^9 \longrightarrow {}_0n^1 + {}_0n^1 + {}_2He^4 + {}_2He^4$$

TECHNICAL NOTE 5-7

Magnetic Containment and Stability

A force is generated when a charged particle moves in a magnetic field. This force is always perpendicular both to the velocity of the charged particle and to the field.

It is then easy to see that in a uniform magnetic field, a charged particle will travel in a circle, the force always acting towards the center of the circle. It seems as if this particle can be contained. But there may be superimposed on this motion a drift out of the plane of the paper, and the charged particle can hit walls.

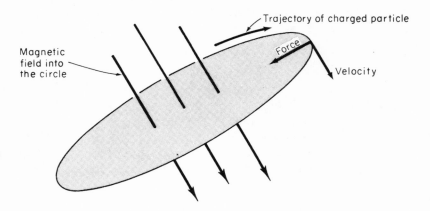

Fig. 5-11. Illustration of a charged particle being kept in a circular orbit by a magnetic field. The force is perpendicular to both the field and the velocity of the particle.

An increase of the field outside the paper can cause a particle tending to drift out of the plane to come back again. We see this by looking in a perpendicular direction and by sketching lines of magnetic field in Fig. 5-12. The strength of the field is proportional to the number of lines (this is not obvious, but is a property of magnetic fields), so that the charged particle has a force to bring it back to the circle. The circular orbit is then said to be stable. This principle is used in circular charged-particle accelerators (cyclotrons, betatrons, synchrotrons) and also in the linear "mirror" fusion devices. These are called Scylla, ISAR I, linear compression machines, or other incomprehensible names. Alternatively, we may build the magnetic field into a toroid, so that the charged particle executes a spiral which closes on itself (see Fig. 5-10). These fusion devices are given fancy names: Stellarator, Tokomak, Screw Pinch.

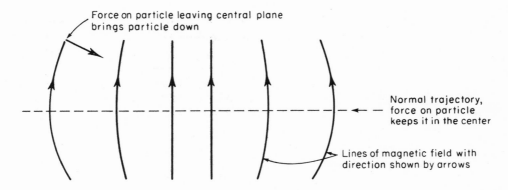

Fig. 5-12.   Force on charged particles moving into the paper.

This containment works for a few particles. But many particles exert electric and magnetic forces on each other. These forces can be stronger than the forces due to the magnetic field. It is hard to calculate the motion of one particle in a magnetic field. It is harder to calculate the motion of millions of particles, all interacting with each other. This study is called magnetohydrodynamics.
   In the first devices built, the forces of particles on each other soon made the orbits unstable. It is these instabilities that limit the maximum density of a plasma and its maximum containment time. Recently, however, progress has been made in understanding these instabilities, and it is widely believed that in larger machines, they will be no problem.

We also must find a way of removing heat from this fusion reaction and conveying it to some sort of heat engine, or whatever.

The lithium blanket, added to produce tritium, is a convenient method. Most of the energy will be absorbed in the lithium and will heat it. It melts at 179° C and will then flow readily. Its chemical properties are similar to those of sodium, in that it reacts with both water and air, though not so vigorously. Therefore, we can anticipate that industrial technology for handling liquid lithium in large quantities will be developed as part of the liquid-metal fast-breeder program (Chapter 4).

The liquid lithium would be pumped to a heat exchanger. At the moment all we can do is make a steam engine at a low temperature, but there is speculation that a turbine working with potassium vapor (boiling point 774° C) can be used.

The magnetic field is large, and we cannot afford to waste power in maintaining it; therefore, the magnet must be superconducting, that is, an almost loss-free magnet. This leads to a heat-insulation problem. Figure 5-13 illustrates various aspects of a conceptual fusion-reactor design. We see that establishing physics feasibility is roughly equivalent to operating the first graphite-moderated fission reactor at Stagg Field, Chicago, in December, 1941. Several other developing technologies must come together to establish engineering feasibility: large superconducting magnets, large vacuum insulation, high-temperature lithium-flow technology, and technology to prevent tritium release.

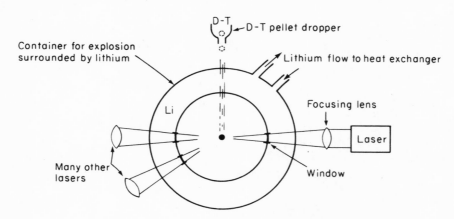

Fig. 5-13. Conceptual laser D-T pellet reactor model.

We now come to another approach to a feasible reactor, which consists of consuming all the fuel at a high temperature *before* heat leaks to the side: laser-induced fusion. A pulsed laser is capable of producing a pulse of coherent light, which when concentrated by a lens, gives a very high energy density. The scheme is simple: a small pellet of solid D-T (kept at 4° above absolute zero to prevent melting) is injected into an explosion vessel. A laser pulse is focused onto the pellet, heating it instantaneously to 10^8 °K, consuming the deuterium and tritium, and giving off heat. Then another pellet is dropped. This then is a series of explosions, rather like an internal combustion engine (Fig. 5-13).

This process may be feasible if a laser is developed that has 100 times the present power density in a pulse. Physical feasibility, however, does not demonstrate financial feasibility, and it is likely that there are many other difficulties ahead.

There are several recent articles about feasibility to which we refer the reader for more details. These are listed as references [13-22]. Reference [13] is especially recommended, as it contains reprints of many of the others.

Environmental Effects

A fusion reactor should be far superior to a fission reactor environmentally. First and foremost, it does not produce, or use, a material such as uranium 235 or plutonium, which can be used to make bombs; the problems of safeguarding the nuclear material and preventing its diversion to military uses do not arise. Laser-induced fusion is not quite so attractive. Anything that can explode in 10^{-9} sec can set off a bomb; and a hydrogen bomb without a uranium-fission bomb trigger may be easier to proliferate.

The attractiveness of fusion lies in the prospects of almost unlimited power, without the environmental disadvantages of fission. Therefore, it is being actively pursued. Varying estimates are given of the prospects for, and the time scale of, success. At budget time, optimists hold sway.

A "reasonable" guess [21] is that feasibility might be demonstrated by 1980 and the first power station by 1990, but not until well into the 21st century will fusion produce even 1% of the electricity we use.

Thermal pollution will occur with a fusion reactor, just as with any other power station using a heat engine. The projections of 50-70% efficiencies that are often quoted assume that in the intervening years high-temperature helium gas or potassium-vapor turbines will be developed. These improvements are likely to be adaptable to fission reactors also. More specific would be the prospects of direct conversion of fusion power to electricity that have been raised by many authors. These, however, are even more speculative than the fusion reactor itself.

What local problems are there of fusion-reactor accidents? They turn out to be few. The plasma only contains enough fuel for a short time, and new fuel has to be fed into it, rather like an oil or gas burner. The reactor operates in a limited regime: too little fuel, and it goes out; too much and power is reduced. Experts [14] have been unable to envision any situation in which a fusion-reactor plasma can cause an explosion, melt down, or even have local hot spots.

We must consider, however, the radiological hazards of escape of the material. Tritium is present in large quantities and must be controlled. The danger is that tritium might enter the water system, and become HTO and then be impossible to separate from common H_2O. However, it is estimated that even the liberation of all the tritium (6×10^7 C) from a reactor, by accident or sabotage, could not be a major catastrophe, because tritium dilutes quickly and in any case has a very low decay energy. This safety arises because the reactor burns its own tritium as fast as it is made.

We must be careful about producing radioactivity from neutron-induced radioactivity. In this regard, the only serious problem is likely to be the superconducting magnet, which must be kept close to the plasma to keep power down. The only acceptable superconducting wire for winding such a magnet is Niobium. On neutron activation the 10^8 gm present will produce 4×10^8 C of Nb^{93m}, which decays with a 5000-day half-life. This is 100 times less than for a fission reactor, and the Niobium is easier to handle.

Table 5-2 shows how the maximum possible steady leakage rate of 0.002%/day is estimated.

TABLE 5-2

Estimate of Tolerable Leakage Rate of Tritium
to the Total Biosphere of the Earth if All Electric
Power Came from Fusion Reactor Plants [20, 21]

Annual dose from natural radioactivity	125 mrem/yr
Assumed allowable dose from tritium	5 mrem/yr
Specific activity of body fluids for 5 mrem/yr	2.8×10^{-5} μCi/cm^3
Volume of water circulating in biosphere	2.7×10^{22} cm^3
Allowable tritium inventory in biosphere	1.5×10^{10} Ci
Allowable annual tritium leakage to biosphere	10^9 Ci/yr
Assumed power capacity per person	1 kW/person
World population in year 2000	6×10^9 people
World power capacity	6×10^6 MW
Allowable annual tritium leakage	0.14 Ci/kW-yr
Estimated tritium inventory in 3000-MW$_e$ CTR plant	6 kg
	(60×10^6 Ci)
	(20 Ci/kW)
Total tritium inventory in world-wide power-plant complex	12×10^{10} Ci
Allowable annual leakage rate of tritium in percent of circulating inventory	0.7%/yr
	(0.002%/day)

REFERENCES

[1] For example, "Handbook of Chemistry and Physics." Chem. Rubber Publ. Co., Cleveland, Ohio. Also, "Chart of the Nuclides." General Electric Co., Nuclear Energy Divn., San Jose, California.

[2] Hoffman, B. (1972). "Albert Einstein, Creator and Rebel." Viking, New York.

[3] Marion, J.B. (1973). "Physical Science in the Modern World." Academic Press, New York and London.

[4] Koch, L.J., and Paxton, H.C. (1959). "Fast Reactors." Ann. Rev. Nucl. Sci. Vol. 9, p.437.

[5] Graham, J. (1971). "Fast Reactor Safety." Academic Press, New York.

[6] Yevick, J.G., ed. (1967). "Fast Reactor Technology." MIT Press, Cambridge, Massachusetts.

[7] Seaborg, G.T., and Bloom, J.L. (1970). "Fast Breeder Reactors." Scientific American Vol. 223, p.13.

[8] Hafele, W., Faude, D., Fischer, E.A., and Lane, H.I. (1970). "Fast Breeder Reactors." Ann. Rev. Nucl. Sci. Vol.20, p.393.

[9] US Congress (1971). AEC authorizing legislation for fiscal year 1972, Hearings before the JCAE, Parts 1 and 2. USGPO.

[10] Rose, D.E. (1971). "LMFBR Safety." Nucl. Safety Vol.12, p.421.

[11] Culler, F., and Harms, J. (1972). "The Fast Breeder Reactor." Physics Today Vol. 24, No.5 (May).

[12] US Congress (1972). Hearings on liquid-metal fast breeder reactor demonstration project. JCAE, USGPO. (September).

[13] US Congress (1973). Hearings on controlled thermonuclear fusion, Part I, Hearings, Part II, Appendices. JCAE, USGPO.

[14] Chen, F.F. (1967). "The Leakage Problem in Fusion Reactors." Scientific American Vol. 220, p. 26 (July).

[15] Rose, D.E. (1971). "Controlled Nuclear Fusion - Status and Outlook." Science Vol. 172, p.797.

[16] Gough, W.C., and Eastland, B.J. (1971). "The Prospects for Fusion Power." Scientific American Vol. 224, p.50 (February).

[17] Lubin, M.J., and Fraas, A.P. (1971). "Fusion by Laser." Scientific American Vol. 224, p.21 (February).

[18] Post, R.F. (1971). "Nuclear Power, the Uncertain Uncertainty." Bull. At. Sci. Vol.27, p.42 (October).

[19] Post, R.F. (1970). "Controlled Fusion Research and High Temperature Plasmas." Ann. Rev. Nucl. Sci. Vol. 20, p.509.

[20] Postma, H. (1970). Nucl. News Vol. 14, p.57.

[21] Tuck, J. (1971). "Outlook for Controlled Fusion Power." Nature Vol. 233, p.593 (October 29).

[22] Nuckolls, J., Emmett, J., and Wood, L. (1973). "Laser-Induced Fusion." Physics Today August, p.46.

5. Nuclear Fission and Fusion

General References for Nuclear Power

Inglis, D. (1973). "Nuclear Energy." Addison-Wesley, Reading, Massachusetts.

Glasstone, S., ed. (1967). "Sourcebook on Atomic Energy." Van Nostrand-Reinhold, Princeton, New Jersey.

Foreman, H., ed. (1970). "Nuclear Power and the Public." Symp. at Univ. of Minnesota. Univ. of Minnesota Press, Minneapolis, Minnesota.

United Nations. Atoms for Peace conference papers, particularly 1971, Geneva. UN Reports, New York.

Ontario Govt., Canada (1973). "Nuclear Power in Ontario." Rept. No. 3 to Executive Council, Govt. of Ontario (February 16). Available from Ontario Govt. Bookstore, 880 Bay Street, Toronto, Ontario, Canada. Gives details of CANDU (heavy-water reactors) and a comparison to other types.

Descriptions of other specific types of reactors can often be obtained free from the advertising of reactor vendors:

PWR:	Westinghouse Electric Systems, Nuclear Power Equipment Divn., Pittsburgh, Pennsylvania
BWR:	Combustion Engineering, 1000 Prospect Hill Road, Windsor, Connecticut
	Babcock & Wilcox, Power Generation Divn., P.O. Box 1260, Lynchburg, Virginia
HTGR:	General Atomic Co. (Gulf-Shell), P.O. Box 608, San Diego, California
English Reactors:	Central Electricity Generating Board, 18 Newgate St., London, England

Other general reports are available from: Atomic Industrial Forum, New York, and Atomic Energy Commission, Washington, D.C.

PROBLEMS

1. Given $_{26}Fe^{56}$ [see Worksheet 5-4], how many protons, neutrons, and electrons are in this atom? Provide the same information for $_{26}Fe^{57}$.

2. 256 g of a radioactive substance decays into 16 g after 2 days. What is the half-life of the material?

3. Write a short essay on the principle and application of radioactive tracers in medicine.

Problems

4. The release of energy in nuclear processes is given by Einstein's equation, $E = mc^2$. Take the energy released in burning coal (Table 2-8) and calculate the change of mass using this equation. What fraction is this of the mass of the coal? Can this be determined by weighing the coal and its combustion products?

5. Compare the burning of coal in a fireplace to the fission of uranium. What in the fireplace corresponds to the critical size of a uranium assembly? What corresponds to the match in the nuclear case?

6. Assume that the first working fission reactor (3000 MW_e) is built in 2000 A.D.; and that 2 years later 2 more are built, 4 years later 4 more are built, 6 years later $2^3 = 8$ more are built, etc. How long will it be before the world's energy demand can be met by fission? (Take the demand figure from Chapter 3.)

7. What are the requirements for a material for a control rod for a nuclear-fusion reactor?

8. Explain the importance of delayed neutrons for reactor control. Is there any difference between uranium and plutonium fission? What other factors are important for reactor control?

9. Compare the fuel requirements of (a) a light-water reactor, (b) a graphite reactor, (c) a heavy-water reactor, and (d) a high-temperature graphite reactor with thorium blanket. How will the use of these reactors change the amount of uranium needed before 1990?

10. What feature of nuclear fission or nuclear fusion makes it unsuitable for direct replacement of oil in the world economy?

11. Can you think of any ways, other than fusion or fission, to produce nuclear power? Are there other sources of fissionable fuel, or fuel for fission? What are their disadvantages?

12. Compare a fusion reactor and a hydrogen bomb, and hence explain why a fusion reactor cannot explode.

13. From an atlas, estimate the volume of the world's oceans. In seawater, deuterium is mixed with ordinary hydrogen to the amount 0.015%. How much deuterium is there? If burned in a D-D reaction, for how many years will this supply the world with energy?

173

14. The following nuclear reaction takes place:

$$_0n^1 + {}_{92}U^{235} \longrightarrow {}_{92}U^{236}$$

$$\longrightarrow {}_{53}I^{139} + {}_{39}Y^{95} + 2{}_0n^1$$

(a) Compute the energy release from this particular mode of fission.

(b) Compute the number of fissions per year to produce 1000 MW_e of power at 30% efficiency and 80% plant availability.

Assume masses are

I^{139}: 138.955, Y^{95}: 94.945, U^{235}: 235.119, C^{12}: 12.000

in units in which

$$(1/12 \text{ mass } C^{12}) = 931.48 \text{ MeV}$$

$$1 \text{ MeV} = 1.602 \times 10^{-13} \text{ j}$$

Extra Question

Consider the possible ways in which a hydrogen bomb might be triggered. Explain why:

(a) A uranium bomb can be used as a trigger;
(b) The sun does not blow up;
(c) A fusion device incorporating a toroidal confinement will not blow up;
(d) Laser fusion research is classified as a military secret in the U.S.

6

Comparisons of Hazards
of Life

INTRODUCTION

In the following chapters we will consider a particular type of environmental problem: the hazard to human life. If there is a hazard to human life, there is likely to be a hazard as well to animal life and wildlife in general. However, in most cases man is more sensitive to chemical and radiation hazards than plants or animals, and therefore by turning our attention to human life we also turn our attention to other environmental effects.

Radiation, sulfur dioxide, and nitrous oxides all produce effects on human beings, even in quantities as small as a hundred times less than cause death to everyone exposed. We observe these effects by considering a large population that is exposed. Some people will die; others will not. It is usually a random process as to which person dies and which does not, and depends on accidental conditions, such as who is tired at the moment of exposure, or even which particular molecules of the body are exposed.

To assess these effects, we need to know how much of a toll will be taken by a given increase in a pollutant. To a physicist, or any scientist who deals in quantitative matters, "to know" means spelling out the cause-and-effect relationship as an equation whereby he can plug in a known cause and solve the equation to predict the magnitude and/or nature of the effect.

6. Comparisons of Hazards of Life

It is a good deal simpler to set up an equation to represent the motion of a falling body than one that will describe human or animal phenomena. Difficult as it may be, a considerable amount of good brain power is going into such efforts. Mathematical economics is a growing field that applies highly sophisticated and even abstract mathematics to develop mathematical models of economic systems. Theoretical biologists do the same for life systems. It would be fantastically useful to have a mathematical model of the human system to predict the effects of a new drug before laboratory tests; or to determine theoretically the information processing of cells with the goal of ultimately creating life. As an exercise for yourself, try to define what constitutes a simple living system. That fundamental problem has yet to be satisfactorily solved since we cannot even define life.

Our goal in this section is to work out a very simple model that will relate pollution to its effects on people.

The least complex model we can choose is a straight-line relation between pollution and, say, deaths. According to this model, twice the pollution gives twice the number of deaths. Examine Fig. 6-1.

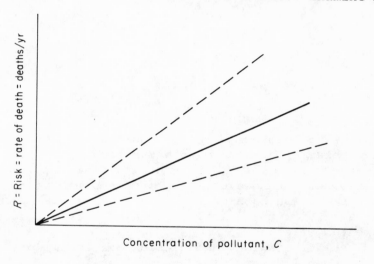

Fig. 6-1. Risk versus concentration of pollutant.

Three lines are drawn. How are we to know which of these or the infinite number of lines that could be drawn from the origin is most satisfactory? We don't know. We will not know until we get some statistics and plug them into the formula for a straight line:

$$R = aC + b$$

where R (the y axis) is the number of deaths each year per million of population exposed to a pollutant with a concentration C. If we obtain some numbers, we should be able to solve for *a*, the slope of the line, and also for the value of *b*, which in this case is zero (*b*=0). In Problem 6-1 further details of this curve will be brought to your attention, including one obvious contradiction with reality.

From this curve, we become abundantly aware that almost anything we do involves a risk, however small. In everyday life we take many risks. We instinctively balance risk and benefit. Risk versus benefit is the key concept to be dealt with in this chapter.

Risk/benefit analysis is anything but a hard and settled science. In fact, such studies are only beginning. How can we measure the relative benefit of an X ray in comparison to nuclear-generated electricity? How can we decide, in terms of policy, what is an acceptable risk? Let us discuss these questions in more detail.

COST/BENEFIT ANALYSIS

In American society, it is more conventional to refer to a cost/benefit analysis than to risk/benefit analysis. The two are similar, being related by the cost we assign to a certain risk.* For example, for diagnostic X rays used in medical practice, the benefit is early diagnosis; the risk is an increased chance of cancer or genetic damage. Increasing care in the administration of X rays can decrease the risk, but if the cost goes up thereby, fewer X rays may be taken and the benefit may therefore go down. Cost is thus an important parameter in estimating benefit.

We must be careful in risk/benefit analysis of not directly equating cost and death rate. We do not want to have to ask the imponderable question, "What is the value of a human life?" This is a theological question. But we can and must ask how much we can, or are willing, to pay to save a life, when by the nature of our precautions we do not know which life we are saving. It is easy to answer that we must pay whatever is required. But the most society can pay for all its many purposes is the total Gross National Product; if we pay too large a portion of it to save one life, we can afford less to pay for another. It is useless to ask a poor man to pay $20,000 to save the life of one child when he can't afford $2000 to feed another. By careful quantitative analysis, we hope to ensure that our efforts are best spent overall.

---

* At times we have been told that no benefit outweighs a risk, and that this is a theological matter. It may be a theological matter, but in life we *do* instinctively compare small benefits and risks; we must do this for public policy also. We may not yet have a theology to cope with this comparison, and our legal system does not do so properly. But these changes must come.

6. *Comparisons of Hazards of Life*

Thus we must not be surprised that a comparison of risk and benefit can lead to a lower standard for one use of radiation than for another, quite apart from the fact that different persons often make the assessments. For this reason, we must be cautious about comparing radiation hazards from nuclear power plants to those from chest X rays or cosmic rays. What must be compared are not the *risks*, but the risk/benefit ratios. For example, we may argue that estimates of the benefits from diagnostic X rays that put the benefit at more than 100 times that from electric power plants are unrealistic, even taking account of the relative cheapness of reducing the radiation from a power plant. Almost intuitively, it seems right to stop calculating in detail once the risk from a pollutant is less than 1% of other risks from similar sources. In the case of radiation, risk cannot be calculated absolutely at this low level because of the uncertainty of the existence of a threshold,* although risks can be compared.

We further emphasize the *necessity* of comparing risks from disparate uses of radiation. Many persons worry about average levels of radiation which are lower than 1% of the normal average background, and lower than 1% of the average diagnostic X-ray dose. It is worth pointing out that the *risk* caused by diagnostic X rays, which as we shall see in Chapter 9 is 100 to 10,000 times larger than the average risk due to radiation from the normal operation of nuclear plants, is believed by many scientists and physicians to be negligible because of a threshold, although the existence of a threshold is, of course, unproven and almost unprovable [see Problem 3].

Cost/benefit analysis takes as a premise that it is logical to consider all deaths as equal, no matter what causes them. That is the perspective we shall adopt in this book: We will express risk in terms of death rate. However, this comparison has three distinct parts: the death rate of persons involved in the enterprise itself, e.g., coal miners, construction workers, and radiation workers; the death rate of the general public, hurt by steady sulfur or radiation pollution; and the death rate of persons killed in accidents.

In the case of electric power, one can argue that a *direct* comparison must be made of the risks of the different methods of producing electric power where the *benefit* is the same. When doing this it is important to note that we know more about the detrimental effects of low-level radiation than we do about those of breathing and inhaling sulfur dioxide, nitrous oxides, mercury, radium, and other noxious materials from burning coal, oil, and even to some extent natural gas. We must not only compare the risks inherent in normal operation, but also the potentials for accident, which are disparate. Hydropower

---

* The point below which radiation has no effect on the organism, if such a "threshold" value for radiation exists. In most cases, we do not have enough data to know whether or not a threshold exists.

kills people by flood when dams break, and natural gas kills by explosion, but coal and oil rarely kill people by accidents of this nature. Nuclear power stations have not killed people yet, but the fear is that the potential for killing becomes greater just as the energy density becomes greater. Tied to the fear of immediate death is the threat of genetic damage and the despoiling of a large area for an indefinite period of time as a result of nuclear plant accidents.

Also disparate are the health and accident hazards to those who produce the power, e.g., coal miners, uranium miners, construction workers. A single coal mine explosion in Rhodesia in 1972 resulted in over 45 deaths to miners, but none to the general public.

To compare all these facets of power production is difficult, but necessary. Comparison of hazards becomes harder still when there is neither a common risk nor a common benefit, for example, in the comparison of hazards due to (tobacco) smoking and those due to automobile accidents. In such cases, we need much bigger differences in the risk/benefit ratio to make any decision.

A leader in attempting to put accidents in quantitative terms is F.R. Farmer [1] of the United Kingdom Atomic Energy Authority, who suggests that we plot both the probability of an accident and the number of persons killed thereby.

We shall assume with Farmer that all causes of death are equally acceptable to the public. Then to follow his reasoning, we turn to Worksheet 6-1 and mark off the following points on the graph:

persons killed in an accident	probability of an accident in a year
1000	10^{-4}
100	10^{-3}
1	10^{-1}

Connect these points by a straight line. Label this line the *accident limit line,* the area above it *unacceptable,* and the area below *acceptable.* According to this, an activity with a probability of one in 10^4 yr of an accident killing 1000 people is equal in acceptability to a probability of one in 10 yr of killing one person. But clearly, large accidents are psychologically much more important and less acceptable than the simple theory would allow. Thus Farmer simply modifies the upper part of his curve to bring it closer to reality. Crude as this model may be, it is at least a start toward finding risk levels acceptable to the public. We see this by an extreme analogy.

Small accidents throughout the world kill about 2 million people each year, or 4 billion people in 2000 years. This is "acceptable" in the sense that society will continue to exist, since births continually replace the deaths. But if a single accident were to kill 4 billion people, that is, the population of the whole world, society could not recover. This would be unacceptable even if it only happened once in 2000 years.

C. Starr [2], an American who is now director of the Electric Power Research Institute, has also urged some interesting ideas in risk/benefit analysis to help in national decision-making. He first tries to discover what level of risk people are willing to accept, and then attempts to relate it to the benefit of the activity. He lists the risk as the number of fatalities per hour a person is exposed. (This is a number much less than one, since we have fewer fatalities than persons exposed.) The benefit is hard to assess: in air travel, he considers benefit as the time saved compared to car travel; in electricity, he obtains the benefit by assuming electricity is a contributing factor to the national income.

The risk of disease can also be included.

Starr finds that for many involuntary activities, that is, activities over which we have little control, the risk is comparable to the risk from disease. This is plotted in Fig. 6-2. The curve here is plotted on semilogarithmic paper. Just as we know the equation for a straight line plotted on conventional cartesian graph paper, so too, we can write down the equation for this straight line on semilog paper.

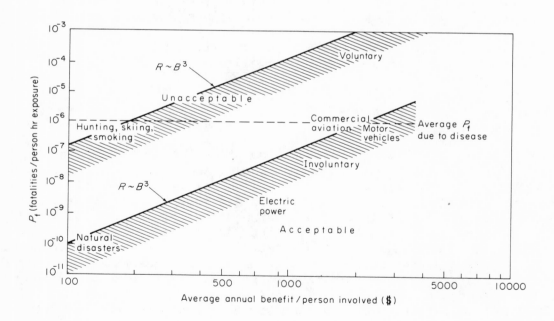

Fig. 6-2. Risk versus benefit for voluntary and involuntary exposure (R = risk; B = benefit) [2].

180

The Accident Limit Line

Assume that accidents that involve over 100 deaths in a single event are publicly unacceptable, no matter how infrequently they occur. Draw a modified limit line that reflects a reduction in the number of deaths per unit time by a factor of 10, i.e., one that would allow no more than 1000 deaths in 10^5 yr instead of 10^4.

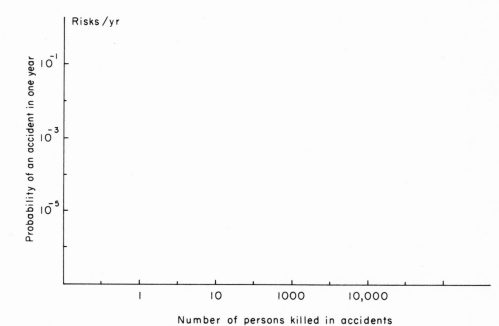

And doing so, the risk is found to be related to the cube of the benefit, that is,

$$R \propto B^3$$

[See Problem 6.]

Some activities on this graph are more dangerous than others, by a factor of about 1000. These are all voluntary activities, that is, work we could stop if we wished. Thus we must consider two separate acceptable risks for voluntary and involuntary exposure.

We have here no more than a very good try at obtaining the answer to the question of how much more risk the public will accept for additional benefits. (You should try to see how closely this applies in your own experience.)

Starr puts matters very well in terms of nuclear plants:

> The nuclear power plant... raises some fundamental questions about our societal approach to public risk. The dramatic aspect of the unfamiliar large catastrophe - but with exceedingly low probability - tends to draw both public attention and concern. Unlike natural catastrophes - earthquakes, typhoons, floods, tidal waves, etc. - society has not learned to place such hypothetical man-made events in an acceptable comparative perspective, particularly when they are poorly understood by the public. If, in fact, the low-release (radioactive) events are of more importance, the concern with imaginary large catastrophes may seriously distort both societal policy decisions and, as a result, engineering design emphasis.
> [3]

Perhaps the reason for the great concern about large accidents is the fear of destroying a whole section of society or even civilization itself, just as a single airplane accident some years ago killed the leading members of the Boston Skating Club and destroyed, for a time, U.S. dominance in international ice-skating competitions.

Other authors have written about various risks in modern life, but these have mostly ignored the risk/benefit criterion. As an example we give Table 6-1 [4], showing a comparison of various occupational risks.

Commoner [5] argues that there should be a third class of risk, less acceptable than the involuntary ones: those which risk destroying a large segment of society. Although it is not clear why this argument is distinct from $R \propto B^3$, using the graph of Starr instead of a linear relation $R \propto B$, we must be especially careful of any genetic damage, and therefore exposure to our young. "Survival of the fittest" has partially disappeared in our society as we struggle to keep everyone alive, but genetic damage is likely to persist through many generations

much more than formerly. For this reason, excessive radiation and
use of drugs by pregnant, or even fertile, women and by children is
of special concern.

TABLE 6-1

Lifetime Risk of Death as a Percentage of Total
Number of People Working in Selected Occupations [4]

Occupation	UK	US
Trawler fishing	5	-
Aircraft crews (civilian)	7	-
Coal mining*	2	5
Pottery (pneumoconiosis)	2	-
Construction	5	-
All manufacturing	0.3	0.5
All industries	-	1
US Atomic Energy Commission	-	0.3
40-yr occupational exposure to 1 rem/yr (all cancers)	0.6	0.6

* Including mining and quarrying.

We will proceed, therefore, to make comparisons in the following
chapters. In order to make these comparisons easy, we will express
them all in the one unit, "deaths per kilowatt-hour" of energy used
(including thermal losses at the power station). In doing this we will
make the assumption, which can be only approximately true, that the
death rate in each case is proportional to the power usage. This will
enable us to compare risks where the same benefit is obtained (e.g.,
energy produced), but not to decide what is an acceptable risk/benefit
ratio.

Life-Shortening

There are two methods proposed for obtaining some idea of what
an individual will accept. One is the concept of average life-shortening
and the other is a monetary estimate of risk. The two are closely
related.
The concept of life-shortening is based on the averaging of a risk
over the entire population. In the U.S., 50,000 people die in automobile
accidents each year, out of 2,000,000 total deaths per year. Each person
who dies loses about 20 years of his life. The average life-shortening
of each member of the population is then 20 yr × 50,000/2,000,000 yr,

or 6 months. There are some specific data on life-shortening due to radiation, which include not only the cancers we will discuss later but all causes of death [6]. It was concluded from a study of 82,000 obituaries of U.S. physicians that U.S. radiologists died 5.2 yr earlier than did other physicians. These radiologists used old practices and were exposed to an average of 1000 R. Thus, assuming a linear theory, an exposure of 500 mrem* shortens life *from all causes* by an average of one day.

We should modify this because exposure early in life may cause more life-shortening because of delayed effects (radiologists start exposure only at age 27-30). Also, the average life expectation is now greater, and delayed effects are therefore more significant. We take as a conservative figure, therefore, that a 100-mrem exposure shortens life by one day. This matches the cancer estimates if we *assume* that each cancer shortens life by 10 years.

No comparable study has been done for air-pollution accidents, but it is reasonable to assume that each air-pollution death is a case of life-shortening by at least a year. Then the life-shortening due to air pollution averaged over the whole population is also about one day.

This concept of average life-shortening has its drawbacks. Why should we average over the whole population and not merely over the part of the population at risk? A perfect safety record in the mines would lengthen life by perhaps a few hours averaged over the whole population, but many months averaged over all mines.

Monetary Value of a Risk

Lederberg [7] suggests that a monetary value be assigned to a risk, so each individual may easily compare risk and benefit. This is particularly easy when the hazard is expressed in an average as a *life-shortening*. None of us wishes to sacrifice a day of his life, but $1000, which could be spent on better medical treatment or on avoidance of a disagreeable task, might compensate.

Assigning what we can afford on a human life can be done in various ways. The total earning power is one: For example, in 45 years of earning, a breadwinner may earn $500,000, and we could afford perhaps that much to save a life. Life insurance is another: A common value for life insurance is $30,000. Still another is the maximum amount that courts can award in Massachusetts for death in an automobile accident, which is $15,000.

To be generous, let us assume we can afford $1,000,000 to save a life. We will later estimate that 2×10^7 men exposed to 1 rem, or 2×10^8 men exposed to 0.1 rem, *may* lead to 5000 deaths; one *man-rem* will give roughly 2.5×10^{-4} deaths, and it is worth $250 to reduce this cost to zero. A typical nuclear power station will add 4 to 400

---

* rem = roentgen equivalent man.

man-rem/yr and will then "cost" $1000-100,000/yr in this way. It does not, *by this reasoning*, seem worthwhile to spend $1,000,000 to reduce radiation to the lower figure; however, the psychological effects of nuclear power, and the involuntary nature of the exposure, make this reduction politically and morally necessary.

Others have given smaller numbers; Lederberg [7] assigns $100-500 per man-rem and Sagan [8] assigns $50. A comparison of such estimates is given by Ottway [9].

The monetary estimates can also be made for air pollution, but they have not been. If we take the most naive and simplest version of the sulfur-pollution problems as discussed in Chapter 8, an exposure to sulfur dioxide at the National Air Quality Standard (0.03 parts sulfur dioxide per million) increases the death rate by 3%. If we can afford the same amount of $1,000,000 for each life we save, we find a cost of $30,000 per lifetime for every person exposed to sulfur at the National Air Quality Standard.

This assessment is crude; it can and must be done better. [See Problem 8.]

POLLUTION TAX

Once we give a monetary value to the risk of a certain pollutant, there is a logical basis for a pollution tax. An obvious criticism of our past energy policy is that energy was artificially cheap because environmental effects were not considered in setting a price. This criticism is independent of the economic system; the company president in the board room and the commissar in the ministry have been equally misled by omission of these charges. It is in order to meet this criticism that a pollution tax is often considered [10].

President Nixon in 1972 proposed a pollution tax of $0.15/lb on sulfur-dioxide emission. As proposed, this tax seems unrelated to environmental consequences. At that time, the cost of removing sulfur from fuel oil at the refinery was $1.50/bbl, which with 3% sulfur in the oil works out to be about $0.10/lb, which is the cost differential between oils of high- and low-sulfur content (see Chapter 3). Such a tax will, therefore, act as an incentive to burn low-sulfur oil.

Much better, however, is a tax based on the consequences of pollution, and we *have* techniques sophisticated enough to devise one. The environmental effect of sulfur-dioxide emission in the oceans is presumed to be less than in New York City: the sulfur is soon absorbed by the ocean, where it becomes a small fraction of the existing sulfuric acid. Nixon's tax plan gave no credit for proper power-plant siting. Any pollution tax should give such credit. For radiation, the numbers exist: the tax for a nuclear power station can equal the integrated

radiation dose in "man-rems" (from a conservative calculation) multiplied by the cost ($250) per man-rem. For a typical power station
this will be between $1000 and $100,000.

The calculation for sulfur *can* be done for each power station.
We note that the average sulfur concentration in the Boston metropolitan
area (population 3,000,000) is about 0.003 parts per million (one-tenth
the National Air Quality Standard); this leads to 90 air pollution
related deaths, or a tax of $90,000,000 to be collected from all the
polluters. Probably $20,000,000 of this should come from the individual
owners of home oil heaters. Refinement of these calculations seems
a most important, but easy, task for public officials [11].

Recently, meteorologists have speculated that a sizable amount
of air pollution in the northeastern states originates at mid- and
far-western power plants. If proven, the issue will become far more
complicated.

REFERENCES

[1] Farmer, F.R. (1967). "Siting Criteria - A New Approach." IAEA
  Symp. on Containment and Siting of Nuclear Power Reactors, Vienna,
  April 1967, IAEA-SM-89/34. IAEA, Vienna.
[2] Starr, C. (1971). "Benefit-Cost Relationships in Socio-Technical
  Systems." In Symp. on Environmental Aspects of Nuclear Power Stations, 1970. IAEA, Vienna.
[3] Starr, C. (1973). "Benefit-Risk Analysis and National Decision-
  Making." American Physical Society Meeting, April,
[4] Sowby, F.D. (1971). In "Environmental Aspects of Nuclear Power
  Stations," p. 919. IAEA, Vienna.
[5] Commoner, B. (1970). In "Nuclear Power and the Public" (H. Foreman,
  ed.). Univ. of Minnesota Press, Minneapolis, Minnesota.
[6] Warren, S. (1956). J. Amer. Med. Assoc., Vol. 162, p. 464.
[7] Lederberg, J. (1971). "Squaring an Infinite Circle: Radiobiology
  and the Value of Life." Bull. At. Sci. Vol. 27, p. 43.
[8] Sagan, L. (1972). Science, Vol. 177, p. 487.
[9] Ottway, J.L., ed. (1971). "Risk vs Benefit: Solution or Dream?"
  Proc. Symp. Los Alamos Scientific Laboratory, Rept. No. LA 4860-MS,
  Los Alamos, New Mexico.
[10] Ramsey, N.F. (1971). "We Need a Pollution Tax." Bull. At. Sci.
  Vol. 26, p. 3.
[11] Wilson, R. (1972). "Tax the Integrated Pollution Exposure."
  Science Vol. 178, p. 182 (October).

General References

At a seminar in Washington, D. C., in 1971, several distinguished
people from many fields presented their views on benefit/risk analysis.

6. *Comparisons of Hazards of Life*

They have been published in an excellent compendium:

"Perspectives in Benefit/Risk Analyses for Decision-Making," Proc. Seminar on Benefit/Risk Analysis, Washington. Natl. Acad. Engineering, Washington, D.C. (1973).

A collection of papers from "Science and Public Affairs," Bull. At. Sci. 1971-72, on the "Energy Crisis" is available from Bull. At. Sci., 1020 E. 58th St., Chicago, Illinois. These contain much risk/benefit analysis.

PROBLEMS

1. Attempt an historical assessment of the risks that society has asked its members to accept. Discuss, for example, the average life insurance per person as a function of time; the average accidental death rate in a selected industry, such as merchant shipping, mining, construction, etc.
By extrapolating such curves to the year 2000, estimate the risks society is likely to ask its members to accept in that year.

2. It costs about $20 for an automobile manufacturer to install seat belts. It has been estimated that 5000 lives are saved every year in the U.S. by their use. About 9 million new cars are bought every year. How much is spent per life saved?
If everyone used seat belts, it is estimated that 15,000 more lives would be saved. How would the answer be changed? We have made no allowance for injuries reduced. Does this raise or lower the figure?

3. Refer to Fig. 6-1. How can we tell that this model will not be valid for all situations? [Hint: what would the curves have to look like when we reach large numbers?]
Why do the curves start at the origin?

4. Prepare an essay dealing with risk/benefit analysis of a long auto vacation trip.

5. Prepare an essay on the risks and benefits of such voluntary activities as flying, smoking, sex, etc., and determine a formula for your own unacceptable cutoff point.

6. Prepare a bibliography of reasonable length, which includes the multiplicity of views on the question of radiation hazards to man. Devise your own weighting scheme to assign some sort of a numerical factor to indicate how valid you find the arguments in each reference. State how you arrived at each value.

7. Let us assume that a new and extremely convenient form of jet aircraft is put into service. (Perhaps it provides greater comfort or speed than present planes.) Let us also assume that it is slightly less safe than present aircraft. If we assume the new plane will contribute 500 additional general aviation deaths per year, how much must the benefits increase before the plane will be found generally acceptable? (Use the formula that R is proportional to B^3, or Fig. 6-2.)

7

Environmental Problems
at the Source

MINING DISEASES

Coal "causeth consumptions, phthisicks and the indisposition of
the lungs... speedily destroy(ing) those who dig it in the mines ...."
So said John Evelyn in 1661; in the 20th century matters are little
better.

Twenty-five percent of coal miners get black-lung disease (pneu-
moconiosis) [1] from ingestion of coal dust. The situation has become
worse as mining efficiency increases, because the coal is broken down
more into slivers. About 4000 miners every year succumb to this disease.
Each of the factors contributing to disease and accident can be reduced,
but coal-mining accidents and black-lung disease have been shameful
facts of our civilization for a long time, and, if the past is any guide,
improvement will be slow. However, in Great Britain, stringent control
measures have reduced the incidence of black-lung disease from 8.1 new
cases per 1000 miners in 1955 to 1.9 per 1000 in 1967.

Now that new mining methods have been introduced to pulverize the
coal and extract it more efficiently, miners absorb it more efficiently
into their lungs! Therefore, until 1969 there was no improvement in
the control of black-lung disease in the U.S. A new law passed in 1969
will eventually force improved standards on mine operators, and we can
only hope that black-lung disease will be much reduced. Fortunately
also, underground mining is being reduced, and strip-mining is taking

over (as shown in Fig. 2-21), but progress is slow. A major business publication recently stated: "The 1969 act is not being fully applied and probably won't be for some time" [2]. Coal owners argue that the law was unnecessary and try to circumvent it, while other people do not think it powerful enough.

However, the miners have largely accepted their hazardous way of life. Those in Appalachia come from poor families and an area with chronic large-scale unemployment. This makes them less able to fight for improvement of their working conditions.

Uranium has been mined for centuries, particularly in Czechoslovakia, and has been used as a source of fluorescent, decorative glass. Uranium miners have been dying from cancer for centuries, as well as within the last decade [3, 4]. In the referenced survey [4], these deaths are classified according to the exposure to radon, a gaseous daughter of radium. A "working level" (WL) is defined as that combination which will give *ultimately* 1.3×10^5 MeV of α-particle energy in one liter of air. The "ultimately" is important because the radioactive substances from radon decay lodge in the lungs, and the subsequent radioactive "daughter" products stay in the body permanently.

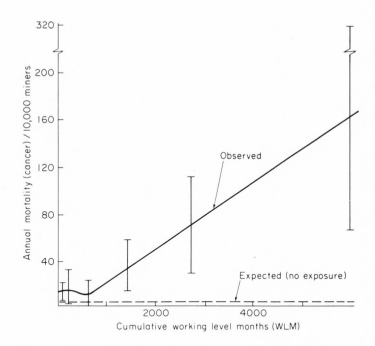

Fig. 7-1. Annual mortality (cancer) versus time on the job [5]. Note that these are well-attested cases *only,* and without allowance for a proportion of uncertain cases. The actual number of cases might be twice as great.

7. *Environmental Problems at the Source*

In Fig. 7-1 the relationship between cancer and exposure is clearly established, but radon may not be the sole cause. Miners of other base metals have three times the U.S. average cancer rate.

TABLE 7-1

Respiratory Cancer Deaths in Uranium Miners [3]

	Smokers	Nonsmokers
Person-years	26,392	9047
Cancers observed	60	2
Cancers expected on average basis	15.5	0.5

An interesting comparison was made by Lundin [5] (see Table 7-1), who correlated the mining cancers with smoking habits for some 3000 miners who had been mining for an average of over 15 years. A strong synergistic effect* was observed. Various reasons for this have been suggested: One is that the radon is preferentially absorbed into the lungs on the smoke particles. We are reminded of a suggestion that the cancers apparently caused by smoking tobacco are themselves due to the absorption of the radioactive element polonium into tobacco smoke and the subsequent ingestion of polonium in the lungs.

ACCIDENTS AT THE SOURCE

Since 1907, 88,000 coal miners have died in mining accidents in the U.S. These deaths are in addition to those caused by occupational diseases. Coal mining is very dangerous, because mines collapse and the methane in them explodes.

Even now, 200 men die each year from coal mining accidents and another 100 die in accidents transporting the coal to the power station. The first of these numbers comes from official U.S. statistics (shown in Table 7-2), the second is an estimate.

Petroleum is safer to produce: Only 150 men die each year in accidents at oil wells and refineries, in spite of the fact that oil supplies twice as much of our energy as coal. No particular disease problems are known.

---

* A synergistic effect is one due to multiple causes, any one of which would not produce the same total effect by itself.

TABLE 7-2

Mining Deaths at Source per Year (Based on 1965 Data) [6]

Fuel source	Accident deaths	Disease deaths (cancer or black lung)	Total deaths	Production (kW_th)	Deaths/kW_th
Coal	259	≈4000	4259	4×10^{12}	1×10^{-9}
Oil and gas	78	–	78	11.7×10^{12}	7×10^{-12}
Uranium*					
U^{235} only	≈20	≈7	≈27	8.6×10^{11}	3×10^{-11}
U^{235} and U^{238}	≈20	≈7	≈27	1.6×10^{13}	1.5×10^{-13}
Hydro, geothermal	–	–	–	–	0

* The production of power in the case of uranium is largely hypothetical, since much of the uranium was stored for bombs. The number given is calculated from the heat content of the fuel. Deaths at purification facilities for uranium are estimated.

191

There were 10 fatalities in uranium mining in 1965. The number in fuel-fabrication and processing plants is not separately available, but is probably about another 10.

Uranium ore is not used directly as it comes from the mines, as is coal; but since only a little uranium is needed, purification, which is necessary for successful reactor operation, does not add much to the cost of power. So far, much of the uranium and plutonium preparation has been for the manufacture of bombs - an activity that we hope will cease.

For bombs, the pure metal is used. When a pure metal is machined, fragments oxidize. This happens with many metals but particularly with uranium and plutonium, which can therefore catch fire. On May 11, 1969, a fire broke out at the bomb-fabrication facility at Rocky Flats, Colorado. Luckily, no member of the public received an overdose of radiation [7], but an overdose could occur at another time. Moreover, it was found that, from other causes, small traces of plutonium had been allowed to seep into the ground. Fortunately, the fuel used in a reactor is an oxide ceramic, so that this particular hazard exists for bombs but not for reactors. However, other hazards do exist.

Uranium is not particularly toxic, but plutonium is. Plutonium is nearly as radioactive as radium and, like radium, concentrates in biological systems. Whereas the total amount of radium in use before 1939 was only a few *grams,* thousands of *tons* of plutonium will be used as fuel for breeder reactors before the end of the 20th century.

"ROAD LIABLE TO SUBSIDENCE"

This is a common sign along roads in Staffordshire, England, where old mine workings, which thread their way beneath roads, fields, and villages, collapse as their wooden "pit props" decay. Figure 7-2 shows an example of such a building collapsing in Pennsylvania. Roads are made unsafe and farms unworkable.

The amount of subsidence varies from place to place. A study in the U.S. [8] shows that for every 1000 tons of coal removed, 0.2 acres of land subsides up to 4 ft. There is an average extraction efficiency of 60%, leading to about 800 acres of land damaged every year to supply a 1000-MW$_e$ power plant.

Solid wastes are produced and then are usually placed in unsightly slag heaps near the mine mouth. In the U.S., these wastes average 36 tons per 1000 tons produced, or 140,000 tons/yr for the 1000-MW$_e$ plant described (or 20 million tons for the whole U.S.). The disposal of these wastes is a formidable problem. The slag heaps are not stable, and in 1966 a slag heap, turned into mud by rain, slid into a school in Aberfan, Wales, killing most of the children. Similar accidents on the same scale occur frequently in the U.S.

Fig. 7-2. Subsidence at Coaldale, Pennsylvania, 1963.

Water must also be used in the mining of coal [9], amounting to
160,000 tons/yr. Estimates of the total acid drainage from underground
coal mines vary from 4,000,000 tons/yr [10] to 8,000,000 tons/yr [1].
This leads to 45,000 tons/yr of acid for the 1000-MW$_e$ plant.

STRIP-MINING

The demand for energy, the reduced amounts of conventional oil
and gas supplies in the U.S., and a reluctance to import as well as
limited imports of both fuels, will, as discussed earlier, lead to a
return to coal. The only way it seems that this can be done fast
enough is by strip-mining. There is plenty of coal near the surface
in the western states, but after a century we will probably have to
return to underground mining.

The environmental hazards of strip-mining are more obvious than
those of underground mining. When the overburden of topsoil is removed,
rainfall can wash onto the coal and lead to large quantities of acid
entering the water supply. Therefore, topsoil must be quickly replaced.
If slopes of more than 13° (1 in 4) are strip-mined, soil erosion is
very serious.

Government estimates [11] suggest that 13 tons of overburden must be removed for every ton of coal mined. Most of it is returned to the pits, but still 1/10 usually remains in dumps. The amount remaining in dumps is especially serious because acid can drain off. A rough estimate, assuming drainage for 10 yr, yields 30,000 tons/yr of acid from the coal needed for the operation of a 1000-MW$_e$ power station.

There is also an increase in the volume of the overburden, which can be greater than the volume of coal removed. If this takes place, geographical contours and the surface run-off patterns are also altered. There exist detailed measurements at a Kentucky strip-mine [12], which show that water run-off carries nearly 2000 tons/yr of suspended solids per square mile of disturbed area. It is probable that this draining and erosion goes on for some time after reclamation has started, which emphasizes the need for fast reclamation.

Fig. 7-3. Strip-mining operation in progress in Ohio (courtesy of American Electric Power Co., New York).

WORKSHEET 7-1

Strip-Mining

Assume that coal is present in a seam 15 ft thick just below the surface of the ground.

(a) How many cubic feet of coal are there per acre? (640 acres = 1 square mile; 1 mile = 5280 ft)

_____

(b) Convert (a) to cubic centimeters (2.54 cm = 1 in.).

_____

(c) Now determine the amount of coal mined:

in tons/acre _____

in grams _____

(Each cubic centimeter of coal is about 2 g.)

(d) With the cost of coal at $10/ton, what fraction of the coal's cost is necessary to reclaim the land?

_____

(e) If the land was worth $100/acre for the original purpose, discuss whether this reclamation will happen, why it should happen, and who should pay for it.

194a

194b

Fig. 7-4. Aftermath of a reclamation project in Ohio (courtesy of American Electric Power Co., New York).

The reclamation costs of strip-mined land are large in absolute amount [13]: about $300/acre for level ground, or $2700/acre for slopes of 13° in the eastern U.S.

On level ground it seems that reclamation may be a relatively inexpensive and easy operation. In Europe, where land is at a premium, it is reclaimed at once. The amount of reclamation necessary can be judged by adding the total amount of land strip-mined and dividing by the coal obtained. In this way, we find that 1500 acres of strip-mining is necessary to provide coal for one 1000-MW_e power station for one year.

Strip-mining reclamation needs water and fertilizer to encourage new growth, which requires more water than old growth. Therefore, it may be almost impossible to reclaim ground where the rainfall is less than 10 in./yr.

Figures 7-3 and 7-4 show strip-mining in progress and the aftermath of a reclamation project, respectively.

At the moment, there is inadequate control in the U.S. Mining companies may be bound by law to replace the landscape after mining, but they often delay, and paper subsidiaries can be formed that go bankrupt before restoration is complete. "Pay as you mine" must be the watchword.

Nor must we be content with forcing the mining companies to pay taxes; local taxes can be diverted to pay for schools or hospitals, leaving nothing for the environment. A trust fund seems like the right solution. Of the mining states, all but Alaska, Arizona, New Mexico, and Missouri have some laws. However, these laws are weak: Among other weaknesses, they only specify steps to be taken and not results to be achieved. Politicians are, at last, becoming concerned [14].

RADIOACTIVE HOUSES

People in Colorado have unknowingly built houses with and on radioactive mine-tailings (the waste from uranium mines). No one is sure of the extent of the hazard, but it has received wide publicity. Men have used radioactive stone and bricks from time immemorial. Grand Central Station in New York City, and the base of the Statue of Liberty, are made of radioactive stone from Millstone Point, Connecticut. The radiation dose at Grand Central is 470 mrem/yr. (The

TABLE 7-3

Radiation from Buildings [15]

	γ radiation (mrem/yr)	Radon-daughter concentration (working levels)
New York City (average)	–	0.002
Grand Central Station	90-550	–
Buildings in Florida phosphate areas	110-500	0.001-0.030
Buildings in Tennessee shale areas	70-190	0.001-0.038
National Capitol	30-180	–
Swedish houses		
Wooden	–	0.005
Brick	–	0.009
Concrete	–	0.018
Grand Junction,		
Colorado area	120-140	0.004
2400 residences	(≈100)	0.01
19 residences	(≈1000)	0.05
Sea-level background	100	–

average dose in buildings in Aberdeen, Scotland, is 250 mrem/yr, compared with the sea-level average of 100 mrem/yr.) This does not excuse the carelessness of mine operators in allowing mine-tailings to be used in construction, but it may put it into perspective. *All* building material, whether mine-tailings or not, should be tested for radioactivity and particularly for anything releasing radon gas, which can be inhaled [7].

In Table 7-3, we show a summary of radioactivity levels for buildings in various places.

REFERENCES

[1] New York Academy of Sciences (1971). The Sciences, June-July. See also US Govt. (1971). Social Security Bulletin Vol. 34, No. 10 (October). HEW, USGPO.

[2] Business Week (1971). "Will Tough Laws Stifle Coal Mining?" Business Week, May 16, p. 31.

[3] Federal Radiation Council (1967). "Guidance for the Control of Radiation Hazards in Uranium Mining." FRC Rept. No. 8, USGPO (also referenced in [4]).

[4] US Congress (1967). "Radiation Exposure of Radiation Miners," Parts I and II. Hearings before the JCAE, May-October. USGPO.

[5] Lundin, F.A., Lloyd, W., Smith, E.M., Archer, V.E., and Haladay, D.A. (1969). Health Phys. Vol. 16, p. 371. (More recent statistics obtained from Dr. Shields Warren compare 160 cancers among smokers and 1 among nonsmokers; see also "Biological Effects of Ionizing Radiation." Natl. Academy of Sciences Report, 1973.)

[6] US Govt. (1965). "Statistical Abstract of the United States"; (1969). "Work Injuries in Atomic Energy." US Dept. of Labor Rept. 385. USGPO.

[7] Giller, E.B. (1969). Testimony to Joint Committee on Atomic Energy, hearings on environmental effect of producing electric power. USGPO.

[8] Delson, J.K., and Frankel, A.J. (no date). "Residuals Management in the Coal-Energy Industry." US Dept. of Interior Rept., USGPO.

[9] US Govt., Dept. of Interior (1966). "Water Use in the Mineral Industry." Bureau of Mines Circular 8285, USGPO.

[10] Fortune, M. (1972). "Environmental Consequences of Extracting Coal - Underground Mining," in "Electrical Power and Human Welfare." Amer. Assoc. Advan. Sci. Rept. (August).

[11] US Govt., Dept. of Interior (1971). "Surface Mining and Our Environment." USGPO.

[12] US Govt., Dept. of Interior (1970). "Influences of Strip-Mining on the Hydrological Environment of Parts of Beaver Creek Basin, Kentucky, 1955-1966." US Geol. Surv. Paper 427C, USGPO.

[13] Walsh, E. (1972). "West Virginia: Strip Mining Issue in Moore-Rockefeller Race." Science Vol. 178, p. 484.
[14] New York Times (1973). (Several articles during the year.)
[15] US Congress (1971). "Use of Uranium Mill-Tailings for Construction Purposes." Hearings before the Subcommittee on Raw Materials of the JCAE, October. USGPO.

General References

A dramatic account of problems facing U.S. coal miners is given in:

Caudill, H.M. (1963). "Night Comes to the Cumberland." Little, Brown, Boston, Massachusetts.

Various references show that even ash can be reclaimed to an agriculturally useful state, on level ground and with adequate rainfall, for example,

Barber, E.C. (no date). "Win Back the Acres: The Treatment and Cultivation of DFA Surfaces." Central Electricity Generating Board Paper, 18 Newgate Street, London.

PROBLEMS

1. From the data of Table 7-1, how much would the risk of lung cancer be reduced if only *nonsmokers* were employed as miners?

2. By what factor must the exposure be reduced so that miners have no more lung cancer than other radiation workers? (Take from Chapter 9, Table 9-5, an "allowance" of 5 rem/yr, and a cancer incidence of 5000 cases/yr per 200 million people per 100-mrem exposure.)

3. Explain how increasing the ventilation in the uranium mines or in the schools built with uranium mine-tailings in Grand Junction, Colorado, can *reduce* the radiation exposure. Comment on what the release of radioactivity from one place to the atmosphere means.

4. Examine Table 7-3 and compare with cancers observed in Fig. 7-1. How many extra cancers would be observed if *all* Americans lived in concrete instead of wood buildings (compare working-level months)? Assign a "cost" of $1,000,000 to each cancer, and with this budget outline a procedure for moving Americans to safer buildings. Is this sensible or is it a fantasy?

5. Draft a strip-mining law with all the environmental and fiscal protection necessary to ensure that any environmental damage is restored and that any left to future generations is prepaid.

6. Assume that we must mine more coal in the next 40 years to satisfy demands for energy. Should the emphasis be on strip-mining or on underground mining? State your reasons clearly and outline the mechanism(s) by which government can direct industry into the desired route.

8

Air Pollution

We believe that all citizens have an inherent right to the enjoyment of pure and uncontaminated air, and water, and soil; that this right should be regarded as belonging to the whole community; and that no one should be allowed to trespass upon it by his carelessness or his avarice, or even by his ignorance. This right is in a great measure recognized by the State, as appears by the General Statutes.

> State Board of Health
> State House
> Boston, Massachusetts
> October 1869

Not for a hundred years were these words heeded; now we have the National Primary Air Quality Standards (Table 8-1). Large U.S. cities already exceed these standards.

PARTICULATE EMISSIONS

It is quite true that perhaps 60 percent of the fly ash goes up through the stack. This ash is of such light fluctuant nature that it is dissipated over a wide area before precipitation occurs and no trouble can be expected from this source, although the... tonnage put out... seems great.

So said Herington [1], referring to the usual type of coal burning done in a pulverized-fuel (PF) plant. This outlook is now unacceptable. Utilities have built higher and higher stacks to spread the particulates over ever wider areas, but the volumes of fuel have increased, and public acceptance of pollution has decreased.

TABLE 8-1

National Primary Air Quality Standards [2]*

Pollutant	Amount in air ($\mu g/m^3$)	Equivalent proportion in air (ppm)	Interpretation
SO_2	80	0.03	Annual arithmetic mean
	365	0.14	Maximum 24-hr concentrations to be exceeded not more than once per year
Particulates	75		Annual arithmetic mean
	260		Maximum 24-hr concentration
CO	10	9	Maximum 8-hr concentration
	40	35	Maximum 1-hr concentration
Photochemical oxidants	160	0.08	Maximum 1-hr concentration
Hydrocarbons	160	0.24	Maximum 3-hr concentration
NO_2	100	0.05	Annual arithmetic mean

* These standards are exceeded in many U.S. cities. For a summary of the evidence for concentrations, release, and medical effects, see the Air Quality Control Criteria reports issued by the U.S. Environmental Protection Agency.

8. Air Pollution

Typically, 10% of the weight of coal goes off as fly ash. This fly ash consists of many small solid particles, which are borne aloft by the gaseous products. We will consider the gaseous products themselves later.

TECHNICAL NOTE 8-1

Stokes' Law

Before we discuss the effect of examinations of these particles, we must discuss a fundamental law of the physics of fluids, Stokes' law. This law tells us the limiting rate of fall of a small spherical particle in a field of force (gravity, centrifuge, electrostatic precipitator) through a fluid (air).

As Galileo was the first to show systematically, large objects fall through the air at the same velocity, independent of their densities; however, this does not apply to small objects, which are subject to air resistance. The frictional force (resistance) on such a small particle is

$$F = -6\pi\eta a v$$

where η is the viscosity of the fluid (molasses is more viscous than water), a the radius of the sphere (for simplicity and to a good approximation, the particles are assumed to be of spherical shape), and v the velocity of the particle.

The limiting velocity, that is, the greatest velocity the particle can have, may be found from the above equation.

When the particle moves at a steady velocity, it is not accelerating. Therefore, the net force on the particle is zero. Thus, when the particle is moving at this steady velocity, the force of friction cancels out the force of gravity. Thus, the force downward, the force of gravity, is equal to the upward or backward force F, as given by Stokes' law. The force due to gravity on the particle is the weight of the particle. As a sequence of equations, we would write:

$$F_{gravity} = F_{friction}$$

$$weight = 6\pi\eta a v$$

from which we can solve for the velocity.

Small particles, those with a diameter of less than 5 μm (microns, 5×10^{-6} m), can stay in the air a long time, since their velocities of fall are less than wind velocities. A centrifuge at the power station can remove particulates, but only the largest ones are removed, not those of less than 5 μm, which continue to float. An electrostatic precipitator can do better; the particles are attracted to metal plates that have a high voltage across them. The force of attraction to these plates is proportional to the area of the particle. The plates are periodically washed. Again, smaller particles, because they are not strongly attracted to the plates, are harder to remove.

We must beware of the significance of statements made by a proud electric utility that 99% of fly ash is removed; this may include only 50% of the small particulates that stay in the air longer and are, therefore, more dangerous than the large ones. The particulates from coal vary with the source of the coal, but we list in Table 8-2 approximate figures for the U.S. in 1966. Some of the impurities are variable and hard to judge. The radium content is based on the same fraction of fly ash as in the Tennessee Valley Authority's Widow's Creek plant. The mercury content has been measured by helicopter observations of coal stacks in Illinois and Missouri and has been found quite large. Most of the mercury entering the human body is introduced through the food chain; the average amount ingested probably does no harm [3], but this is a different method for ingestion into the body and can add to the problem. Other heavy elements may be released in similar quantities. A more complete study of mercury release by coal burning *worldwide* has been made by Joensu [4]. We divide this by 3 (the United States burns about 1/3 of the total amount) to get an estimate of the pollution in this country. Estimates for other trace elements are gleaned from various sources [5,6,7].

SULFUR-DIOXIDE POLLUTION FROM FOSSIL-FUEL PLANTS

Sulfur is an impurity in most coals and oils, and, as these fuels are burned in the power stations, sulfur dioxide (SO_2) is among the exhaust gases. This gas has well-known effects on human beings [7, 8]. Most individuals show bronchial response to SO_2 at concentrations of 5 ppm (parts per million) (14 mg/m^3), and more sensitive people at 1 ppm. The odor can be noticed at concentrations which are 10 times lower. Sulfuric-acid mist (formed by interaction of the SO_2 with water vapor) is 10 times more irritating, but its effects are highly dependent on the size of the particles that are in the atmosphere with the SO_2. In addition, there seems to be a synergistic effect with particulate matter when the particulates promote the conversion of SO_2 to sulfuric acid (H_2SO_4). Indeed, Ferris [7] suggests a "mixed" air quality standard - particulate concentration multiplied by SO_2 concentration to be less than 4000 $(\mu g/m^3)^2$.* [See Technical Note 8-2.]

TABLE 8-2

Particulate Emissions in U.S., 1966 [4,6,8]

	Millions of tons	Kilograms per person
Total coal consumed	600	3000
Fly ash *released*		
Electric power stations	2	10
Other stationary coal stations	6	30
Transportation	1	5
Miscellaneous	12	60
Radium-thorium released*	1×10^{-10}	5×10^{-10}
(all coal)	(100 Ci)	(1/2 μCi)
Mercury released**	10^{-3}	5×10^{-3}
Vanadium (400 ppm in oil)	≈ 0.2	≈ 1
Other		
Nickel	≈ 0.1	$\approx 1/2$
Beryllium	≈ 0.001	≈ 0.005

   * Based on radium-thorium in Widow's Creek coal, assumed all radium [5, 6].
   ** Based on 1 ton/yr in Illinois and Kansas as representative of the country [4].

TECHNICAL NOTE 8-2

Catalysis

   A catalyst is a substance that increases the rate at which a chemical reaction takes place. Many industrial processes would be impossible without catalysts. Recently, catalytic converters for automobile exhausts have been in the news (see Problem   ).
   There is yet another important property of catalysts beyond their affecting the speed of chemical reactions. The catalyst is recovered chemically unchanged at the end of the reaction. Although the catalyst

---

   * 1 μg (microgram) = 0.000001 g.

Sulfur-Dioxide Pollution from Fossil-Fuel Plants

is not consumed, it is universally agreed that the catalyst enters into the chemical reaction but is subsequently regenerated. Let us look at an example. The following reaction is slow:

(1) $2SO_2 + O_2 \xrightarrow{slow} 2SO_3$ (sulfur dioxide to sulfur trioxide)

The combination of nitrogen oxide with oxygen is a fast one, as is combination of nitrogen dioxide and sulfur dioxide. These two reactions are written as:

(2) $2NO + O_2 \xrightarrow{fast} 2NO_2$

(3) $2NO_2 + 2SO_2 \xrightarrow{fast} 2NO + 2SO_3$

Going back to reaction (1) and adding NO to the SO_2 and O_2, we would have

$$2NO + 2SO_2 + O_2 \xrightarrow{fast} 2SO_3 + 2NO$$

In the end, the NO will not have been consumed, but it took part in the reaction. The catalytic reaction of concern to us on p. 203 is

$$2SO_2 + O_2 + 2SO_3 \longrightarrow SO_3 + H_2O \longrightarrow H_2SO_4$$

In this case, many catalysts are effective. Particulates and the nitrogen oxides are probably the most important for air pollution, since particulates and oxides are usually present simultaneously.

Finally, an epidemiological study of acute air-pollution "episodes" suggests that much lower SO_2 concentrations (0.1 ppm) can be detrimental to health. Although the cause is not conclusively demonstrated to be SO_2, this seems the most likely cause (provided that particulates are also present).

Table 8-3 shows the total emissions of SO_2 in the U.S. in 1963, 1966, and 1970; Table 8-4 shows the emissions in selected large cities. The amount is huge and is still increasing. We must, however, relate this to the concentration at various parts of the cities. The total man-made SO_2 is only 10% of that released naturally worldwide, yet it is obvious that the concentration in the cities is mostly man-made, and the increase over the natural background amount is very large.

Among the cities listed in Table 8-4, Chicago suffers the greatest amount of SO_2 release, with approximately 600,000 tons/yr. Clearly, 600,000 tons is not to be found in the air of that city at any given time. We see from the table that when a sample of air is analyzed, 0.12 ppm of that sample are SO_2. In Worksheet 8-1 we use this datum to determine the average life of the SO_2 in the air. It is found to be three days.

TABLE 8-3

Atmospheric Sulfur-Dioxide Emissions by Source: 1963, 1966, 1968 [11]*

Process	1963		1966		1968	
	Tons $\times 10^3$	% of total emissions	Tons $\times 10^3$	% of total emissions	Tons $\times 10^3$	% of total emissions
Burning of coal						
Power generation (211,189,000 tons, 1963 data)	9580	41.0	11,925	41.6		
Other combustion (112,630,000 tons, 1963 data)	4449	19.0	4700	16.6		
Subtotal	14,029	60.0	16,625	58.2	20,100	60.9
Combustion of petroleum products						
Residual oil	3703	15.9	4386	15.3		
Other products	1114	4.8	1218	4.3		
Subtotal	4817	20.7	5604	19.6		
Refinery operations	1583	6.8	1583	5.5		
Smelting of ores	1735	7.4	3500	12.2		
Coke processing	462	2.0	500	1.8		
Sulfuric acid manufacture	451	1.9	550	1.9		
Coal refuse banks	183	0.8	100	0.4		
Refuse incineration	100	0.4	100	0.4		
Total emissions	23,360	100.0	23,562	100.0	33,200	100.0

* A small amount of this tonnage is converted to sulfuric-acid mist before discharge to the atmosphere. The rest is eventually oxidized and/or washed out. Only under unusual meteorologic conditions does accumulation occur. The increasing output of sulfur oxides due to increasing power demand is evident.

TABLE 8-4

Sulfur Dioxide and Nitrogen Dioxide: Emissions and Releases
for Selected Cities, 1966 [8]

		Average concentrations, 1962-67 (ppm)	
	SO_2 (tons)	SO_2	NO_2
Chicago	600,000	0.12	0.14
Pittsburgh	400,000	-	-
Philadelphia	200,000	0.09	0.08
Los Angeles	180,000	0.02	0.12
Washington	35,000	0.04	0.07
Denver	33,000	0.01	0.06
1971 Air Quality Standard*		0.03	0.05

* Listed for comparison.

It is clear that the SO_2 concentration in Chicago exceeded the
National Air Quality standard, for short times, of 0.1 ppm (3×10^{-4}
g/m^3) more than half the time!
A study of how air pollutants distribute themselves from their
source shows that the way they will spread is determined by the wind,
how high above the ground they are released, the temperature, the
general weather conditions, as well as other factors. This information
is put into an *experimentally* derived equation, which requires assigning numerical values to the plume of a smokestack and plugging in the
weather conditions to allow the observer to predict the spread of the
pollutant. [See Technical Note 8-3.]

TECHNICAL NOTE 8-3

The Spread of Pollution; Chimneys

*The spread of pollution from a stationary source can be calculated
using the following equation developed by Sutton:*

$$C = \frac{Q}{2\pi u_x \sigma_y \sigma_z} \exp\left(\frac{-y^2}{2\sigma_y^2}\right) \left\{ \exp\left[-\frac{(z-h)}{2\sigma_z^2}\right] + \exp\left[-\frac{(z+h)^2}{2\sigma_z^2}\right] \right\}$$

8. Air Pollution

where C is the pollutant concentration in quantity per unit time;
Q is the total quantity of pollutant emitted in a given time by a
chimney stack of height h; the coordinate axes are taken as x along
the wind, y perpendicular to the wind, and z vertical; u_x is the wind
velocity; σ_y and σ_z are arbitrary constants that are determined by
the weather conditions and vary with x.

   Note that much empirical data must be available in order to use
this equation and predict the spread of pollution.

   As shown in Table 8-5, σ_x and σ_y increase with x. This equation
becomes useful when we put in average meteorological conditions. Pasquill [12] listed several typical conditions, which bear his name (Pasquill A, Pasquill F, etc.). Pasquill A is very turbulent air, Pasquill
F steady air. Rogers and Gamertsfelder [13] have tabulated values of
σ_y and σ_z for typical meteorological conditions, with f, the frequency
of occurrence. (A detailed discussion of this equation is given in
[14].)

TABLE 8-5

Meteorological Data for Atmospheric Release Calculations*

Weather type	A	B	C	D	E	F	G
Probability of weather condition	0.019	0.081	0.136	0.44	0.121	0.122	0.08
Wind velocity, u_x (m/sec)	2	3	5	7	3	2	1
Distance, x (m)				σ_z (m)			
200	28.8	20.3	14	8.4	6.3	4.05	2.63
500	100	51	32	18	13	8.4	5.5
1000	470	110	59	32	21.5	14	9.2
2000	3000	350	111	51	34	21.5	13.7
5000	–	1900	230	90	57	35	23
10,000	–	–	400	140	80	47	31
20,000	–	–	650	200	110	58	37
50,000	–	–	1200	310	150	75	48
100,000	–	–	1800	420	180	90	55

* Table adapted from [13].

Lifetime of SO_2 over Chicago

This is a rough calculation that will tell us the average lifetime of SO_2 in the Chicago area. It is again another example of how to make a rough calculation without elaborate mathematics or detailed data. For the purposes of our estimate, we would be satisfied to know the answer to an accuracy of several days.

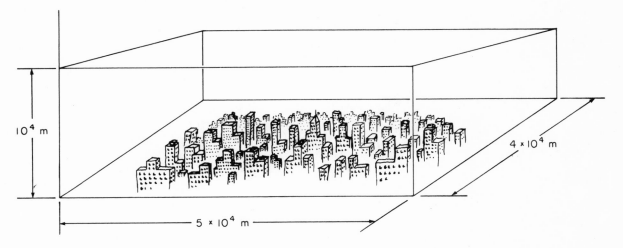

Assume the volume of the air in metropolitan Chicago to be as shown in the diagram.

(a) Calculate this volume.

_____

(b) Given that the 600,000 tons/yr of SO_2 is equivalent to 6×10^{11} g/yr, how many grams of SO_2 per cubic meter would be in the air of Chicago if all 600,000 tons were contained at one time?

_____

(c) The average concentration of particles in the air of Chicago at any time is 0.12 ppm. Refer to Table 8-1 and work out a conversion factor that will give this density in grams/meter^3.

_____ g/m^3

(d) From the answers to (b) and (c), show that the average life-time of SO_2 in the Chicago atmosphere is 3 days.

Sulfur-Dioxide Pollution from Fossil-Fuel Plants

However, a very important general prediction can be made from this equation: the concentration of the pollutant can be reduced by a tall stack. Not only does this increase the sideways distance until the plume hits the ground, but, in a case of temperature inversion, the hot gases can break through the inversion layer to calmer air above.

In Tennessee (TVA) smokestacks of 1000 ft are now built, and 800-ft stacks are being built in England. This has almost completely avoided the old problem of air trapped in a temperature inversion; however, the SO_2 gets spread more widely. Unofficial complaints have been made by Swedish officials to the United Kingdom Central Electricity Generating Board (400 miles away!). When asked to comment, an engineer said, "When we started on this programme we never dreamt we would be so successful; I still don't quite believe it."

The prevailing wind suggests that Sweden actually gets its increased SO_2 concentration from Germany and that the increased sulfuric-acid concentration in Norwegian waters can be laid at England's door. However, this is not proven, and work with radioactive sulfur as a tracer is being started to understand these plumes in detail [15].

A secretary of a local conservation society recently suggested how to clean the air: "Find the president of the local electric utility company and leap for his jugular vein." This was a good first approximation a few years ago, but in large cities the polluters are now those with small smokestacks: hospitals, industries, houses, and autos. In other words - *us*.

The ultimate fate of SO_2 is probably the ocean, which can absorb much more than we are now producing. The lifetime of SO_2 in the atmosphere is much shorter than that of CO_2, which is several years. The emissions of SO_2 are 20 times less than those of CO_2, but background air concentrations are a million times less.

Junge [16,17] estimates a lifetime for *industrial* SO_2 of 4 to 21 days, and a lifetime in the troposphere of 21 to 40 days.

Sulfur Reduction

There are many ways of reducing SO_2 concentrations, and most are being attempted. First, we can burn low-sulfur fuel. Coal has a sulfur content ranging up to 3.4%, but in the Arizona strip mines coal with a sulfur content of only 1% is found. Low-sulfur oil is found in Nigeria and Libya. Also, it is possible to extract the sulfur from the fuel. For oil this is fairly simple and is being done at some refineries.

Prior to the 1973 Middle East price increases, low-sulfur oil commanded what was then a premium price; in 1972 it was $4.75/bbl, as compared with $3.25/bbl for 2-1/2% sulfur oil. In 1972, low-sulfur oil increased the cost of electricity by $0.007/kWh, or 7 mils/kWh (1 mil = $1/1000). The premium price of $1.50/bbl for low-sulfur oil was determined by the cost of refining the oil. This price, and the difficulty of refining a solid like coal, led to the development of procedures for removal of SO_2 in the flue gases.

Early attempts (1935) at Battersea and Fulham power stations in London met with limited success and were later abandoned: by washing the stack gases, they washed sulfuric acid into the river Thames. At the time the Thames was totally polluted, but fish have recently been seen at Westminster Bridge, and pollution of the river is no longer acceptable.

From 1965 onwards, work has intensified. Some procedures that are being developed are listed in Table 8-6. The catalysts vary: limestone, potassium, magnesium. The magnesium-oxide (MgO) method by Chemco has the interesting feature that the sulfur recovery (in the form of sulfuric acid) can take place at another location [18]. The cost estimates vary and depend heavily on the value of the sulfuric acid produced. If *all* the SO_2 were converted to sulfuric acid, the value of the sulfuric acid would drop to zero and might even represent a disposal problem. These methods can follow electrostatic precipitation for fly ash and can remove the last traces of large (bigger than 5 μm) particulates.

We must note, however, one important feature of all these methods: the thermal efficiency of the power station is reduced by 6%. Moreover, none yet work reliably in large units. The limestone, dry [lignite, $Ca(OH)_2$] or wet (limestone), methods produce calcium-sulfite crystals ($CaSO_3$) or calcium sulfate (gypsum or plaster of paris, $CaSO_4$), which block the system. (These systems are summarized by Spaite [19].)

A much better procedure would be to change the combustion process. Squires [20] argues that "paths of technological development exist that could lead to suppression of SO_2 from coal and at the same time to a lower cost of power."

All our great power-generating stations based on coal use pulverized-fuel (PF) firing. This could ultimately be replaced by high-temperature traveling (fluidized) fuel beds, where the coal is powdered into a "fluid," which can be on a conveyor belt. Above 1100° C, ash sticks to ash and no longer comes out of the stack. Squires [20] lists many ideas for possible new coal-burning plants. One is shown in Fig. 8-1.

The coal is partially burned in a "fluidized bed"; the "lean" (short of oxygen) fuel gas is burned to run a high-temperature gas turbine, and the volume of gas is low enough at this stage that cleaning is cheap.

Another method of sulfur-oxide reduction is the removal of power stations to rural areas, so that the problems are more widely diffused. However, this is not acceptable to the inhabitants of these rural areas. The power-station complex near Four Corners, Arizona, is an example. The first power station produces 400 tons of SO_2 a day.

TABLE 8-6

Methods of Sulfur-Dioxide Removal from Stack Gases [8,20,21]

Method	Developer	Removal fraction (%)	Comments
Dry			
$MgO \longrightarrow MgSO_3$	Chemco (Boston Edison)	90	High temperature necessary
Absorption on alumina (Al_2O_3)	US Bureau of Mines	85 (small scale)	
Absorption on manganese (Mn)	Mitsubishi (Japan) (oil only, so far)	90	Emission of Mn compounds
Absorption on lignite (CaOH)		80	
Wet			
Calcium, manganese	Combustion Engineering (St. Louis, Kansas)	80	Also removes particulates; clogs badly
$K_2SO_3 \longrightarrow K_2S_2O_5$	Wellman-Lord	90	
Li, Na, K carbonates sulfates	North American Rockwell	95	Proposal only
$NH_3 + H_2O \longrightarrow NH_4SO_3$	Mitsubishi (Japan)	90	5-MW test only
MnO, MnOH absorption	A.G. für Zinkindustrie Wilhelm Grillo (Germany)	90	
$SO_2 \longrightarrow SO_3 \longrightarrow H_2SO_4$ (plus catalyst)	Monsanto	90	Temperature control needed
Coke absorption	Reinluft (Germany)	95	Large recirculation requirement; self-ignition of coke
$NH_3 + SO_3 + H_2O \longrightarrow (NH_4)_2SO_4$ (V_2O_5 catalysis)	Kiyoura (Japan)	93	

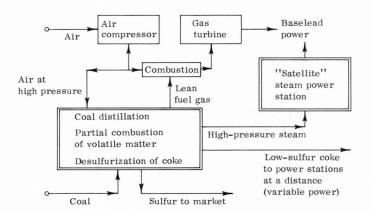

Fig. 8-1. A pioneering Coalplex directed toward recovery of sulfur and generation of clean power [20].

This is five times less than the amount produced in Chicago, yet the air in the area was normally so clear that the pollution from this station affects the air for 200 miles! Four more stations are under construction at this location. Fortunately, if particulate and sulfur controls are installed, air pollution from five can be less severe than that from the first one alone.

That techniques for abatement of SO_2 can be successful is already clear from results in New York City. Figure 8-2 shows the average sulfur concentration in the air of Manhattan from 1965 to 1970. The improvement is obvious and can occur in any city that wishes to take the trouble.

The effect of the improvement of burning habits in cities since 1960-65 is very obvious. In England the "London Law" banned the use of soft coal (containing much sulfur) from the center of London and other cities. Electricity companies installed high smokestacks. The SO_2 and particulate concentrations have dropped dramatically, by about a factor of 3.

In Chicago, for example, home heating by coal has almost vanished since 1972; natural gas is now the most commonly used fuel for this purpose. The Commonwealth Edison Company of Chicago uses natural gas to generate electricity during the worst air-pollution months (around September), and Commonwealth Edison is the principal user of nuclear power in the United States as of 1974. As a result, the SO_2 concentration (annual average) has dropped from 0.1 to 0.03 ppm over most of the city, but this cannot continue as long as natural gas is running short. There are two remaining areas of high SO_2 concentration: in Hyde Park, where a group of old homes near the University of Chicago

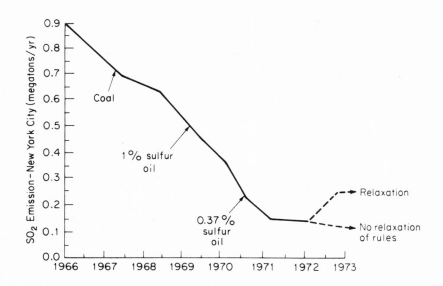

Fig. 8-2. Amount of sulfur dioxide emitted from sites within New York City in recent years, according to estimates by the New York City Dept. of Air Resources. [Figure adapted from Harte, J., and Socolow, R.H., eds. (1972). "Patient Earth." Holt, New York.]

still burns soft coal, and near some new apartment buildings, which are heated with oil that is burned without a smokestack. In this case, there is no plume to carry the SO_2 high into the air; since it is heavier than air, the SO_2 hangs close to the ground.

Gasification of Coal

Another way to avoid many of the environmental problems of coal is to convert it into gas at the coal mine and then transport the gas by pipeline. SO_2 would be converted to H_2S gas, which is easily removed, and the fly ash would be left behind.

Coal gas has been known for nearly 100 years but, as traditionally made, had a low heat content and was always made locally. Research is now in progress toward a cheap method of making coal gas with a high heat content, so that transportation costs are not prohibitive.

The techniques for coal gasification are economically viable [22] and have been the subject of important recommendations to the President of the U.S.

Presently [23] the price of natural gas in New England depends on the supplier. The gas at the end of the pipeline from Texas costs $0.42/1000 ft^3. Liquified natural gas imported from Algeria costs

$1.37/1000 ft^3. It is estimated that the gas from coal will cost $0.90/1000 ft^3 at the coal mine [23]. We note that a residential customer pays for an average of all these, plus a distribution cost. It is about $2.00/1000 ft^3. If gasification becomes cheaper (or natural gas becomes more scarce), it will become, once more, one of the important methods of using energy and will replace a direct use of coal. It deserves, and is getting, a natural priority for research funds.

NITROGEN OXIDES FROM FOSSIL-FUEL PLANTS

As utilities in eastern U.S. cities have switched from oil to gas (to avoid SO_2 pollution), nitric-oxide (NO) emission (the principal source of photochemical smog) has increased, due to an increase in combustion temperature. NO is not an irritant in itself, but under certain circumstances it can combine with oxygen to form the more toxic and irritant nitrogen dioxide (NO_2), or other equally hazardous compounds. Although NO_2 reacts with water to form nitric acid,

$$3NO_2 + H_2O \longrightarrow 2HNO_3 + NO$$

just as SO_2 reacts to form sulfuric acid, the nitric acid does not seem to cause the same sort of pollution problems as sulfuric acid. Nitrogen dioxide, a reddish-brown gas with a pungent odor, is a primary cause of urban smog. The presence of nitrogen dioxide also enhances the SO_2 reaction to sulfuric acid. The combination of scattering of light by aerosols (droplets of liquid), and absorption of light by nitrogen dioxide, produces the visibility reduction noticeable with photochemical smog.

The major source of nitric oxide is the natural decay of biological sources; these, and man-made sources in the U.S., are listed in Table 8-7. Since the nitrogen oxides so readily convert into each other, they are listed together as NO_x. (As usual with pollutants, the U.S. produces about half the world's man-made nitric oxide.) The man-made sources are relatively unimportant except in cities. In cities on the U.S. East Coast, the stationary power sources, in particular those burning natural gas, dominate automobiles in producing the nitrogen oxides. The switch from oil to natural gas in some of the major eastern U.S. electrical utilities has helped to reduce SO_2 emission, but may have made smog worse by increasing nitrogen-oxide emission. (In a similar way, the initial reduction of hydrocarbons in automobile exhaust also increased nitrogen-oxide emissions!)

The levels of nitrogen-oxide concentration at which there are air-pollution problems depend on the presence of oxidants, such as carbon monoxide or ozone, in the air that can set up the NO $\longrightarrow$ NO_2

Nitrogen Oxides from Fossil-Fuel Plants

TABLE 8-7

Summary of Annual Nationwide Emissions of Nitrogen Oxides, 1966-1968 [24]*

Source category	1966	1967	1968	Change, 1966-1968
Transportation	7.6	7.6	8.1	+0.5
Motor vehicles	6.6	6.7	7.2	+0.6
Other	1.0	0.9	0.9	-0.1
Fuel combustion	6.7	9.5	10.0	+3.3
Coal	4.0	3.8	4.0	N**
Fuel oil	0.9	1.0	1.0	+0.1
Natural gas	1.6	4.2	4.5	+2.9[†]
Wood	0.2	0.2	0.2	N
LPG and kerosene	–	0.3	0.3	+0.3[†]
Industrial processes	0.2	0.2	0.2	N
Solid-waste disposal	0.5	0.6	0.6	+0.1
Miscellaneous	1.7	1.7	1.7	N
Man-made	0.5	0.5	0.5	N
Forest fires	1.2	1.2	1.2	N
Total				
Man-made	16.7	19.6	20.6	+3.9
Natural sources	500	500	500	

* Figures given in tons × 10^6.
** N = negligible.
[†] Apparent change. (Emission estimates added in 1968 from sources not included in 1966.)

reaction. Levels of 0.1 ppm are high. This is clearly exceeded in many cities, but levels of 0.02 ppm are found in less heavily populated areas. There is a variation during the day. Figure 8-3 shows the variation in concentrations for selected pollutants on one day in Los Angeles. The nitric oxide converts to nitrogen dioxide when the oxidants are present simultaneously with sunlight.

Reducing Nitrogen-Oxide Emission

"No proven process... is currently available for substantial removal of NO_x from combustion stack gases" [25]. Possibilities include reduction of temperature in combustion, reduction of excess air in combustion, flue-gas recirculation, scrubbing, catalytic oxidation

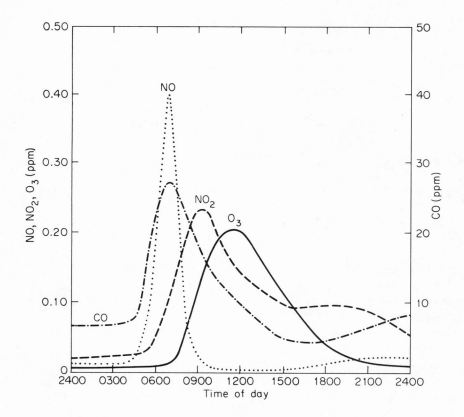

Fig. 8-3. Average daily 1-hr concentration of selected pollutants in Los Angeles, California, July 19, 1965 [14].

using ammonia, absorption on charcoal or other solids. If, as we described in Chapter 5, magnetohydrodynamics (MHD) works, the combustion temperature will be increased, and the nitrogen-oxide problem made worse [15].

    If we burn oil or natural gas, the flow of fuel can be carefully controlled and air supplied in no more than exactly the correct amount. NO formation will then be reduced. This is not so easy to control as for coal. Another procedure is to adjust the burners for tangential firing instead of horizontal firing. This reduces the flame temperatures and hence the NO concentration by 50%. In all cases, individual adjustment of the burners seems necessary. Catalysis, decomposition, and absorption do not seem practical for large burners, although catalytic decomposition seems to be the preferred method for automobile exhausts. A good review of these methods is given in Sensenbaugh [26].

    If, however, nitrogen oxides can be widely dispersed over the countryside (and this dispersal must clearly be over an area much larger than Los Angeles County), they may be beneficial as a very effective method of wide dissemination of nitrogen fertilizers.

EPIDEMIOLOGICAL EFFECTS OF AIR POLLUTION

It is hard to measure and isolate the epidemiological effects of any one variable in the presence of so many others. We show two examples of work in the field: first, a plot of deaths in Oslo, Norway, as a function of SO_2 concentration (Fig. 8-4) [27]. A linear curve fits well, and we see that the death rate would be doubled at a concentration of 1 ppm. This study suggests that even if U.S. cities kept to the National Primary Air Quality Standards, 3% more people would die than would if the air were pure. This is less than 3% of all deaths, since we should not apply the increase to effects unrelated to pollution. This leads to 50,000 deaths per year. (See Problem 2.)

Confirming evidence comes from Japan [28]. Figures 8-5, 8-6, and 8-7 show the incidence of chronic bronchitis as a function of SO_2 *released* in several cities; again, the U.S. air quality standards are shown, and, again, there is an effect that is linear even at low concentrations. This effect is the same for men and for women and *adds* to the effect from tobacco smoking.

Since SO_2 cannot be isolated from the other air-pollution effects, these graphs should be considered to include deaths from *all* air-pollution sources. Of course, the deaths might have nothing at all to do with air pollution; SO_2 concentrations are high in cities and so are the tensions of modern life. Thus some deaths might simply be due to these tensions! Nevertheless, we tentatively ascribe them to air pollution.

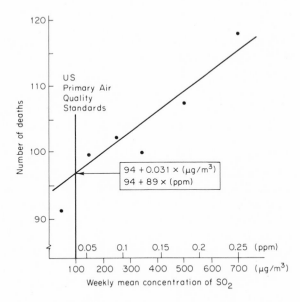

Fig. 8-4. Total number of deaths for 156 winter weeks in Oslo, Norway (1958/9 to 1964/5) [27].

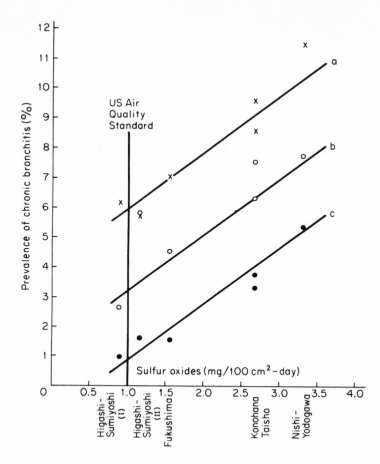

Fig. 8-5. Correlation between the prevalence of chronic bronchitis and sulfur-oxide precipitation for several Japanese cities. Curve a, 11-20 cigarettes/day; curve b, 1-10 cigarettes/day; curve c, nonsmokers [28].

A more systematic correlation between death rate and air pollution has been described in a series of papers by Lave and Seskin [29,30, 31]. They considered many variables in a systematic study of the causes of deaths in the U.S. for the years 1960 and 1961: average particulate concentrations C ($\mu g/m^3$), sulfate (SO_2) concentrations S ($\mu g/m^3$), population density in persons per square mile (P/mile^2), proportion of nonwhites in the population (NW), proportion of old people in the population ($\geq$65).

They find an equation for the death rate (deaths/10,000 yr) DR:

$$DR = 20 + 0.04C + 0.7S_{min} + 0.001(P/mile^2) + 40(NW) + 700(\geq 65)$$

$$= 20 + 4.5 + 3.3 + 0.7 + 5 + 58$$

$$= 91 \quad \text{(for 1961 deaths)}$$

218

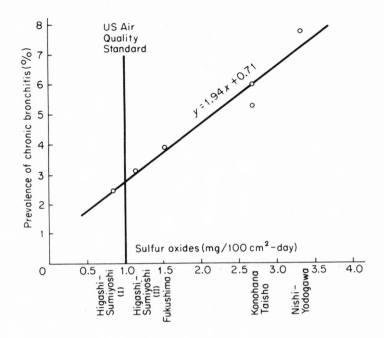

Fig. 8-6. Correlation between the prevalence of chronic bronchitis and sulfur-oxide precipitation in Japan without separation of smokers and nonsmokers [28].

(We have rounded off the numbers and simplified the notation.) The correlation is with the minimum biweekly value (S_{min}) of the sulfate concentration, and the arithmetic mean is about two to three times this value. For the 1961 data used by Lave and Seskin, the total deaths in the U.S. is 60,000 from sulfate pollution and 80,000 from particulates.

This yields a number within a factor of 3 of what we obtained from a naive look at the Norwegian data.

An important feature of the Lave and Seskin study is that it seems to confirm that *low levels* of sulfur concentrations are very important. Public attention has been focused on air pollution "episodes" in which many people have died in a few days. The major health hazard seems to be the wide distribution of low sulfur concentrations. This cannot be confirmed in laboratory experiments, and it may be a spurious effect, but we must, at the moment, give it serious consideration. The importance of widespread low concentrations of pollutants is the main thrust of many recent papers and books on pollution.

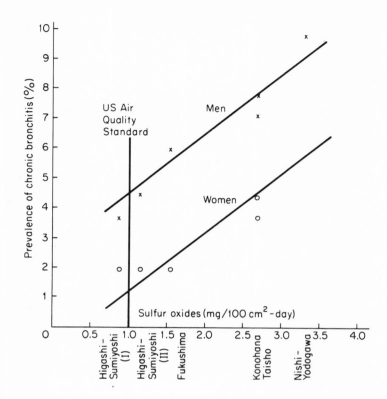

Fig. 8-7. Correlation between the prevalence of chronic bronchitis and sulfur-oxide precipitation in Japan. Data are separated by **sex** [28].

Lave and Seskin [30] emphasize the difficulties of this type of study:

> As happened with the association between smoking and lung cancer, statistical investigations are always subject to the charge that the association is really only a spurious correlation. The only way of ruling out spurious correlation is to observe all the variables which are causes of mortality and to control for each, explicitly or implicitly. There are an indefinitely large number of possible "true causes" that can be thought up by an imaginative critic. Here, and elsewhere, we have attempted to control for relevant factors which could be the "true causes" (for which we could obtain data). Unless the relationship between air pollution and mortality is specified formally in a theory, no conclusions about causation can be drawn.

Our explorations of the association may or may not be indicative of a causal relation; they do explore the empirical relationships in some detail.

When pathologists try to describe such a linear graph of death rate versus concentration on a detailed basis, they run into trouble. It is well known that the human body has many repair mechanisms to adjust small insults to the system, and this suggests that there might be a concentration threshold below which there is no effect.

But a linear relationship *is* suggested by the data; it is conceivable that a different mechanism, without repair, operates for low concentrations. This could account for the death of old and sick people at quite low concentration levels, followed by the death of healthy people as the concentration increases. We will see in Chapter 9 the paucity of evidence for or against a threshold in radiation-induced leukemias and other cancers. Although the mechanisms are almost certainly different in the two cases, prudent public policy demands that we take the conservative linear approach in each case.

Hot air would normally rise from a city, but if there is a temperature inversion at a certain altitude, the hot air cannot rise, and the air beneath is trapped. This effect is shown in Fig. 8-8.

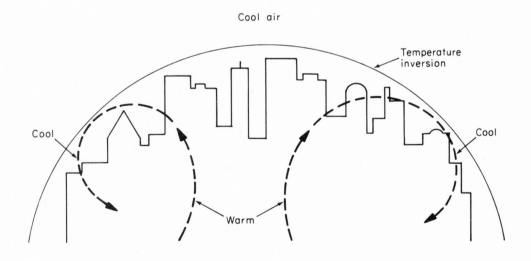

Fig. 8-8. The temperature inversion over cities' air traps the air; over rural areas there is no trapping.

The death rate from heart trouble, pneumonia, and bronchial diseases increases markedly during such periods. Although a causal connection between the death or illness rate and air pollution is suggested, we must not forget that the possible cause of any such death or illness could have been the sudden changes in weather which caused the air pollution.

In Table 8-8, we list some of these air-pollution episodes. Assuming that the death rate is due to the same cause as the Oslo deaths, and that the SO_2 concentration is a good index of that cause, we calculate the excess deaths for each of these episodes. (Note that in December, 1952, nearly 4000 more Londoners died in the space of one week than is usual.) The agreement indicates that there may be some truth in this sort of reasoning.

In spite of the uncertainty as to medical cause, we tentatively assign 50,000 deaths/yr to air pollution caused by the 16×10^{12}-kWh/yr energy usage in 1965 (Table 8-9). Then air pollution causes 3×10^{-9} deaths/kWh. We hope this is decreasing. We note this figure is 1/3 of Lave and Seskin's figure for 1961.

TABLE 8-8

Some Air-Pollution "Episodes" [8,24,32,33,34]*

		SO_2 level (ppm)	Excess deaths	Rough prediction from observed Oslo data
Dec. 1930	Meuse Valley, Belgium	9	63	?
Oct. 1948	Donora, Pennsylvania	1	20	?
Dec. 1952	Greater London	1.5	3900	3000
Nov. 1953	New York City	0.2	360	400
Jan. 1955	Greater London	0.3	240	700
Jan. 1956	Greater London	0.5	1000	1000
Dec. 1956	Greater London	0.3	400	700
Dec. 1957	Greater London	0.5	800	1000
Jan. 1959	Greater London	0.2	200	400
Dec. 1962	Greater London	1.0	850	2000
Dec. 1962	Osaka, Japan	0.1	60	?
Nov. 1966	New York City	0.5	168	500

* In all cases, particulate matter was also present.

TABLE 8-9

Public Pollution Deaths, 1965*

	Total power produced, including losses (kWh)	Deaths	Deaths/kWh
Coal and oil (mostly SO_2)	1.57×10^{13}	50,000	3×10^{-9}
Hydro	0.19×10^{12}	<1	$<5 \times 10^{-12}$
Nuclear (radiation hazard)	3.00×10^{11}	<1	$<3 \times 10^{-12}$

* For nuclear power we take 1970 figures.

REFERENCES

[1] Herington, C.F. (1970) "Powdered Coal as a Fuel," p.273. Van Nostrand-Reinhold, Princeton, New Jersey.

[2] US Govt. (1971). "Federal Register." USGPO.

[3] Goldwater (1971). Scientific American.

[4] Joensu, O. (1971). "Fossil Fuels as a Source of Mercury Pollution." Science Vol.172, p.1027.

[5] Chou, J.J., and Earl, J.L. (1972). "Lead Isotopes in North American Coal." Science Vol.176, p.150.

[6] Dole, S.H., and Papetti, R.A. (1973). "Environmental Factors in the Production and Use of Energy." Rept. R 992 RF, Rockefeller Foundation, New York.

[7] Shroeder, H. (1970). "A Sensible Look at Air Pollution from Metals." Arch. Environmental Health Vol.21, December.

[8] US Congress (1970). "The Environmental Effects of Producing Electric Power," Vol.1, Parts 1,2, Vol.2, Part 2, combined index Vol.2, Part 2, pp.810,1733. Hearings before the JCAE, USGPO.

[9] Martin, J.E., Hayward, E.D., and Oakley, D.T. (1969). US Public Health Service Rept. reprinted in [5, pp.773-810].

[10] Ferris, W. (1971). "Report on SO_2 Pollution to the World Health Organization." UN, New York.

[11] US Govt. (1970). "Air Quality Control Criteria for Sulfur Oxides." US Dept. of Health, Education, and Welfare, Environmental Protection Agency Report. AP-50. USGPO.

[12] Pasquill, F. (1961). "Atmospheric Diffusion." Van Nostrand-Reinhold, Princeton, New Jersey.

[13] Rogers, T., and Gametsfelder, C.C. (1971). In Proc. Conf. on Environmental Effects of Nuclear Power Stations Vienna, 1970. IAEA, Vienna.

[14] Turner, J. (no date). "Handbook for Atmospheric Dispersion Estimates." Dept. of Housing, Education, and Welfare, Environmental Protection Agency, USGPO.

[15] In [8], p.452.

[16] Junge, C.E. (1960). J. Geophysics Res. Vol.65, p.227.

[17] Junge, C.E. (1963). "Air Chemistry and Radioactivity." Academic Press, New York and London.

[18] Shah, I.S., and Quigley, C.P. (1971). In Proc. Amer. Inst. Chem. Engineers Meeting Aug. 29-Sept. 1, New York. AICE, New York.

[19] Spaite, P.W. (1972). Power Engineering Vol.10, p.34.

[20] Squires, A.M. (1970). Science Vol.169, p.821.

[21] Maurin, P.G., and Jonakin, J. (1970). "Removing Sulphur Oxides from Stack Gases." Chem. Eng., April 27, p.1.

[22] Hottel, H.C., and Howard, J.B. (1972). "New Energy Technology." MIT Press, Cambridge, Massachusetts.

[23] FPC (1972). FPC Opinion and Order Authorizing Distrigas to Import LNG, March 9, 1972 (DC 54); FPC Presiding Examiners Initial Decision upon Applications to Import LNG, May 22, 1972 (DC-51). USGPO.

[24] US Govt. (1970). "Air Quality Control Criteria for Nitrogen Oxides." HEW, Environmental Protection Agency Report, AP-84. USGPO.

[25] National Academy of Engineering (1971). Report on Abatement of Nitrogen Oxides from Stationary Sources, COPAC 4 (NAE-NRC 472), Natl. Research Council Panel on Air Quality Management. NAE, Washington, D.C.

[26] Sensenbaugh, J.D. (1966). "Formation and Control of Oxides of Nitrogen." Combustion Engineering, Windsor, Connecticut.

[27] Lindberg, W. (1968). "Den Alminnilige Luftforurensnig i Norge" ("General Air Pollution in Norway"). Utgitt av Røykskaderädet (Smoke Damage Council), Oslo.

[28] Nishiwaki, Y., Tsunetoshi, Y., Shimuzu, T., Ueda, M., Nakayama, N., Takahashi, H., Ichinosawa, A., Kajihara, S., Oshino, A., Agino, M., and Sakaki, K. (1971). "Atmospheric Contamination of Industrial Areas Including Fossil-Fuel Stations, and a Method of Evaluating Possible Effects on Inhabitants." IAEA-SM-146/16, IAEA, Vienna.

[29] Lave, L., and Seskin, E. (1970). "Air Pollution and Human Health." Science Vol.169, p.723.

[30] Lave, L., and Seskin, E. (1971). "An Analysis of the Association between US Mortality and Air Pollution." Univ. of Pittsburgh rept., Pittsburgh, Pennsylvania.

[31] Lave, L., and Seskin, E. (1971). "Does Air Pollution Cause ill Health?" Univ. of Pittsburgh Rept., Pittsburgh, Pennsylvania.

[32] Donora (1949). "The Donora Smog Disaster." Hygenia Vol.27, p.684.

[33] Logan, W.P.D. (1949). "The London Fog of 1948." Lancet Vol.256, p.78.

[34] Ferris, B.G., and Frank, N.R. (1970). Anesthesiology Vol.25, No.4.

Problems

Extra Reference

Finklea et al. (1973). "Health Consequences of Sulfur Oxides." Human
  Studies Lab., EPA, Washington, D.C. (August 15).

PROBLEMS

1. The second line on p. 204 ends with $(\mu g/m^3)^2$. What does this
unit mean?

2. Define epidemiology.

3. Imagine yourself a health minister in the Norwegian government
attempting to prove that the increase in SO_2 concentration in the Norwegian countryside is due to English power stations. What steps would
you take if: (a) England cooperated? (b) England did not cooperate?

4. Assume a pollution tax proportional to the persons affected
($1,000,000 per life) and use the Norwegian figures for deaths due to air
pollution (Fig. 8-4). What would have been the tax paid for the various
air-pollution episodes of Table 8-8? Who would have paid it, and how
could it have been collected?

5. Fit the data of the Norwegian Smoke Damage Council (Fig. 8-4)
by various curves: (a) linear in SO_2 concentration, (b) quadratic
in SO_2 concentration.
  Assume that Chicago has a population of 5,000,000, with average
life expectation of 50 years, spread uniformly over a semicircle of
50,000 m radius (Lake Michigan is the other semicircle). Calculate
that part of the death rate due to the SO_2 concentrations calculated
in Problem 1 with each of these assumptions.

6. Discuss some "models" of how death rate, or disease rate, can
vary with pollution concentration.
  Should it be linear?

$$\text{Death rate} = A \times C \qquad (C = \text{concentration})$$

Should it be linear with a threshold C_0?

$$\text{Death rate} = A \times (C - C_0)$$

Should it be quadratic?

$$\text{Death rate} = A \times C^2$$

8. Air Pollution

Consider a *linear* curve, but with different constants *A* for different parts of the population (children, old people, etc.). What is the combined curve?

Should death rate vary with concentration averaged over a year, or with total exposure? What equation or curve can illustrate repair of damaged cells?

What reasons can you guess for treating radiation, SO_2, CO, or NO differently from each other?

[*Note:* In this question, use your imagination and express the answer quantitatively for possible comparison with experiment.]

9

Radiation Hazards

ENVIRONMENTAL RADIATION

Nuclear power stations avoid many of the environmental problems of fossil-fuel plants: there is no fly-ash or noxious gases; the plant is smaller and better looking; fuel arrives less frequently; and there is no large coal tip or smelly oil tank. Two environmental effects are shared with fossil-fuel plants: thermal pollution and the transmission lines. However, there is a unique problem in nuclear power generation: the radiation from the decay products of nuclear fission. If these decay products are not contained within the reactor, they can cause a severe health hazard, which by comparison dwarfs most of the other hazards we have discussed. Accordingly, we will now discuss this health hazard and the efforts that are necessary, and that are so far successful, to confine the radioactivity. We do this because there are many misconceptions about radiation. There have been many detailed reviews made of radiation hazards [1, 2, 3, 4]; here, we will simplify.

We note that the only important environmental effect of radiation is the hazard to man. Animals, plants, and lower forms of life are less sensitive to radiation than is man; moreover, a radioactive forest or mountain is as beautiful as a nonradioactive one, and perhaps more so. For centuries we have admired uranium glass made luminescent by radioactivity.

9. Radiation Hazards

RADIATION DOSAGE

The unit by which we measure exposure to radiation is the *roentgen* (R). Thus, we say a certain amount of radium may emit so many roentgens. The unit by which we measure how much radiation is absorbed by a substance, including living tissue, is the *rad*.

Recall that radiation is a form of energy, and therefore there exists a relation, or conversion factor if you like, between roentgens or rads and joules, as follows:

With 1 rad of absorbed dose, 1 g of material absorbs 10^{-5} j. Notice that since you wish to know how much energy the material absorbs, you must specify how much material is involved, or adjust your figure to a standard gram of material.

In line with this reasoning, it is conventional to speak of the number of rads of energy absorbed per roentgen emitted. For example, it is found experimentally that if we expose air to 1 R, 1 kg of air will absorb 87.7×10^{-5} j. Therefore, the number of rads per roentgen in air is 0.877.

Different types of radiation cause slightly different effects on biological systems. Thus when comparing different sources of radiation, we use the unit *roentgen-equivalent-man*, or *rem*. For gamma radiation and electrons, 1 rem = 1 R. For α-particle radiation, 1 rem is greater than 1 R. For the sort of accuracy with which we are concerned, 1 rem = 1 R produces with each exposure approximately 1 rad of absorbed dose.

With these definitions out of the way, we now consider the medical effects caused by 1 R of exposure to radiation and, in turn, how much exposure is caused by how much radioactivity.

TABLE 9-1

Expected Effects of Acute, Whole-Body Radiation Exposures [2]

Dose (rem)	Effect
10,000	Tissue destroyed*
500	Half of those exposed would die
100-200	Nausea and fatigue
25-50	Slight temporary blood change
0-25	No detectable effects

* Used locally for radiotherapy, e.g., irradiation of the pituitary gland, instead of surgical removal, at Harvard University. This dose is given in one minute. The doses considered from the power stations are *yearly* averages and are a million times less!

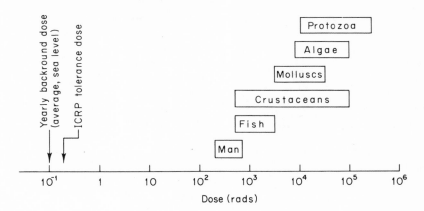

Fig. 9-1. Relative tolerance of different groups of organisms to radiation. Listed is dose required to kill 50% of individuals in a short time [5].

In Table 9-1 we show the effects of acute radiation exposures as demonstrated by a variety of radiation accidents. These doses could be tolerated by the body if taken slowly. Over the years, procedures have been developed for diagnosing acute radiation sickness and for facilitating recovery.

The effects of radiation on man are far more serious than on other organisms. For example, we show in Fig. 9-1 the relative tolerance of various marine organisms to radiation, as measured in atomic-bomb tests [5, 6]. One surprising feature of these numbers is that small organisms survive doses larger than those necessary to destroy a single cell.

We need not discuss this peculiarity here but merely remind ourselves that if we protect man adequately from radiation we have also protected other organisms adequately.

In addition to the direct clinical effects in Table 9-1, there are two other effects: the inducing of cancers and the problems of genetic damage. These do not occur often and can be seen only when averaged over a very large number of people. Since, however, we are contemplating the possible irradiation of many people, these effects are very important. The cancer cases are the best understood and will be outlined in the discussion that follows. Data are scarce; our knowledge comes from those cases that are the results of accidents.

In discussing these data, we compare two possibilities. The first is a pessimistic model called the *linear theory*. Once again we deal with a model whose numbers are related by a straight line on a graph, and which tell us, among other things, that when the dose is doubled, its effect is doubled. According to the linear theory,

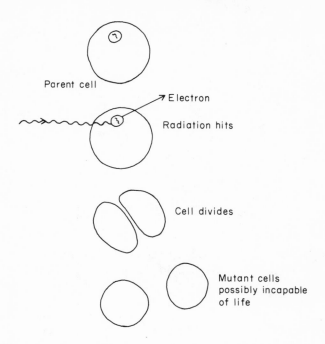

Fig. 9-2. Schematic of cancer, genetic damage, or death following division of a parent cell irradiated by a γ-ray.

the probability of cancer is therefore proportional to the dose, but not to the *dose rate*. To elaborate, this model says you have the same likelihood of developing a cancer whether you are exposed to "*x*" number of roentgens over the course of an hour or over the course of a year. If this theory is wrong and the dose rate is the more important factor, then the short concentrated burst of radiation is more likely to produce a cancer.

This follows a theoretical idea, illustrated in Fig. 9-2, that a dose of radiation acts as a carcinogen to form an abnormal cell, and this damaged cell is never destroyed and never heals. This may not always be true; healing effects are known to exist for various species [7, 8].

The second theory is that there is a *threshold* below which no cancer effect is produced by radiation. This could occur because an abnormal cell may heal with time when the dose and the dose rate are small.

Experiments with onion root tips [9] show that caffeine and alcohol cause changes, maybe by destroying the repair mechanism. A possible synergistic effect of tobacco smoking and radiation was mentioned earlier, in connection with uranium miners. But these effects have not been confirmed with mice [10], and certainly not with people.

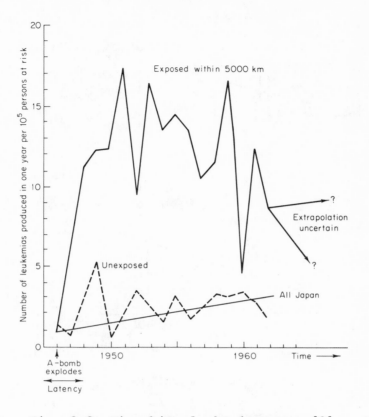

Fig. 9-3. Hiroshima leukemia cases [2].

Prudent public policy demands that we ignore the possibility of a threshold in considering environmental effects and assume a linear theory as we did for SO_2 pollution earlier. But at some stage we may get large doses of radiation by accident or, in the case of X rays, by mistaken design. In such a case then, all hopes of a repair mechanism should be considered as a basis for our preventive actions:

1. Refrain from caffeine (tea, coffee, cola-based drinks) for 24 hours before and after fluoroscopic X-ray examinations;
2. After an unusual X-ray dose, refrain from procreation for perhaps a year (if possible!);
3. In view of the Stewart and Kneale [11] data showing possible increased sensitivity to radiation of humans *in utero*, fertile women should refrain from X rays during the first two weeks after their menstrual periods (when they *might* become pregnant) [12].

231

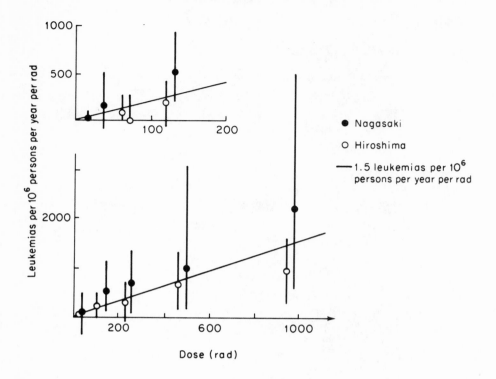

Fig. 9-4. Hiroshima and Nagasaki leukemia rate [13]. Later reports change the dose scale and reduce the hazard to about 0.8 leukemias per 10^6 persons per year per rad. *Note:* there is some indication that the dose scale may be low by a factor of 2.

EXPERIMENTAL DATA

Out of a vast mass of data in the general references, we choose five particularly interesting mistakes in which large radiation insults were received by people who have since been carefully studied. We must, however, keep in mind that these are almost always selected populations. X rays are more often given to sick people than to healthy people. In the atomic-bomb studies, follow-up work was done only on those who *survived* the explosion; presumably these were people in good enough health to overcome the initial insult.

1. In Fig. 9-3, we show leukemia (see Problem 1) cases from irradiated persons who were within 5000 km of the bomb explosion at Hiroshima. The ordinate is the number of leukemias produced in a year for 10^5 persons at risk; leukemias continued to be found for 25 years following the explosion. The rate of occurrence of leukemias for both Hiroshima and Nagasaki is plotted against radiation dose in Fig. 9-4.

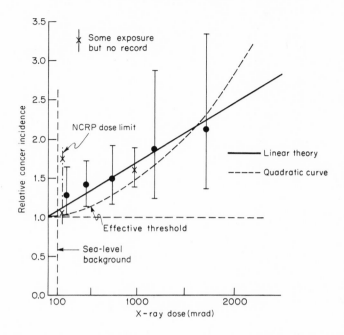

Fig. 9-5. Relative cancer incidence for children whose mothers were irradiated during pregnancy. Data from [11].

The points can be fitted by a straight line through the origin, or by any threshold below 100 rad. Using the straight line, we find 1.5 leukemias per million persons per year per rad. Since these cancer cases continue appearing for about 25 years, we find 40 leukemias per 10^6 persons per rad, or (8000/6) leukemias for 200 million people exposed to 170 mrem. This assumes that no one dies of anything else before dying of cancer. Thus, it might be an overestimate by a factor of 2. The Hiroshima and Nagasaki data collected by the Atomic Bomb Casualty Commission (ABCC) [2] also show about five other cancer cases for each leukemia - leading to 8000 cancers for 170 mrem per year.

2. There were many persons with cases of ankylizing spondylitis who were given large radiation doses in attempts to cure them. These have been analyzed by Court and Brown [14], who found leukemias and cancers. The sensitivity is consistent with the ABCC series. The doses were too large to indicate anything about a threshold.

3. X rays used to be taken of the pelvis of pregnant women [15]. This practice has been shown to lead to excess cancer cases in children. In one of these studies, by Stewart and Kneale [11], the cancer risk was originally plotted against the number of X-ray films taken. The

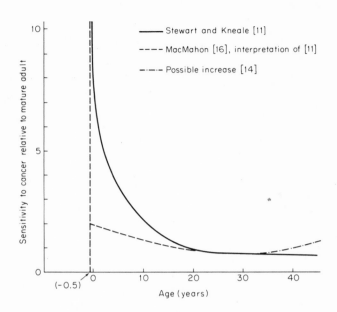

Fig. 9-6. Assumed sensitivity to radiation-induced cancer.

number of films was used because the X-ray dosage was uncertain. If a dosage of 500 mrem per film is assumed, the data can be plotted (Fig. 9-5). We find that the fetus has 10 times the sensitivity of a mature adult, as shown in Fig. 9-6. Other studies do not show such a strong effect [15]. Let us analyze this figure together.

100 mrad is normally absorbed from natural background sources at sea level. This is represented by the dashed line near the vertical axis. Notice next that each of the heavy points has a vertical line through it, which is flattened off at each end. Normally one plots a curve by connecting "points." If the data are very inaccurate, "points" are not meaningful. Thus looking near the beginning of the line, from the limited data available, the best that can be said is that the first point of the curve can be anywhere from just over 1.0 to about 1.7. That means our straight-line curve, which represents the linear theory, can have a pretty wide range of slopes - all of which would seem to fit the data. You will note that the straight curve is drawn pretty much through the center of the aggregate of vertical lines.

On the other hand, using the lower limits of the data line, we can speculate on the existence of the dashed (quadratic) curve, and that would tell us the threshold value of the radiation, the least amount that would produce a certain number of cancers. However, even this datum tells us that the linear theory cannot be so easily discarded.

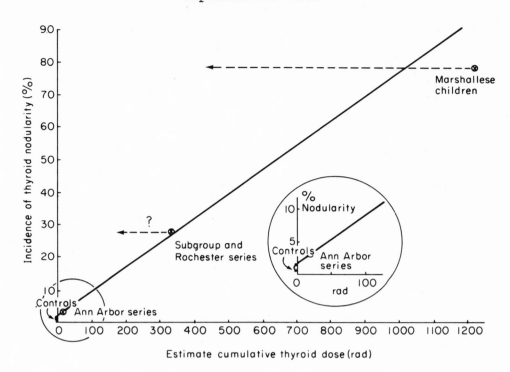

Fig. 9-7. Incidence of thyroid nodularity in relation to estimated cumulative dose to the thyroid gland [18].

A similar sensitivity was confirmed by MacMahon [16] but with a smaller absolute effect. Moreover, MacMahon finds that the excess risk disappears at age 8, rather than at 25 for the ABCC series. This is illustrated in Fig. 9-6. Gibson et al. [17] take similar data and show that the increased cancer risk due to radiation was only present when there was *another* pathological condition. Presumably, the pathological condition was what caused the X ray to be taken. Nonetheless, we take a conservative view and assume that there is, as suggested by these data, a linear risk-to-dose curve down to about 1 r. This is the best linear curve we have for low-intensity radiation, and the dashed curve shows that a quadratic with an "effective" threshold of 1/2 r fits as well.

4. There have been studies of thyroid cancer in children. Because the cancer *itself* is rare, Hempelman [18] studied *any* nodularity. Figure 9-7 shows that linearity seems to hold down to 20 r.

5. A survey that seems to indicate a threshold is one in which persons who painted radium on clock and watch dials then sucked their paint brushes to make fine points on them [19, 20]. These people have

235

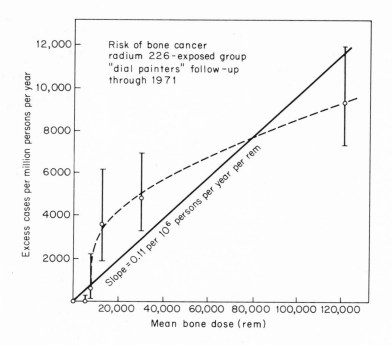

Fig. 9-8. Radiation tumor incidence for radium-dial painters [4].

ingested radium "daughters" in their bones. The dose is well determined, because the radium remains in the bones and there is no difficulty at all in remeasuring the dose. The cancer incidence is compared with both the linear and threshold theories in Fig. 9-8. It seems that there may be a threshold at 1000 rad *cumulative* dose, or about 50 rad/yr. There exist other data on mice, rats, dogs, and pigs showing a linearity if alpha-particle emitters are used [21], but a threshold of about 20 rad/yr if beta emitters are used [22, 23].

It is hard to reconcile these data. There seem to be two possibilities: One is that the medical data really do follow a threshold behavior, but the dose scale is incorrect. Possibly there is a threshold only for people who are physically fit. Second, we could argue that, as noted above, *for doses given at a slow rate,* some form of healing occurs. This could be an extension of the latency period, since when this period equals the human lifetime the risk vanishes. Table 9-2 shows a list of latency periods as a function of dose as suggested by Evans [19]. We see that, if we are lucky, slow rate doses give no risk.

TABLE 9-2

Evans' Suggestion for Latency Period of Cancer [19]

Cumulative dose (rad)	Latency period (yr)
700	45-110
600	50-125
500	60-150
400	70-175
250	100-250

Here is what is most important in terms of nuclear power plants. If a threshold of 50 r/yr is correct, then the radiation from cosmic rays at any altitude, or from the normal operation of nuclear power plants, will give no extra cancers. Excessive X rays, given in one dose, could still cause problems, as could doses given suddenly because of reactor malfunction. In other sections we show that normal operation of a power plant can give very low radiation with no undue expense; however, since accidents and X rays are important, taking a linear theory seems not only conservative but justified.

GENETIC HAZARDS

The study of genetic damage is much harder to undertake than that of cancer, because genetic changes are not as easy to identify as cancer cases. Therefore, we depend even more upon theory, and upon experiments with mice. Results for mice show that genetic changes are linear with dose for males but follow a nonlinear relationship for females, with a threshold [8, 10, 24]. Since, at the present level of human development, we depend upon both for continuing the human race, we calculate using a linear theory. (Of course, there is no need to bother about genetic effect caused by radiation for people beyond childbearing age.)

No one is sure how many genetic changes *homo sapiens* can stand. People have lived for generations at high altitudes (e.g., the Andes), where the radiation dose from cosmic rays is up to 300 mrem/yr. There are no obvious effects, although detailed studies might show some important effects. It seems that genetic changes from additional radiation of up to 50 mrem/yr could be tolerated [8]; still, there is every reason to keep the dose to children small.

9. *Radiation Hazards*

There are studies showing differences in height and weight at menarche for persons living in Denver, Colorado, as compared to those living at sea level [25]. Denver girls are born smaller, grow at slower rates, and attain menarche at a later age. All these differences are, however, attributed to fetal hypoxia (a deficiency of oxygen in tissues) rather than to radiation. The difficulty of matching cause with effect should be apparent.

COMPARISON OF ESTIMATES

Other estimates have been given of cancer incidence. Gofman [26] assumes the worst: that the fetus is ten times more sensitive than the adult (as compared with MacMahon's factor of 2); and he allows for a continuation of the latent period for 20, 30, or an infinite number of years, in spite of evidence mentioned earlier that it may be about 8 for children and 25 for adults. Moreover, he assumes that there are 30 cancer cases per leukemia (which is not consistent with the ABCC data, but is consistent with the ankylizing spondilitis cases because of the possible error in evaluating the dose distribution over the body). Pauling's estimate [27] allows an even larger factor of 50 in cancer cases or leukemia. These large factors are based on the simple idea that radiation increases the incidence of each type of cancer in proportion to the dose; in this way, a dose that doubles the incidence of leukemias will also double that of all other cancers. This idea has an attractive simplicity. Authorities claim it is contrary to present evidence, but authorities have been wrong before. Early references give this factor as unity. Storer [28] assumes that a semithreshold is operating and that small doses give very small effects. Tables 9-3 and 9-4 show a summary of experiments and risk estimates.

As a result of a detailed examination of data, the International Commission on Radiological Protection (ICRP) and, in the U.S., the Federal Radiation Council (FRC) and the National Council for Radiological Protection (NCRP) have established upper limits for all man-made radiation (except that produced by diagnostic or therapeutic X rays). These dose limits are different for different organs of the body, but we are here concerned with the whole-body dose. The guidelines recommended by the ICRP, FRC, and NCRP are listed in Table 9-5. We note that, for the whole population, the guide is on the order of the natural background, which itself fluctuates widely. If we are concerned about smaller levels than this (and we are), we should also be concerned about reducing natural background.

In the rest of the book we will not refer to the ICRP guidelines but rather to the cancer incidence as calculated earlier.

238

TABLE 9-3

Summary of Long-Term Effects of Radiation

Mistake	Reference	Dose range (rem)	Dose rate	Linearity	Leukemias per 10^6 persons per year per rad	All cancers**
Hiroshima/ Nagasaki	[13]	100-200	instantaneous	yes	1-2	4
X ray of spine for ankylizing spondylitis	[14]	100-200	few single irradiations	yes	0.7	3
X ray in pregnancy (sensitivity of embryo)	[11, 16]	1-20	0.5 r per picture*	yes	10	60
Irradiation of thyroid, often by iodine	[18]	20-1000	8 days	yes	–	–
Radium dial painters	[20]	10-1000	continuous	100-r threshold	1 at 200 r	
Mice experiments					Genetic sensitivity	
Male	[10]	10-1000	variable	yes	1	
Female	[10]	10-1000	variable	40-r threshold	1/3	

* MacMahon would put 2 to 4 r per picture and reduce the number of leukemias per rad by a factor of 4 to 8.

** Gofman puts a factor of 30 for all leukemias to cancers, based on [14]. He probably underestimated the dose to the rest of the body. Pauling seems to agree with his ratio of 30, but no one else seems to.

239

9. Radiation Hazards

TABLE 9-4

Annual Increment in Radiation-Induced Cancer*

Estimator	Years of latency assumed	Cases per year	Man-rads for one cancer per year
Pauling [27]	50	100,000	300
Gofman [26]	infinite	108,000	300
	30	74,000	400
	20	9000	3000
Sagan [29], Morgan [1], Hamilton [30], ICRP [4]	25	1500	18,000
Storer [28]	20	160	180,000
Used in text	25	8000	3000

   * For dose rate of 170 mrem/yr and population of 200 million persons.

   The ICRP also recommends that in all cases radiation levels be reduced to "as low as practicable." The ICRP is an international organization and has no responsibility for national actions. National agencies must define what is practicable by comparing risk and benefit.

OTHER EPIDEMIOLOGICAL STUDIES OF RADIATION

   The most important of the epidemiological studies that have been done on radiation are those associated with excessive use of X rays, as noted earlier. These have the advantage that there is a control group with similar social and environmental circumstances.
   There is a large dose in certain parts of the world from background radioactivity; for example, Kerala, India, has monazite sands containing much thorium, and the inhabitants receive ten times the average sea-level background dose. Studies [32] show no significant health effects in comparison with other parts of India. These studies, however, are not sensitive enough. Cancers appear at age 50 and above, and in an undeveloped country like India people usually die before reaching that age.
   A serious study has been made of health conditions of people working and living in Hanford, Washington, where nuclear work has been going on for 30 years. This study [33] shows that the people of Hanford

TABLE 9-5

1971 Dose-Limiting Recommendations (ICRP, FRC, and NCRP) [31]

Maximum permissible dose equivalent for:

Occupational exposure (combined whole-body)	
Prospective annual limit	5 rem in any one year
Retrospective annual limit	10-15 rem in any one year
Long-term accumulation to age *N* years	(N-18) × 5 rem
Skin	15 rem in any one year
Hands	75 rem in any one year (25/qtr)
Forearms	30 rem in any one year (10/qtr)
Other organs, tissues, and organ systems	15 rem in any one year (5/qtr)
Fertile women (with respect to fetus)	0.5 rem in gestation period
Dose limits for:	
The public	0.5 rem in any one year
Individual or occasional students	0.1 rem in any one year
Population dose limits:	
Genetic	0.17 rem average per year
Somatic	0.17 rem average per year
Emergency dose limits, life saving:	
Individual (older than 45 years if possible)	100 rem
Hands and forearms	200 rem additional (300 rem total)
Emergency dose limits, less urgent:	
Individual	25 rem
Hands and forearms	100 rem total
Family of radioactive patients:	
Individual (under age 45)	0.5 rem in any one year
Individual (over age 45)	5 rem in any one year

are healthier than those in surrounding counties in spite of radiation
releases, both gaseous and liquid, greater than now allowed. The reason is clear: these people have had better medical care as part of
the study!

Attempts to compare people living at high and at low altitudes
are also hard to carry out; at high altitudes the lack of oxygen causes
much more observable effects [25].

Another approach to studying the effects of radiation has been
made in a series of papers by Sternglass [34-38]. This is similar in
concept to the epidemiological studies of the effects of sulfur dioxide
discussed earlier; some parameter (usually infant mortality) is plotted,
and a search is made for any deviation from a smooth curve, together
with any reason for it.

In Fig. 9-9, we present data given by Sternglass of infant mortality in Westchester County before and after the operation of the Indian
Point No. 1 nuclear power station at Buchanan, New York. From the
points marked with the arrows, Sternglass claimed there was a possible

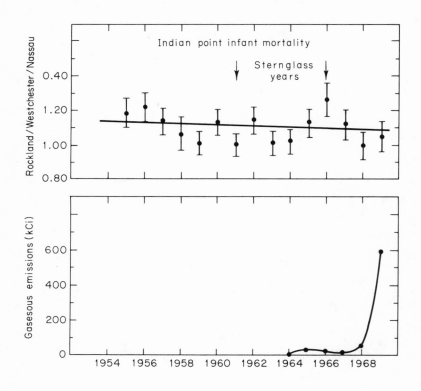

Fig. 9-9. Infant mortality near Indian Point, New York, showing
attempts to find an effect due to the Indian Point No. 1 nuclear
power station [39].

effect of the power station. This shows, however, that the increase in infant mortality is not sustained over a period of years, and that the increase occurred before any major release of radioactivity. Thus Sternglass' specific claim seems invalid, but he has performed the valuable task of spurring others on to make careful studies.

A more systematic epidemiological procedure would be to plot the increase of infant mortality against calculated exposure, just as the Oslo and Japanese data were plotted against sulfur-dioxide concentration in Chapter 8. The work of Sternglass cannot, therefore, be considered in the same class as the epidemiology referred to there. In these sulfur-dioxide cases, we made many cautionary remarks about other possible interpretations of the data. These apply with still greater force to the work of Sternglass.

SOURCES OF RADIATION

Man has always been exposed to radiation, and he always will be. His body contains sodium and potassium, some of which is radioactive. From this he cannot escape.

As we look at the list of radiation doses to which man is subject (Table 9-6), we note that radiation from the present uses of nuclear power is among the smallest values. These facts are little understood. In a recent survey of 1700 college students (from Harvard, MIT, and Princeton), Red [40] found that very few could list radiation sources in the correct order of hazard. The variability of the background is one of the important features; another is the huge effect due to diagnostic medical X rays [41]. While it is not the primary purpose of this book to criticize the medical profession, we feel that a small effort spent on reducing the huge 95 mrem/yr from medical X rays to a more reasonable 5 mrem/yr would enhance the health of the U.S. population more than the current criticism of the nuclear power industry, which already keeps radiation doses down to an average of less than 0.1 mrem/yr.

COMPARISON OF GUIDELINES

It is instructive to compare radiation guidelines with the air quality criteria we discussed earlier. If everyone in the U.S. were exposed to doses at the level of radiation guidelines, we estimate there would be 8000 extra cancer deaths. If everyone were exposed to sulfur dioxide and particulates at the level of U.S. Primary Air Quality Standards, we estimate 50,000 extra deaths. In each case, Gofman [26]

9. *Radiation Hazards*

TABLE 9-6

Some Typical Radiation Doses*

Source	Dose (mrem/yr)	Radiation cancers/yr if all U.S. population so exposed
Potassium 40 naturally occurring in body	20	1000
Potassium 40 naturally occurring in neighboring body	2	100
Gamma rays from neighboring soil and rocks (av.)	50	2500
Gamma rays inside brick or stone buildings	30-500	1500-24,000
Cosmic rays at Vernon, Vermont	30	2000
Background dose at sea level (av.)	100	5000
Background dose at sea level in Kerala, India (av.)	500-2000	25,000-100,000
Cosmic rays at Denver, Colorado	67	3000
3-hr jet-plane flight	2	100
60 hr/month of jet-plane flight (pilot)	500	24,000
Medical diagnostic X rays in U.K. (av.)	14	1000
Medical diagnostic X rays in U.S. (av.)		
1964	55	2600
1970	95	5000
Weapons tests "fall-out"	3	150
AEC "design criteria" for reactor boundary (upper limits for actual use)	5	250
Within 20-mile boundary of BWR with 1-day hold-up but leaky fuel (gaseous emission) (av.)	0.1	250
Within 20-mile boundary of PWR with leaky fuel (av.)	0.002	0.02
Within 20-mile boundary of coal plant (av.)	0.01	0.1

   * Lists such as this can be combined from various general sources: [1, 2, 42, 43, 44, 45, 46, 47].

244

guesses a factor 4 higher. These numbers are of the same order of magnitude, showing that regulatory agencies think alike about acceptable risks. There is one interesting difference. The natural background for air quality is near zero, whereas the air in our cities equals or exceeds the standard, due to energy use. On the other hand, the natural background for radiation is close to the ICRP standard, and power use (if controlled as properly as is now being done) adds less than 0.1%.

LONG-LIVED RADIOACTIVITY

We have seen in Chapter 5 that fission of the nucleus $_{92}U^{235}$ leads to two other nuclei with masses in the regions of 100 and 135. (Each fission is slightly different from others.) The relevant fission-product nuclei (e.g., $_{40}Zr^{191}$ and $_{52}Te^{134}$) each have 5 or 6 too many neutrons to be stable; thus they are very radioactive. The nearest stable nuclei with these atomic numbers would be $_{52}Te^{130}$ and $_{40}Zr^{96}$. The fission products are called *neutron rich*.

92% of the total energy of the fission is in the kinetic energy of the fission fragments and soon converts to heat. But 8% is in this decay radioactivity. Each of the fission products decays by a chain of radioactive nuclei, for example:

$$_{52}Te^{134} \longrightarrow {}_{53}I^{134} \qquad (\beta \text{ decay; 42 min})$$
$$\text{(tellurium)} \qquad \text{(iodine)}$$

$$_{53}I^{134} \longrightarrow {}_{54}Xe^{134} \qquad (\beta \text{ decay; 53 min})$$
$$\text{(xenon)}$$
$$\textit{stable}$$

The amount of such decay radioactivity after a long irradiation is shown in Fig. 9-10. Since irradiations typically last 3 years, and since most activities have shorter half-lives than this, this is a useful graph.

The concept of a *half-life* is basic to all physical phenomena [see Technical Note 5-4]. If 1 Ci of Te^{134} is produced, after 42 min, 1/2 Ci will have decayed and 1/2 Ci will be left; after 84 min, 1/4 Ci will be left; after 126 min, 1/8 Ci will be left; and so on. The half-life of Te^{134} is therefore 42 min. There is no way of altering these half-lives.

The total quantity of radioactivity produced is large, and this is what gives nuclear power its unique environmental hazard. A nuclear reactor of our standard size (1000 MW_e) contains 10,000 *million* Ci of radioactivity during ordinary operation. 1 Ci is that amount of radioactive substance that gives 3.7×10^{10} disintegrations/sec (for radium,

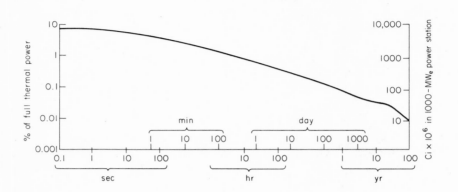

Fig. 9-10. Decay power after infinite irradiation.

almost exactly 1 g). As we have seen, 1 Ci badly handled can cause illness and even death. Thus the radioactivity must be contained at all times, or else diluted until it is insignificant. Containment is the usual course.

The other reduction factor is distance.

For example, the dose rate at 1 m from a 1-Ci source of cobalt 60 (Co^{60}) is 1.25 r/hr. At 1 km, it would take a 1 million-Ci source to produce this dose. Likewise, a lead absorber of 5-cm thickness reduces the dose to 91 mr/hr, a reduction of 14.

It is therefore easy to protect even the reactor operators from the 10 billion Ci, *if it remains contained in the reactor*.

RELEASE OF RADIOACTIVITY FROM POWER STATIONS

Let us assume we are facing a radioactive source in a vacuum where there is no air or other medium to absorb the radiation of the source. We would find that the radiation gets weaker as we move away from the source, as we doubled our distance from the source we would measure the radiation as 1/4 of its original strength. This is an example of $1/r^2$ law. [See Technical Note 9-1.]

TECHNICAL NOTE 9-1

The Inverse Square Law

    Briefly stated by means of an example, the inverse square law refers to the following phenomena: Assume a radioactive element is at some distance, say 1 m, from a measuring device. If the distance between the element and the measuring instrument is doubled to 2 m, the intensity of the radiation would be 1/4 of the measurement at the 1-m point. Upon separating the source and the measuring instrument by 3 m, the intensity would be 1/9 that of the original measurement.

    Let us tabulate the above figures by assigning a numerical value to the intensity of radiation, and, for simplicity, let us say that the radioactive source at one meter gives a reading of 1 R.

Distance between
source & measuring

instrument (D)	Intensity
1 m	1 R
2 m	1/4 R
3 m	1/9 R

We see that as D gets large, the intensity gets smaller by an amount $1/D^2$. Gravitational, electric, magnetic (and therefore light) fields all obey this inverse square.

    We can see why this is so. Think of the source (of light radio-activity) as being at the center of a sphere. And again for simplicity, assume the source is actually small enough to be a point.

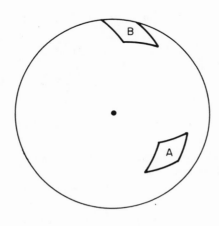

9. Radiation Hazards

On the imaginary sphere, let us mark off two equal areas, A and B. Since nature does not play favorites, as much radiation will pass through A as through B. Now imagine two spheres centered about the source and look at area A and area A^1 on the larger sphere. All the radiation passing through A will pass through A', no more and no less. But A' is larger than A, and therefore the "concentration" of the radiation at any point will be less.

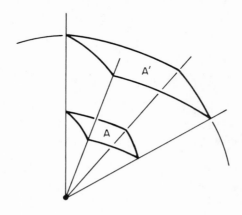

Finally, we must recall that the area of a sphere is given by:

$$A = 4\pi r^2 \qquad \textit{where r is its radius.}$$

Therefore, as r gets larger, the area gets larger by r^2. In terms of the radiation, as r (the distance from the source to the surface) increases, the radiation has to spread itself out over an area that has increased by r^2.

On the other hand, if we had a leak of radioactive material, the material itself would distribute itself so as to be most concentrated at the source of the leak and less concentrated away from the leak following a 1/r law, that is, at twice the distance from the leak, the concentration of material would be half what it was at the source, and this is indeed serious. Radioactivity releases must be given special attention.

The public is protected from the reactor fission products by a set of barriers:

1. The uranium fuel is in a form [usually uranium dioxide (UO_2) ceramic] that tends to retain the fission products, even those which are gaseous.

2. The UO_2 fuel is made in pellets, which are placed in long tubes (nowadays of a zirconium alloy called zircalloy) and sealed. But the weld that seals the tube can develop a pinhole leak and allow gas to escape.

3. In the light-water reactors used in the U.S., the primary coolant circuit of hot pressurized water or steam is itself isolated from the environment.

4. There is a secondary containment vessel of reinforced concrete in case the other barriers fail.

These barriers are adequate, in ordinary operation, to keep all fission product activity under control. A small amount of fission product gases (krypton, xenon, and iodine) do leak through the pinhole leaks to the primary coolant circuit. It is convenient to release these to the environment, and, since the amount is small, this is usually done in a controlled and monitored way. The gases are taken through a hold-up tank where the shorter-lived products decay. Then the gases are released through a stack together with hot air to make them rise and disperse (see Chapter 5).

The calculation of dispersal is identical to that we showed for sulfur dioxides; now, however, we are not concerned with concentrations of gas, but with the radiation doses from the radioactive gas. A cloud of radioactivity 250 m high can still cause a ground-level dose by γ-radiation, although some of the radioactivity can decay as it disperses. Since the numbers will be seen to be small and may easily be reduced further, we can afford to be pessimistic in the calculation. Figure 9-11 shows the results of such an integration by Rogers and Gamertsfelder [48], including averaging over weather conditions, for a BWR (mostly γ-rays emitted) and a PWR (mostly β-rays). The gases emitted are mostly xenon and krypton with perhaps 10 ppm of iodine.

In a BWR of design until 1971, the time in the hold-up tank had been one-half hour, but since 1972 it has been one day or more. For a PWR, 30 to 60 days is more usual. Thus, a PWR releases much less gas than does a BWR, and these (Xe^{133} and Kr^{85}) are mostly β-emitters. Taking a typical population distribution, we get the dose, which is very small, in Table 9-6. This assumes that about 0.1% of the fuel has pinhole leaks, leading to emission of 50,000 μCi/sec from an old BWR with one-half hour hold-up, or 1 μCi/sec for a new PWR. These numbers can be compared to official AEC records [49] or to utility company reports.

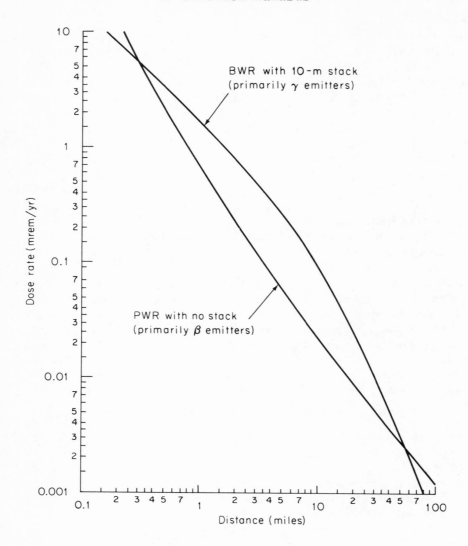

Fig. 9-11. Dose rates as a function of distance for a BWR and a PWR normalized to give 5 mrem/yr at 0.31 miles (500 m) [48].

There has been a lot of confusion about these releases. The AEC has set limits corresponding to the ICRP/FRC/NCRP radiation guidelines for 24-hr occupancy of the worst area of the boundary fence "fence post," or for drinking the reactor effluent, which comes from various waste processes. These limits are set for each power station following the Code of Federal Regulations Title 10, Part 20 (10CFR20). No power station has exceeded these limits. The releases tend to increase with time; this is primarily because the pinhole leaks in the fuel elements increase with time. This has been noted with alarm by many authors [50, 51], who extrapolated to the year 2000. However, every three years the fuel is replaced, so that the releases will go down again! Experience proves this.

It seems sensible always to compare a dose to background or to multiply the dose by the population to obtain an integrated dose. Thus, the background dose for 30,000 people at sea level is 3000 man-rems; if they are within 20 miles of a PWR with leaky fuel, the dose is increased by 60 *milli*-man-rems. The relative importance is then abundantly clear.

Some radioactivity also appears in the coolant. This comes mainly from elements (iron, cobalt) that come from corrosion of the metal by the water; these elements are made radioactive by neutron capture. The quantity of these is kept under control by continuous purification of the water. In addition, a small amount of tritium from fission products is present in the water as T_2O. The radioactive products from the filtration are usually taken away, but small quantities are released to the reactor coolant water, after monitoring.

BIOLOGICAL CONCENTRATION OF RADIOACTIVE ELEMENTS

The calculation of doses from radioactive sources is simple. If the sources are emissions that disperse from a power station, the calculation is not so precise, but it is possible to make it. Sources that will disperse are the chemically inert rare gases, such as krypton and xenon, which are emitted from nuclear power stations.

However, some substances will be biologically concentrated. Of those potentially emitted by power stations, iodine, strontium, radium, plutonium, and caesium are probably the most important.

For example, iodine can fall on grassland and be eaten by cows; it will then be concentrated in the milk. The milk, when ingested by humans, will lead to radioactive iodine concentrated in the thyroid [52].

These "pathways" for radioactive materials through the ecological system are illustrated in Figs. 9-12 and 9-13 for airborne and water-borne releases. The radioactive iodine is particularly important in an accident situation, because, being gaseous, it is easily released.

Therefore, we must study these concentration factors in great detail. In this book, we could go into further detail, but instead we refer the reader to Table 9-7 and references [42-47, 53, 54].

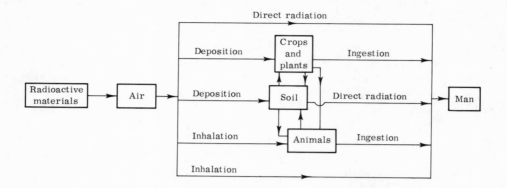

Fig. 9-12. Exposure pathways for radioactive materials released to the atmosphere.

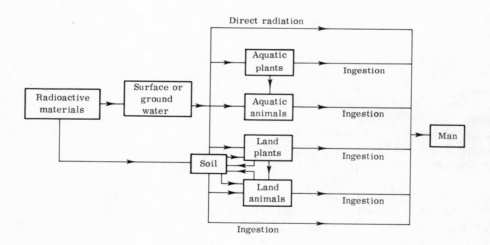

Fig. 9-13. Exposure pathways for radioactive materials released to ground and surface water.

TABLE 9-7

Aquatic and Terrestrial Food-Chain Concentration of Elements [54, 55]

Trophic level*		Element concentration factors**						
		Ca	Sr	K	Cs	Na	Co	Zn
Aquatic								
Water		1.0	1.0	1.0	1.0	1.0	1.0	1.0
Algae and higher plants		1-400	10-3000		50-25,000		2500-6200	140-33,500
Invertebrates	S	16	10-4000		60-11,000		325	
	H		1		600			150
	C				800			
Fish	O		1	300-2500	125-6000			
	C	0.5-300	1-150	400-2700	640-9500			4-40
Terrestrial								
Plants		1.0	1.0	1.0	1.0	1.0	1.0	1.0
Invertebrates	S	0.1-18		3.5	0.2	17		
	H	0.1	0.1	3.0	0.3-0.5	21	0.4	
	C	0.1	0.1	2.0	0.1-0.5	27	0.5	
Mammals	H		0.5-4.5		0.3-2.0		0.3	
	O				1.2-2.0			
	C				3.8-7.0			

Trophic level*		Mn	Ru	Fe	H	P	Ra	I
Aquatic								
Water		1.0	1.0	1.0	1.0	1.0	1.0	1.0
Algae and higher plants		700-35,000	80-2000	2400-200,000		36,000-50,000	0.5	60-200
Invertebrates	S	6000-140,000	130			2-100,000	0.5	20-1000
	H			125		2000		
	C							
Fish	O			10,000		3000-100,000	0.5	25-50
	C						1.5	
Terrestrial								
Plants		1.0	1.0	1.0	1.0	1.0	1.0	1.0
Invertebrates	S				0.6	11		
	H		0.4			17		
	C		1.2			18		
Mammals	H		0.4	0.8	0.6		0.01	0.5
	O			0.2				0.2
	C							0.1

* S = saprovore (detritus feeder); H = herbivore; C = carnivore; O = omnivore.
** Ratio of element level in consumer to element level in food-chain base, with base value normalized at 1.0.

RADIATION FROM COAL

Coal can also emit radioactivity, in this case, the naturally occurring elements radium and thorium. These elements can be inhaled and absorbed by the human body and end up in the bones. The bone marrow is peculiarly sensitive to radiation. Man obtains a dose of about 2 mrem/yr from ingested radium. The dose rate obtained by replacing the nuclear power station by coal is estimated by Martin, et al. [56]. If the coal has the composition used in the Tennessee Valley Authority's Widow's Creek Plant, and the same 97.5% fly-ash suppression, we find 0.1 mrem/yr averaged over 20 miles. A coal station in London or New York, with a population of 5,000,000 within 20 miles, gives 500 man-rem, which is greater than the AEC allows for reactor designs of the same power!

253

9. Radiation Hazards

REFERENCES

[1] Morgan, K.Z., and Turner, J.E. (1967). "Principles of Radiation Protection." Wiley, New York.

[2] United Nations (1964). Report of the United Nations Subcommittee on Effects of Atomic Radiation. United Nations, New York.

[3] Natl. Academy of Sciences (1972). "The Effects on Population of Exposure to Low Levels of Ionizing Radiation." Rept. of Committee on Biological Effects of Ionizing Radiations, NAS, Natl. Res. Council Rept., Washington, D.C.

[4] International Commission on Radiological Protection (1966). Recommendation of the International Commission on Radiological Protection, ICRP Publ. 9. Pergamon, Oxford. [Other ICRP reports are also useful.]

[5] Donaldson, L.K. (1964). "Evaluation of Radioactivity in the Marine Environment of the Pacific Proving Ground." In "Nuclear Detonations and Marine Explosions" (S.M. Small, ed.). Norwegian Defense Res. Est., Kjellet, Norway, pp.73-83.

[6] Kinne, O. (ed.) (1972). "Marine Ecology." Wiley, New York.

[7] Watson, J.D. (1965). "Molecular Biology of the Gene," pp.292 ff., 597 ff. Benjamin, New York.

[8] Brookhaven Natl. Lab. (1967). "Recovery and Repair Mechanisms in Radiobiology," Symp. No.20. Brookhaven National Laboratory, Upton, New York.

[9] Sax, K., and Sax, H.J. (1966). Proc. Natl. Acad. Sci. Vol.55, p.1431.

[10] Russell, W.L. (1965). "Studies in Mammalian Radiation Genetics." Nucleonics Vol.23 (1), p.53.

[11] Stewart, A., and Kneale, G.W. (1970). "Radiation Dose Effects in Relation to Obstetric X Rays and Childhood Cancers." The Lancet, June 6, pp. 1185-88.

[12] US Govt. (1971). "X Ray Examinations: A Guide to Good Practice." Rept. prepared for US Dept. of Health, Education, and Welfare, Public Health Service, USGPO.

[13] Brill, A.B., Tomanaga, M., Heyssel, R.M. (1962). Ann. Internal Medicine Vol.56, p.590. [Later reports change the dose scale and reduce the hazard to about 0.8 leukemias per 10^6 per year per rad.]

[14] Court, W.M., and Brown, D.R. (1965). Brit. Med. J. Vol.2, p.1327.

[15] AEC (1961). "Prenatal X Rays and Childhood Neoplasms." Rept. by Atomic Energy Commission, Division of Biology and Medicine, TID-12373, USGPO.

[16] Macmahon, B. (1963). "X Ray Exposure and Malignancy." J. Amer. Med. Assoc. Vol.183, p.721.

[17] Gibson, R.W., Bross, I.D.J., Graham, S., Lilienfeld, A.M., Schuman, L.M., Levin, M.L., and Dowd, J.E. (1968). New England J. Med. Vol.279, p.906.

References

[18] Hempelman, L.H. (1968). "Risk of Thyroid Neoplasms after Irradiation in Childhood." Science Vol.160, p.159.

[19] Evans, R.D., Keane, A.T., Kolenkow, R.J., Neal, W.R., and
Shanahan, M.M. (1969). In "Delayed Effects of Bone-Seeking Radio-
nuclides" (C.W. Mays et al. eds). Univ. of Utah Press, Salt Lake
City, Utah.

[20] Rowland, R.E., Pailla, P.M., Keane, A.T., and Stehney, A.F. (1970).
"Some Dose Response Relationships for Tumor Incidence in Radium
Patients." Argonne Natl. Lab. Rept. ANL-7760-11, Argonne, Illinois.

[21] Mays, C.W., and Lloyd, R.D. (1971). In "Radiobiology of Plutonium"
(Jee and Stover, eds.).

[22] Mays, C.W. (1970). Testimony to the Joint Committee on Atomic
Energy. USGPO.

[23] Mays, C.W., and Lloyd, R.D. (1971). "Biological Implications of
Radiostrontium" (Conf. rept.).

[24] Russell, W.L. (1969). Rept. in "Biological Implications of the
Nuclear Age." Symp. Lawrence Radiation Lab. USAEC, USGPO.

[25] Frisch, R.E., and Revelle, R. (1970). Science Vol.169, p.397.

[26] Gofman, J. (1971). Many papers, including Amer. Phys. Soc., April
meeting, Washington, D.C., and testimony before JCAE. In [49].

[27] Pauling, L. (1970). Bull. At. Sci., September.

[28] Storer, J. (1970). Testimony before the JCAE. In [49,p.653].

[29] Sagan, L. (1972). Science Vol.177, p.487.

[30] Hamilton, L.D. (1971). Paper presented to Amer. Phys. Soc. Meeting,
April, Washington, D.C.

[31] Natl. Council on Radiation Protection and Measurements (1971).
"Basic Radiation Protection Criteria." NCRP Rept. No.39, Washington,
D.C.

[32] Gopal-Ayengar, A.R., et al. (1971). "Evaluation of the Long-Term
Effects of High Background Radiation on Selected Population Groups
of the Kerala Coast." Nuclear News, October 15.

[33] US Govt. (1971). AEC Authorizing Legislation for Fiscal Year 1972,
p.96 JCAE, USGPO.

[34] Sternglass, E.J. (1965). "Environmental Radiation and Human Health."
Univ. of Pittsburgh Press, Pittsburgh, Pennsylvania.

[35] Sternglass, E.J. (1969). "Has Nuclear Testing Caused Infant Deaths?"
New Scientist, July 24.

[36] Sternglass, E.J. (1970). "Infant Mortality and Nuclear Power Generation." Privately circulated rept. (October 18).

[37] Sternglass, E.J. (1971). "Effects of Low-Level Environmental
Radiation on Infants and Children." March 30.

[38] Sternglass, E.J. (1971). "Estimated Risks of Health Effects to
Infants and Children From Low-Level Radiation Exposure prior to
Birth." April 20.

[39] Hull, A.P. (1972). Nuclear News Vol.15, p.53.

[40] Red, I. (1972). Term paper presented at Harvard University.

[41] Gitlin, J.N., and Lawrence, P.S. (1966). US Public Health Service Bulls. 1519, 2001.

[42] Eisenbud, M. (1963). "Environmental Radioactivity." McGraw-Hill, New York.

[43-47] Mitchell, N.T. (1967, 1968, 1969, 1970, 1971). Radioactivity in Surface and Coastal Waters of the British Isles." Ministry of Agriculture, Fisheries, and Food, Repts. FRL1, FRL2, FRL5, FRL6, FRL7. HM Stationery Office, London.

[48] Rogers, T., and Gametsfelder, C.C. (1971). Paper in 1970 Conf. on Environmental Effects of Nuclear Power Stations. IAEA, Vienna.

[49] US Govt. (1970). "Environmental Effects of Producing Electric Power." Hearings before the JCAE, Parts 1, 2 (combined index Part 2). USGPO.

[50] Abrahamson, D. (1970). "Environmental Cost of Electric Power." (workbook). Scientists Committee for Public Information, New York.

[51] Caldecott, R.S., and Snyder, L.A. (eds.) (1960). Proc. Symp. on Radioisotopes in the Biosphere. Univ. of Minnesota, Minneapolis, Minnesota.

[52] Woodwell, G.M. (1967). Scientific American Vol.216,p.24.

[53] Polikardov, G.G. (1960). "Radio-Ecology of Aquatic Organisms." Reinhold, New York.

[54] Reichle, D.E., Dunaway, P.B., and Nelson, D.J. (1970). Nucl. Safety Vol.11, (January).

[55] Martin, J.E., Hayward, E.D., and Oakley, D.T. (1969). US Public Health Service Rept., reprinted in [49, Part 1, pp.773,810].

General Reference

Sonnenblick, B.J. (1972). "Low and Very Low Dose Influences of Ionizing Radiations on Cells and Organisms Including Man, a Bibliography." US Dept. of Health, Education, and Welfare, BRH/DBE 72-1, USGPO.

PROBLEMS

1. Define leukemia and ankylizing spondylitis. What are regarded as the "natural causes" of these diseases?

2. Make a survey of what people regard as potential sources of dangerous radiation by having them put the following hazards in order:

fall-out from bomb tests
diagnostic X rays
color television sets

controlled use of nuclear power (no accidents)
frequent airplane flight (to professional pilots, for example)
living in a stone house
living at 6000 ft above sea level

3. When taken internally, the elements listed below each migrate to a different part of the body. If they were radioactive isotopes, they might produce a cancer at the site where they concentrate. What type of cancer is each likely to produce?

iodine, phosphorus, sodium, strontium, caesium

4. Why are the "noble gases," krypton and xenon, less important than iodine or strontium? What are the chemical properties of these elements that account for the difference? What happens to strontium and iodine in the body?

5. If gaseous iodine is released in a metal container, will it (a) diffuse? (b) combine chemically? Is there a difference between steady-state operation and an accident situation? If so, what?

6. Assume that *all* cancers in the US are caused by radiation (300,000 cases/year). Use the data in Table 9-6 and calculate the maximum number of cases that might be caused by controlled uses of nuclear power, given a linear relation of cancer incidence to dose. Is this estimate plausible?

7. What reasons are there to expect that the body of a healthy person will repair damage to cells if it occurs slowly? Does the evidence for or against a threshold theory occur for healthy or sick people? Outline a possible way to study this question. (Expense is no object.)

8. Assuming that Kr^{85} is released either at the power station or fuel-reprocessing plant, stays in the northern hemisphere, and diffuses to a height of 10 km, what is the density of Kr^{85} in Ci/cm^3 from a single 1000-MW_e power station (see problem in Chapter V)

9. What is the average dose to a man (skin dose) from Kr^{85} in the year 2000 from 500 1000-MW_e power plants and associated reprocessing stations? [*Hint:* Take the range of the β-particles (1m of air) and calculate the amount of Kr within that range.]

10. Assume that a correlation suggested by Sternglass between nuclear power and infant mortality is real (in spite of data presented in this chapter). What other causes aside from radiation could account for this?

11. Assume you live ten miles from a radio transmitter and then move to 50 miles away from it. How much weaker will your signal be in the new location as compared to your original signal if you apply the inverse square law? [*Note:* radio and tv stations intentionally do not send their signals out uniformly in all directions, so the inverse square law in its simplest form does not apply directly.]

10

Accidents and Sabotage

INTRODUCTION

The normal operation of power plants and power usage has been discussed, but while we have discussed accidents as they occur at the source - mine, processing plant, or oil well - we have not fully discussed the possibility of an accident due to power usage itself.

The larger the power plant, the larger the potential accident. Although it appears reasonable, at first sight, to express the accident hazard directly in terms of the benefit produced (i.e., deaths/kWh), man does not think this way. Man shudders at the thought of many simultaneous deaths within a group in society. Reluctant though man is to accept death, however, 50,000 automobile accident deaths each year are accepted, and a major airplane accident with 100 deaths is front-page news. Man seems still more concerned about anything that might "wipe out the family name" or destroy society by genetic effects passed on to his children.

As we consider larger and larger power stations, we find it harder and harder to compare the accident potential, because the accidents, instead of being small and happening frequently, are potentially large and happen rarely or never at all! Thus in this chapter we will have to compare frequent small accidents with hopefully unnecessary speculations. Some will consider us foolhardy in assigning numbers to our

speculations. Maybe it is foolhardy, but we believe it is necessary.
In this we believe with William Thomson, Lord Kelvin (1824-1907),
that: "When you cannot measure it, when you cannot express it in
numbers - you have scarcely in your thoughts advanced to the stage
of Science, whatever the matter may be." Another problem with estimates is that often they are not made on similar bases. We hope that
our estimates can, in fact, be compared, one to another.

Although not the direct purpose of this book, we feel that a list
of natural and man-made disasters will set a perspective (Table 10-1).

There are three basic approaches to accident analysis. The first,
and easiest, is to use actual performance history (such as this list
of disasters) to estimate the probability of various events. This
gives good estimates for small, frequent accidents, such as automobile
accidents, but only upper limits for infrequent accidents.

Second, we can estimate accident probability (or risk) by measuring the reliability of individual components and calculating the failure probability of the whole system. This is used by NASA for space
flights and by the nuclear industry.

Third, and most common, is the intuitive judgment (or guess) of
experts in the field.

HYDROELECTRIC POWER

In the United States, about one dam gives way per year. These
are small accidents and usually cause rather few deaths. For purposes
of our later tabulations, we shall assume that these accidents cause
5 deaths/year. However, many people use hydroelectric reservoirs for
recreation, and 7000 drownings per year can be attributed to this fact.
We shall discount these drownings in our considerations; had the dam
and its reservoir not been available, these people would have gone
elsewhere, and a similar figure for deaths due to drowning would probably have been transplanted to other sites. We shall attribute only
about ten deaths per year to hydroelectric power itself.

Of course, large dam failures fall into the realm of major disasters. In 1962 in Vaiont, Italy, a mountainside gave way and fell into
the reservoir. The valley flooded. Two thousand people were killed,
and about 50,000 were left homeless. It must also be presumed that
the homeless had more than their usual share of disease in the following year, yielding a similar number of "related" deaths. Another
catastrophic dam failure also occurred above Frejus in France. Due
to the Los Angeles earthquake of 1971, a small dam above the San Fer-
nando Valley cracked. It is widely believed that this dam would have
given way had not the relatively high demand for electricity at the
time caused it to be partially empty.

TABLE 10-1

A Selection of Large World Disasters*

Incident	Place	Date	Deaths
Black death (bubonic plague)	worldwide	1347-1351	75,000,000
War	USSR	1941-1945	30,000,000
War and revolution	China	1913-1960	30,000,000
Cholera epidemic	worldwide	1840-1862	10,000,000
Famine	China	1877-1878	10,000,000
Flood (Yellow River)	Honan, China	1887	900,000
Earthquake	Shansi, China	1/24/1556	800,000
Fire in theatre	Canton, China	1845	1700
Explosion (ammunition dump)	Halifax, Canada	12/6/17	1900
Reservoir overflow (caused by land-slide)	Vaiont, Italy	10/9/63	2000
Mine explosion	Courrieres, France	3/10/05	1050
Ship sinking (Canadian Pacific Empress of Ireland)	St. Lawrence River, Canada	5/29/14	1624
Mine accident	Honkeiko, Manchuria	4/26/42	1549
Explosion, ammonium nitrate (fertilizer)	Oppau, Germany	9/21/21	600
Explosion, ammonium nitrate (fertilizer)	Texas City, US	4/16/47	561
Aircraft collision	New York City, US	12/16/60	134
LNG tank failure and subsequent fire	Cleveland, Ohio, US	10/20/44	133
Coal-tip slide (into school)	Aberfan, Glamorgan, Wales	10/21/66	144
Fire (Coconut Grove nightclub)	Boston, Mass., US	11/21/42	492
Forest fire	Wisconsin and Minnesota, US	10/13-15/18	1000
Tornado (twister)	Texas, Kansas, and Oklahoma, US	4/9/47	167
Aircraft hit bldg. (Empire State Bldg.)	New York City, US	7/28/45	13

* Detailed lists can be found in [1].

We accordingly estimate that there is one major dam failure of "Vaiont" size every 50 years in the U.S. About 2.1×10^{11} kWh of electricity are produced by hydroelectric power every year. With the number of drownings noted above, we calculate 3×10^{-10} direct deaths/kWh from major failures of hydroelectric facilities, and another 3×10^{-10}/kWh from related deaths (subsequent disease, etc.). We shall compare these figures with other hazards of power production (see Table 15-1).

NATURAL GAS

Gas explosions are frequent. In 1971, 45 persons in the U.S. lost their lives in gas main explosions [2]. Small domestic fires and explosions are frequent but are not separately listed. We estimate that about 100 persons per year lose their lives in this way. Finally, we find that 500 people per year are poisoned by gas. The total energy usage from natural gas is 5.2×10^{12} kWh/yr. So we find that gas kills a total of 10^{-11} persons/kWh by accident.

This neglects the possibility of a really major catastrophic accident. Ships containing liquified natural gas (LNG) contain 1 billion cubic feet of liquified methane (=290 million kWh). These tankers are presently brought into heavily populated areas (e.g., Everett, Massachusetts, 1-1/2 miles from downtown Boston). It is argued that these tankers cannot explode (because to explode the liquid would have to be mixed with air), but there seem to be few data on this. Certainly there could be a "big fire": no one has tried creating an accident and lighting a match. Also, huge storage tanks for liquified natural gas are placed near big cities. A large explosion of these tanks, setting off all the underground pipes beneath, say, Manhattan Island, does not seem impossible. Such a catastrophe would paralyze New York and, like the San Francisco earthquake of 1905, would cause fires and make many homeless by secondary causes.

However, a large LNG accident has taken place. On October 20, 1944 (as noted in Table 10-1), LNG tanks in Cleveland, Ohio exploded. The tanks were *not* surrounded by an earthen dike to contain the liquid. The LNG entered sewers, causing fires and the death of 133 people. The volume of gas involved was only 50 million cubic feet - 1/20 of that now stored in large LNG tanks.

A more recent LNG tank accident (February 10, 1973) had smaller effects. An empty tank exploded, and its inflammable lining burned, killing 33 people. If an empty tank can kill 33 people, what can a full one do?

Large quantities of gas stored in a rather small volume make LNG a threat for a major accident. Methane is lighter than air, so that small spills will quickly disperse. However, large spills of LNG will not evaporate so readily. Large volumes will stay cold. They will heat up enough from the ground to rise a few feet, but then they will become a neutrally buoyant cloud and stay close to the ground.

In addition to the danger of fire and explosion, there is also a hazard of asphyxiation. Individuals use gas ovens to commit suicide; a bank of gas 1000 ft × 2000 ft × 1000 ft can asphyxiate a city.

The huge energy content leads to a hazard somewhat like the potential nuclear accident; LNG involves less energy, but it is more explosive. In any case, both energy sources require the same precautions. These include keeping the ships and storage areas away from population centers, maintaining an efficient regulatory staff, holding public hearings complete with mandatory environmental impact statements, and estimating accident potential. So far, the environmental statements are meager and do not discuss these accidents [3]. Although probably in violation of the National Environmental Policy Act (NEPA), this omission has not been challenged in court.

A most obvious problem with liquified natural gas has been the occasion of "explosion" of LNG as it hits water. Such explosions were observed at the Bureau of Mines, U.S. Dept. of the Interior, in 1969 [4]. A more recent study [5] shows that these explosions are not chemical but are due to a sudden evaporation; they are noisy but contain very little energy. However, this is only one of the hazards and has only, so far, reached the "report" stage, which cannot be considered publication in the usual sense.

All this is speculation, but as each component of industry gets bigger, small accidents become less frequent, and the potential severity of large accidents becomes greater. Speculation about potential accidents becomes vital so that we may plan to avoid them. Such speculation has only been done in the nuclear industry, which was begun by dedicated scientists. Personnel in older industries are slow to initiate studies of such accidents; they would prefer not to have public attention called to such possibilities. Our comments are therefore speculative and badly documented. In our view, this fact in itself should show that this is a place where intense public pressure must be brought to bear on public and private authorities [6, 7].

COAL

Accidents in the use of coal are not probable. Unlike gas, it will not explode. A major fire of a coal dump could cause a few deaths; so also could the extra air pollution. Minor house fires set by coal occur more rarely than formerly, since many home owners have changed from coal to oil, gas, or electricity. We estimate 10 deaths/year from these causes.

10. Accidents and Sabotage

OIL

As is true for coal, small oil-caused fires are common, particularly house fires. Probably 200 persons/year die in these fires. This small, steady hazard gives 4×10^{-11} deaths/kWh.

In the early days of the oil industry, oil-tanker fires and explosions were frequently set off during the connecting of oil pipes in harbor by an electric spark. This happens less frequently because of greater care. Yet, for every 1000-MW$_e$ power station, one supertanker enters a city harbor every week. A fire and explosion could destroy the whole waterfront and kill hundreds of people. This is a particularly severe potential hazard in the older U.S. cities. In Salem, Massachusetts, for example, there are facilities for about 1000 MW$_e$ already, and as much again is being built. Yet an accident could send burning oil over a town in which half the buildings are made of wood.

A 1000-MW$_e$ power station will burn 40,000 bbl/day of oil. About six weeks' supply will normally be kept on hand: around 2,000,000 bbl.

This is a large quantity of oil, and it is subject to accident and sabotage. Large oil fires are common in time of war. A particularly nasty accident can occur if an oil fire produces heavy smoke, and there are unfavorable meteorological conditions that keep the smoke close to the ground. If this happens in the summer (when windows are open), at nighttime (when people are asleep), and with a light wind blowing over the nearest city, people could be fumigated and would suffocate.

Calculations of such large-scale accidents are few and far between, although occasional deaths have occurred in smaller fires. The accident as it develops could be similar to the hypothetical serious accident in a nuclear power reactor, where radioactive gases can be spread over the countryside and kill hundreds of people; both accidents are serious only in adverse meteorological conditions.

On January 6, 1973, an oil fire started in Bayonne, New Jersey, as a result of the collision of two ships (Fig. 10-1). The black smoke was denser than that in London in December, 1952, when, as noted in Chapter 8 (Table 8-7), 3000 excess deaths were caused by the resulting air pollution. The photograph shows that the citizens of New York were lucky; the wind was blowing away from Manhattan and moreover was turbulent enough to disperse the smoke. If the wind had been blowing toward Manhattan, and especially if there had been a temperature inversion, it is probable that there would have been a marked increase in respiratory ailments.

In a report to the Resources Agency of California, Starr, et al. [8] calculate the accident probabilities for oil-powered, oil-fired power stations. Starr [9] estimates the probability of a major fire by taking American Petroleum Institute fire statistics (1966-1970) for bulk terminals and pipeline stations. These are plotted in

Fig. 10-1. Oil fire in Bayonne, New Jersey, January 6, 1973.

Fig. 10-2. From this graph, Starr calculates the various pollutants
released in such a fire, and through atmospheric dispersion calculations the pollutant concentrations. Finally, through data similar to
those discussed in Chapter 7, he calculates the public impact in deaths
per accident.

The accident is clearly worse if the pollutant spreads slowly
and steadily over a city. These are the Pasquill A conditions. If
air is turbulent, the pollutants disperse; if stagnant, they do not
spread.

The results are shown in Fig. 10-3, where they are also compared
with similar calculations for a nuclear accident which we discuss
next. Starr's calculations suggest that a large fossil-fuel power
plant is worse than a nuclear plant at the same site, except possibly
for the most extreme accident probability.

NUCLEAR ACCIDENTS

Because of the large amount of radioactivity that remains even
after a power station is switched off, the potential hazard of the
spread of radioactivity is huge. This sort of release could happen
in any one of four places: at the power station, in transit to the

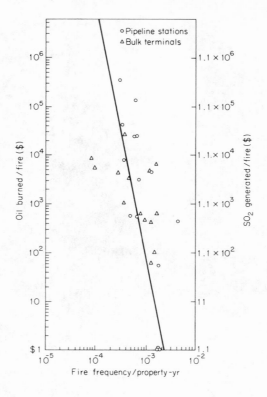

Fig. 10-2. Size of oil fire versus frequency of occurrence.

reprocessing plant, at the reprocessing plant, or at the ultimate storage place of the spent radioactive fuel. The question then arises: How would the radioactivity be dispersed?

Clearly, the gaseous fission products can be dispersed easily if the various barriers or containers are broken. About 25% of the fission products are gaseous, mostly krypton, xenon, and iodine. If the fuel is allowed to decay for three months, the only remaining significant gaseous activity is krypton 85 (Kr^{85}). As we shall see, this Kr^{85} is almost all liberated at the reprocessing plants anyway. We should therefore pay particular attention to conditions at the power station or elsewhere in which the fuel could be broken up into particulate form. In this section we will arbitrarily restrict ourselves to accidents at the power station.

There is a whole spectrum of possible accidents in a power station, but the only one that causes much effect outside the power station is one in which most of the fuel melts, releasing radioactivity. Hypothetical accidents are discussed in many papers and books, but

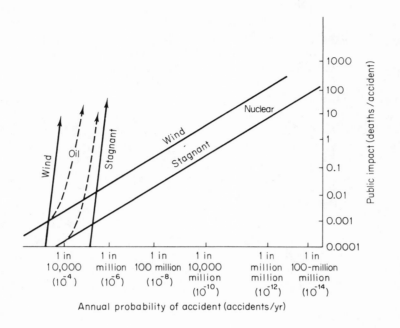

Fig. 10-3. Comparison of public risk from individual accidents, as calculated by Starr [9] for oil fires, and by Ottway [10] and Starr [9] for nuclear accidents. The dashed lines are our pessimistic guess, to be discussed later.

the best reference is Thompson and Beckersley [11]. Unfortunately, this reference does not include the "loss of coolant accident" (LOCA), which we will now describe.

The potential hazard involved in an LOCA in a nuclear power station can be very simply seen and calculated; indeed, it was recognized very early. The first report of the Committee to Study Atomic Energy of the National Academy of Sciences [12] mentioned the possibility of radioactive poisons as a deadly form of warfare. A detailed report by Wigner (Nobel prize winner and professor at Princeton University) and Smyth (recently U.S. Ambassador to the International Atomic Energy Agency) [13] showed that a 100-MW reactor could produce enough radioactivity in *one day* to render one hundred square miles uninhabitable. Nor was this danger withheld from the public; the famous Smyth report on the Manhattan project [14] refers to this. The safety of nuclear power reactors has been of paramount consideration from the start, and experience of normal operation enables safety to be improved continuously.

10. Accidents and Sabotage

The first detailed description of the effects of a large nuclear accident is in an unpublished AEC report [15], according to which an accident could, under adverse meteorological conditions, kill 3000 people and injure tens of thousands. Two other estimates exist [16, 17] that give larger figures, particularly because we now have larger reactors. But none of these estimates considers the large reduction in casualties possible with reasonably prompt evacuation procedures.

Some of the best theoretical studies of the consequences of major radioactivity releases have been performed in the United Kingdom. Beattie [18] confirms the major importance of radioactive iodine in such a release, both inhaled and ingested with milk. The ingestion of iodine in milk can be minimized by impounding milk after an accident.

The radioactive iodine, even when inhaled, can concentrate in a human thyroid and cause cancer. For all but the worst accidents, the iodine release can be estimated and its effect calculated. This is shown in Fig. 10-3, which is based on accident probability calculations by Otway [10], but we venture to suggest that the small probabilities are overoptimistic and our guess is the more realistic dashed curve.

The most obvious feature of accidents is that they occur in a manner, a place, or a time that is unexpected. Nonetheless, accident probabilities can be reduced by considerable advanced planning and thought. Outside the reactor vessel itself is built a concrete containment vessel to contain radioactivity in case of most accidents. Unfortunately, the total energy is so large that it is not practicable to make this vessel large enough to handle the worst conceivable accident. To reduce the effects of an accident, nuclear power stations are built outside cities, so that evacuation would involve a limited number of people, perhaps 10,000.

As an example of the care with which a reactor must be designed, we discuss below a hypothetical LOCA that attracted much public attention in 1971-72. No such accident has occurred, and we hope that none ever will, but in the view of some people, largely because of the way the AEC handled the matter [19], there is insufficient assurance that such an accident will not soon take place.

The reactor core is hot and is cooled by a circulating fluid. If this coolant is removed, the reactor will shut down: automatically if the fluid is also the moderator, and by control rods otherwise. But the decay power (Fig. 9-10) would remain; for a large reactor of 1000 MW_e and 3000 MW_t, this is still 100 MW! As the temperature rises, the zircalloy cladding would chemically interact with any water present; as the temperature rises further, the cladding would melt. Then, the fuel would melt. The chain of critical temperatures is shown in Fig. 10-4.

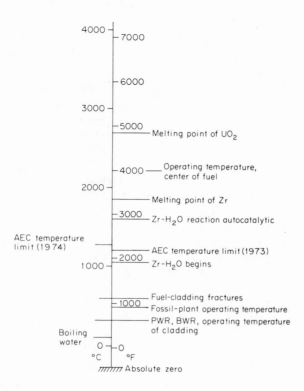

Fig. 10-4. Critical temperatures in reactor operation.

What happens then is uncertain; the worst is that the molten fuel forms a spherical ball and thus has a reduced surface for cooling. The ball might then melt through the bottom of the reactor vessel, through the concrete containment vessel, and eventually (some months later) solidify at a depth of several hundred feet. For obvious reasons, this is called the "China Syndrome." Perhaps the Chinese have an equivalent name for the phenomenon, should one occur on their soil.

If we could be sure that the fuel - with its inventory of 300 million curies of fission products - would stay down in the ground, this would be an "economic accident" but not a "personal accident"; that is, the power station would be destroyed but with no one hurt. However, we cannot be sure; the radioactivity might instead be spread over the countryside; explosions could occur as the molten metal meets the remaining water, and it could violate the containment. Therefore, we must make sure that this accident never happens, and if the cooling fluid (water) is removed, we must replace it as soon as possible.

269

The LOCA is probably the accident that has the most serious consequences in a light-water reactor. As described in Chapter 5, a light-water reactor uses ordinary water (H_2O) both as a neutron moderator and as a working fluid. There are two types: the pressurized water reactor (PWR) and the boiling water reactor (BWR). Therefore, all possible steps are taken to avoid it - by quality control of components - and to mitigate any consequences should it occur - by an emergency core cooling system (ECCS). The LOCA is defined by the AEC as the maximum credible accident for a light-water reactor and is discussed in the safety analysis report of every reactor. For the same reason, it is the accident most discussed by nuclear critics [19-28].

We will go through the course of such an accident in some detail, outlining what is reliable knowledge and what is not. We will first, however, go through the steps taken to prevent its occurrence. We do this for one type of reactor manufactured by General Electric Co., the boiling water reactor (BWR). We study this particular reactor because of the existence of a good company report on it [29], an official AEC report [30], and a detailed review by Ybarrondo, et al. [31].

First, the reactor vessel and the pipe for the primary circuit are made of the best possible materials and are subjected to extensive tests; they are X-rayed for flaws, and every weld is X-rayed at the fabrication plant. The vessels are tested hydrostatically for leaks and are tested ultrasonically. Unfortunately, ultrasonic tests sometimes produce signals with no flaws because of spurious low-level signals (background "noise") in the system itself. It is only used to produce a record, so that later tests can show there has been no change and, therefore, no developing flaw.

On installation, the hydrostatic and ultrasonic tests are repeated and are repeated again every 15 months thereafter. Any change in the ultrasonic signal necessitates an immediate reweld. Any pipe improperly mounted may have excessive strain; this is checked at the same time. The reactor vessel itself is designed and tested so that it is believed by most engineers that it cannot split apart suddenly to cause a catastrophic accident. Unfortunately, splitting apart would not violate an obvious law of nature, and it is possible to prove solely by direct tests that a vessel will *never* fail: we must rely on the experience of the designer.

Experience with steam piping shows that there occur many breaks of vessels and welds that have not been subjected to the exhaustive testing noted above, for example, at laundries. We are primarily concerned with the large pipe break: a double-ended, guillotine break of the largest pipe in the system. We are trying to obtain information on such breaks; at present we know of three at (fossil-fuel) power stations. One pipe that broke in a New Orleans power station was knowingly made in wartime of poor material, not meeting the code of the American Society of Metallurgical Engineers (ASME). Two others, Canal Plant in Massachusetts and one in Pittsburgh, were made of Chromak steel, also not meeting the ASME code. Moreover, all of these were used at higher temperatures and pressures than there would have been in a reactor. There has been no break in any pipe meeting ASME codes in reactor primary-system piping. (There have been breaks in pre-operative tests of secondary systems: Turkey Point No. 3 and Robinson No. 2.)

Therefore, a LOCA is very unlikely. If the accident severity is near that for the "maximum credible accident" (as defined by the AEC), the power station would be shut down for some years for investigation and study. The whole reactor vessel and primary-circuit piping would be replaced. The power company takes every known step to prevent its occurrence in order to protect its investment; in this respect, the protection of the investment and the protection of the public are co-incident goals.

How likely is the accident? Certainly less than once in 100 reactor years, for we have had none yet. Failures in untested pipe are about one in 10,000 operating years, and failures in tested pipes (with less severe operation) should be less than this, perhaps one in 100,000 years.

Unfortunately, no one seems willing to make in writing even the sort of crude estimates given here, so that some people think of such an accident as a very probable occurrence. It is a surprise to us that the nuclear industry and the AEC do not have a detailed report on this, but they do not.

In the maximum credible accident, a large pipe break occurs at the lowest point in the reactor vessel. The water is at a temperature of 600° F (320° C, 593° K) and a pressure of 2250 psi (155 atm). The pressure falls and a steam-water mixture leaves the reactor. The duration of the "blowdown" is easy to calculate; it depends very little on details of reactor shape. Tests have been made with vessels of various shapes and sizes up to a diameter of 5 ft and a length of 30 ft, and, in all cases, the calculation fits the experiment. The scaling laws that allow comparison with a full-size unit are therefore known. We show in Fig. 10-5 a comparison with experiment.

Details of the blowdown, however, are harder to calculate. How much water and how much steam come out? (The ratio of water to steam at any moment is called the *quality* of the fluid.) Is any water left in the vessel at the end? For a BWR, the hydraulic situation is simple enough that we can assume a little is left. For a PWR, we do not know, and small-scale tests are not fitted by the simple calculations. We must therefore assume the worst: that *no* water stays in the vessel.

What happens now depends on the reactor; in the gas-cooled, graphite-moderated reactors (as used in England and the U.S.S.R. and built by Gulf-Atomic), loss of coolant is little problem; the graphite has enough heat capacity to absorb the decay heat for an hour before excessive temperatures are reached. In the liquid-metal (sodium)-

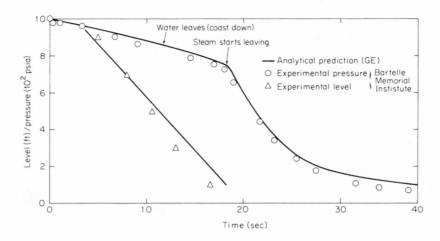

Fig. 10-5. Blow-down test comparison (bottom break). Initial pressure: 1005 psia; initial level: 10.1 ft; pipe diameter: 3/4 in. (Source: [29]).

cooled fast breeder reactors (LMFBR) under development in many countries (particularly the pool type), the coolant is at ordinary atmospheric pressure, and if a leak develops, the coolant will not be pushed out rapidly. If circulation is stopped, the time before corrective action *must* be taken is even longer than for a gas-cooled reactor; the sodium can absorb the decay heat for hours before action need be taken. Moreover, after several hours the decay heat will have fallen, by a factor of 5 to 10, as shown in Fig. 9-9. But for the light-water reactors presently in use in the U.S., immediate action is necessary. The fuel temperature of an isolated element rises at an initial rate of 100° F/sec. For the PWRs (built by Westinghouse, Combustion Engineering, and Babcock & Wilcox) corrective action may be needed within 20 sec. For BWRs (built by General Electric) the power density is lower; it is assumed that to commence corrective action within 30 sec is enough. Several pumps are kept in readiness to put water back into the reactor immediately, and the 30 sec may be needed to start them. In a typical BWR, there are four low-pressure core injection (LPCI) pumps to flood the reactor from the bottom, and two independent core sprays to flood and cool from the top.

If power coming from a generator or the power grid is available, refill can start at once. The reactor is then quickly cooled; however, the LOCA as defined in safety-analysis reports, and as discussed in the public press, assumes that on-site power fails simultaneously with the accident (even though two independent power lines are available to the power station), and also that one of two emergency diesel generators fails to work. This redundancy gives a high probability of *something* working. (A rough guess puts it at 99.9%.) In what follows,

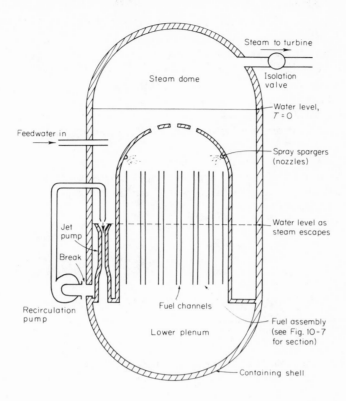

Fig. 10-6. Simplified boiling-water reactor vessel, showing double-ended guillotine break.

we will assume the worst case; that only the core sprayers operate, and only after 30 sec. (The diesels should actually start in 7 sec, and the core sprayers should be at full load in about 25 sec.)

An Accident Analysis

We shall subject the GE BWR to a theoretical accident and analyze its consequences. This particular reactor is simpler than the PWR types and for that reason alone may be a safer unit. Figure 10-6 shows a simplified diagram of the reactor.

Take note of the design of the containing shell. The lower plenum (bottom) of the reactor vessel is essentially isolated from the upper part, in particular, the topmost section or steam dome. Notice that water is fed into the lower plenum by a jet pump and that the lower plenum has no direct entry lines to the outside. The jet pump effectively works in one direction only, downward as shown by the arrow.

10. Accidents and Sabotage

Thus given a whole range of possible accidents, there is a maximum probability of the coolant being retained.

A second important design feature is in the distribution of the fuel. The fuel is divided into groups of 49 rods and each group is surrounded by a metal channel. This further helps isolate an accident in one part of the reactor from the other parts.

After the reactor depressurizing (blowdown) is complete and there is relative calm, water can stay in the reactor vessel covering most of the core without flowing out of the break.

We will consider the break occurring at the input to the recirculation pump. You may wish to refer to Table 10-2 as to the external steps that would be taken, while we discuss what is happening in the interior of the reactor.

TABLE 10-2

Sequence of Events in an LOCA (for a BWR)

Time (sec)	Event
0	Major break in water line
1	Reactor shut-down rods inserted, pumps started, emergency diesel engines started
0-7	Water/steam mixture leaves reactor, some cooling of fuel rods persists
7	Reactor core isolated
8-10	Water in lower plenum of reactor vessel boils rapidly (flashes) causing fluid to cool core partially
10-30	Reactor core temperature may be rising rapidly.
30	Pumps assumed to be at full rated flow, reactor core begins to be sprayed from the top and flooded from the bottom
1-2 min	Full rod fractures may occur
1 min	Full channel, if previously dried out, rewets
3 min	Core is re-covered with water

In the BWR, there are 5-8 sec after the break while water pours out, and before the pressure drops rapidly and the core uncovers. We might guess that superheated, pure water would come out in a jet from the reactor break. But experiments indicate that the water flashes to steam on many surfaces and that a mixture of water and steam escapes. This is called Moody two-phase flow (liquid and gas phase), and it is

274

slower than the ejection of pure water. Until the water level flows below the core, relatively normal cooling of the core will continue. Below the level shown by the dashed line in Fig. 10-6, the height of the jet-pump inlet, steam begins to escape, and the pressure reduction (blowdown) becomes very rapid. The core is quickly uncovered, and for a second or two there is no cooling and the core may dry out. Very soon, however, the pressure falls until the water in the lower plenum reaches the boiling point, and the water rapidly boils. The steam pressure in the core area was pushing the water out through the jet pumps. But now, as the water boils, bubbles are formed, and this will cause a lowering of pressure in the core area, which will draw up the water to cover the core. Measurements have been made of this *level swelling*, which indicate that the water level will go to the top of the core, although as of early 1972 no explicit tests have been made with a break level so low on a real reactor.

The blowdown we have just discussed is the worst possible case. If we take account of the resistive flow properties of the water, the effect is equivalent to that of a break of half the size, and the blowdown will take longer. To be conservative, the AEC will not allow this to be assumed in the safety analysis.

The Fuel Rods

Having looked at what happens to the fluid in the system during a blowdown, let us now focus our attention on what may happen to the fuel rods while the rest of the events are going on.

The reactor engineer must know how fast heat can be carried away or transferred from the rods as he reintroduces the cooling liquid into the reactor. Will the fluid boil as it comes into contact with the rods, will it form a film of steam? The AEC conservatively insists that industry, in its safety analysis, assume a rate of heat transfer for film boiling that is 100 times lower than that for nucleate boiling.

The engineer must also know how much heat is actually stored in the fuel and how much must be "disposed of," so to speak.

The total heat stored in the fuel will depend primarily on the reactor power for the day preceding the accident; even the decay heat will be dominated by short-period radioactivities. The heat generated in the fuel should be well known, but the present industry standard assumes an error of 20%. The temperature of the fuel cladding will rise as heat from the inside of the fuel elements comes to the outside. Also, there will be a pressure stress on the fuel elements. Each fuel element has a small space filled with helium gas; at blowdown, due to the increased heat, this gas and the gas coming from the fission products will expand and build up pressure within the rods. The pressure will tend to push out the zircalloy cladding surrounding the rods. The cladding itself will weaken at the increased temperature and will

275

burst at about 1100° F (600° C, 900° K). In the worst postulated
accident, it is calculated that most fuel rods will bow and burst.
This poses new hazards to the reactor and its environment. Obviously,
it will be harder to salvage the reactor and bring it under control.

Because of this danger, there have been many tests of how fuel
rods will burst [31], but these tests have not been fully satisfactory.
In most cases, the test rods are filled with aluminum oxide (alumina),
not UO$_2$, because alumina is a good insulator for the electrical heaters
that are used to bring the rods up to temperature.

The bursting or bending of a fuel rod can complicate the overall
situation by blocking coolant passages to some extent. If the blockage is complete, some sections of the reactor will be without any
coolant.

Restating some of the above, the rods burst when the internal
pressure exceeds the external pressure, and the rods are at the same
time hot enough for the zircalloy to melt and flow. The internal
pressure of the rods increases as their internal temperature increases,
whereas the external pressure of the steam/water mixture surrounding
the rods falls during blowdown. Tests must be made with a variety of
initial internal pressures to encompass all possibilities. The worst
blocking occurs, it seems, with low initial pressures, such that the
fuel rods expand for a long time before breaking.

Tests at these low pressures are sparse; they are mostly with
unirradiated zirconium and are out of the reactor. The maximum is
therefore ill defined. There is some indication that complete blockage of one channel may occur at some pressure, but the greatest blockage yet observed in any *one* coolant channel (between two rods) is 94%
[32].

This point has been stressed by a group of critics [20, 22] who
argue that channel blockage is not adequately taken into account. The
points they make must be considered, but their arguments are not so
ironclad as to be immune from challenge. Neither the rebuttals nor
the arguments has been conclusively demonstrated.

For example, some tests indicate that blockages up to 90% have
been shown to increase heat transfer because of turbulence, and total
blockages of 16 adjacent channels cause no problem. These tests are
not, however, universally accepted [28]. Moreover, as we shall see,
radiation plays the major part in keeping a BWR core cold.

Although the melting of the cladding occurs at 3400° F (1900° C,
2200° K), at 2100° F there is a reaction between the zinc in the zircalloy and steam. Before melting becomes important, brittle fracture
of the material can occur, and bits of cladding can block the coolant
channel.

The reaction between the zinc-alloy cladding and the steam is
one where the zinc takes an oxygen molecule from the water to become
zinc oxide, useless as a cladding. This process of oxidation is accelerated by the rupture of the cladding, as both sides of the cladding

are then exposed to the steam. As noted, the water/zinc-alloy reaction
starts at 2100° F but becomes automatic and rapid at 2800° F. Thus,
to be conservative, the AEC sets a limit of 2300° F on the fuel temperature.

While on the subject of the rods, we should recognize that there
is some indication of *propagating* fuel failures. The uranium-oxide
pellets sometimes fragment into chips; a chip might be forcibly ejected
from one rod as it breaks and force a break in an adjacent one. This
effect is probably small.

If we now assume that the core spray is used to cool the core,
we might guess that the spray is pushed away from the hot rods by upwelling steam; tests [29] show that this is indeed correct. In the
BWR, however, the rods are contained in a 7 × 7 array in a solid channel; water can flow between channels, and therefore the channel walls
stay cold.

The tests that have been done on this core spray are extensive,
although only one test used pressurized zirconium rods. This one test
is itself open to much question. The temperature was measured with
a device standard to physics laboratories called a thermocouple.* But
the thermocouples were operating near their melting point, making the
temperature readings quite uncertain. Worse still, two of the heaters
failed. Critics have stressed with much validity that this particular
test is very hard to interpret reliably [28, 33].

Were this test to be repeated with high enough starting temperatures, with all heaters properly operating, and were it to simulate
correctly a BWR, the thermocouples would be unimportant. For safety,
we need to know that the fuel rods did not fall apart after the test
from oxidation and embrittlement. We would like such a test to be
repeated ten times for statistical reliability. Thus we could bypass
many arguments.

When the fuel rods are sprayed with water from above, it is a
long time before they are wetted and cooled, as this happens only when
the reactor is flooded. The channel is wetted quite early, but the
exact time is unimportant. The rods are finally wetted when the reactor fills from the bottom.

The last unknown factor about which engineers must speculate is
the degree to which different parts of the reactor core behave differently. The outside fuel rods are always at higher power than the
inside ones, because these outside rods are closer to the moderator.

----

* The thermocouple is a temperature-measuring device consisting
of two dissimilar metals that generate a small voltage, the size of
which depends on the temperature applied to the junction. Such a device
is particularly useful for making temperature measurements at a distance
simply by connecting the thermocouple in a normal electrical circuit
to a meter near the experimenter.

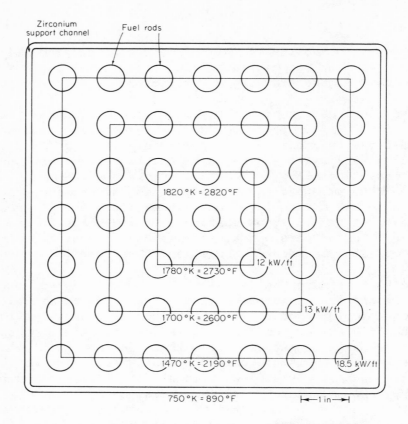

Fig. 10-7. Top view of section of GE 7 × 7 fuel bundle, showing approximation for radiation calculation. Temperatures in equilibrium at 3% of full power shown.

To estimate how hot the core is and how long it will take to cool, we must know the temperature distribution of the fuel rods. Recall that, in the BWR, the rods are set in groups of 49; they are in fact contained within a 7 × 7 array as in Fig. 10-7.

By calculation, it is possible to show that the sudden temperature change of the outer rods ends sooner than that of the inner ones. These rods radiate heat to the inner ones and to the channel walls. After the short-term heat exchange is complete, the inner rods are at a higher temperature than the ones near the outer wall. Better temperature estimates can be made using more sophisticated computer models.

The temperature here is above the AEC's criterion of 2300° F, which was chosen to prevent oxidization and fuel fragmentation, but, if the channel is blocked already, further fragmentation can do no more harm, and the next temperature limit is 3400° F, the melting point of zircalloy.

278

Thus we see that for a GE BWR the jet pumps and the channeling of the core enable us to understand some features simply. There are several features that may be overly conservative, but only further experiment can show this:

1. The AEC insists on an assumption of a higher decay heat than is probably the case;
2. Core flow is assumed to cease and the core to dry out just before the water in the lower plenum flashes to steam;
3. A low heat-transfer coefficient, that given by stable-film boiling, is assumed during the lower-plenum flashing. Calculations can be made of the rewetting of the surfaces. Some experiments by Groenveld [34] indicate that rewetting actually occurs sooner than calculation suggests;
4. Only the spray system is assumed to work, and only after the pumps have reached full power;
5. Even if all flow channels in a 7 × 7 array become blocked completely, which is unlikely, radiation to the channel wall could prevent fuel melting, as demonstrated by the simple argument above.

Safety is too important to be left to experts, and we must all study it. But we must be careful of negative criticism, namely, criticism without suggestions of what to do next, or instead. We should show how the phenomena can be simply described and where further work can be done, and then urge this knowledge directly on the persons who count. We feel nervous when a large 1100-MW$_e$ reactor *just* meets the AEC criteria. Indeed, to meet the criteria by a large margin can inspire confidence and save weeks of public hearings.

The most obvious approach to the problem is to demand a full-scale test of a reactor. A special PWR is being built for the AEC by the Aerojet Nuclear Corp. in Idaho; but this is proceeding *very* slowly. The project was started, with a high priority in 1966, when many high-power reactors were begun. A utility company (e.g., Connecticut Yankee) can build a reactor in three years. Yet in 1972, the projected completion date of the test reactor for the Loss of Fluid Test (LOFT) program is still 1975. This program is under attack by industry, the AEC, and environmental critics, and it is hard to judge how to proceed. A new test program could be started, but in the meantime the country is left with a hiatus that is almost intolerable. We could impose a moratorium on nuclear power, which would mean more pollution and possibly also fuel shortages. Alternatively, we can rely on calculations or the partial tests. More partial tests can, we believe, be applied easily.

In the GE reactors it seems that one profitable place to apply our efforts is in studying the heat transfer during the time when water in the lower plenum flashes to steam. Calculated temperatures might then drop 1000° F. This would obviate discussing the complicated and unverifiable problems of fuel-rod bowing. We urge, therefore, an intensive study of the appropriate heat-transfer mechanisms; we suspect that the AEC interim criteria of June 1971 already have spurred the industry to intensive work in this direction, and that we will soon see such data.

Another alternative is to repeat the zinc-alloy tests with conditions designed to meet the critical objections mentioned earlier [28]. These could include:

1. A start at the highest temperature yet calculated;
2. The use of rods prepressurized to the *worst* calculated pressure;
3. Simulation of decay heat *plus* the 20% uncertainty, for the *worst* rod bundle;
4. Repetition of the test 10 times to ensure repeatability.

As a temporary measure, a power reduction can make the operation more conservative. Over a longer term, GE plans to use redesigned fuel rods anyway. Experience at the Dresden II (Illinois) power station shows that high central temperatures of the fuel rods lead to cracking when fuel is used to high burn-up. Therefore, GE plans to use smaller rods and to have 8 × 8 (=64) in a bundle instead of 7 × 7 (=49). The lower central temperature and the larger surface area for cooling will also reduce the "calculated" maximum accident temperature by 500 to 1800° F lower than many critics have requested.

Another question that has been raised is whether GE should try to inject cooling water sooner, perhaps from a storage tank of water under pressure (an accumulator). We instinctively prefer such static devices, which depend only on a check valve; that is because we often fail to make gadgets work.

Of course, the estimates of accident probabilities above should be multiplied. This multiplication gives a rate per reactor year, for catastrophic accidents, of

$$\underbrace{\frac{1}{100,000}}_{\text{(pipe failure)}} \cdot \underbrace{\frac{1}{100}}_{\text{(pump failure)}} \simeq 10^{-7}$$

This is ridiculously small and hard to believe. All it tells us is that the accident may occur some other way, for example, by the deliberate action of enemies or crackpots. (These possibilities are discussed in the following section.)

The PWR is a much more complicated reactor and is, therefore, inherently less safe, for there are more ways for things to go wrong.

TABLE 10-3

Accident Probability in Reactors

Type	Manufacturer	Major problem
Light-water reactor (PWR)	Westinghouse Babcock & Wilcox Combustion Engineering Kraftweek Union	LOCA
Light-water reactor with jet pumps (BWR)	General Electric	LOCA
Liquid-sodium fast breeder (LMFBR)	US AEC UK AEA USSR France	Local sodium voids
Heavy-water reactor with light-water circuits: (a) CANDU (Gentilly type), (b) SGHWR	AECL (Canada) UK AEA	LOCA
Heavy-water reactor with separate coolant loops and heat exchanger (CANDU)	AECL (Canada)	LOCA
Advanced gas-cooled AGR and gas-cooled Magnox	UK AEA	Corrosion of fuel
Graphite-moderated water-cooled	USSR	LOCA
High-temperature gas-cooled (graphite) reactor (HTGR), with uranium-carbide fuel	Gulf-Atomic UK AEA "Dragon"	"Rod drop"

In Table 10-3, we present our own list of accident problems in different reactors in order of their inherent safety (the safest at the bottom). We recognize that, while knowledgeable, we are not experts on reactor safety; moreover, inherent safety problems can be overcome by safeguards. We are reminded of the fact that aspirin is inherently safer than cyanide, but more people die of aspirin overdoses than by cyanide poisoning.

We guess that by the year 2000 there will be 500 nuclear power stations in the U.S. One serious LOCA might occur every 100,000 reactor years, or at one reactor in 200 years. We tentatively assume that *some* serious accident can occur more often than this. Moreover, even in the WASH 740 report of the AEC [15], a serious accident might cause no deaths if the meteorology is favorable. We will assume an accident, with unfavorable meteorology, once every 30 years, so that 3000 people die. We have no justification for such pessimism but derive therefrom 1×10^{-11} deaths/kWh.

10. Accidents and Sabotage

It is the PWR safety that has particularly triggered recent public attention on the LOCA. One of the authors [35] has written a survey of the technical problems at issue for the PWR and some bumbling of the AEC in dealing with these problems. Gilette [19] has outlined many of the bureaucratic errors in dealing with these. Another recent review of the calculated ECCS capability is given by Leeper [36].

The preceding was a detailed discussion of one particular type of reactor and illustrates the detailed study necessary. Detailed discussions are available for other reactors and accidents: for the sodium-cooled fast breeder, we particularly recommend Farmer's [37] collection and Rose [38]; for light-water reactors, Bright [39]; and for the gas-cooled reactor, Kaplan [40].

Actual Accidents

We should remember that there have been only 4 major reactor accidents in the western world (Table 10-4). At Windscale in England, a plutonium-production (military) graphite reactor caught fire, and most of its fission products went up the chimney. The hazard to the general public was reduced by impounding milk supplies, which could otherwise have given overdoses to the human thyroid.

At Chalk River, Canada, an experimental heavy-water reactor leaked and had to be replaced.

At the Fermi reactor, Laguna Beach, near Detroit, coolant flow channels in the liquid-metal fast-breeder became accidentally blocked; several fuel-rod assemblies partially melted, but there was no excessive radiation leak.

Finally, at an Army test reactor in Idaho (SL 1) a shutdown rod was disconnected and removed, causing a reactor accident that killed three technicians.

In present power reactors, design precludes accidents, proceeding in exactly the same way as the above; also none of these four accidents injured any member of the public. The problem is to maintain this safety with many more reactors in service.

SABOTAGE

Sabotage can be a serious problem in modern life. We may carefully design a modern power station so that accidents will not normally occur; there are many safeguards in the chain and the probability of any one of them failing is small. These small probabilities multiply, giving a negligible probability of an overall accident. But if someone deliberately sets out to cause an accident, redundant safety systems *can* be bypassed. It seems that to cause a major accident, several conditions are necessary.

TABLE 10-4

Major Reactor Accidents in the Western World

Location	Date	Type of accident
Chalk River, Canada	1952	Coolant blockage caused partial fuel melt-down and hydrogen explosion in heavy-water reactor. The core was destroyed, but no injuries or deaths
Windscale, England	1957	A plutonium-production reactor was overheated due to the Wigner effect in the graphite moderator and caught fire. 20,000 Ci of iodine 131 was liberated to the environment, and milk was impounded. No radiation injuries or deaths
SL 1, National Reactor Testing Station, Idaho, USA	1961	A shutdown rod in an Army test reactor was removed and caused sudden criticality. Although radiation contributed to the death of 3 Army technicians, there was no large release to the environment or injury to the public
Enrico Fermi Reactor, Laguna Beach, Michigan, USA	1966	The sodium coolant was blocked in a section of this experimental breeder reactor, causing melt-down of some fuel subassemblies. No large radiation release, injuries, or deaths

1. The saboteur must know enough about the specific power station oil-storage farm, dam, or reactor to know how to do the most damage. Presumably a bomb placed 30 ft below the water surface could blow a dam, or one placed inside the reactor containment vessel could cause an LOCA. These places should be made inaccessible during operation. This is true of reactors, but similar precautions have not been taken for dams or oil- and gas-storage tanks.

2. For reactors, engineered safeguards operate automatically to prevent environmental hazards. These cannot be short-circuited in advance, for the reactor would be shut down. Simultaneous destruction of safeguards would hence be needed.

3. Any saboteur from outside would have to pass a security fence and guard system. Nuclear reactors are well guarded, but dams and other energy-storage areas are not.

4. The saboteur would have to be a person who wanted to kill others as well as himself. In fact, saboteurs usually stop short of destroying many other people; there seems to be a mental block here. This is fortunate, because otherwise the human race would probably have been destroyed long ago.

The most common types of saboteurs are the enemy agent and the educated madman. Their motives are different. It seems that oil tanks, gas-storage tanks, and dams are easier to destroy than are nuclear power stations, and their destruction can cause as much or more havoc. However, the peculiar nature of radiation, and the spectacular manner in which nuclear power came to public attention in 1945, might combine to make a power station peculiarly attractive to someone who wants to "go out" in a "big way."

To guard against sabotage, we need a good security plan, which must be kept secret just as the location of a home burglar alarm is kept secret. The U.S. Continental Army Command (CONARC) inspects many sensitive industries, including all large power stations. Although any army's mandate is to guard against enemy action, it is wise also to guard against the madman.

Probably the most likely saboteur is a former, disgruntled employee of the power company. Some years ago, such an ex-employee of Consolidated Edison Co. of New York went around blowing up substations. He destroyed several before he was caught. More recently, in October, 1971, a fire destroyed the control room of the just completed Indian Point 2 nuclear power station. In March, 1972, a mechanic employed by Consolidated Edison was indicted for setting the fire.

In 1961, at the National Reactor Testing Station in Idaho, there was an accident at an army test reactor (SL 1). Most of the uranium was spattered around the laboratory building, which had no containment vessel. The three operators died.

The course of events in this accident has been traced by experts [11]. A shut-down rod was removed by hand to start this criticality accident. No one knows why, and the report (in a footnote) speculated that the operator deliberately committed suicide. Nuclear power reactors are designed so that this particular accident could not take place, but there might be some other method of committing suicide in the grand manner. A study of the possibilities of such an accident is an engineer's job; the prevention of it is a policeman's or a psychiatrist's job. All three jointly should study how to prevent sabotage.

Sabotage prevention plans should also be made for all other energy devices, dams, and oil-storage farms.

HAZARDS OF LIQUID SODIUM

The most usual working fluid for heat engines has been water; it is plentiful and well understood. However, as we have noted, obtaining a high efficiency depends upon a high temperature of the working fluid. Water boils at 212° F (100° C, 373° K) at atmospheric pressure, and to obtain higher temperatures high pressures are necessary. This leads to problems with strengths of materials, and with nuclear reactors it leads to an accident potential.

Accordingly, searches are continuously made for materials that can work at higher temperatures. Gases, helium and carbon dioxide, are obvious choices, but their heat capacities are small. The choice seems to be the alkali metals, lithium, sodium, and potassium. These are liquid at atmospheric pressure at over 1000° F (with boiling points of 2373, 1616, and 1400° F, respectively). They also have, however, the disadvantage, well known by most schoolboys, of rapid chemical interaction with air or water. The accident potential of large quantities of alkali metals is therefore large and must be studied.

The first use of liquid sodium has been in the nuclear field; it was the working fluid for the thermal neutron reactor in the submarine *Sea Wolf* and is the working fluid for the fast breeder reactors that are in the prototype stages in France, U.S.S.R., U.K., and, shortly, the U.S., Japan, and Italy. Lithium is a good absorber of neutrons and also regenerates tritium in the reaction

$$_0n^1 + {_3}Li^7 \longrightarrow {_2}He^5 + {_1}T^3$$

This reaction makes lithium useful both as a reflecting blanket and as a heat-transfer medium for fusion reactions using the deuterium - tritium cycle, which is that cycle most likely to be used first. Liquid sodium has also been proposed for use in the solar power project of Meinel and Meinel (discussed in previous chapters).

The development of the technology of liquid sodium has taken a long time and is not yet finished. This is one of the major tasks of the fast-breeder-reactor development program.

One container holding 2000 tons of liquid sodium seems very unsafe. Studies of the safety have been made [41]: Small leaks of 1-10 lb of sodium are likely. They would oxidize and form a spray, preventing easy location of the leak. The sodium oxide (NaO) is caustic and can destroy skin and nasal mucus. Larger spills can occur at fuel handling. Thus the sodium can become a personnel hazard, but it is unlikely to be a hazard to the general public.

TABLE 10-5

Summary of Environmental Problems of Fuels

Fuel	Accidents and diseases	Emissions	Thermal effects	Supply in US at 1970 rate (yr) (assuming one fuel only)
Nonreplenishable				
Coal	Mining accidents Black lung disease Strip-mining ravages	NO_2, NO, SO_2, CO_2, CO, mercury, radium, fly-ash	Adds	400
Oil	Spills Well accidents Fires	SO_2, NO_2, NO, CO_2, CO, vanadium, ash	Adds	13 (excluding oil shales)
Gas	Explosions at well, pipeline, or ship	NO_2, NO, CO_2	Adds	16
U^{235} (fission)	Mining radiation hazard; spills of stored or transported radioactive waste (10^{10} Ci stored in equilibrium)	Kr^{85}, Xe^{133}	Adds	>14 (at \$20/lb)
U^{238}	Diversion of plutonium to bombs		Adds	30,000
Th^{233} (breeder)	Reactor accidents, spill of radioactivity (10^{10} Ci in reactor)	I^{131}		100,000
D, Li	Does not yet work; 10^7 Ci tritium produced per day	T	Adds	1,000,000,000

Replenishable (apparently)			
Solar	Impractical, large area needed		800
Hydro	Ecology changed; dams silt up and break; valuable land used up		1/10
Tidal	Expensive		1/10
Geothermal	May last 30 years, may last 10,000 years; possible earthquakes; salt-dirty water brought to surface	Adds	1/10-10

287

10. Accidents and Sabotage

ACCIDENT INSURANCE

"This policy does not insure against loss caused by... any earth movement, including but not limited to earthquake, caused by... flood, surface water, water which backs up through sewers... ."

Every insurance policy has these and other clauses, including some for radiation hazards. These exclusions mean that a major catastrophe leaves people unprotected. Every year the President of the U.S. has to declare a disaster situation in one or another state as a result of some catastrophe. Large power stations can produce large accidents.

Unfortunately, large-scale accident insurance is still rare. The Price-Anderson Act [42] introduced some insurance for nuclear power, but not for hydroelectric dam failures. The act has been criticized because it was designed as both stimulant and subsidy for nuclear power, but we should examine its *present* effects.

The federal law now insists [43] that every nuclear power station be insured against liability for $560,000,000, of which $85,000,000 is presently held by private insurance pools and the rest by the federal government. Above $560,000,000, liability ceases. This limitation of liability has been criticized, but it is better than the limitation of zero for floods! Removal of this limitation of liability will probably not help the public. Limitation of liability is characteristic of a private enterprise system; most companies go bankrupt with a smaller claim than $500 million. Moreover, major industries are adept at creating subsidiary companies, so that a bankruptcy can occur in a subsidiary without bringing the parent to his knees. We need a systematic catastrophe insurance system, for all large hazards, with a maximum of $10 billion or more. A limitation of liability above this amount probably makes no difference in practice, but, since it seems to alarm some members of the public, it should be omitted.

So far, the insurance industry and the government have done well, since there have been almost no claims [44]. This does not, however, mean that the insurance is unnecessary.

SUMMARY OF ENVIRONMENTAL PROBLEMS OF FUELS

Table 10-5 presents a summary of the environmental problems caused by the fuels we have discussed up to this point.

REFERENCES

[1] New York Times (1973). "New York Times Encyclopedic Almanac." New York Times, New York. Also "Guinness Book of World Records" (annual). Sterling, New York; and Metropolitan Life Insurance Co. Statistical Bulletin (annual).

[2] US Govt (1971). 4th Annual Rept. of the US Secretary of Transportation on the Administration of the National Pipeline Safety Act, 1968 (Appendix 1). Dept. of Transportation, USGPO.

[3] FPC (1972). FPC Opinion and Order Authorizing Distrigas to Import LNG, March 9, 1972 (DC 54); and FPC Presiding Examiner's Initial Decision upon Applications to Import LNG, May 22, 1972 (DC-51). USGPO. [Since the text was written, the FPC has produced three detailed environmental statements: "Draft Environmental Statements for Importation of Liquified Natural Gas to Staten Island, New York, Everett, Massachusetts, and Providence, Rhode Island," October, 1973.]

[4] Burgess, D.S., Murphy, J.N., and Zabetakis, M.G. (1970). "Hazards Associated with the Spillage of Liquified Natural Gas on Water." Rept. of Investigation 7448, US Dept. of the Interior, Bureau of Mines, USGPO (November).

[5] Enger, T., and Hartman, D.E. (1972). "Mechanics of the Liquified Natural Gas-Water Interaction." Shell Pipeline Corp., Research and Development Lab., Houston, Texas.

[6] Wilson, R. (1973). "Natural Gas Is a Beautiful Thing." Bull. At. Sci., September.

[7] Fay, J., and Mackenzie, J. (1972). "Cold Cargo." Environment, November 19.

[8] Starr, C., Greenfield, M.A., and Hausknecht, D.F. (1972). Nuclear News Vol.15, p.37.

[9] Starr, C., Greenfield, M.A., and Hausknecht, D.F. (1972). Rept. to State of California on Safety of Steam Generating Power Stations. Available from Engineering Dept., Univ. of California at Los Angeles, Los Angeles, California.

[10] Ottway, H.H., and Erdman, R.C.E. (1970). Nucl. Engineering Design Vol.13, p.365.

[11] Thompson, T.J., and Beckerley, J.G. (eds.) (1964). "The Technology of Reactor Safety." MIT Univ. Press, Cambridge, Massachusetts.

[12] National Academy of Sciences (1941). 1st Rept. of Committee to Study Atomic Energy. NAS, Washington, D.C.

[13] Wigner, E., and Smyth, H.D. (1945). Report quoted in [14].

[14] Smyth, H.D. (ed.) (1945). "Atomic Energy for Military Purposes," Official rept on the development of the atomic bomb, p.65. Reprinted by Princeton Univ. Press, Princeton, New Jersey (1948).

[15] US Govt. (1957). "Theoretical Possibilities and Consequences of Major Accidents in Large Nuclear Power Plants." USAEC Rept. WASH-740, USGPO.

10. Accidents and Sabotage

[16] Atomic Power Development Associates (1957). "A Report on the Possible Effects at Laguna Beach, Michigan." Prepared for the Atomic Power Development Associates, Detroit, Michigan.

[17] Mattison, L., and Daly, R. (1964). Science and Citizen, April.

[18] Beattie, J.R., and Bryant, P.M. (1970). "Assessment of Environmental Hazards from Reactor Fission Product Releases." Rept. AHSB(S)R135. Available from HM Stationery Office, London.

[19] Gillette, R. (1972). Science Vol.177, pp.771,867,970.

[20] Forbes, I.A., Ford, D.F., Kendall, H.W., and MacKenzie, J.J. (1971). Nuclear News Vol.14, p.32.

[21] Forbes, I.A., Ford, D.F., Kendall, H.W., and MacKenzie, J.J. (1972). Environment Vol.14, p.40.

[22] Ford, N.C., and Kane, J.W. (1971). Bull. At. Sci. Vol.27, p.27.

[23] Ford, D.F., Kendall, H.W., and MacKenzie, J.J. (1972). Nuclear News Vol.15, p.28.

[24] Lapp, R.E. (1971). "A Citizen's Guide to Nuclear Power." New Republic, Washington, D.C.

[25] Bryerton, G. (1970). "Nuclear Dilemma." Ballantine, New York.

[26] Curtis, R., and Hogan, E. (1972). "Perils of the Peaceful Atom." Ballantine, New York.

[27] Novick, S. (1969). "The Careless Atom." Houghton-Mifflin, New York.

[28] Union of Concerned Scientists (1972). "Affirmative Testimony in Public Hearing of Emergency Core Cooling Systems." UCS, Washington, D.C., March 23.

[29] Slifer, B.C. (1971). Topical Rept. NEDO 10329, including appendices and errata, General Electric Co., New York (April).

[30] US Govt. (1972). "Statistical Abstract of the United States." USGPO.

[31] Ybarrondo, L.J., Solbrig, C.W., and Isbin, H.S. (1972). "The Calculated Loss-of-Coolant Accident - A Review." Amer. Inst. Chem. Eng.

[32] Rittenhouse, P.L. (1971). Nuclear Safety, August-September.

[33] Aerojet Nuclear Corp. (1972). Testimony of Dr. Brackett of ANC at ECCS hearings, March.

[34] Groenveld, D.C. (1970). Rept. No. AECL-3281. Atomic Energy of Canada, Ltd., Ottawa, Canada.

[35] Leeper, C.K. (1973). Physics Today Vol.26, p.39.

[36] Wilson, R. (1973). Nature, February 9.

[37] Farmer, F.R. (ed.) (1970). "Fast Reactor Safety." UK AEC, London.

[38] Rose, D.E. (1971). "LMFBR Safety." Nuclear Safety Vol.12, p.421.

[39] Bright, G.O. (1971). "Light Water Reactor Safety." Nuclear Safety Vol.12, p.421.

[40] Kaplan, S.I. (1971). "HTGR Safety." Nuclear Safety Vol.12, p.421.

[41] First, M.W. (1972). Nuclear Safety Vol.13, p.37. [And other sources.]

[42] US Govt. (1965). "Selected Materials on Atomic Energy Indemnity Utilization," and hearings on proposed extension of AEC indemnity legislation. AEC, USGPO.

[43] Trosten, L.M., and England, W.T. (1968). Nuclear Safety Vol.9. p.343.
[44] Marrone, J. (1971). Nuclear Safety Vol.12, p.291.

Additional Recent References

US Congress (1974). Hearings on Light-Water Reactor Safety. JCAE, USGPO (January).
Rasmussen, N. (1974). "Reactor Safety." Rept. to AEC, USGPO (April).
AEC (1974). Rept on Reactor Vessel Failure. Advisory Committee on Reactor Safeguards to the AEC, USGPO (January).
AEC (1974). Draft Envionmental Impact Statement for the Liquid-Metal Fast Breeder Reactor Program (LMFBR). AEC Rept. WASH 1535, USGPO.
Weinberg. A. (1972). "The Moral Imperatives of Nuclear Energy." Science, July.
Emelyanov, V.S. (1971). "Nuclear Energy in the Soviet Union." Bull. At. Sci. November, p.38.
Union of Concerned Scientists (1972-1974). Various reports; "Nuclear Safety: An Evaluation of Recent Reports." P.O. Box 289, MIT Station, Cambridge, Massachusetts.
Natl. Academy of Sciences - Natl. Research Council (1972). "LNG Transportation and Terminal Safety." Rept. of Conf. Boston, 1972.
Edsall, J.T. (1974). "Hazards of Nuclear Fission Power and the Choice of Attenuators." J. Environ. Conservation Vol.1 (1), Spring.

PROBLEMS

1. Look up the area of the U.S. in an atlas and check the number of aircraft accidents in a year (from statistical abstracts). If these occur randomly, what is the chance of an aircraft hitting within 100 ft of a nuclear reactor or LNG storage tank?´ (Assume 500 of the former and 2000 of the latter exist, randomly spaced, in the whole continental U.S.) How much is this chance increased if the reactors lie on aircraft traffic lanes? Or on an airport approach path? (Note that not only is the area smaller, but most accidents happen on landing and takeoff.)

2. Discuss the relative hazard of a Boeing 747 hitting: (i) a nuclear reactor with containment vessel; (ii) an LNG storage tank; (iii) an LNG ship in harbor next to a large city; (iv) a crowded football stadium.

3. What is a 6 months' supply of oil for an oil-fired 1000-MW$_e$ power station? Assuming this oil has $\frac{1}{2}$% sulfur by weight, how much sulfur is there?

10. Accidents and Sabotage

Assume all this oil burns in a short time at *ground level* under bad meteorological conditions (1 mph wind; Pasquill F stability) in a city with a population density of 40 persons/acre (25,000/square mile). Assuming that an SO_2 concentration of 0.03 ppm increases the death rate by 3% and the effect is linear with concentration, estimate the increase in mortality due to the accident. (Use Sutton's equation, Chapter 8, to evaluate the concentration.)

4. Approximately 50,000 persons are killed in automobile accidents every year in the U.S. Of these, one-half are "innocent" bystanders, and their death must be considered involuntary. Determine from governmental authorities the total amount of money spent on automobile safety in the U.S. Assume that spending the same amount again could halve the death rate. To how much does this correspond per death? per involuntary death? Compare with the other values used in this chapter.

5. Why is it important, for reactor safety, to maintain good thermal contact between the fuel and the moderator?

6. Summarize those features that make a liquid-sodium-cooled reactor *safer* than a light-water reactor, and those that make it more dangerous.

7. What features of the design of a fast neutron reactor prevent it from exploding like a bomb? Do these features apply to thermal neutron reactors?

8. What happens if a local void (bubble) occurs in the fluid of one of the following reactors: (a) pressurized-water reactor; (b) boiling-water reactor; (c) liquid-sodium fast breeder. Is the effect stabilizing or destabilizing? (d) Does this make these reactors dangerous or not?

11

Transportation of Fuel
and Wastes

FOSSIL FUELS

Traditionally, the cost of transportation of fuel was sufficiently large so that for centuries it was used where it was found. The industrial revolution brought towns and factories to the coal in northern England, the Rhine Valley, the Lehigh Valley in Pennsylvania, and in many other places. Only as the transportation costs have come down (relative to other costs) has it been possible to spread the use of fossil fuels over wider areas (and hence the spread of pollution).

Since the transportation costs influence environmental decisions, in Fig. 11-1 we summarize the costs, as best known in 1972, of transporting energy. The cheapest energy to transport is the nuclear energy in uranium: so cheap, in fact, that the cost of transportation is never a serious factor in siting nuclear power plants. Next cheapest is the transportation of oil by oil tanker; and we see that the transportation of oil several thousand miles barely increases its cost.

Transmission of electricity by cable seems so simple to the private householder that it is the first suggestion for transporting energy, but it is only the simplest for distances of a mile or less. It is for this reason that transmission of electricity from the western U.S. (where coal is plentiful) to the eastern U.S. (where a large demand exists) is not seriously proposed, although it is now transported

293

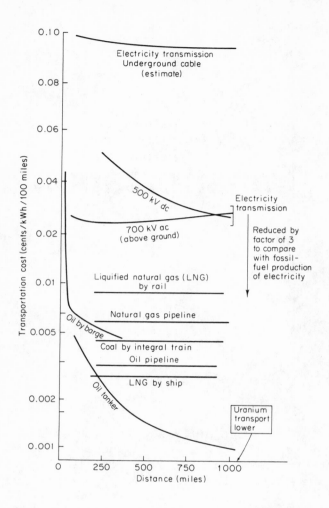

Fig. 11-1. Energy transportation costs, adapted from [1].

1000 miles from the "four corners" area (Arizona, New Mexico, Colorado, Utah) to Los Angeles county at a cost of 3 mils (0.3 cents)/kWh. Already 1% of the cost of electricity is transmission costs.

These numbers are important because it is easiest to insist on good environmental controls for the cheapest method of transportation. The increased cost will be small and will not drive industry to an environmentally inferior method.

The low cost of transporting oil and liquified natural gas (LNG) by ship allows for large-scale use of oil and gas by nonproducing countries. An increasing portion (rising from 25%, or 3 million bbl/day in 1970 to 50% or 11 million bbl/day estimated in 1980) of U.S.

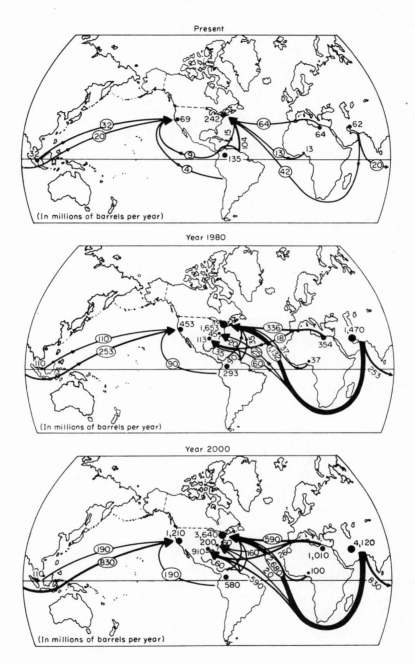

Fig. 11-2. Present and future oil importation to the U.S. according
to U.S. Dept. of Commerce projections. The thickness of the line is
proportional to the amount of oil shipped on the route, and the numbers thereon are in millions of barrels per year.

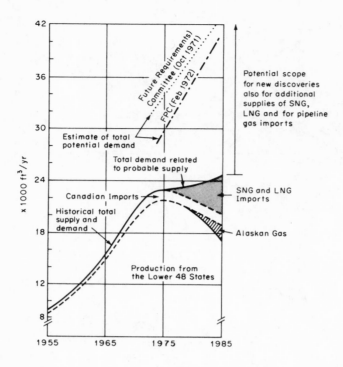

Fig. 11-3. The demand for natural gas in the U.S., showing the projected availability of supply and the projected demand; the gap is obvious.

oil requirements are met this way. About half the tonnage of world trade is oil. In Fig. 11-2 we illustrate this transportation of oil, as projected by the U.S. Department of Commerce.

The gas picture is more complex. The increase in cost of transporting LNG over oil by tanker is mainly due to the safety features necessary (Chapter 10). If the gasification of coal becomes as cheap as present, shipment by pipeline for 2000 miles in the U.S. will be cheaper than shipment by LNG tanker over 4000 miles. The price of foreign gas is unpredictable. With these uncertainties in mind, Fig. 11-3 gives presently predicted demand for natural gas and presently planned sources of supply - showing an energy gap.

When oil is transported, there is still another choice: shall the oil be refined at the oil well or at the location of the consumer? A refinery can produce many petrochemicals useful in medicine and industry, and this suggests a location near the consumer; also an oil company likes to have control over this part of the business, and it is hard to have such control in a foreign country. On the other hand, an oil-well refinery allows the oil company to transport only refined products, leaving waste behind for someone else. Again, the environmental concerns are large and obvious - and usually neglected.

This large increase in oil and LNG importation will be in mammoth tankers: 200,000 deadweight tons, containing 4 million bbl or 225 million gal. Terminals must be equally large. Some safety features of a large-scale accident due, for example, to earthquake or sabotage, have already been discussed.

The large tankers will require new deep-water berths, which fortunately will keep them away from major cities but may extend pollution to presently untainted estuaries or sections of estuaries. At these major terminals, oil and LNG will be distributed by barge, and the number of small spills will increase with the volume of oil transshipped and the number of transshipments.

Oil Spills

In 1967 the Esso ship Torrey Canyon ran aground on some rocks off the southwest coast of England. The ship had been sailing under automatic pilot, which had been incorrectly set. In the course of the accident 50,000 tons (29,000,000 gal) of oil were spilled onto the ocean. Attempts to clean up the mess with detergent led to worse problems. Fortunately, after some agitation, we now have better procedures.

These large spills make news, but in 1970 one million tons of oil were spilled in over 3700 spills in the western hemisphere. According to Thor Heyerdahl [2], the major Atlantic trade routes are covered not only with flotsam and jetsam but with an almost continuous oil slick.

In Tables 11-1 and 11-2, we list the recorded oil spills of over 42,000 gal for the years 1957-1971. The *total* oil spilled in the U.S. and territorial waters alone is nearly 9,000,000 gal in 1971, as shown in Fig. 11-2. The effect of one such small spill has been recorded in detail [5].

We see that the large numbers of small spills dominate the total oil spilled. However, it is the large spills that can endanger a whole species of fish, by destroying a complete hatchery, for example. Thus the ecological problems of spills are not directly proportional to the amount spilled, and we should probably have a similar separation approach between large and small spills, as discussed by Farmer and Starr (Chapter 6, Figs. 6-1 and 6-2), for the human death rate due to accidents.

The effects of these oil spills are many and varied. Even small quantities of oil can spoil the pleasure of a bathing beach by covering it with globules of tar. The beaches in California were probably always somewhat contaminated by the local oil, but the beaches in England were clean until 1940; by 1960, oil spills and a prevailing westerly wind and surface current made them less pleasant.

Oil is particularly serious because it spreads on the surface due to its low surface tension; this reduces the oxygen intake of the sea and can kill fish. Pouring oil on troubled waters to calm them is traditional, but not ecologically sound. It is for this reason

TABLE 11-1

Reported Tanker Spills in Excess of 42,000 gal, 1957-1971 [3]

Name/location	Date	Cause	Material	Est. spill (gal)
Torrey Canyon, Scillies	3/18/67	Grounding	Crude	29,000,000
World Glory, South Africa	6/13/68	Hull failure	Crude	13,500,000
Keo, Massachusetts	11/5/69	Hull failure	#4	8,800,000
R.C. Stoner, Wake Island	9/6/67	Grounding	Mixed	6,250,000
A.M. Browig, 35 mi W, Heligoland	2/20/66	Collision	Crude	5,300,000
Andron, west coast of Africa	5/5/68	Sinking	Crude	5,000,000
Ocean Eagle, Puerto Rico	3/3/68	Grounding	Crude	3,500,000
Polycommander, Spain	5/5/70	Grounding	Crude	3,500,000
Tampico, Baja California	3/57	Grounding	Diesel	2,500,000
Arrow, Straits of Canso	2/70	Grounding	Bunker C	1,500,000
Pacific Glory, 6 mi NW, Isle of Wight	10/21/70	Collision	?	1,400,000
Gen. Colocotronis, Bahamas	3/7/68	Grounding	Crude	1,300,000
Esso Essen, South Africa	4/29/68	Grounding	Crude	1,300,000
Argea Prima, Puerto Rico	7/17/62	Grounding	Crude	1,200,000
Ocean Grandeur, Australia	3/3/70	Grounding	Crude	900,000
Oregon Standard, San Francisco	1/18/71	Collision	Bunker C	840,000
Esso Gettysburg, Connecticut	1/22/71	Grounding	Kerosene, #2	780,000
Otto N. Miller, 10 mi S, Beachy Head	3/27/65	Collision	?	730,000
Witwater, Canal Zone	12/13/68	Hull failure	Mixed	630,000
Benedicte, 13 mi off Trelleborg	5/31/69	Collision	Crude	590,000
Floreal, 2 mi off Gibraltar	9/11/65	Collision	?	560,000
Evje, Alaska	5/2/67	Grounding	Jet	420,000
Gironde, off Brittany	8/19/69	Collision	?	420,000
Tim, Pennsylvania	2/18/68	Sinking	#6	290,000

	Date	Cause	Type	Amount
Efthycosts, Bristol Channel	3/8/70	Collision	?	220,000
Esso Wandsworth, Thames	9/23/65	Collision	?	220,000
Hamilton Trader, Liverpool Bay	4/30/69	Collision	Resid	210,000
Barge, New York	12/27/70	Grounding	#2	200,000
R.L. Polling, N.H.	5/10/69	Collision	#2	200,000
Marita, California	9/20/62	Collision	Bunker C	180,000
Florida, W. Falmouth, Mass.	9/10/69	Grounding	#2	172,000
Algol, New York	2/9/69	Grounding	#6	168,000
Hullgate, 4 mi off Beachy Head	4/8/71	Collision	?	165,000
Monti Ulia, Coryton	7/27/70	Grounding	?	140,000
Barge, New York Bay	5/22/70	Collision	#6	131,000
Barge, Florida	5/26/70	Collision	Gas	84,000
Texaco Caribbean, 9 mi off Dungeness	1/11/71	Collision	?	84,000
Barge, Louisiana	5/23/69	?	#2	76,000
Heruluv, 2 mi ENE, South Goodwin Light Vessel	5/15/71	Collision	?	72,000
Barge, Maryland	7/12/70	Human error	#6	67,000
Barge, Louisiana	5/26/70	Collision	Crude	67,000
Kenai Peninsula, Pennsylvania	11/5/68	Collision	Crude	42,000
Otello, Lindal Sound	3/20/70	Collision	?	serious leakage
Lutsk, Bosphorus	3/1/66	Collision	?	serious leakage
Mosli, N. Atlantic	7/13/66	Collision	?	serious leakage
Beefeater, Thames	11/5/68	Collision	?	some leakage

11. Transportation of Fuel and Wastes

TABLE 11-2

Recorded Large Spills Involving Pipelines,
Refineries, Bulk Storage and Transfer,
1967-1971, Spills > 42,000 gal [4]

Location	Cause	Reported amount	Date
Pipelines			
West Delta Area, LA, OCS	Anchor dragging	6,600,000	10/15/67
Persian Gulf	Break	4,000,000	4/20/70
Buckeye, Lima, OH	Unknown	690,000	1/14/69
Alabama	Rupture	590,000	12/10/70
Chevron, MP 299, LA, OCS	Unknown	310,000	2/11/69
Gulf, St. 131, LA, OCS	Anchor dragging	250,000	3/12/68
Michigan	Human error	210,000	10/7/71
Tennessee	Break	184,000	10/6/71
Louisiana	Unknown	155,000	3/17/71
Missouri	Human error	147,000	12/20/71
Texas	Rupture	140,000	12/6/71
Kansas	Rupture	118,000	10/18/71
Illinois	Break	108,000	7/23/71
Tennessee	Vandalism	100,000	12/26/71
North Dakota	Unknown	84,000	5/4/70
Wyoming	Break	84,000	3/3/69
Immigration Canyon, Utah	Rupture	84,000	9/7/69
Indiana	Leak	60,000	1/9/70
Virginia	Rupture	75,000	5/6/71
Illinois	Break	63,000	7/8/71
Indiana	Break	60,000	5/9/71
Mississippi	Break	55,000	3/5/71
Texas	Break	42,000	11/21/71
Pennsylvania	Break	42,000	11/28/71
Texas	Struck by bulldozer	42,000	6/23/71
New Mexico	Unknown	42,000	7/14/71
Refineries			
Moron, Venezuela	Dumped thru sewer	678,000	3/29/68
Humbolt Bay, CA	Hose eruption	60,000	12/68
Bulk storage and transfer			
Seawarren, NJ	Tank failure	8,400,000	11/69
Indiana	Tank collapse	3,500,000	11/23/70

that breaking the oil up into globules by the chemical action of detergents is so important. No one seems sure of the long-term fate of the oil and whether the oil lasts forever like DDT. Radioactive tracers have been suggested for following this long-term fate.

Regulation of Oil Spills

A particularly obnoxious feature of large or small spills is that probably half are deliberate. Oil tankers coming to the U.S. often take back grain as a return load. Their tanks must be cleaned. Although they could be cleaned in port and the water stored, this would hold up the ship an extra valuable day. A deliberate "accidental" oil spill on the high seas is the method too often adopted.

To stop these spills we need accountability, and this may mean strong international controls. The cost of oil spills is estimated to be about $10/gal spilled, which does not include "hidden" ecological costs.

Tagging of oil with radioactive tracers may allow tracing a culprit; the number of international traders in oil is small enough so that a different isotope could be used for each trader. The company could then be held to account. Deliberate oil spilling, if and when detected, could be followed by a ban on all ships of that company from the ports of the civilized world.

Coal Transportation

Coal is not transported as much as oil; and coal does not spread upon the surface of the water. However, coal dust can be spilled along railroad lines and cause local environmental nuisance.

Transportation of Wastes

Oil and gas produce almost no waste to be removed. But coal leaves 10% ash, which has often been left at the power stations or mine site. However, this is slowly changing. Ash can be transported back to a mine and replaced where it came from. On the way it can be spilled. This problem is, fortunately, a relatively small one.

NUCLEAR FUELS

Spent nuclear fuel is a very different problem. It is highly radioactive, and this radioactivity must not be spilled. We will outline the usual procedures in its disposal.

11. *Transportation of Fuel and Wastes*

First, in ordinary situations the fuel elements remain intact. They are left in a spent-fuel pool at the reactor site for at least 90 days, after which some of the activity has decayed. (This time may be reduced with breeder reactors, because the value of the spent fuel is great, so that to keep it idle is costly.) It is then transported in specially designed casks built to withstand a 30-ft drop onto a concrete floor, and a fire of 1350° F for three hours. Therefore, an ordinary transportation accident should not result in the breaking of a fuel element. Suppose, however, that by some combination of errors the fuel cask broke and came open. The only gaseous fission products left in any quantity are krypton 85 and caesium 136. The first is a relatively small hazard because of the low-energy beta ray and its lack of chemical activity. The other fission products will mostly be retained by the uranium-oxide ceramic, but some could get into drinking water if the fuel fell into a river. It seems, therefore, that although the major hazards demand prompt action, such action can reduce the hazard to small proportions. The hazards of spent-fuel transportation in California have been evaluated in a report by Yadigaroglu et al. [6], who find little hazard.

Shipments of radioactive fuel will increase as the generation of electricity by nuclear power increases up to 9000 railroad shipments (of 30 tons each) per year, or 30,000 road movements (of 10 tons each). If shipments are for about 400 miles, major accidents will occur at 1.5 per year (rail) or 15 per year (road), according to present figures. In spite of the precautions to keep the fuel cask intact in an accident, this is a source of worry and suggests that power stations, fuel reprocessing plants, and, possibly, waste-disposal facilities should all be placed together in one complex (sometimes called a "nuclear park"). Uranium should go in, and electricity, but no radioactivity, should come out.

It is probable that such nuclear complexes will be built in the U.S.S.R.; however, it should not be necessary to have a socialist economy to ensure the necessary coordination. Perhaps a state could buy the land and refuse to allow a power station to be built anywhere else; then the individual power companies could build together just as several large department stores build in one suburban shopping center.

Meanwhile, any shipping should be done with the greatest safety and expediency possible. Turnpike and toll-bridge authorities in the U.S. do not allow potentially hazardous cargoes on their roads, for fear of losing revenue if the road is blocked. Hazardous cargoes must then travel along crowded roads in the centers of cities, where the accident probability is larger by a factor of 4, and the problems of an accident worse by an even larger factor. This is neither the first nor the only example of a supposedly public authority ignoring the public interest, nor is it the first time that a common hazard is first brought to light by nuclear power.

TRANSMISSION LINES

Electricity has to be transmitted from the generator to the user. For a given power, we can choose either high voltage and low current, or low voltage and high current. Since losses due to wire resistance (ohmic losses) are proportional to current, the former is preferred. Voltages as high as 500 kV are now in use in the U.S. The upper voltage limit is given by corona losses at the insulators, and finally by breakdown of the insulator. An insulator can no more stand arbitrarily high voltages than can a floor arbitrarily large weights.

Electricity is usually generated and supplied as alternating current (ac), because transformers to change from high to low voltage can be readily made.

There were 250,000 miles of transmission lines in the U.S. in 1970. Because of the trend for power stations to be built away from cities, this length will increase markedly.

The environmental effects of transmission lines are obvious: the right-of-way cuts a great swath across hill and dale, and landowners often object. In bad weather, the increased corona discharge across the insulators interferes with radio communication, aircraft navigation, and television reception. In forest areas, the right-of-way often interrupts the passage of wild animals. This effect can be mitigated by planting undergrowth and trees that cannot grow tall enough to interrupt the transmission line. There are at present several proposals to reduce the problems:

1. We can design and build more attractive (i.e., less ugly) transmission-line towers. The usual spidery steel towers can be replaced by slender concrete ones that can, depending upon one's taste, mitigate the problems.

2. In Figs. 11-4 and 11-5, we show two typical transmission-line towers. The former is the usual steel-lattice construction and takes two 3-phase 150-kV circuits. It is preferred by utility companies since it can be easily rebuilt, like Meccano or an Erector set, to accommodate changing requirements. The latter is a concrete tower carrying two 345-kV circuits and was specially built to satisfy neighborhood standards.

3. We can concentrate several lines along one right-of-way, or along a highway, to concentrate the environmental impact. However, this desire to concentrate the environmental impact conflicts with a need to maintain several independent utility corridors in case one is put out of action by accident, earthquake, or sabotage. We can also combine the right-of-way with an open way for recreational walking, a need that is becoming ever more apparent near U.S. cities.

4. We can put selected sections of line underground. This is *very* expensive. Sixteen hundred miles (300 miles in New York City) are underground [7]. For long distances, where high voltages are

Fig. 11-4. Twin 3-phase 138-kV transmission lines with steel towers (Commonwealth Edison Co.).

used, this costs $5 million/mile for 2000 MW, ten times the cost of overhead cable. The usual cable is a pipe cable, insulated with paper, and filled with oil under high pressure. A small oil-pumping station is placed on the surface every mile. This makes the reliability much less than for an overhead line, and maintenance costs ten times as much. West [8] maintains that a compressed-gas-insulated cable will be very attractive for the future. Often scientists talk about a superconducting underground cable to enable large (dc) currents to be carried with minimal losses. At the moment, superconductors have to be at temperatures of -442° F (-253° C, 20° K) or less. The energy requirements of cooling this line exceed the losses of an ordinary line. If a superconductor were found at liquid-nitrogen temperatures (-346° F, -210° C, 53° K), the whole economic question would change. There is no sign of this, but again we must remember that, 15 years ago before the Bardeen, Cooper, Schrieffer theory of superconductivity,

Fig. 11-5. Twin 3-phase 345-kV transmission lines at Oak Brook, Illinois (Commonwealth Edison Co.). The cost of each tower is 2-1/2 times that of a steel tower.

high-field superconductors were unknown. There seems no fundamental reason why a superconductor at 53° K should not exist, and this in itself seems adequate reason for continuing basic research on super-conductivity. A good summary is given by Forsyth [9].

We must beware of overestimating the environmental degradation of transmission lines; it does not yet approach that caused by roads.

REFERENCES

[1] Hottel, H.C., and Howard, J.B. (1972). "New Energy Technology,"
    p.72. MIT Press, Cambridge, Massachusetts.
[2] Heyerdahl, T. (1971). "The Ra Expeditions." Doubleday, New York.

[3] The Georges Bank Petroleum Study (1973). Rept. No. MIT SG 73-5. MIT Press, Cambridge, Massachusetts.
[4] US Geol. Survey, Conservation Divn. (1971). "Recorded Oil Spill Accidents Involving 1000 or More Barrels since 1957," July 29; revisions Sept.1, Dec.30. USGPO.
[5] Anon. (1973). "A Small Spill." New Yorker, Fall.
[6] Yadigaroglu, G., Reinking, A.G., and Schrock, V.E. (1972). Nuclear News, November, p.71. Also part of Rept. UCLA-ENG-7242 (C. Starr and M.A. Greenfield, principal investigators), for Resources Agency of California.
[7] FPC (1970). "1970 National Power Survey," Parts I-IV. USGPO.
[8] West, J.R. (1970). "In Support of CGI Cable." Power Engineering Vol.74, p.42, March.
[9] Forsyth, E.B. (1972). "Warm Watts and Cool Currents: Power Transmission by Superconducting Cable." Brookhaven Lecture Ser. BNL 50384 (available from Natl. Tech. Inf. Service).

PROBLEMS

1. Reference [2] of this chapter is to Thor Heyerdahl. Who is he? Can his observations be regarded as valid and important?

2. When was the phenomenon of superconductivity discovered? Describe this phenomenon. List three superconducting materials. Briefly describe and discuss one present or expected application of superconductivity.

3. Refer to Table 11 - 1. Determine how many of the ports listed might berth tankers that deliver liquified natural gas. Assume that the fleet of LNG tankers will be 20% as large as the fleet of oil tankers. How many accidents might we expect in a 14- to 15-yr period unless extraordinary precautions are taken?

4. Discuss how oil discharged at sea by ships could be tagged. Describe the logistics of doing so and develop arguments for and against taking such a step.

5. Compare the capacity of an oil pipeline and a trainload of tank cars. [Note: first estimate the speed at which oil travels in a pipeline and the capacity of 100 tank cars.]

6. Potentially hazardous cargos are not allowed on many toll roads. Compare the hazards to society of transportation of nuclear fuel or wastes, gasoline, or poisonous gases along a toll road through your state or along the adjacent ordinary road. Draw up draft regulations to establish optimum safety procedures for society.

7. Are offshore deepwater terminals safer or less safe for oil and LNG transportation than existing US ports? What are the environmental issues relevant to their use?

8. Find out what you can do about the breakdown of oil in seawater. With the present rate of oil spills, how much is the concentration of oil in the world's oceans increasing? What will be the ultimate limit of these concentrations if the present rate of oil spillage continues indefinitely? Compare this with the equivalent problem of nuclear wastes in Chapter 12.

12

Energy Converters

INTRODUCTION

Apart from nuclear energy, energy is most cheaply transported in the form of oil (by tanker). Yet for stationary applications it is most easily used in the form of electricity. Intermediate in ease both of transportation and use is natural gas. Thus it is very important to find the most plentiful and environmentally safest fuel and then to convert it into the most convenient forms for transportation and use. Of course, the generation of electricity is just such a method of conversion, and its use is implicit in most of this book.

In Chapter 8 we discussed briefly the gasification of coal as a method of "purifying" the coal before use, so that sulfur dioxide and particulates will not be produced. Just as important as the purification, however, is the fact that the resultant gas becomes easier to use than coal. It is sometimes said that the cost of transmission of energy by gas pipeline is cheap enough to command attention, but an examination of Fig. 11-1 shows that the "unit train" for shipment of coal is just as cheap.

Oil is needed for operation of our extensive transportation system, and, as we saw in Table 3-1, the transportation industry uses up 20% of our total energy supply, mostly in the form of petroleum products. There is no easy substitute for light distillates (oil) for airplanes. In Germany during World War II, oil was in short supply and had to be made from coal.

The only method now in use for commercial production of oil is the combining of hydrogen and a carbon-monoxide mixture to produce hydrocarbons by catalytic synthesis (Fischer-Tropsch synthesis). This is done in South Africa. But other methods are avilable in pilot form, as summarized by Holtel and Howard [1], who estimate a cost of $4.00/ bbl of oil, at the coal mine and at 1970 prices. This is sulfur-free oil and compares favorably with the $4.75/bbl paid by Boston Edison Co. in 1972 (Chapter 3). During November 1973, just a few weeks after the Mideast embargo on oil shipments to the U.S., Nigerian oil was selling for $16.80/bbl. Moreover, oil costs half as much to move by pipeline as does gas. This, therefore, seems a valuable project to pursue.

DUAL-FUEL ENGINES

We have seen that gas is environmentally superior to coal and possibly to oil. Yet gas is in short supply. Accordingly, engines and power stations are being built to work on either fuel.

The electric utility industry already uses natural gas whenever possible. In the major cities of the U.S., it is, however, only available as an interruptible supply, and the industry is permitted by regulatory authorities to use natural gas only when there is plenty available, mainly during the summer months. A situation where plenty of gas is available during the summer is fortunate for Chicago, where, during the months of August and September, the weather leads to temperature inversions and air pollution. Commonwealth Edison Co. of Chicago is able to burn gas instead of coal at this time and thus can avoid adding to the pollution problem.

There are a few automobiles in California which have been converted to burn natural gas. The equipment for one such car weighs about half a ton and occupies all the luggage space of a standard car. But the fuel economy is good, wear on the engine is exceptionally low, and the pollution is low. By proper adjustment of the engine, even NO_x is reduced to a fifth of that from a conventional automobile. This leads to a speculation that all internal combustion engines eventually may be compelled to burn natural gas within city boundaries. This will put still more strain on this scarce fuel resource.

HYDROGEN GENERATION

The possibility of the vanishing of liquid fuels has spurred the study of other fuels for the transportation industry. We have discussed batteries (Chapter 3); a variant is the generation of hydrogen electrolytically for subsequent use in an automobile. Hydrogen explodes easily, but if safety matters can be solved it burns with little environmental impact, the residue being water. We must not, however, forget that nitrous oxide is produced if *air*, rather than pure oxygen, is used to burn the hydrogen.

An alternative to hydrogen gas or liquid is lithium hydride, a solid which may be produced electrolytically and which can be burned to produce energy.

METHANOL

Methanol, a form of alcohol, is a serious contender as a substitute fuel for light distillate petroleum. That is, it can be used instead of or mixed with gasoline and fuel oils used in heating and electric-power production [2].

Methanol can be made from natural gas, coal, petroleum, vegetation, animal and human wastes, and garbage. While it is possible to manu-facture methanol (gas) or methanol from agricultural wastes, livestock wastes, garbage, and sewage, the amounts of methanol obtainable are nowhere near the amount possible if one converts coal to this methanol.

Excess associated natural gas from the oil-producing countries of the Arabian Gulf and North Africa has been hampered by the cost and difficulty of transporting the gas over long distances. The same ap-plies to gas at Prudoe Bay and McKenzie Bay at the Arctic Ocean. Some has been liquified, but the costs are high and the transport ships are highly specialized in design and not capable of being used for any other type of cargo. The dangers are discussed in Chapter 10.

Production of methanol from natural gas is less efficient and more expensive than the liquifaction of gas. However, methanol can be shipped in conventional oil tankers and at the final destination can be used directly or gasified back to methane gas, depending on the market.

The conversion of the vast U.S. coal reserves into gas or methanol is possible and is now, early 1974, economically justified, in addition to minimizing the U.S. dependence on imported petroleum.

If the methanol were used instead of gasoline in transportation, then the surface transportation needs for regular petroleum could be almost eliminated.

The total U.S. coal resources were estimated earlier, in Chapter 2. The major problem in coal supply is meeting the provisions of the Clean Air Act of 1967 and the 1970 amendment to the act, as much of Eastern and Midwestern coal has a high sulfur content.

Western coal (Wyoming) has a low-sulfur content and is classified as surface coal that can be strip mined. The problems associated with strip mining have been discussed elsewhere. Other coal areas have high sulfur content and require either deep mining or surface (strip) mining.

Methanol

There are adequate quantities of coal, the nation's most abundant fossil fuel, and proven technologies for mining, liquifaction, "clean-up," and transportation of the methanol.

Methanol may be added to gasoline up to about 10% by volume without necessary adjustment to an automobile engine. The methanol and gasoline separate at low temperatures, but nonpollutant-type additives can be used to prevent this.

Methanol can be used in automobile engines up to 100% but requires almost a trivially modified or adjustable carburetor [3].

The addition of methanol to gasoline or complete substitution eliminates the need for lead additives. Methanol-burning automobiles can easily meet the Clean Air Act requirements of 1975 [4]. (See Table 12-1.)

TABLE 12-1

Emissions from a 1972 Gremlin (i) that uses gasoline and (ii) that was modified for use with methanol fuel and equipped with a catalytic converter. Projected (as of 1973) federal standards (for 1975 to 1976) are included for comparison [2].

| Fuel | Emissions (gal/mile) | | |
	Unburned hydrocarbons	CO	NO
Gasoline	2.20	32.5	3.2
Methanol	0.32	3.9	0.35
Federal standards	0.41	3.4	0.40

The chemical process for conversion of coal and coke to methanol proceeds as follows in simplified chemical shorthand [coal is represented as C (carbon)]:

$$C + 2H_2O \longrightarrow CO_2 + 2H_2$$

$$2[C + H_2O \longrightarrow CO + H_2]$$

$$2[CO + 2H_2 \longrightarrow CH_3OH]$$
$$\text{methanol}$$

The chemical formula is CH_3OH, but for many purposes it can be considered to have the formula $CH_2 \cdot H_2O$. Since gasoline has approximately the formula $(CH_2)^n$, methanol can be considered to be a 50:50 mixture of gasoline and water.

A gallon of methanol then has about one-half the energy of a gallon of gasoline; a car that consumes 1 gal of gasoline to travel 15 miles will consume 2 gal of methanol to travel the same distance.

We refer to "gasoline equivalent" when we speak of gasoline substitutes. A "methanol-gallon equivalent" is 1/2 gal of gasoline. The price of methanol must be about one-half the cost of gasoline in order to receive public acceptance, provided gasoline is available. In order to preserve petroleum, the government might either prohibit the sale of gasoline for surface transportation or apply taxes so that it would not be economically attractive when compared with methanol.

We anticipate that methanol (produced from coal or natural gas that would be otherwise "flared" or reinjected into the ground) will become a major fuel. Several years will be needed to complete the system (mining, liquifaction, distribution, etc.).

The gain in availability of fuels for transportation would be great; the advantage of reduction or possible elimination of U.S. dependence on oil imports, tremendous.

Methanol is also suitable for use in fuel cells for electric power generation. Its employment in this application alone is sufficient impetus for a major effort in the establishment of a methanol production and distribution system [5].

OTHER ENERGY CONVERTERS

The waste of energy in using a heat engine to generate electricity can be considerable (as shown in Table 4-2). We therefore would like to avoid this indirect energy conversion if possible.

At the Bunsen Gesellschaft (Society) in 1894, Ostwald [6] pointed out that if chemical reactions were carried out electrochemically, it would, in principle, be possible for the entire free-energy change of a reaction to be converted directly into electricity. Until quite recently, this involved a very high capital cost. The "direct conversion" of chemical energy into electrical energy was used, therefore, only for very special and extremely low-power purposes (such as batteries). The history of development and the principles of operation of the fuel cell can be found in the standard text by Bockris and Srinivasan [7], starting from the old "dry cell" and lead-acid "accumulator."

Fuel cells are divided into two classes: "primary" batteries and "secondary" batteries. The primary battery, also known as the "dry cell," is really a fuel cell. Its reactants are converted, during the chemical process, into other products and electricity. The original chemicals are consumed.

Secondary batteries, also known as "storage batteries," are best known in the form of lead-sulfide "wet" "accumulators" as found in automobiles. They are reversible devices because they are charged with electricity and discharge electricity into appropriate loads. The original chemical materials are not consumed in the complete charge and discharge cycle.

A fuel cell that is practical for large-scale power generation was not realized until quite recently due to a lack of understanding of electron transfer reactions across interfaces. The first modern fuel cell was described by Bacon [8]. These fuel cells rapidly reached such a stage of perfection, efficiency, and weight that hydrogen-oxygen fuel cells have provided auxiliary power in American space vehicles since 1966.

There are many types of fuel cells both in development and in use. The fuels may be solid, liquid, or gaseous. Metals, gases, hydrocarbons, and even biochemicals are being explored. We describe in Technical Note 12-1 the operation of a basic unit which uses hydrogen and oxygen as reactants.

TECHNICAL NOTE 12-1

The Fuel Cell

The basic fuel cell uses the reaction between hydrogen and oxygen to form water. The rapid combustion of hydrogen that we are most familiar with is an explosion giving off heat and light. In the fuel cell, the reaction will be carried out in a controlled manner. The fuel cell may be said to belong to the class of devices commonly referred to as batteries. It differs from the wet cell (of our automobiles) and dry cell (of our flashlights) in that these are closed systems, chemically speaking, while the fuel cell is constantly fed fresh reactants and the products of the reaction are constantly removed. To date, the most workable fuel cells are expensive and large.

The posts to which the wires are attached on a battery or fuel cell are called the electrodes. One is a positive (+) electrode and one is a negative (-) electrode. The positive electrode (called the anode) gives off electrons; when all of its electrons are gone, it is left with a positive charge. Similarly, the negative electrode (the cathode) collects, or attracts, electrons.

By attaching some sort of load between the electrodes, as, for example, a motor, the electrons will flow from the anode, through the wire, through the load, to the cathode (see Fig. 12-1). The dry cell has a limited amount of stored charge dependent on the amount of chemical potential energy stored within it. The wet cell can be recharged;

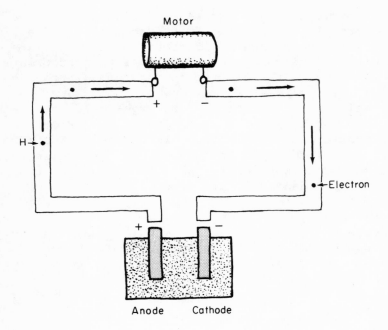

Fig. 12-1.

thus when its chemical potential energy is nearly exhausted, by recharging the battery, electrical energy is converted back into chemical
energy for later use. The fuel cell is refueled to replenish its
chemical energy.

A schematic of the fuel cell is shown in Fig. 3-6 (p. 87). The
electrolyte is a solid membrane with the property of giving up H_3O^+
ions that react with hydrogen and give off two free electrons:

$$H_2 + 2H_2O \longrightarrow 2H_3O^+ + 2e^-$$

The oxygen comes into the picture to react as follows:

$$1/2\ O_2 + 2H_3O^+ + 2e^- \longrightarrow 3H_2O$$

The energy released in this reaction is 1.229 V. The only product
discharged by the cell should be pure water. The electrolyte that
has this convenient property to make the cell work is an ion-exchange
material. A material with similar overall properties but which deals
with sodium and calcium ions is used in water softeners.

This particular reaction is not of direct use since hydrogen is not an available fuel. However, combined with the inverse reaction, the electrolysis of water, it can make an energy-storage mechanism.

Hydrogen can be produced in a nuclear electrical complex remote from population centers and used to operate fuel cells in cities, as demand requires. The fuel cell would make a pollution-free engine, although hydrogen gas is explosive and thus presents safety problems that would need to be solved.

More interesting would be the use of propane, which can be produced from oil. In Table 12-2, we compare the steps in using propane in a fuel cell and using it in a "conventional" steam electric-power plant. These fuel cells produce a potential of about 1 V and a current of several hundred amperes. They are connected in series and parallel to form a useful dc supply.

TABLE 12-2

Essential Steps in the Production of Energy by the "Hot" (Heat Engine) and "Cold" (Electrochemical Energy Converter) Combustion of Propane

Hot combustion (thermal method)	Cold combustion (electrochemical method)	
Produce heat energy (burning)	Chemical reaction at anode produces excess electrons	Chemical reaction at cathode produces excess positive charges
Heat energy ⟶ KE of gas molecules (air?) ⟶ expansion of gases		
Expanding gas delivers *some part* of its energy to piston-balance heat energy wasted as thermal energy of products	Electrons flow through "load" from anode to cathode, delivering electrical energy	
Energy of piston ⟶ motion of generator ⟶ drives electrons through wires ⟶ electrical energy		

In 1972, a group of electrical utilities entered into a development contract with Pratt & Whitney Aircraft for a 26-MW$_e$ fuel cell for distributed use. The whole process includes production of hydrogen from oil and is expected to be 27% efficient. Very few atmospheric pollutants will be produced, the waste heat will be dissipated into the air, and the cost is expected to be comparable to the cost of other methods of generating electricity from fossil fuels.

THERMOELECTRIC ENERGY CONVERTERS

There are other heat-to-electricity converters. These are of less interest because they do not avoid the heat wastage involved in the Carnot cycle [refer back to Technical Note 2-4]. There are three thermoelectric effects that are related: the Seebeck, the Peltier, and the Thomson. Two junctions are made between two dissimilar metals; when one is heated and the other cooled, a voltage is created and a current can be made to flow. The thermoelectric effect gives low voltages and high currents and is useful mainly in small units.

THERMIONIC ENERGY CONVERTERS

Thermionic energy conversion is the direct conversion of heat to electricity by the heating of an emitter (cathode) to a high temperature, which causes an emission of electrons from the cathode. The electrons travel to a collector (anode), which is at a lower temperature, and then pass through an external circuit and return to the cathode. The emission of electrons from a heated metal was first observed by Thomas Edison in 1880.

Again, the efficiency of the thermionic energy converter is expressed by, and limited to, the Carnot efficiency formula, which applies to all heat-energy conversion machines. The best efficiency for the present state-of-the-art devices is about 11%. There are some space activities for which thermionic converters have application.

PHOTOVOLTAIC ENERGY CONVERTERS (SOLAR CELLS)

Photovoltaic energy conversion is a direct energy conversion in that light energy is converted to electric energy without intermediate mechanical or heat involvement. The efficiency is limited by the

316

Carnot cycle only to the extent that the source has a temperature equal to that of the surface of the sun (which is high), leading to a high efficiency.

A photoelectric energy converter is made by exposing light to a semiconductor (pn) junction. A photon transfers its energy to an electron when the two collide. The electron may then have sufficient energy to become free; in leaving its atom it creates a hole. The hole is filled by an electron from another atom, which in turn leaves a hole to be filled by another electron, and so forth. In this way a current can be made to flow in an external circuit.

The maximum predicted efficiency for solar cells is on the order of 20%. Present-day cells are about 11% efficient. The fuel cost for a solar cell is zero. The measure of efficiency is the electricity produced for surface exposure and converted light energy.

Solar cells of the silicon type produce electricity at a cost of \$400/W with an efficiency of 15%; cadmium-sulfide cells operate for \$50/W with an efficiency of 4%.

Solar cells ranging in power levels from a few hundred milliwatts to a kilowatt have been developed for space applications. It is necessary to couple solar cells with storage devices in order to ensure a continuous supply of electricity over the 24 hours of the day, or during long periods of relative darkness.

MAGNETOHYDRODYNAMIC (MHD) ENERGY CONVERTERS

As long as we employ heat engines, there will be a search for the high-temperature working fluids necessary to obtain a high efficiency in the Carnot cycle. One possibility is a magnetohydrodynamic (MHD) plasma. An MHD plasma is basically a mixture of positive and negative ions that moves through a magnetic field in a direction perpendicular to the field. Under these conditions, an electric field is induced in a direction mutually perpendicular to the direction of the magnetic field and to the direction of motion of the particles. The positive ions and electrons will be directed toward opposite electrodes.

If the two electrodes are connected externally through a load, then a current will flow through the circuit. Thus in an MHD energy converter, the translational energy of the ionized particles is converted to electrical energy. The efficiencies should reach 50 to 60%.

The gas that leaves the energy-conversion chamber is at a temperature high enough to be used to generate steam as in a conventional plant. The steam may then drive a turbine-generator to produce electricity. The gas is then returned to the boiler for reuse. A schematic of a speculative system is shown in Fig. 12-2.

12. Energy Converters

TABLE 12-3

Comparison of Available Data and Maximum Feasible Performance Data of Energy Converters [ ]

Method of energy conversion	Efficiency (%)		Power/wt (hp/lb)		Power/vol (hp/ft)	
	Best available till 1969	Maximum feasible	Best available till 1969	Maximum feasible	Best available till 1969	Maximum feasible
Thermoelectric	10	12	0.03	0.1	1.1	2
Thermionic	22	32	0.03	0.1	1	3
Photovoltaic	15	25	0.6	1.0	80	130
Magneto-hydrodynamic	60	70	1.6	2	1200	20,000
Low-temperature fuel cells	70	90	0.04	1	3	30
High-temperature fuel cells	60	90	0.2	2	10	50
Gas turbine	28	-	1	-	70	-
Internal-combustion engine	27	-	0.3	-	7	-
Diesel engine	42	-	0.2	0.2	8	-

Magnetohydrodynamic (MHD) Energy Converters

Life expectation (yr)		Cost/power ($/hp)		Intangible factors	Comments
Best available till 1969	Minimum feasible	Best available till 1969	Minimum feasible		
3	Greater than 10	400	200	No moving parts, virtually maintenance free. Noise free, will operate over wide temperature range. Efficiency independent of size.	Cost relatively high. Covers wide range in power levels.
1-1/2	Greater than 10	400	100	Same as thermoelectric materials problems owing to high temperature and Cs vapor.	High temperature necessary, 2000° K. Covers wide range of power levels.
5	Greater than 10	70,000	40,000	Simplest device. Long life. High temperature not required.	Wide range of power levels. Cost too high. Necessary to develop types other than silicon solar cells. Needs energy storage (fuel cells).
Tests carried out for 1 wk	Greater than 10	70	45	Same as thermionics but higher temperatures cause more problems.	Only for high power levels (>1 MW). Field in infancy.
Greater than 2	Greater than 10	400	100	High efficiency at low temperatures. Easy to operate. No problem of corrosion.	H_2-O_2 cells best developed. Cost of H_2 and its storage are main problems.
1	Greater than 10	100	30	Polarization is low at both electrodes. Carbonaceous fuels may be used in molten carbonate or solid electrolytes.	Problems of corrosion. Wide range of power levels.
1	–	25	–	Many moving parts.	Low initial costs, cheap fuel. No cooling or ignition.
5	–	3	–	Many moving parts.	Low initial costs. Operates well over wide range of temperatures and pressures.
10	–	3	–	Many moving parts.	Low fuel costs. Hard starting in cold weather (below 5° C).

12. Energy Converters

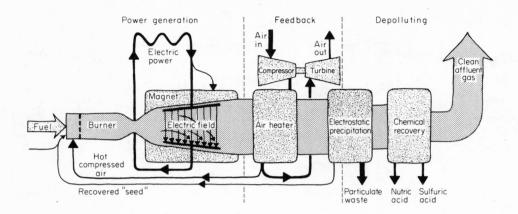

Fig. 12-2. Essential steps in the production of energy by the "hot" (heat engine) and "cold" (electrochemical energy converter) combustion of propane .

MHD units must be quite large in order to be economical. Practical power plants are some years away from actuality.

(A comparison of some of these unconventional generation methods is shown in Table 12-3.)

REFERENCES

[1] Hottel, H.C., and Howard, J.B. (1972). "New Energy Technology."
    MIT Press, Cambridge, Massachusetts.
[2] Reed, T.B., and Lerner, R.M. (1973). "Methanol: A Versatile Fuel
    for Immediate Use." Science Vol.182, No.4119 (December 28).
[3] Ebersole, G.D., and Manning, F.S. (1972). "Engine Performance and
    Exhaust Emissions: Methanol versus Isooctane." Paper 720692,
    presented at the Soc. Auto Engineers, Natl. West Coast Meeting,
    San Francisco, California, August 21-24.
[4] National Academy of Sciences (1973). Rept. by the Committee on
    Motor Vehicle Emissions. NAS, Washington, D.C. (February).
[5] Baudendistel et al. (1972). Proc. 7th Intersoc. Energy Conversion
    Engineering Conference, Paper 729004.
[6] Ostwald, W. (1894). Elektrochem. Vol.1, p.122.
[7] Bockris, J.O., and Srinivasan, T. (1969). "Fuel Cells: Their
    Electrochemistry." McGraw-Hill, New York.
[8] Brescia, F., Arents, J., Meislich, H., and Turk, A. (1970).
    "Fundamentals of Chemistry." Academic Press, New York and London.

General References

United Nations (1972). "Hydrogenation of Coal Tars," review and
  bibliography. UN Rept. E 72 II B27, United Nations, New York
  Available from UNIPUB, P.O. Box 433, New York, New York.
United Nations (1973). "Carbonization and Hydrogenation of Coal."
  UN Rept. E 72 II B26, United Nations, New York.
Perry, H. (1973). "Gasification of Coal." Scientific American Vol.230,
  p.19, (March).

PROBLEMS

   1. Prepare a brief report on the present methods for the
commercial preparation of oil.

   2. Since fossil fuels are not easily replaceable, proposals have
been made to raise an annual crop that can be burned as a fuel. Along
these lines, corn has been suggested as a source of fuel alcohol.
Develop a feasibility report on the use of corn as a fuel that discusses
all aspects of this idea, from the environmental impact of new corn-
fields to the chemical processing of the crop.

   3. List a number of present uses of fuel cells.

4. Prepare a report on how the Wankel engine differs from the internal combustion engine in present automotive use.

5. Look up and list the various forms of alcohol, along with how they differ from each other. What form of alcohol is used in liquor?

6. Prepare three graphs of money versus year, each of which depicts the amount of money spent from 1950 through 1970 on research to harness: nuclear power, fusion power, and MHD. Can a comparison of these graphs be used to generalize the government policy-making apparatus? Discuss your answer.

13

Waste Disposal

FOSSIL FUELS

In the consumption of any fuel, a residue of some sort is left. In burning fossil fuels, we produce the gases SO_2, NO_x, CO, and CO_2, as discussed in Chapter 8. These gases are objectionable in large concentrations, but they can be and are dispersed, and since man only produces about 20% of those released by natural processes, they are (with the exception of CO_2) easily absorbed.

As noted also in Chapter 8, we attempt to prevent the liberation of fly ash, but 90 million tons of ash are produced every year in the U.S. by coal burning. Coal mines produce several hundred million tons of slag, which is often forgotten but which must be included when we consider the total fuel cycle.

This ash, or slag, is often piled into heaps near the mines, but they make unstable soil. One of these slag heaps slipped at Aberfan in South Wales, and the landslide destroyed a school, killing 150 people. On February 26, 1952, a dam built out of slag collapsed and killed 125 people in Logan County, West Virginia.

13. Waste Disposal

Slag heaps can also cause poisons to be leached into drinking water. These are often acid, and valuable water supplies can be and are destroyed. Fortunately, most of the impurities are poisonous only in large concentrations, which are and have been easily observed and avoided. Moreover, these slag heaps are ugly - a more conventional environmental problem we all understand and need not discuss.

It would seem logical to use coal mines, or surface coal areas, as places to deposit these wastes, which cannot exceed in quantity the fuel taken out. Furthermore, this would prevent the subsidence of the soil above the mines or earthquakes caused by deep mines. This step has until recently been considered too expensive. National and international attention is being paid to the whole waste problem, of which this is one part, and the cheaper disposal methods are being deemed unacceptable. So this solution may be used.

Oil and gas burning produce few solid wastes, but we must still consider the debris from refining processes or the calcium sulfate thrown away after use in the limestone scrubbing process to remove SO_2. For a given amount of energy produced, a smaller amount of waste is produced from oil or gas than coal, but it is still important.

NUCLEAR WASTES

When nuclear fuel is used to produce electricity, we have seen (Table 1-1) that the weight of the uranium fuel needed is 1 million times less than that of fossil fuels. The wastes produced will have proportionately less weight. Therefore, using the energy figures of Chapter 3, we can guess that 100 tons of waste will be produced per year in the U.S. in the year 2000. This seems very little and would be no problem at all were it not radioactive.

The amount of radioactivity from a 1000-MW$_e$ power station was shown in Fig. 9-7. After a few years, the radiation level is still 10 million curies. In Table 13-1, we show the total amount produced in the U.S. in the year 2000, assuming the nuclear power demand (2×10^{12} W$_t$) we projected in Chapter 3. As a rough guide, we must remember that, before 1939, a radioactive source of 1 Ci was rare, but if used carelessly it could kill. Yet sources of 10,000 Ci of cobalt 60 are used routinely in hospitals for radiotherapy.

Where should we place these wastes? This is a problem similar to disposal of any waste. Should we keep these poisons in the initial concentrated form in one - or a few - locations, or should we allow them to be diluted in the deep oceans? Once a material is diluted, it is hard to concentrate, and particularly hard to separate from other isotopes of the same chemical species. An attempt to dilute is therefore not easy to reverse.

TABLE 13-1

Long-Lived Activities in Wastes, 2×10^{12} W_t Installed Capacity*

Nuclide	Mean life (1.5 × half-life, yr)	MCi/yr generated	Total accumulated in steady state (MCi)	Concentration if diluted in oceans (μCi/cm³)	Fraction of US drinking water standards of Public Health Service
Sr^{90}	40.4	1300	50,000	5×10^{-7}	2
Cs^{137}	43.2	1900	80,000	8×10^{-7}	4×10^{-2}
I^{129}	2.5×10^{7}	0.0006	16,000	1.6×10^{-7}	2
Kr^{85}	15.2	190	3000	3×10^{-8}	
T^{3}	17.7	12	200	2×10^{-9}	1×10^{-5}
Tc^{99}	3.0×10^{6}	0.2	7.5×10^{5}	7.5×10^{-6}	2×10^{-2}
Pu^{238}	128	1.8	230	2×10^{-9}	1×10^{-3}
Pu^{239}	35,200	0.03	1000	1×10^{-8}	2×10^{-3}
Pu^{240}	9750	0.08	750	7.5×10^{-9}	1×10^{-3}
Am^{241}	660	3	2000	2×10^{-8}	5×10^{-3}
Am^{243}	11,000	0.3	3000	3×10^{-8}	1×10^{-2}
Cm^{244}	26.1	40	1000	1×10^{-8}	2×10^{-3}

* Adapted from [1].

13. Waste Disposal

Dilution might just be possible for the amount of waste we consider here. The world's oceans are vast, and if the wastes could be mixed with water in the deep oceans, Table 13-1 shows that the concentrations could be only just above U.S. drinking water standards, which allow for concentration by the biological systems. But no one knows how to mix the ocean's surface and its deep.

Another elementary calculation illustrates that the problem may not be so great as often assumed. Figure 9-7 shows that a 1000-MW$_e$ power station in operation contains within its reactor vessel 10,000 million curies. If the wastes are collected and put in a tank, the radioactivity never reaches that in the original reactor! Since we have successfully kept the activity enclosed in a reactor, it only remains to continue to do so.

Still a third calculation can give us some perspective. Table 13-1 shows that in the wastes from one year's operation, strontium 90 and caesium 137 dominate until they have decayed. After several hundred years, we will be left with technicium (which is biologically not a severe hazard), iodine, and various "transuranic" elements, plutonium, americium, and curium. The specific activity of these would be about the same as the one *pitchblende* that occurs in nature. If the iodine and transuranic elements were removed, the activity would be close to that of ordinary uranium ore and little more hazardous (of course uranium ore is hazardous, but a hazard that is not too troublesome).

One possibility is to use secondary processing for these long-lived materials, or continue to recycle them into reactors!

At present, in Great Britain (where 20% of the electricity is produced by nuclear power) fifteen 150-gal steel tanks store the wastes in liquid (acid) form. These tanks are below ground and must be cooled. Each tank is surrounded by another tank to catch the drippings if it leaks, and any leaky tank can be emptied and repaired. This method is satisfactory up to a point: it requires continuous surveillance. Accordingly, people are searching for ways to store the wastes forever, without any intervention. Since *forever* is a big word, we also want a method whereby the wastes can be retrieved if anything unforeseen goes wrong.

In the U.S., larger tanks are used than in the U.K., and many of them have leaked. When they have done so, the liquid leaked onto soil at Hanford, Washington. Surveillance has been very bad, and in 1973 a tank was leaking for 6 weeks without being noticed. Although it would be at least 100 years for this liquid to reach drinkable water supplies, these procedures are obviously inadequate.

Storage of the wastes in a concentrated form has therefore been the decision of all countries, and many countries have decided to make a solid glass out of the wastes so that they can be less easily dissolved in ground water.

326

One plan was to dump wastes into the deep ocean trenches where the water does not mix with the surface, and it was hoped that after some years the wastes would be "subducted" or sucked into the earth's mantle and permanently removed from the earth's surface. But it now appears that the removal may be neither complete nor permanent and certainly not retrievable.

A plan to deposit wastes in deserted ice caps would only work on a short time scale. Over a geological time scale the results are quite transient.

SALT MINES

In 1957, an advisory committee of the National Academy of Sciences [2] recommended that high-level radioactive wastes be buried in excavations in bedded salt deposits. There are several reasons for considering salt mines:

1. A highly radioactive source separated from the environment by a thickness of good-quality bedded salt in an area of tectonic stability is effectively isolated from that environment for at least 1000 years and probably for significantly longer.

2. Bedded salt has a high compressive strength but flows plastically at relatively low temperatures and pressures. This will relieve stress concentrations produced by the mining operation or by the heat generated by the radioactive waste.

3. Fractures that might develop in bedded salt are "self-healing." This is indicated in part by the absence of solution cavities in the rock salt that has been studied.

4. The natural plasticity of the salt at the temperature imposed by the highly radioactive waste will effectively seal the remnants of the containers in cells of crystalline salt. Should man, for a now unforeseen reason, have to remove the buried radioactive waste, it could be accomplished with specialized mining equipment, albeit with considerable difficulty and effort.

5. Bedded salt permits the dissipation of larger quantities of heat than is possible in other types of rock.

6. Rock salt is approximately equal to concrete for gamma-ray shielding. Experimental radiation exposure has caused very little detectable radiolytic change in rock salt.

7. The loss of our salt resources would be negligible. There is a great abundance of bedded salt in the U.S. (particularly in Kansas) that is of satisfactory quality and in suitable geological environments that can be used for the burial of specified radioactive wastes produced by the nuclear plants that are anticipated in the U.S. over the next two to three decades.

8. The burial of the radioactive wastes under consideration in deep-bedded salt greatly reduces chances for release by accidental or malicious acts in both the near and distant future.

However, a subsequent committee [3] recommends five studies before committing wastes to the salt beds:

1. In order to plan the location of the shafts and the distribution of the rooms in which disposal will be made, it is essential that the uniformity in quality and thickness of the salt beds be known. In order to obtain this information, some subsurface exploration is necessary.
Recommendation: Four cored and logged drill holes through the salt should be sunk at the corners of the approximately 1100-acre proposed disposal site.

2. Location of previous oil and gas wells and inspection of records, where available, should determine if these former wells have been adequately plugged to avoid an entrance of water to the salt.
Recommendation: A survey should be made of neighboring wells in order to avoid threats to the integrity of the proposed bedded-salt disposal site.

3. Subsidence in the distant future may result from void spaces after the rooms are backfilled with crushed salt.
Recommendation: An answer to this problem is required in order to determine the best mode of mining and backfilling. Model studies are suggested, e.g., block mining and block backfilling.

4. The possibility of a metamict (Wigner) effect due to high gamma radiation and the uncertainty about the accompanying marked temperature rise is a matter of moderate concern. (If this effect occurred, the γ-rays could displace atoms from their location in the salt crystals and lead to energy storage. Later, this energy might be released suddenly and explosively.)
Recommendation: Experimental determination of the metamict effect in salt should be made using γ-ray dosages equivalent to those expected under storage conditions.

5. A surrounding peripheral zone of approximately 1000-1500 ft in width must be protected from accidental drilling that might adversely affect the integrity of the demonstration site.
Recommendation: Control of this peripheral zone by purchase, lease, or other legal agreement is recommended.

Have these precautions been taken, and will they be taken in the
future? The safety of storage in salt has been questioned by several
authors [4, 5]. There are many cases of careless storage of wastes;
the use of uranium mine-tailings in building, mentioned earlier, is
probably the most serious. It will be hard to reverse any mistake,
so this is a matter of unusual concern.

The original hope was that the wastes could be left for 1000 years
with no attention, and no provision was made for possible retrieval.
However, it is already clear that we should have provisions for our
grandchildren to make a different decision, and the proposal is being
postponed pending further study.

STORAGE IN UNDERGROUND ROCK

Another proposal for long-term storage of radioactive wastes
seems, at first sight, to be more attractive. A hole can be drilled
down into deep rock (10,000 ft underground) and below any possible
ground water. An atomic bomb exploded there will produce a cavern,
and the walls of the cavern would be sealed by the heat, which makes
a glass-like surface.

A fuel-processing plant can then be placed on the surface, and
wastes injected below. The heat of activity will steadily evaporate
any liquid solvent, and this or additional liquid will keep it cool.
After 50 years or so, the cavern can be sealed, the decay heat will
then melt the surrounding rock, and after cooling 20 years later the
whole will be sealed in a rock tomb beyond the reach of ground water.

This idea may have its faults, but it looks attractive enough
to warrant extensive study.

The general problem of disposal of radioactive wastes has been
studied much more extensively than we suggest here. A very readable
general article has been written by Blomeke and others [6]. (For
more detailed references we suggest [7, 8, 9].) It is an important
subject that has caused much public concern. The idea of passing on
a problem to our grandchildren is unacceptable to many people. Brower
[10] articulates this particularly clearly. But we must be sure that
the alternative is not also passing on to our grandchildren a *different*
problem and one that may be less understood: a problem of excessive
pollution from other causes, or a problem of a stagnant economy.

Suppose 1% of the stored waste were to escape from storage.
Could we recover from this, or would it be an uncontrollable disaster?
From the figures above, we see that we could do one of several things:
evacuate the area of that particular storage area and allow that part
to decay; or, at the other extreme, dilute this waste as soon as possible. Since man can drink water polluted at the drinking water

standards forever without undue hazard, it may be that such a leakage, though a catastrophe, would not be of unprecedented magnitude. However, the fear is that this argument is wrong, and a spill could almost destroy civilization.

It is therefore important to understand this question: Do nuclear wastes pose a problem significantly worse than fossil-fuel wastes? Present plans are to keep nuclear waste under control, and there are as yet no such plans for fossil fuels. But if the plans fail, is the problem worse or better? Such comparisons have not been documented.

FUEL REPROCESSING

In the light-water reactors used in the U.S., the uranium fuel is enriched over the natural 0.71% U^{235} to 3% U^{235}. After use, the enrichment has dropped to about 0.8%, and plutonium has been produced with a weight 0.54% of the weight of the uranium. Only a third of the fissile material is left; it might then appear sensible to "throw away" the fuel. Certainly, it is possible to store it for some time, and it often is stored for several years. From an environmental point of view, this would have the advantage of disturbing it as little as possible. Economic considerations, however, suggest that the useful uranium and plutonium be separated from the radioactive wastes, particularly when a breeder-reactor program is in progress. Possibly also some particular isotopes can be extracted for medical or industrial use. Similar problems arise with other types of reactors.

A reprocessing plant can process the fuel from many power stations. Fuel is transported there, cut up, and dissolved. In principle, all the radioactivity can be contained, but in practice some radioactivity is released into the environment. The amounts released have always been low enough so that exposures to the public have never exceeded ICRP guidelines. This has been documented in several public health service reports [11, 12]. However, these reports were written at a time when very little fuel was being processed and can only be considered as tests of equipment. Radioactivity releases at that time ranged up to 50% of that allowed by federal regulations (10 CFR 20). An increase of a factor of 100 as our use of power increases would be insupportable, and in any case public concern with the environment has demanded that better care be taken. Therefore, the reprocessing plants were shut down during 1971 and are being improved. In 1972, the radioactivity of the liquids released from reprocessing plants should have been as low as that from the cooling water of a power station (i.e., reduced by a factor of 1000). But krypton 85 will still be released to the air, and tritium to the air or water.

Problems

There remains a potential for accident. At the reprocessing plant it is possible that a fire could spread the activity, but this is probably less serious a threat than a power-station accident. Moreover, the reprocessing plant can, and probably should, be in a place more isolated than a power station site, since there is no reason for it to be placed near an electricity load center.

The nuclear center (or "park") discussed earlier could include, at one location, several nuclear power stations, a reprocessing plant, a fabrication plant for plutonium fuel, and a waste-disposal unit. Thus problems of transportation and the possibility of theft could be minimized.

REFERENCES

[1] Weinberg, A.M., and Hammond, R.P. (1970). Amer. Sci. Vol.58,p.412.
[2] Natl. Academy of Sciences (1957). Natl. Research Council Rept. on Storage of High-Level Radioactive Waste. NAS, Washington, D.C.
[3] Natl. Academy of Sciences (1970). Natl. Research Council Rept. on Storage of High-Level Radioactive Waste. NAS, Washington, D.C.
[4] Hambleton, W.W. (1972). "The Unsolved Problems of Nuclear Wastes." Tech. Rev. Vol.74,p.15.
[5] Lewis, R.S. (1971). Bull At. Sci. Vol.27, No.6,p.27.
[6] Blomeke, J.O., Nichols, J.P., McClain, W.C. (1973). Physics Today Vol.26,p.36 (August).
[7] Mattison, L., and Daly, R. (1964). Science and Citizen (April).
[8] Glueckauf, E., ed. (1961). "Atomic Energy Waste." Wiley Interscience, New York.
[9] Blomeke, J.O., and Roberts, J.T. (1965). Ann. Rev. Nucl. Sci. Vol.15,p.151.
[10] US Congress (1972). Hearings on liquid-metal fast breeder reactor demonstration project, September 1972. JCAE, USGPO.
[11] Shlien, B. (1970). "An estimate of radiation doses received by individuals living in the vicinity of a nuclear fuel reprocessing plant in 1960." Rept. BRH/NERHL 70-1. Dept. of Health, Education, and Welfare, USGPO.
[12] Magno, P., Reavery, T., and Apidiamakis, J. (1970). "Liquid waste effluents from a nuclear fuel reprocessing plant." Rept. BRH/NERHL 70-2. Dept. of Health, Education, and Welfare, USGPO.

PROBLEMS

1. Consider the possibility of disposing of radioactive wastes in outer space. Prepare a report describing how this could be

accomplished in terms of cost and complete facilities (including bringing the fuel to the launch site), in its many positive and negative ramifications. Introduce as many safety factors as possible. Determine a target in space.

2. Prepare a short report on garbage disposal in the oceans and its consequences. Use presently known data to project what we might expect if radioactive wastes were disposed of in a similar manner.

14

Regulation of Energy Industry

REGULATION AND LICENSING, BACKGROUND

Government regulation of the energy industry began when public utilities commissions were established to ensure that, in the monopoly situation in which much of the energy industry operates, prices are not set exorbitantly high. The U.S. Federal Power Commission (FPC) has this task, but it also has a promotional function: to ensure an adequate supply of electricity and natural gas. The protection of the environment has added still a third function.

These functions have not always worked well in the same commission. There is constant public outcry to separate the regulatory and promotional aspects of power. This has particularly arisen now that one agency, the Atomic Energy Commission, has the responsibility both for promoting nuclear energy and for regulating its safety and environmental effects [1]. The FPC is concerned with prices, but no one makes proper environmental comparisons between fuels.

From the outset, regulation of the nuclear industry was the only course in light of the awful demonstrations of its capacity for evil at Hiroshima and Nagasaki and the fear that it would be controlled by military establishments. In the U.S., the regulatory function is performed by the AEC under the Atomic Energy Act of 1954. The fabrication of power stations is done by giant private corporations (Westinghouse,

14. Regulation of Energy Industry

General Electric, Gulf-Atomic, Combustion Engineering, Babcock & Wilcox), and the utility industry is separate again (although the utility company may be a public corporation like the Tennessee Valley Authority, which builds dams and power stations and sells electricity). As stated here, this sounds like an excellent separation of functions, but the electrical industry has been slow to promote nuclear power. Following congressional urging, the AEC has taken an active lead in promoting nuclear power, thereby somewhat compromising its regulatory function. In the U.K., the public Central Electricity Generating Board is the utility company, the Atomic Energy Authority the development agency, and the Nuclear Installations Inspectorate of the Dept. of Trade and Industry the regulatory body. In Canada, the utilities are private or provincial. Nuclear power station manufacture is federal (Atomic Energy of Canada, Ltd.), and its principal user (Ontario Hydro) provincial. There is a separate government regulatory authority. Whether the functions are separated in different agencies in the U.S.S.R. is unknown to the authors. (A detailed account of the structure of the AEC can be found in [2].)

The U.S. Atomic Energy Act specifies two public hearings for every nuclear power station, one before construction and one before operation. Originally these hearings were only concerned with radiation and safety, since these were the special new concerns about nuclear power at the time. Under the Environmental Protection Act of 1969, as interpreted in July 1971 by the U.S. Court of Appeals in the "Calvert Cliffs" case, the same licensing board must now consider all environmental effects.

Licensing for other power stations has been less rigorous. An inland power station not on a navigable waterway usually has only to pass a state hearing, and until three or four years ago these hearings were almost nonexistent. Now state laws demand restrictions on sulfur-dioxide emissions to satisfy the National Air Quality Standards, and also on water and chemical releases to meet water quality standards. However, there is only one public hearing for each of these, and that on a state level, which is usually less rigorous than the federal hearings. A power station on a navigable waterway must, in addition, have federal hearings before the Army Corps of Engineers, which, like the AEC, must consider all environmental effects.

The total number of permits that must be obtained for the operation of a single nuclear power station (including such matters as septic tanks!) is over 96; this suggests a reorganization of such hearings. The advantage to the utility companies is obvious; not so obvious, but even greater, are the potential advantages to the environment. Uniform hearings procedures enable comparisons to be made so that the best power sources for a given situation may be chosen. The possibility of an early power-plant siting hearing is being discussed on both federal and state levels. Such a hearing would enable the public to choose the best of many sites, rather than merely to accept or reject the one

334

chosen solely for the financial advantage of the power company. This early search for sites will enable many sensible decisions to be made. These suggestions were incorporated into a report by the President's Office of Science and Technology [3], and in 1971 no fewer than six different bills on power-plant siting were before Congress. A state could select a large, isolated area for a nuclear power complex, complete with its own fuel fabrication, reprocessing, and waste storage facilities, thereby limiting potential transportation and plutonium theft problems.

It is probable that these nuclear complexes will be adopted in the U.S.S.R., but in the U.S., the nation that started the supermarket and the suburban shopping center, a workable system can surely be found.

LEGAL PRECEDENTS

The granddaddy of environmental cases in the power field is Scenic Hudson Preservation Society versus the Federal Power Commission [4,5]. In 1962, Consolidated Edison Co. of New York City proposed to build a pumped-storage power station at Cornwall, N.Y., on the Hudson River. The 2000-MW_e power station was to be on the banks of the Hudson, the water to be pumped up 1000 ft under Storm King Mountain to a reservoir in Black Rock Forest. The objections were primarily in regard to destruction of the scenic section of the river.

In 1965 the FPC, after a public hearing, issued a permit. It was overturned by the Court of Appeals on the grounds that the FPC had not considered alternatives. A new plan, with an underground power station and underground transmission lines, was presented to the FPC. After a long public hearing in 1969, the FPC issued its permit in August 1970, and the Court of Appeals upheld this in July 1971. Meanwhile, the arguments in this case were a major stimulation to the enactment of the National Environmental Policy Act of 1969 (Public Law 91-190), which came into force on January 1, 1970. This act enjoins each and every federal agency to consider all alternatives to actions that have adverse environmental consequences. Conservation societies in the case argued that the full requirements of NEPA have not been met and appealed the case to the Supreme Court; the Supreme Court did not agree, and by an 8 to 1 decision denied a writ of certiorari.

In this case, conservation societies have already won the underground placement of power station and transmission lines, have inspired NEPA, and may win a complete abandonment of the project by further actions in state courts. One of the issues that has arisen since the FPC decision is the realization, noted earlier, that fish larvae could be killed by passing through the turbines, thus severely depleting the population of striped bass. This case, and the consequent birth of environmentalism, is well documented in [6].

The next interesting case was that of Calvert Cliffs Coordinating Committee, Inc., versus U.S. AEC [7]. The AEC had issued a permit to Baltimore Gas and Electric Co. to construct a nuclear power station in Calvert Cliffs, Maryland, on the banks of Chesapeake Bay. The AEC is subject to NEPA when it issues a construction or operating license for a power station. The AEC had proposed to accept, for those aspects of environmental quality for which it is responsible, the certification of other relevant state and federal agencies. However, such a certification does not assure that no unnecessary hazard to the environment exists; for example, certification that water quality standards have been met does not mean that there is no water pollution. Accordingly, the U.S. Court of Appeals insisted that the AEC independently compare cost and benefit and consider these matters in its public hearings. This will apply to all federal agencies.

The third case of importance is the Quad Cities case [8]. In this case, it was ruled that the AEC had no right to issue even a low-power testing license without a full environmental statement and hearing. This particular case means that considerable delays occurred for those power stations ready for licensing when NEPA took effect, and temporary authority was enacted in 1972 to allow such temporary licensing. Conservation groups considered this to be an undermining of NEPA; however, the authority was temporary and should be no problem.

In the fourth case [9], the Secretary of the Army, through the Army Corps of Engineers, is enjoined to issue an environmental statement before permitting the deposit of "refuse" in navigable waters under the River and Harbors Act of 1899. Hot water from power stations comes under the "refuse" classification, so that tens of thousands of permits are required throughout the United States. This is a vital function of NEPA, because under federal review it brings a multitude of small actions, whose cumulative effect may exceed that of the few large actions previously considered.

In the fifth case [10], the scope of the NEPA requirement that the environmental impact statement contain a discussion of alternatives was defined. In this case the Department of the Interior proposed to lease submerged off-shore lands for oil exploration and exploitation. They should have compared this with the possible importation of oil and with the use of nuclear power. Moreover, the court found that "the mere fact that an alternative requires legislative implementation does not automatically establish it as beyond the domain of what is required for discussion."

In the first four of these cases, the agency concerned was making an effort to comply with NEPA, but was faced with an interim situation due to urgent permit applications in progress. In Quad Cities, the immediate increase in environmental damage was not obvious; it is hard to see how 1% of the design power allowed by the interim license could lead to permanent environmental damage. Legal points must be fought when they are found, but it would be preferable to fight them on more obvious cases, otherwise a large backlash against conservation societies is created. The National Environmental Protection Act, these discussions, and comments thereon are collected in a very useful volume by the Joint Committee on Atomic Energy [11].

All of these cases illustrate the major change in environmental concern that has taken place during the decade of the 1960's. Before 1960 an objector had to prove environmental damage; now a power company must prove the lack of it. It is this change in onus of proof which is so important for the environment. Some of this is not a change in the letter of the law, but only in public opinion and a willingness and ability to take legal action.

In a sixth case, Sierra Club versus EPA [12], the Sierra Club objected to EPA rules governing air quality in certain rural areas. In many rural areas, the air is much purer at the present time than the National Air Quality Standard. EPA rules would have permitted the air quality to be degraded until the Air Quality Standard is reached. The Sierra Club argued that the National Environmental Policy Act allows no significant degradation of air quality even for air which is pure. The Federal District Court ruled in favor of the Sierra Club, and the Supreme Court refused to review the case.

This leaves certain antipollution measures in limbo; the British and German method of dispersing electricity generating stations in the countryside to reduce pollution in the towns would not be allowed under this ruling, not would it be possible to have significant industrial development where none now exists. The full ramifications are not yet clear.

These cases establish legal precedents for the decision makers. In order to aid the public in understanding these, there exists the Freedom of Information Act; within very broad units, the information used by the agencies in arriving at their opinions must be available to the public. Even the wastebaskets of the AEC seem to be emptied into the *in* trays of intervening lawyers. The public can therefore, if it wishes, be well informed. Finally, we note that every state has a wealth of environmental legislation in addition to the federal environmental legislation.

Using public information, public action can begin; this too is becoming easier. The AEC is altering its hearings procedures to make it simpler for citizens to ask questions and present their views without need of a lawyer. State laws are allowing class-action suits. The threat of a legal action is now always present, and energy companies and government agencies alike have to be more careful than before.

However, there are not always enough informed members of the public to take action, and they are not always well financed. Two lawyers feel that there is still need for change in attitudes of regulatory authorities, and if public concern about the environment wanes, this may not be forthcoming [13,14].

14. *Regulation of Energy Industry*

The saga of the Alaskan oil pipeline is an example of how proper environmental concerns may well be introduced too late in our decision-making processes.

Most people agree that eventually Alaskan oil will be brought to the U.S. market. But concerns were expressed over the problems of a large pipeline in the tundra and oil spills on the Canadian west coast. Alternative routes were not adequately considered. Finally, the court ruled that the environmental statement of the Department of the Interior was inadequate, and a new one was made in several volumes. This too was being challenged, but the oil crisis of 1973, together with an embargo on oil from the Middle East, urged Congress to act to declare this environmental statement adequate. Many felt that a pipeline through Canada would be superior, but the oil companies persuasively argued that the nation could not afford the delay.

Several lessons can be learned. First, the major decisions are taken early, and often secretly, by industry. By the time these reach the public, industry is committed and unwilling to consider changes. Future laws and regulations should bring the public into the process earlier.

Second, environmental matters are quickly brushed aside when crises occur, and national independence in energy policy is of vital concern to most Americans. We are reminded that Edward I of England banned the burning of coal on environmental grounds, but when the wood was all gone, there was no alternative, and environmental issues were forgotten.

PLUTONIUM POLITICS

The projected large increase in nuclear power will produce a large amount of plutonium that will be recycled back as fuel. This plutonium is radioactive (α-decay) and is itself as serious a hazard as are the long-lived, high-level wastes. A 1-μg ingested dose of plutonium is hazardous, yet 100,000 tons (10^{19} times as much) will be within the U.S. at any one time. This plutonium will *not* be put into long-term waste disposal, but will be used in the power stations.

The place where this hazard of plutonium is greatest is in the fuel reprocessing plant. In the reactor it is in oxide ceramic or carbide form; hence, it is solid and cannot burn. But the transportation and processing of it is, in principle, hazardous.

A more serious worry about the plutonium is the fact that fuels meant for nuclear reactors can become fuels for bombs: if these fuels are made in the correct chemical form and have a high concentration of the fissile isotope. Only 5 kg of Pu^{239}, or 25 kg of U^{235}, is needed, and several tons are present in a reactor. It is for this reason that the nations of the world, through the International Atomic

338

Energy Authority (IAEA) have formed a *safeguards* program to keep track
of all production and use of fissile material, to prevent theft or possible hijacking during transportation. It is important to realize that
the IAEA can only detect violations of the safeguards programs and the
production of fissile materials. At any time a country could break away
from the IAEA and, within some months, make a bomb.

If a source of pure U^{235} were available, it would be quite easy
to make a bomb. But the facilities to separate this isotope are expensive, and only a few countries have them. The enrichment used for most
nuclear power plants (3% U^{235}) is inadequate for a bomb; a bomb can only
work with greater than 50%. The fuel for an HTGR is, however, enriched
to 80% and is suitable. It is, therefore, important that it be closely
guarded between enrichment and fabrication into the carbide fuel.

The capital cost of existing gaseous diffusion isotope separation
plants is $1,000,000,000 and cannot be afforded by small countries.
However, the centrifuge method of isotope separation is being developed
and will reduce the cost of isotope separation to $100,000,000 capital
cost. Worse still, isotope separation by optical excitation of the
different isotopes (using the monochromaticity of laser light) is being
developed and will need still lower capital investment: about $100,000.

At first sight, it seems easier to use plutonium. As discussed
in Chapter 5, plutonium is produced in large quantities, and we plan
to produce thousands of tons of it per year. A chemical separation is
all that is necessary to make the plutonium pure. Unless we make a firm
decision otherwise, pure plutonium will travel from fuel-fabrication
plants to power stations and can be hijacked en route.

But even with pure material, a plutonium bomb is harder to make
than a uranium bomb. The technology required is large enough that,
as emphasized at a recent conference [15], the Russians are not much
alarmed about a criminal group making a device themselves. But even
for a small nation, it is too easy, and anyone could put plutonium up
for sale on the black market. But not everyone agrees with this assessment: T.B. Taylor [16,17,18], one of the foremost bomb designers in the
U.S., believes it is easy to make a bomb in the garage once plutonium
is available.

The plutonium isotope that is available for a bomb is Pu^{239}. In
those reactors designed for production of plutonium for bombs such as
those at Hanford in the U.S. or Windscale in the U.K., the fuel is
continually reprocessed. If, however, the Pu^{239} stays in the reactor,
the isotope Pu^{240} is formed by neutron capture. This cannot be chemically separated from Pu^{239}. The large number of spontaneous fissions
complicates the making of an efficient bomb, since "preignition" can
occur as the bomb is being assembled. The natural uranium reactors
often have "on-line" refueling, which might lend itself to clandestine
production of pure plutonium, but the constant switching on and off of

one of the U.S. light-water reactors could easily be detected. In the breeder reactors, half the plutonium would be produced in the blanket and would be Pu^{229}.

It has been suggested that the use of oxide of plutonium in reactors prevents the use of it in a bomb (in addition to the advantage of noninflammability noted earlier); this is not entirely true. Oxygen is not a poison. It is, however, a moderator, but a less efficient bomb could still be made [19].

Many people find the possibility of diversion of plutonium to criminal uses so serious that this is adequate reason to stop nuclear power development [20,21,22]. Others argue that we should at least guard all pure plutonium, dilute it with Pu^{240} and elements chemically similar when possible, and reduce transportation as much as possible.

It is beyond the scope of this book to go into these matters, vital though they are, in detail. Other books and articles discuss them more thoroughly [15,16,17,18,19,23,24,25,26].

OIL POLITICS

The political dangers of plentiful plutonium may not be the most dangerous political aspect of energy. The major oil supplies are located in the Middle East (well known for its political instability), and as the oil runs out, a major war is not inconceivable. The danger of this war is increased by the fact that storage of oil is adequate only for a few months' supply, so that time may not exist for the subsidence of passion.

This type of war is unlikely for nuclear fuels. Ten years' forward supply is easy to stockpile, and, apart from distribution, there seems to be no shortage.

REFERENCES

[1] In 1974, various bills are before the US Congress, which will reorganize the energy agencies of the US. They all separate the regulatory function of the AEC in a Nuclear Energy Commission from the research and development agency.
[2] Green, H.P., and Rosenthal, A. (1963). "Government and the Atom." Atherton, New York.
[3] US Govt. (1970). "Electric Power and the Environment." Office of Science and Technology, USGPO.
[4] Scenic Hudson (1971). Scenic Hudson Preservation Conference *et al.* vs. Federal Power Commission's US Petition for a Writ of Appeals Dockett. Certiorari US Supreme Court Docket 71-1219, 71-1220, 71-1221.
[5] US Govt. (1970). FPC Opinions, Decisions, and Orders Vol.44,p.350. USGPO.

References

[6] Talbut, A.R. (1972). "Power Along the Hudson." Dutton, New York.

[7] Calvert Cliffs (1971). Calvert Cliffs Coordinating Committee vs. AEC. US Court of Appeals for DC Circuit, Case No. 24,839.

[8] Quad Cities (1971). Izaak Walton League vs. James Sesehinger *et al.* US District Court for DC, Docket Nos. 2207-71 and 2208-71.

[9] Kalur and Large (1971). Kalur and Large vs. Secretary of the Army *et al.* US District Court for DC, Docket No. 1331-71.

[10] NRDC (1972). Natural Resources Defense Council vs. Morton as Secretary of the Dept. of the Interior. US Court of Appeals for DC Circuit, Case No. 71-2031.

[11] US Govt. (1972). "Selected Materials on the Calvert Cliffs Decision, Its Origin, and Aftermath." JCAE, USGPO (February).

[12] Sierra Club (1972). Case of Sierra Club vs. Ruckelshaus. US Court of Appeals for DC Circuit, Nov. 1, 1972, and Environmental Law Reporter 20656. Affirmed by the US Supreme Court in a 4-4 decision 412 vs. 541 3, Environmental Law Reporter 20684. In this case, the court affirmed that the air quality may not be significantly degraded even though it would satisfy the National Air Quality Standards.

[13] Sherrill, R. (1971) "Power Play." Playboy Vol.18, p.113; reprinted in Congressional Record, 17 May.

[14] Green, M.J., et al., eds. (1972). "The Closed Enterprise System." Grossman, New York.

[15] Willrich, M. (1971). "Civil Nuclear Power and International Security." Praeger, New York.

[16] Taylor, T.B. (1974). Testimony before the JCAE, January. USGPO.

[17] Anon. (1973). "The Curve of Binding Energy," profile of T.B. Taylor. New Yorker, December 3,10,17.

[18] Taylor, T.B. (1973). "Diversion by Nongovernmental Organizations," in "International Safeguards and Nuclear Industry" (M. Willrich, ed.). Johns Hopkins Press, Baltimore, Maryland.

[19] Hall, D.V. (1972). "Adaptability of Fissile Materials to Nuclear Explosives," in Symp. Implementing Nuclear Safeguards, Kansas State Univ. Praeger, New York.

[20] Brower, D.B. (1972). Testimony in hearings on the liquid-metal fast-breeder demonstration plant. JCAE, USGPO.

[21] Geesaman, D. (1971). Bull. At. Sci. September.

[22] Geesaman, D. (1972). "Plutonium Diversion." Testimony to California Legislature, June 15.

[23] Willrich, M. (1971). "Global Politics of Nuclear Energy." Praeger, New York.

[24] Higginbotham, W.A. (1969). Physics Today, p.33 (November).

[25] AEC (1969). Proc. 10th Annual Meeting, Inst. Nuc. Materials Management. [See J. Ramey's speech.]

[26] AEC (1969). Proc. AEC Symp. on Safeguards Research and Development, WASH 1147.

14. Regulation of Energy Industry

PROBLEMS

1. We noted in this chapter that over 96 permits are required to build a nuclear power plant. Name several of the Federal permits that are necessary and several of the permits necessary in your home state. How do these permits differ from nuclear and fossil-fuel plants?

2. Compare the regulations on nuclear power plants and the handling and transportation of nuclear materials in your state and adjacent states.

3. Locate the nearest nuclear facility to you, or the nearest proposed facility, and obtain copies of the environmental impact statement and safety analysis reports prepared by the organization in question. As an exercise, challenge as many points in these statements as you can.

4. Repeat the last question for the nearest fossil-fuel power plant.

5. The need for national security often seems to conflict with environmental and safety issues. Outline the various national security problems that imported oil poses. Which of these is improved by the use of Alaskan oil with pipelines to the Pacific Ocean?

6. Should electricity-generating stations be in the city or in the surrounding countryside? Write outlines (preferably in the form of legal briefs) of the case for each of these alternatives. How can this conflict be resolved and who should resolve it?

342

15

Summary Tables

In this book we have endeavored to present the problems of power generation and use in such a way as to enable cross comparisons between different energy sources to be made

Most authors discuss one energy source at a time. We include here some flowsheets of various electric-power technologies, from an excellent report prepared for Teknekron, Inc., by T.H. Pigford.

From these flowsheets, we also take our own summary tables. [*Note:* in the flowsheets, Te is metric tons, MPC maximum permissible concentration.]

Fossil Fueled Power Plant 1000 Mwe
Fueled With Clean Power Gas Made From 3%-S Coal
Material And Environmental Release Flowsheet

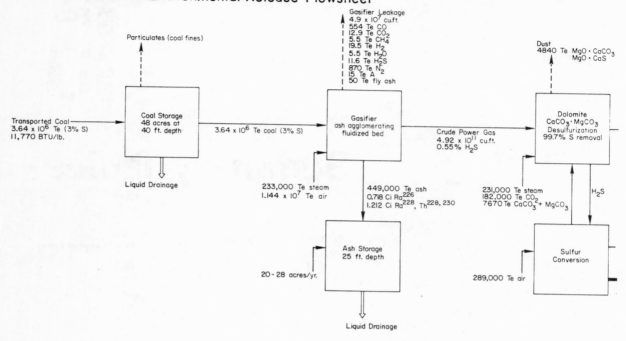

Natural Gas Power Plant 1000 Mwe
Material And Environmental Release Flowsheet

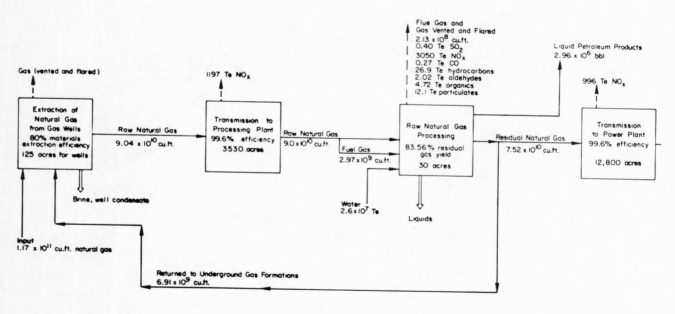

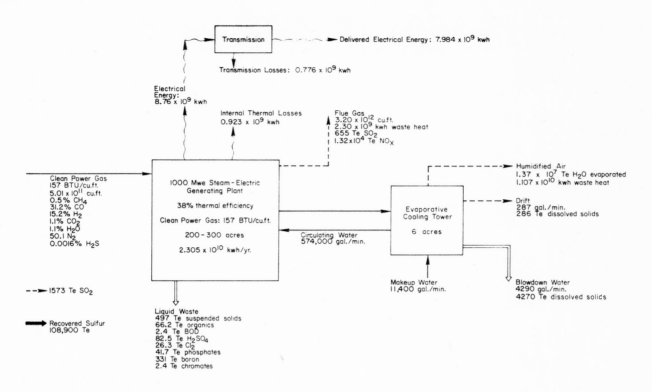

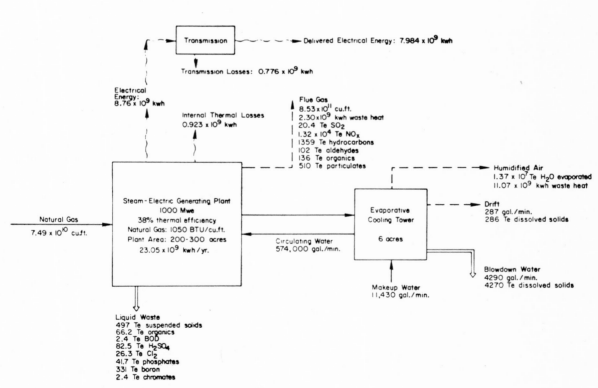

Residual Fuel Oil Power Plant   1000 Mwe
Material And Environmental Release Flowsheet

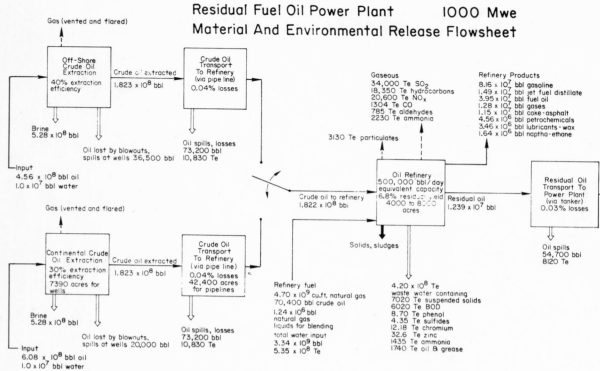

Gas (vented and flared)

Off-Shore
Crude Oil
Extraction
40% extraction
efficiency

Crude oil extracted
1.823 x 10⁸ bbl

Crude Oil
Transport
To Refinery
(via pipe line)
0.04% losses

Brine
5.28 x 10⁸ bbl

Oil lost by blowouts,
spills at wells 36,500 bbl

Oil spills, losses
73,200 bbl
10,830 Te

Input
4.56 x 10⁸ bbl oil
1.0 x 10⁷ bbl water

Gaseous
34,000 Te SO₂
18,350 Te hydrocarbons
20,600 Te NOₓ
1304 Te CO
785 Te aldehydes
2230 Te ammonia

Refinery Products
8.16 x 10⁷ bbl gasoline
1.49 x 10⁷ bbl jet fuel distillate
3.95 x 10⁷ bbl fuel oil
1.28 x 10⁷ bbl gases
1.15 x 10⁷ bbl coke-asphalt
4.56 x 10⁶ bbl petrochemicals
3.46 x 10⁶ bbl lubricants-wax
1.64 x 10⁶ bbl naptha-ethane

3130 Te particulates

Oil Refinery
500,000 bbl/day
equivalent capacity
6.8% residual yield
4000 to 8000
acres

Crude oil to refinery
1.822 x 10⁸ bbl

Residual oil
1.239 x 10⁷ bbl

Residual Oil
Transport To
Power Plant
(via tanker)
0.03% losses

Oil spills
54,700 bbl
8120 Te

Solids, sludges

Gas (vented and flared)

Continental Crude
Oil Extraction
30% extraction
efficiency
7390 acres for
wells

Crude oil extracted
1.823 x 10⁸ bbl

Crude Oil
Transport
To Refinery
(via pipe line)
0.04% losses
42,400 acres
for pipelines

Brine
5.28 x 10⁸ bbl

Oil lost by blowouts,
spills at wells 20,000 bbl

Oil spills, losses
73,200 bbl
10,830 Te

Input
6.08 x 10⁸ bbl oil
1.0 x 10⁷ bbl water

Refinery fuel
4.70 x 10⁹ cu.ft. natural gas
70,400 bbl crude oil
1.24 x 10⁶ bbl
natural gas
liquids for blending
total water input
3.34 x 10⁹ bbl
5.35 x 10⁸ Te

4.20 x 10⁸ Te
waste water containing
7020 Te suspended solids
6020 Te BOD
8.70 Te phenol
4.35 Te sulfides
12.18 Te chromium
32.6 Te zinc
1435 Te ammonia
1740 Te oil & grease

Bituminous Coal Power Plant   1000 Mwe
Material And Environmental Release Flowsheet

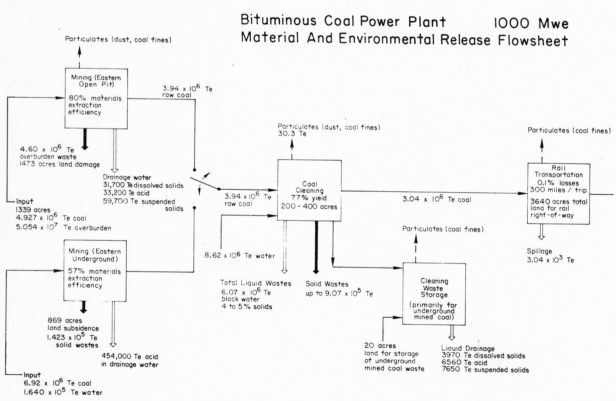

Particulates (dust, coal fines)

Mining (Eastern
Open Pit)
80% materials
extraction
efficiency

3.94 x 10⁶ Te
raw coal

4.60 x 10⁶ Te
overburden waste
1473 acres land damage

Drainage water
31,700 Te dissolved solids
33,200 Te acid
59,700 Te suspended
solids

Input
1339 acres
4.927 x 10⁶ Te coal
5.054 x 10⁷ Te overburden

3.94 x 10⁶ Te
raw coal

Particulates (dust, coal fines)
30.3 Te

Coal
Cleaning
77% yield
200 - 400 acres

3.04 x 10⁶ Te coal

Particulates (coal fines)

Rail
Transportation
0.1% losses
300 miles / trip
3640 acres total
land for rail
right-of-way

Spillage
3.04 x 10³ Te

8.62 x 10⁶ Te water

Mining (Eastern
Underground)
57% materials
extraction
efficiency

Total Liquid Wastes
6.07 x 10⁶ Te
black water
4 to 5% solids

Solid Wastes
up to 9.07 x 10⁵ Te

Particulates (coal fines)

Cleaning
Waste
Storage
(primarily for
underground
mined coal)

869 acres
land subsidence
1.423 x 10⁵ Te
solid wastes

454,000 Te acid
in drainage water

20 acres
land for storage
of underground
mined coal waste

Liquid Drainage
3970 Te dissolved solids
6560 Te acid
7650 Te suspended solids

Input
6.92 x 10⁶ Te coal
1.640 x 10⁵ Te water

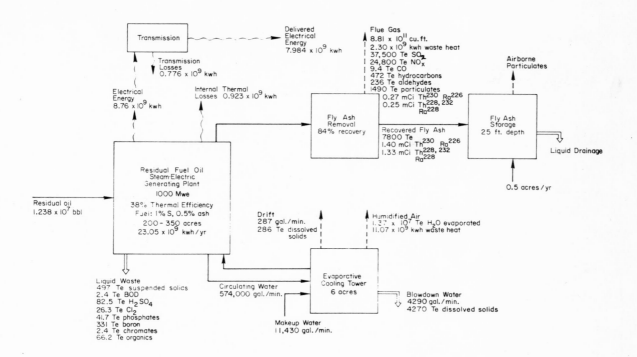

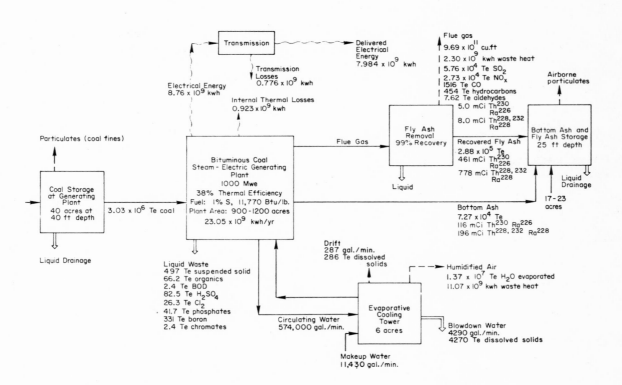

Light Water Reactor Nuclear Power Plant   1000 Mwe
Material And Environmental Release Flowsheet

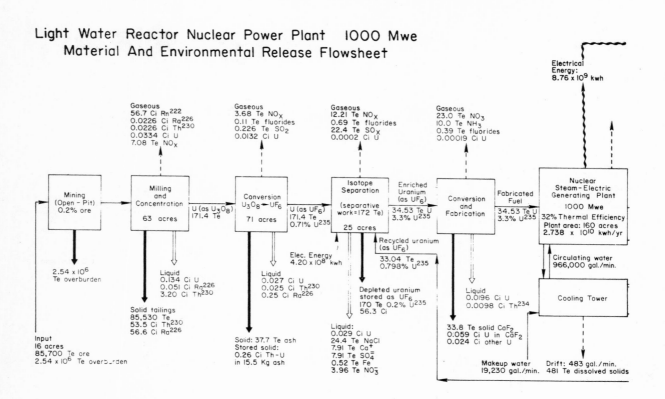

TABLE 15-1

Miscellaneous Environmental Costs

	Tons/kWh
Oil spills (1970)	5×10^{-7}
SO_2 (crude oil)	5×10^{-6}
Fly ash (coal)	5×10^{-6}
NO_x (oil, coal, or gas)	1×10^{-6}

15. Summary Tables

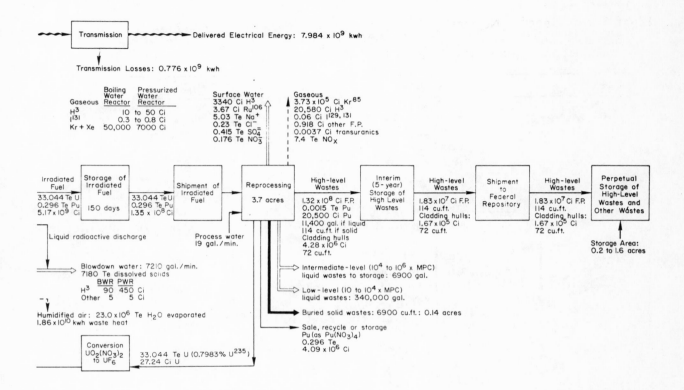

TABLE 15-2

Land Used for 1000-MW$_e$ Electrical Plant
(Producing Approximately 6×10^6 kWh/yr)

Fuel		Use	Land (acres)
Coal		Power station	1000
		Cooling tower	6
		Coal storage	40
		Railroad	3000
		Coal cleaning	300
		Total	~4300
	also:	Strip-mining	1500 /yr
		Underground mining	870 /yr subsidence
Oil		Power station	300
		Cooling tower (fraction for fuel oil)	600
		Pipeline (fraction for fuel oil)	3000
		Oil well (fraction for fuel oil)	500
		Total	4400
Gas		Power station	300
		Cooling tower	6
		Pipeline	16,000
		Gas well	125
		Total	~16,400
Light-water reactor		Power station	160
		Milling/conversion/ isotope separation }	160
		Reprocessing	
		Total	320
	also:	Mining	16/yr
		Storage of wastes	1.6/yr
Hydro		Lakes of hydro	20,000 (typical)
			300,000 (western US)
Geothermal		Geysers plant (California)	1000

TABLE 15-3

Deaths Due to Electricity Use in the US
(1965 Figures Unless Stated Otherwise)

	Deaths/kWh$_t$	Deaths/ 10^9 MWh
Fossil fuels		
Air pollution (undifferentiated)	3×10^{-9}	3000
Coal mining		
Black-lung disease	1×10^{-9}	1000
Accidents	6×10^{-11}	60
Total	$\sim 4 \times 10^{-9}$	~ 4000
Petroleum refining and oil-well accidents	7×10^{-12}	7
Total	3×10^{-9}	3000
Gas		
Main explosions (1971)	1×10^{-11}	10
Poisoning	3×10^{-11}	30
Explosions and fires caused in homes	1×10^{-11}	10
Total	5×10^{-11}	50
Hydroelectric dam failures		
One failure per 50 years as at Vaiont, Italy		
Direct deaths	3×10^{-10}	300
Indirect deaths	3×10^{-10}	300
Miscellaneous small failures	2×10^{-11}	20
Drownings (estimate)	1×10^{-11}	10
Total (actual electricity)	$\sim 6 \times 10^{-10}$	~ 600
Nuclear fuels (fission)		
Uranium mining cancers, if fuel used for:		
Breeder reactors	7×10^{-14}	0.07
Light-water reactors	1.5×10^{-11}	15
Uranium processing and fuel-fabrication accidents, if fuel used for:		
Breeder reactors	2×10^{-13}	0.2
Light-water reactors	2×10^{-11}	20
Radiation cancers from normal operation of 500 reactors and processing plants (0.1 mrem/yr)	3×10^{-13}	0.03
Potential reactor accidents: 1/30 yr of WASH 740 severity by year 2000		
Direct deaths	1×10^{-11}	10
Extra cancers	1×10^{-12}	1
Other indirect deaths	6×10^{-12}	6
Total	$\sim 5 \times 10^{-11}$	~ 50

16

Some Possible
Term-Paper Topics

1. The ecological effects of hydropower
2. Public safety concerns about hydropower
3. LNG storage and transportation accidents
4. The impact of Section 102 of NEPA
5. Solar sea power, using the thermocline in tropical oceans: (a) technology, (b) ecological impact
6. Coal-mine safety in the U.S.: (a) technical, (b) political
7. Strip-mining: its ecological dangers and their avoidance
8. Off-shore drilling versus oil importation, a comparison of environmental problems
9. The potential for solar power
10. Reducing power demand
11. How to finance utility companies
12. Pollution in Lake Michigan: can we control the ecology?
13. Power and fuel reserves in underdeveloped countries
14. Oil pipelines in Alaska and Northern Canada
15. Storage of wastes: (a) radioactive, (b) mine-tailings
16. Nuclear power and its impact on world politics
17. The world struggle for oil
18. How not to regulate an industry: a comparison of FPC and AEC procedures

19. A pollution tax: how to tax pollution in order to give incentives to clean up pollution and compensate its victims

20. Setting utility rate to encourage economy and efficiency

21. A comparison of different energy-storage mechnisms